A WISCONSIN GARDEN GUIDE

Jerry Minnich

Stanton & Lee Publishers, Inc.

Sauk City, Wisconsin 53583

First Wisconsin House Printing, April 1975
Second Printing, May 1975
Third Printing, March 1976
First Stanton & Lee Printing, January 1979

Wisconsin House is an imprint of Stanton & Lee Publishers, Inc.

ISBN 0-88361-036-1 (paper)
ISBN 0-88361-037-X (cloth)

Library of Congress Card Number 75-1945

Printed in the United States of America
by Straus Printing & Publishing Co., Inc.,
Madison, Wisconsin

Table of Contents

Tables

Maps

FOREWORD

"When should I plant potatoes here in Beaver Dam?"

"Is there a peach tree that we can really trust in Stevens Point?"

"When can I expect the first fall frost around Sturgeon Bay ... Marshfield ... Spooner?"

At long last, Wisconsin gardeners can get the answers to these and many, many other questions in a book especially written for them — their climate, their soils, their specific regional conditions. And as far as I'm concerned, Jerry Minnich is the perfect author to have written the book, *A Wisconsin Garden Guide*.

Some twenty years ago, Jerry and I began our editing careers in Emmaus, Pennsylvania. The publishing company was Rodale Press, and there were a couple of small magazines we worked on called *Organic Gardening and Farming* and *Prevention*.

Back in those days, assistant editors did all sorts of things — rewrite, interviews, picture-taking, experiment station visiting, paste-up and dummying, copywriting, etc. We would go out to see everyone from backyard gardeners to dairy farmers, from African violet fanciers to operators of compost factories. In any one issue, we would write three, four, or five articles or more. To keep the readers (and ourselves as well) from getting bored with the same by-lines, we used pen names. One of Jerry Minnich's favorites was Uncle Jasper. And it was with readers, too. When Jerry left OGF, the name of "Uncle Jasper" was permanently retired.

Fortunately, Jerry Minnich kept up his interest in gardening in general — and in organic gardening, in particular — when he moved to Wisconsin. While I personally believe that the true green thumbs in the Minnich family belong to Julie, John, and Becky — nevertheless, the task of communicating how-to garden advice to his Wisconsin neighbors falls on Uncle Jasper himself. He has fulfilled that task extremely well, as you are about to find out for yourself.

Never has gardening been more popular in the United States than in 1975. Pollsters tell us that there are more than 40 million, and if you are fortunate enough to live in or near Wisconsin, you are bound to have one of the best gardens by following the advice offered in *A Wisconsin Garden Guide*.

Jerome Goldstein
Executive Editor
ORGANIC GARDENING AND FARMING
January 28, 1975

Preface

I decided to write this book one day in late February 1973. Since my family and I had moved to Wisconsin some years before, I had been troubled by reading gardening advice — particularly concerning planting times — that was not really trustworthy for Wisconsin. I was never sure of those annual vegetables that would grow to maturity in our short season, or those perennials that were safe to plant in a country where winter temperatures can dip to twenty-five degrees below zero. And I imagined that the problem was even worse for those in the northern reaches of the state.

But it was on that day in late February that I received the real impetus to begin in earnest. I read in a magazine that folks in my area should plant their peas by Washington's Birthday. It was then a few days past Washington's Birthday. I looked out the window at the snow, imagined the frozen ground beneath it, and I knew that the only way I was going to plant peas that day was with a snow shovel, a power drill, and my best quarter-inch bit.

For the next nine months, I formulated plans. I visited the horticultural department at the University of Wisconsin-Madison. I telephoned friends at *Organic Gardening and Farming* magazine, where I had worked for a number of years as an editor and writer, and enlisted their support. I did a fair amount of basic research. I kept my own garden diary, and I made mental and written notes of my observations. Finally, in December, I decided to seek a potential publisher for the nonexistent work. I turned to Wisconsin House, where Editor Mark E. Lefebvre, himself an enthusiastic organic gardener, was immediately interested. With his continuing encouragement, I put the book together over the next ten months. During that time, I wrote to every county Extension agent in the state asking about his county's soil, climate, most popular vegetables and fruits for home gardens, and about any special gardening problems in his area. I visited the Pennsylvania offices of *Organic Gardening and Farming*, where I received all the help I requested, and more. I talked with Wisconsin gardeners, to horticultural experts at the university, and to seedsmen and nurserymen, in order to get other people's views on the major problems of Wisconsin home gardeners. And now, with the help of these people and many more, this book is finished.

I wish that I could claim to be a gardening expert. I am not. I am a gardener, true, and I have been gardening ever since my father put me to work catching insects in our World War II victory garden in Allentown, Pennsylvania. I have published probably fifty or more articles on gardening in the last twenty years, and I have contributed to other books on gardening. I hope that I am a fair garden writer, but I am still no garden expert. I depend on the neighbors to identify wild flowers for me, I have never grown a rutabaga, and my lawn has never been mistaken for a golf putting green.

This book, then, far from being the summary of wisdom of a single gardening expert, is the collective work and wisdom of others — hundreds of others, and perhaps thousands, including professionals and laymen alike — horticulturists, entomologists, botanists, soil scientists, county agents, other garden writers, and many ordinary gardeners who have been willing to share their experiences with others.

In collecting and presenting this work, and adding those few observations of my own, I have striven for three goals: (1) to present information that will be of genuine help in attacking the specific soil and climate problems of Wisconsin gardeners; (2) to supplement that specific information with general and practical gardening advice, so that the book will be, insofar as possible, a complete gardening guide; and (3) to be accurate in the information I present.

It is the last of these in which I seek the reader's help. Any book of this kind, which presents literally thousands of bits of information, is bound to contain some errors. Any of these mistakes are mine and mine alone. If the reader notes any inaccuracies in this edition, I would be most grateful to have them called to my attention. With this help, the next edition of this book will be even more helpful to all Wisconsin gardeners.

I would like to acknowledge my thanks to many people in the preparation of this book. First, of course, thanks must go to Rodale Press, to its publication *Organic Gardening and Farming*, and to the editors of that magazine who were kind enough to give me advice, encouragement, lists of various kinds, permission to quote freely from many of their sources, and many of the photographs that you see in this book: Bob Rodale, Jerry Goldstein, Lee Goldman, Maury Franz, Jeff Cox, Tom Gettings, and Betty Frederick — thank you.

Thanks also to the University of Wisconsin-Extension for their continuing work in researching the special problems of Wisconsin gardeners and in presenting the useful results of that research in the form of low-cost or free publications. This book could not have been written without this research, which I consider a happy example of the rewards reaped by all Wisconsin taxpayers for their support of the university. And special thanks must go to the faculty of the University of Wisconsin-Madison Departments of Horticulture, Entomology, and Soil Science, who were always ready to answer specific questions and resolve doubts whenever I had them. There are others to thank — Ruth Hine of the Wisconsin Department of Natural Resources for her good advice on wild flowers, Martha Fager of McFarland House for her help with herbs, the Madison United States Department of Agriculture office for leading me to reliable climatological data, Wisconsin's county Extension agents for willingly answering my questions, Laureen Seefeldt Thorstad for her valuable guidance in preparing the manuscript, and many, many others who offered encouragement, advice, and useful information to make my job easier and this book more helpful to all Wisconsin gardeners.

For Julia,
who really does the gardening,
and for John and Becky

Half of our misery and weakness derives from the fact that we have broken with the soil and that we have allowed the roots that bound us to the earth to rot. We have become detached from the earth, we have abandoned her. And a man who abandons nature has begun to abandon himself.

—Pierre Van Paassen
That Day Alone (1941)

Chapter One

It All Begins In The Soil

What is this soil, this good earth that Van Paassen accuses us of abandoning?

Go to a poet and he will fill your imagination with pictures of the soil as the giver of life: Mother Earth, the patient, forgiving, and generous bearer of us all. Choosing a favorite poetic passage about the earth is as difficult as choosing the most perfect flower in the world. But who can resist John Milton's tribute?

> Sweet is the breadth of morn, her rising sweet,
> With charm of earliest birds; pleasant the sun
> When first on this delightful land he spreads
> His orient beams on herb, tree, fruit, and flower,
> Glist'ring with dew; fragrant the fertile earth
> After soft showers; and sweet the coming on
> Of grateful ev'ning mild, then silent night
> With this her solemn bird, and this fair moon,
> And these the gems of heaven, her starry train.
> *Paradise Lost*, 4-639

Go to a Wisconsin geologist and you will get quite a different picture. He will talk of residual soils and transported soils, and bowldery sand, and glacial gravel, and stratified clay. He will tell you how modern alluvium was laid down by rivers, how peat bogs were formed by a hundred centuries of vegetable accumulation, and how great valleys were formed by the land's erosion. His eyes will brighten when he tells you about the great continental glacier of twenty thousand years ago, and how it drastically altered the face of three-fourths of Wisconsin's landmass. He would love to show you the mesas and buttes at Camp Douglas, and he would have no trouble giving you the history of your own garden soil no matter where in Wisconsin you live. Geologists are interesting people. They can instill in us a respect for the land by giving us its history.

Go to a soil scientist and he will tell his own story of soil. He will speak of silt loams, red clays, and green sands. He will discuss soil texture and water-holding capacities. He will bring out profile charts and point to A_1 horizons and A_2 horizons. He will bring out multicolored soil maps, and he will be able to tell you more about your soil than you ever knew, even though he has never seen it. He will slap a label on your garden soil, because soil scientists are compelled to attach labels. You might find that you have a Bergland deep black topsoil over bluish gray clay over red clay, if you live near Superior. Or, if you happen to be in Janesville, you might find yourself living on a Carlisle muck.

There are hundreds of different soil types in Wisconsin, and the soil scientists haven't made it any easier for us poor amateurs by deciding, somewhere along the line, to give soil types (or *series*) the names of the places where they were first discovered. Thus, you might have a Dubuque soil if you live in Menomonie, or a Kewanee soil if you live in Whitefish Bay. Wisconsin soil scientists seem to have one aim in life — to survey and classify every cubic foot of the state's soil above bedrock. These dedicated people are integral to the success of Wisconsin agriculture, and they can be quite a bit of help to us home gardeners too.

Ask a farmer about soil and he will most likely speak of productivity. For him, the soil is a way to make a living. And, sad to say, many farmers today see the soil as little more than that. Whereas farming was, not too long ago, a way of life for a large segment of America, it has gradually and surely followed a clear trend: fewer and larger farms, more crop specialization, intense emphasis on yield rather than quality, increasing dependence on chemicals for land and crop management, and a widening separation of the farmer from the land that supports him. This trend has led us from traditional farming to modern agribusiness and corporate enterprise. Respect for the soil is lost, here, in deference to the greater respect for profits. The soil becomes little more than a convenient substance to hold plants upright. It is mined of its natural productivity, and crops are virtually spoon-fed the minerals they need for growth. Vegetable varieties are chosen not for taste or nutritional quality, but for their easy handling by the harvesting machines, for their uniform size, for their attractive color, shipping qualities, yield per acre, and for any other purpose that might add to corporate profits. Certainly there are many farmers in Wisconsin who still hold a proper respect for the soil, and there are still family farms in nearly every part of the state. But the economic pressures brought on by modern agribusiness have made family farming difficult for most, and impossible for many, all to the ultimate detriment of the soil.

What has this trend done to the soil? Here in the United States we have lost an estimated 50 to 60 percent of our topsoil in less than two hundred years of farming. Indeed, most farms west of the Middle Atlantic states are less than one hundred years old. Then we look at the farmers of China, who have lived from the soil for more than *four thousand years*, by returning all organic wastes to the soil. The American record speaks for itself, and the trend is obvious for all to see.

Talk to an organic farmer and you will get a different story. He is the one who is holding onto — or recapturing — traditional respect for the land. The organic farmer is an ecologist. He sees the soil as a vital part of a life community. He studies its character and needs. And he feeds the soil, not the plants. He knows that a healthy soil will produce healthy plants, and that a sick soil can be mined for only so long before its patience wears thin. He tries to keep a natural balance on his farm at all times, encouraging insect-eating birds, and pollinating honeybees, and soil-enriching earthworms. He returns all plant wastes to the land, because he knows he cannot keep taking from the soil without replacing the things he takes.

Perhaps the difference between an agribusinessman and an organic farmer is that one thinks of himself as owning the land, while the other thinks of himself as a visitor there. And the organic farmer is right. We are all visitors on the land, for the land was here long before we came, and it will be here long after we are gone. The land, the soil, has been a mighty gracious host, too, since it has sustained each of us for all our lives. We, as guests, must remember our manners if we want the land to treat our grandchildren in the same hospitable manner.

IN THIS SOIL

The soil in your garden is, indeed, part of a vital life community — an ecosystem, if you will — and it is teeming with life. In your garden soil are countless billions of microorganisms. Some cause plant troubles, but most are friendly creatures, working ceaselessly to break down plant and animal residues, and to liberate nutrients for all your garden plants. In a single gram of garden soil, there are more than a billion bacteria, a veritable soil-conditioning army. There are millions of actinomycetes, which help in the decomposition process and which make minerals available to growing plants. The familiar odor of freshly turned soil in the spring is caused by the products of these actinomycetes. There are fungi of many kinds, and they, too, break down organic matter and improve soil texture. There are millions of algae which, when exposed to sunlight, form chlorophyll and change carbon dioxide from the air into organic matter for the soil. And there are other

living microorganisms, including protozoa and yeast, which also
aid in soil conditioning and in making nutrients available to
plants. During the long Wisconsin winter, these creatures are slow
to move. But in spring they begin to stir into action, and by
midsummer they are in a frenzy of activity.

In your garden soil, there are (I hope) thousands of earthworms, burrowing, tunneling, aerating the soil, creating water
passages, eating the very earth as they go, and leaving behind
their castings, which are far richer than the soil from which they
are made. Earthworms are held in such high regard by organic
gardeners and farmers that many either buy or raise them for
introduction into the soil.

There are also thousands of insects in your soil in both summer and winter. Some are good for the garden and some are bad;
but in the end, all leave their bodies to be claimed by the good
earth and digested by microorganisms, thus further enriching the
soil.

All these creatures call the dark, moist earth their home, and
together they work in relative harmony, living from the products
of plant life and, in turn, enabling plants to live and flourish.

Organic matter. Despite their staggering numbers, all the microorganisms and the earthworms and the insects form an infintes-
imal percentage of the total soil body. In fact, all the living creatures and all the once-living creatures, including both plant and
animal life, account for perhaps no more than *1 or 2 percent* of the
soil in the average garden. These once-living things constitute, in
the soil, its *organic matter*. With ample organic matter, the soil can
carry on the never-ending processes of decay and rebirth which
make it a vital life community. Without organic matter, the soil
will be lifeless and barren, incapable of supporting any significant
plant life.

But what is in the other 98 or 99 percent of the soil body? This
consists of air (perhaps 25 percent), minerals (49 percent), and
water (25 percent). The proportions vary, of course, according to
the soil, and often they vary dramatically. But an average productive garden or farm soil might have these percentages.

Air. Soil cannot support life without air. A lack of sufficient air
will inhibit or stop the important work of microorganisms; it will
cause plant roots to suffocate and die; it will cause the soil to
become hard, dense, and compact; it will prevent the oxidation of
mineral matter, making it unavailable to plants; and it will destroy the vital chemical balance of the soil. You can insure adequate soil aeration, however, by the introduction of organic matter, the addition of rock powders, proper cultivation, and proper
planning for soil drainage. More about all these, later.

Minerals. The mineral content of your soil, which accounts for
about half the total volume, comes from the age-old crust of the
earth itself. When this land we call Wisconsin was very young, it

was covered by barren rock and water. Through eons of time, the upper layers of rock were upheaved, broken, crushed, and ground, through the effects of underground disturbances and atmospheric weathering, and particularly by the alternate freezing and thawing of water and the advance of the great ice sheets. Soon after the first crude plant life appeared, its deposited remains combined with smaller mineral particles, and with water and air, to form soil. Thus did both soil and plant life multiply together, each encouraging the other, until the Wisconsin landscape was changed from a barren and desolate wasteland to a world of green and living things.

Mineral matter is a necessary ingredient of soil, since plants need many different mineral elements to carry on their life processes. The most important are phosphorus and potassium, which, along with nitrogen, comprise most standard chemical fertilizers. But there are many other essential mineral elements needed in smaller amounts: aluminum, calcium, iron, magnesium, manganese, sulphur, titanium, and others. When minerals are needed in very small amounts, they are called *trace minerals* or *trace elements*.

Water. No one needs to be told of the importance of water to a garden. Suffice it to say that water acts as the transportation system of the soil's life community, carrying every molecule of every nutrient from the soil to the plant roots, and from the roots to the stem, leaves, and fruit. Water enables bacteria and other microorganisms to liberate mineral elements for plant use. Without sufficient water, element transportation comes to a screeching halt, and life processes of every kind come to an end. More will be said later about ways to provide ample water for optimum soil and plant health.

WHAT KIND OF SOIL IS THAT?

You can take perfectly good care of your own garden soil without learning the hundreds of specialized terms used by geologists, soil scientists, and agronomists. But there are a few terms that you should know, since we do run into them fairly often in receiving, and giving, soil-care advice.

Soil profile. A side view of your garden soil, beginning with the bedrock below and running all the way up to the surface, is called its profile. Soil profiles are comprised of layers (called *horizons*) which include the topsoil, various layers of subsoil, parent materials, and eventually bedrock.

Texture. This refers to the proportional amounts of the various-sized particles that make up your soil. Gravel, of course, is very large. Sand is smaller, but still coarse in soil terms. Silt particles are still smaller (from 8/100,000 inches to 2/1,000 inches), while clay particles are the smallest recognized. You can get some idea of the composition of any soil by rubbing a bit of it between your thumb and index finger. Sand will feel gritty. Silt will feel floury. And clay will feel sticky.

Structure. In good garden soils, the individual particles of sand, clay, and silt will naturally group together into larger units, called *granules* or *aggregates*. This process is necessary to a good garden soil, since it promotes aeration and water drainage. And the success of your soil in forming these aggregates is called its *structure*, or *crumb structure*. Sandy soils will have poor structure, since the sand is too coarse to form aggregates, while a heavy clay will become compact and dense when wet, inhibiting good plant growth.

Porosity. This term refers to the pore spaces in your soil, i.e., all the space not occupied by soil itself. The pores may be filled with either air or water, and should occupy from 40 to 60 percent of a good soil's total volume. Good soil structure will encourage good porosity. A heavy clay, with poor structure, will not allow enough room for pore spaces. A light sandy soil may have good porosity, but its light character will make it unable to hold water, filling most of the pores with air. The excess air will cause soil nitrogen to be released too quickly, and a nitrogen shortage will result. Gardeners should work for a good medium loam with good structure and porosity.

pH. This is a symbol used in discussing the soil's acid or alkaline nature. The midpoint on the pH scale is 7. A soil with pH of 7 is neutral — neither acid nor alkaline. Numbers above 7 indicate an alkaline soil; those under 7, an acid soil. Since all plants express a preference for soil in a certain range of the pH scale, it is important that you test your soil's pH and, if necessary, correct the soil to bring it within the proper range. Full directions for managing soil pH are given later in this chapter.

Soil groups. Soils are grouped according to their textures. The *sand group* includes soils with less than 20 percent of silt and clay. Soils in the *clay group* have less than 20 percent of sand. The *loam group* includes soils of a happy medium, containing good proportions of sand, silt, and clay. These are best for general gardening.

It must be said here that the definitions, especially regarding percentages, are far from definitive. Some scientists try to establish mathematical relationships in order to classify, while others pay scant attention to the percentages. Francis D. Hole and Gerhard B. Lee, in their booklet *Introduction to the Soils of Wisconsin*, identify a loam as containing about 20 percent clay, 40 percent silt, and 40 percent sand.

Actual soils, naturally, do not fall into these neat categories. Therefore, we break down the three major groups into subgroups. Sandy soils may be, in order of coarseness, gravelly sands, coarse sands, medium sands, fine sands, or loamy sands. Loams may be coarse sandy loams, medium sandy loams, fine sandy loams, silty loams, or clay loams. Clay soils can be stony clays, gravelly clays, sandy clays, silty clays, or pure clays.

Soil series. Soil groups are further divided into soil series. The series is named, as mentioned before, for the name of a place where it was first found and identified. For instance, the series *Hixton sandy loam* was named after the village of Hixton, in Jackson County, where it was first studied.

Soil classification. Soils are also herded into broader groups, called classifications. *Podzol* is one important classification, referring to a soil where once forests or heaths stood, making the soil quite acid over the years. Often, the soil structure is poor and the soil is low in organic matter. It tends to erode easily and aeration is often insufficient. About one-fifth of the soil in the United States is podzolic; the percentage in Wisconsin is higher, covering most of the northern half of the state and dipping southward in the eastern half, through Manitowoc County. Any area which supports natural coniferous (cone-bearing) forest is apt to offer podzolic soil.

Alluvial soils are named for alluvium, the fine-particle clay carried from uplands by streams and rivers and redeposited in bottomlands. A great alluvial valley has been created by the Mississippi River, which has affected the soils of western Wisconsin (although far less than it has affected Southern states). There are also large areas of alluvial soils surrounding many Wisconsin waterways. Some of the world's great agricultural lands are alluvial, and some of Wisconsin's best gardening soil is, too. It is apt to be moderately well-drained silt loam, rich in nutrients and ready for planting with little or no structural repair.

Peat and muck are related terms, often used loosely, although mucks are usually said to contain under 50 percent of organic matter, while peats contain more than 50 percent. Both, however, refer to wet, spongy, acid soils, composed mainly of decayed vegetable matter and very high in organic content. Their water-retaining capacities are extraordinarily high, particularly peats, which can hold up to thirteen times their dry weight in water. Sphagnum moss, which is the principle ingredient of Wisconsin's peat bogs, is always in demand among florists, creating a nice little industry for many people in the bog-rich central counties of Wisconsin.

Raw sphagnum peat is rich in total nitrogen content, but this nitrogen is not in a form available to plants. So poor is this soil in available nitrogen, in fact, that some of the most common wild plants in bogs are the insectivorous species. These plants — including the pitcher plant, the sundews, and the bladderworts — find no nitrogen in the soil, and so they get their nourishment from the insects which they trap and devour! Peat is equally low in mineral elements, too, and so it does not, by itself, make good garden soil. Properly treated, muck soils can make one of the best producing

vegetable soils of any in America. But, except for cranberry production, peat bogs are better utilized to gather materials to add to
more promising soils. Peat moss is extremly valuable in breaking
up heavy clay soils and in adding good texture and structure to
sandy soils.

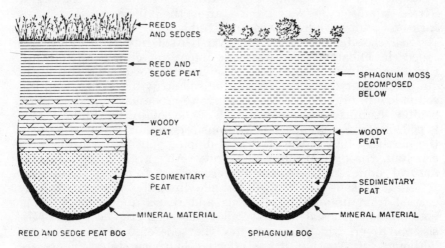

The above illustration, prepared by the United States Department of Agriculture, shows a typical profile of a peat formed mainly from sedges and
reeds; another composed chiefly from sphagnum moss.

In Wisconsin, most of the peat bogs are located in the northern and eastern parts of the state, although there are some
impressive old bogs in the Kettle Moraine district of Waukesha
and Walworth counties, and others in Jefferson and Columbia
counties. These bogs are very old and very deep. It has been
estimated that it takes nature from 100 to 800 years to lay down a
single foot of peat moss, and many Wisconsin bogs are more than
fifty feet deep.

Prairie soils are much like podzols, except that they were
formed without the contribution of trees. The organic content of
these soils is high, the granular structure is good, and their general fertility is high. Prairie soils make up some of the best agricultural lands in the nation. Most of Iowa's soil is prairie, about
three-fourths of Illinois', and a portion of Minnesota's. Wisconsin is
on the northeastern boundary of the great American prairie, and
so its prairie area is largely confined to the southwestern part of
the state. Draw a triangle on a state map, with the three points
being Racine, Grant, and Polk counties, and you will have fairly
well encompassed Wisconsin's prairie area. Gardeners in this region are fortunate, in that nature has provided them with the best
of materials to work with.

There are many, many other classifications of soils — chernozem, laterite, tundra, planosol, and rendzina, to name just a few. There is no need to go into them here, since there is neither the space nor the need. Soil science is a highly developed field of inquiry, and could turn into a consuming interest if you are so inclined. But the home gardener should be able to make intelligent decisions with only scant knowledge of these matters. After all, it is his own soil which holds the keenest interest for him, and he needs not study the soils of the world to get to know his own backyard.

THE SOILS OF WISCONSIN

Wisconsin has a wide variety of soils, the result of the great glacier (which missed about a fourth of the state, called the Driftless Area) and the influence of the Mississippi River and Lakes Superior and Michigan. Other influences have been the intrusion of the great prairie into Wisconsin's southwest and the extensive stands of pine and hardwood forests throughout the north.

In the center of the state is a large region of light, sandy soils, bounded roughly by Portage and Wisconsin Dells on the south, Stevens Point and Wisconsin Rapids on the north, Waupaca and Berlin on the east, and Black River Falls and Sparta on the west. A similar section is found in the northeastern part of the state, beginning around Shawano and running northeastward through Marinette County. Still a third sandy area is located in the northwest, beginning in Burnett County and running northeastward through Douglas and Bayfield counties (but excluding the Superior area). A fourth area, including parts of Forest, Langlade, Lincoln, Oneida, and Vilas counties, is not wholly sandy but has some sandy areas in among loams.

There is a fairly extensive region of fine sandy loam northwest of Black River Falls, running across Jackson, Eau Claire, Chippewa, and Dunn counties and including the southern part of Barron County. Soils in the rest of the state usually run to silt loams, except for red clay areas running along the shore of Lake Michigan, beginning at Milwaukee and going northward, and another such area running along Lake Superior.

The map showing major soil regions (map 1) should give you some idea of the kind of soil which is common in your area. You can get far more detailed information by taking advantage of some of the useful publications offered by the University of Wisconsin Geological and Natural History Survey. Most of these are somewhat technical and detailed, providing information not really essential for the home gardener's needs. But you might find some of the publications to be very interesting, particularly if you want to go deeper into the study of soils. There are, for instance, soil surveys of some Wisconsin counties, most available for one dollar

MAP 1

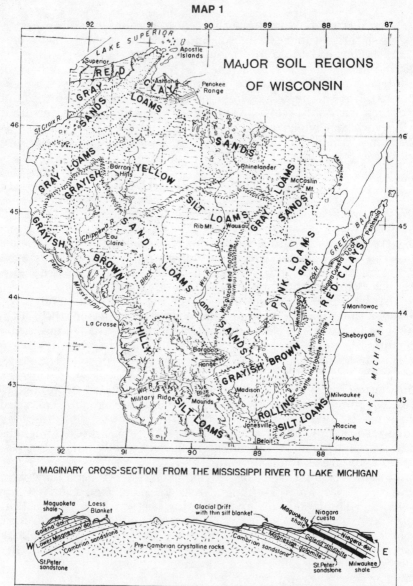

MAJOR SOIL REGIONS OF WISCONSIN

IMAGINARY CROSS-SECTION FROM THE MISSISSIPPI RIVER TO LAKE MICHIGAN

THE SOIL SURVEY DIVISION, WISCONSIN GEOLOGICAL AND NATURAL HISTORY SURVEY

each. There are also soils maps, including a beautiful forty-six by thirty-six inch multicolored wall map of the entire state ($1.00) which pinpoints 190 different soil groups. If you do refer to a soils map, you should also ask for the sixteen-page booklet, *What's In That Soil Map?* (5c), and the previously mentioned *Introduction to the Soils of Wisconsin* (10c). These publications, and more, can be seen in your local public library, at the office of your county

Extension agent, or by writing for a complete list of publications to the University of Wisconsin Geological and Natural History Survey, 1815 University Avenue, Madison, Wisconsin 53706.

BUT HOW ABOUT YOUR SOIL?

Let's get to *your* soil. What is it like? How does it rate in terms of structure, porosity, organic content, and supplies of all the essential and trace mineral elements? Are you working with sand, clay, or an ideal garden loam? Are earthworms in plentiful supply? Are conditions right for your army of microorganisms?

If you have been working with your soil for some time, you probably know the answers to these questions. You may have become intimately acquainted with your soil over the years, learning its needs and capabilities as you would those of a dear friend. But, if you are going to work a garden plot for the first time, you must spend some time in analyzing your soil. Even if you have been gardening in one spot for some years, you might not be happy with the results you have been getting. If this is the case, the first place to look for answers is in the soil — where it all begins.

Soil type. You can easily determine your soil type by checking a detailed soil map or by calling your county horticultural or agricultural agent. If you find that your soil type is not well suited to gardening, do not despair. Samuel Ogden, a Vermont gardener with more than forty years of experience, works a large plot on a soil called Stony Berkshire, which he describes as "just about the worst soil classification that there is in the United States." Yet, Ogden achieves tremendous results with vegetables of all kinds, by following standard organic practices and his good common sense. In speaking of soil types and classifications in his book *Step-by-Step to Organic Vegetable Growing* (Rodale Press, 1971) Ogden says:

> I came to the conclusion that there is very little, if any, relationship between the nature of the soil and the kind of parent rock which lies beneath the surface, and I returned to my previously held conviction, which came as the result of practical experience, that the most important aspect of a soil is its physical or mechanical condition. In other words, the important factors are not the derivation of the soil, or its classification, but rather its texture, its depth, its content of air and moisture, the presence or lack thereof of rocks and stones, etc.

I tend to follow Ogden's common sense, here. Much of the advice of experts is geared to the farmer or the commercial grower, and the experts tend to forget that the home gardener can afford to treat his soil in ways that the large-scale grower would find unfeasible or uneconomic. Especially if you have only one likely spot for your garden, then, do not be discouraged in discovering that your soil type is not the best for growing things.

Structure, texture, and drainage. If at all possible, try to observe your prospective garden soil after a heavy rain. If, after a few hours, the soil has not absorbed the rain, then you might well have a drainage problem. The soil might be too heavy, loaded with clay and lacking in porosity. Or, you might find that the topsoil is shallow, overlying a dense hardpan or rock bed. You can deal with a clay topsoil; but a shallow topsoil over rock or hardpan requires a job scarcely worth the undertaking. Dig a hole two feet deep in several parts of your garden to get an informal soil profile for yourself, and to get some idea of soil texture and structure at different levels. Look at it, feel it, crumble some in your hands. Look for earthworms and evidence of root growth.

If you want a better idea of the soil structure, try the bottle test. Fill a quart or pint bottle one-fourth full of a representative soil sample. (Try to get a straight cylinder of soil for an accurate sample.) Fill the rest of the bottle with water and shake vigorously until a homogenous mixture is obtained, and then put the bottle on a shelf for half a day. The sand will sink quickly to the bottom, the silt will settle on top of the sand, and the fine clay particles will slowly filter down to form a top layer. By measuring with a ruler, you can get a rough idea of the proportions of these various materials in your soil.

Of course, you might find yourself to have the opposite problem — too much drainage, or, a lack of water-holding capacity. I remember visiting Richard Higby's Adams County place several years ago, my first visit to a "sand county" farm. There had been a terrific rainstorm the night before. Three inches had fallen, and the rain had not subsided until an hour before I pulled into the front yard. I was there to observe a composting demonstration that Mr. Higby had organized, and I had expected to be walking in mire up to my ankles. Much to my surprise, the ground was scarcely damp. The rain had been absorbed as quickly as it had fallen, drawn deeply underground where growing plants cannot reach, carrying valuable nutrients with it. Fortunately, you can deal with a soil of this nature (as Mr. Higby proved in an impressive manner that day). It takes some substantial initial effort, but it is a job well worth the doing.

Another factor affecting drainage is the garden's position on the lay of the land. Lowlands will tend to receive the water runoff and drainage from higher lands and will thus drain more slowly. Fine clay particles are gradually carried downhill where they might improve sandy soils. If you find that your soil is heavy, a higher spot on the hill might afford advantages. Conversely, a lowland sand will have a better chance at water retention than one at a higher elevation. Again, look at the soil, dig into it, touch it, feel it. Get to know your soil.

What's growing now? Another quick indicator of a soil's potential is its present performance. Is the area rampant with weed growth? Is there a healthy stand of quack grass? If so, you can be fairly sure that the soil is capable of growing other plants of your own choosing. If, on the other hand, weed growth is sparse and there are large bare areas, you can suspect that something is wrong with this soil. It might be a problem easily corrected, such as a lack of minerals or of organic matter. But, on the other hand, the problem might go deeper, involving basic structural flaws. Investigate.

Table 1. WEEDS AS INDICATORS OF SOIL TYPE

The weeds growing on your land are not an infallible guide to soil type, but they do provide some clues. The following soils will provide good environments for the weeds listed opposite.

WET LAND	Ferns, horsetail, sedge, rush, cattail, buttercup, pennywort. *The surface may be dry but these weeds are a sure indication that the land is wet below. There may be a drainage problem.*
SOUR LAND (ACID)	Sorrel, dock, wild strawberry, bramble. *The soil should be limed.*
POOR, DRY SOIL	Devil's paintbrush, spurge. *Manures and sludge are needed.*
TIGHT, COM-PRESSED SOIL	Knotwood. *Break up surface, work in sand, manure, compost, and peat moss.*
DEEP CLAY	Self-heal, wild onion. *Needs compost and sand.*
LIMESTONE	Chicory, Teasel. *Check pH.*

Courtesy, *Organic Gardening and Farming*

Soil testing. Your soil should be tested if you have never tested it before, or if you have not had it tested within the past couple of years, or if you are having problems and are unsure of the reasons for those problems. If you know your soil intimately, have been following a comprehensive feeding and conditioning program, and have been satisfied with year-end results, there might be no need to test. I suspect that few gardeners fall into this last category, however, and so a professional soil test is recommended. The information it provides can be both interesting and valuable.

In Wisconsin, we are fortunate to have one of the best soil testing programs of any state in the nation, run by the University of Wisconsin. You may have your soil tested for pH (acidity-alkalinity), organic matter content, phosphorus, potassium, and soluble salts, for a fee of only two dollars. For another two dollars, you can have a physical analysis made, telling you the percentage of sand, silt, and clay (which will be more accurate, doubtless, than your home "bottle test"). And, for an extra dollar, you may have the same soil tested for calcium, magnesium, manganese, boron, and zinc. Not only will the university test for all these characteristics, but you will be sent specific fertilizing recommendations made especially for the crops or plants you specify, whether they be rhubarb, lawn grass, spinach, chrysanthemums, or your favorite dogwood tree.

Getting a soil test is fairly simple. Write or call your county Extension agent and say that you want to have a soil test made. Ask for a copy of Circular 670, *Sampling Lawn and Garden Soils*, as many plastic-lined soil sample bags as you will need (one for each sample), and an information sheet which you must fill in and return with each soil sample. Or, if you prefer, you may obtain the informational booklet and sample bags directly from the State Soils Laboratory, Route 2, Marshfield, Wisconsin 54449. After you have taken the samples, you may, if you choose, send them back directly to the laboratory at Marshfield. But it is better to work with your county agent, who will be happy to forward them for you. In fact, it will pay you to get on a first name basis with him, since the day will come when you will want his expert advice on one point or another.

The last word about soil testing is one of caution. Remember that the test results will be only as good as the samples you take, and that your samples might not necessarily be representative of your general garden soil (although you can swing the odds heavily in accuracy's favor by taking samples at different locations in the garden). Some successful gardeners, in fact, have little or no faith at all in the tests. Prominent among these is Leonard Wickenden, author of the popular book *Gardening with Nature* (Devin-Adair Co., 1954), who makes the interesting observation that, whereas soil samples are taken at a depth of only six or eight inches, the roots of common garden plants might reach down six or eight *feet* into the soil to draw up nutrients. Those deep-lying nutrients will not show up on your soil test. He also makes the point that testing procedures vary from laboratory to laboratory, and so do results. I have more faith in the tests than Mr. Wickenden, but it is important to remember that the test results should be regarded as helpful, rather than sacred.

CORRECTING BASIC FLAWS

Improving a sandy soil. A representative "light sandy" soil might contain 70 percent sand, 20 percent silt, and 10 percent clay. You can work with a soil like this, but you will get better results by changing these percentages. And if the percentage of sand is significantly higher than 70 percent, it is essential that you correct it.

The answer to a sandy soil is the addition of organic matter. Some experts advise the addition of heavy clay, but this is difficult and often produces unsatisfactory results. The clay is difficult to break apart and incorporate with the sand. It adheres to itself, and you are likely to be left with the same old sandy soil, sprinkled with clay lumps. Organic matter, on the other hand, is lighter in consistency and will mix in more readily.

If you have the money, of course, you can have several truckloads of rich topsoil brought in and spread to a depth of from four to six inches or more. This is the quickest way to cure a sandy soil, but it is horribly expensive. And if you do choose this course, be absolutely certain of the quality of that topsoil. It will probably be good, having been scraped off the site of a new building project — but not every dark-colored soil is good garden soil. If you intend to invest this kind of money in topsoil, insist on a state test before buying.

More likely, you will want to take on the enrichment project yourself. And for this you will need all the organic materials you can possibly find and haul back to your garden. Gardeners in Dane County, for instance, can pick up the aquatic weeds that are harvested from the Madison lakes. Milwaukee area gardeners should have little trouble coming upon spent hops from the breweries. Canning factories offer abundant organic matter, rich in minerals. Those in forested regions can bring home bushels and bushels of well-rotted leaf mold (which is likely to be very acid, and should be neutralized with ground limestone). Spoiled hay can be picked up from many farmers, often for nothing, sometimes for fifty cents a bale. Remember that anything once living can be used to enrich a sandy soil. Chapter 2 includes a representative list of organic materials (page 45) that will give you some ideas to pursue. Look over the possibilities in your area and begin to investigate. Call the city or county parks department and ask what happens to the leaves that they collect in fall. They may dump them in huge heaps in a forgotten corner of the county. And if they do, you will find beautiful, brown, crumbly leaf mold on the insides of those heaps. Is there a sawmill nearby? Sweep up baskets full of sawdust, which makes an excellent conditioner for sandy soils.

There are two ways you can incorporate these organic materials into the soil. You can build a compost heap (for which directions are given in the next chapter) or you can begin the practice of *sheet composting*. In traditional composting, you build the heap, wait for months for it to decay and mature, then dig it into the soil in the fall or early spring, before planting. In sheet composting, you spread the raw materials directly over the soil, till or dig them under, and let the composting process take place right in your soil. The advantage of sheet composting is that it takes far less work; the disadvantage is that it will take that part of your garden plot out of production for a year.

Another important way to add organic matter to the soil is through *green manuring*. Here, a cover crop is grown for the sole purpose of being plowed or tilled under. The process is not difficult, and the results are very good. You can add literally tons of organic matter in this way without the burden of hauling it to your land. Whichever method you choose — composting, sheet composting, or green manuring — you must add all the organic matter you possibly can to correct a sandy soil in the shortest possible time.

If you are planting trees, shrubs, perennials, or foundation plants in a sandy soil, you might not want to wait for the time it takes to turn your entire soil body into an ideal structure. You might wish to spot treat the soil in these cases. Dig the planting hole about twice as large as recommended for any plant. Fill the hole with four parts good topsoil, one part rotted manure, and one part peat moss. Add a little sand from your own soil. This mixture will give nearly any plant a good start, and should serve its needs until the surrounding soil has been corrected. (Note: Allow for the pH preference of any plant variety by the addition of necessary limestone.)

The proper treatment for sandy and clay soils is essentially the same — the incorporation of plenty of organic matter.

When growing anything in sandy soil, remember also to apply a mulch. The water in sandy soils evaporates quickly, and a good mulch will retard that evaporation, preserving precious moisture. The mulch will also break down slowly at the soil surface, and can be tilled under after each growing season, adding still more organic matter. Further information about cover crops, green manuring, and mulching is given later.

Victory over clay. Far more difficult than building up sandy soil is the process of breaking down a heavy clay. Your soil may be in a natural clay region, or you may have purchased a new home where the builder has stripped the topsoil, leveled out the lot with clay subsoil from the basement excavation, and spread an inch or so of topsoil over it, just enough to support a scraggly lawn. Whichever way you got your clay, you are stuck with it, in more ways than one. Even if you buy good topsoil to spread, you might well have a drainage problem that will keep your soil waterlogged and unproductive.

The treatment for a clay soil is essentially the same as for a sandy soil. You must incorporate all the organic matter you can, and you can do it by composting, sheet composting, or green manuring. The difference is that, in attacking clay, you should also incorporate quantities of builder's sand.

No one has to tell you that clay is sticky. It sticks to your garden tools, it sticks to your children's shoes, it sticks to your dog — and it sticks to itself. And because it sticks to itself, it tends to resist homogenization when other materials are introduced to the soil. Peat is an especially good material to add, because of its light and porous character. But any organic material is better than none, and you should spend a great deal of time during the first two years to incorporate that material. The rewards later will more than repay your early efforts.

Some gardeners report victory over clay with *strip composting.* This is a form of sheet composting in which the entire garden plot is divided into strips, perhaps three feet wide, running the entire length of the plot. Alternate strips are used for sheet composting. All collected organic matter is put into these strips and tilled under periodically — perhaps once a month during the growing season. The final tilling is done in the fall, and the land is left in rough condition so that some heaving will take place during winter's freezes and thaws. The following year, the composted strips are used for planting and the alternate strips are used for composting. In this way, you can plant half of your garden space each year, while building up the soil at the same time. Only when your soil reaches what you consider to be optimum condition will you begin to use the entire plot for annual plantings.

If your soil has a severe drainage problem, it must be solved before you can expect to have a productive garden of any kind. And if the drainage problem lies in the subsoil, rather than just the topsoil, all the foregoing suggestions still will not lead to a satisfactory garden soil. After all your work, rainwater will be absorbed into the renovated topsoil, but will be held on the subsoil like water in a basin. Your soil will remain cold, sour, and unfit for any of the flowers and vegetables you want to grow.

The breaking up of a clay subsoil or hardpan might require extraordinary measures, including subsoiling, trenching, or the laying of drainage tiles. *Subsoiling* is done with a special plow — a subsoiler — which breaks up the subsoil but does not bring it up to the surface. If you have a hardpan horizon in your soil profile, this might do the trick, for a hardpan is nothing more than a layer of subsoil whose pores have been filled in with fine clay particles, eventually forming a cement-like substance, impervious to water. The subsoil under the hardpan might be perfectly good and well drained, but the water never gets past the hardpan. A subsoiler can break up the hardpan in a matter of hours.

Trenching is a method of exchanging the top foot of soil (or the depth of one spade blade) with the foot of soil beneath it. This is a long and back-breaking job, since it is done by hand, row by row, but it might be the answer when you are presented with good topsoil over heavy clay. By placing the topsoil in the bottom position, you can improve the clay more easily on the top, and in the end you will have twice as much good topsoil and far better drainage. I have read of trenching often, but I have never known anyone who has actually done it. Personally, I hesitate to recommend this laborious procedure to anyone, but I present it here as another method you might wish to investigate.

Drainage tiles might also be the answer to inadequate subsurface drainage. These tiles are actually ceramic tubes which come in lengths of from two to eight feet. A common diameter is four inches. The tiles are laid two feet or more underground, and are slanted downhill and toward a natural drainage area or dry well. As with the other procedures, drainage tiling is a major operation involving some expense. You might find, however, that this procedure will give your soil the drainage it needs to become productive.

Before you undertake any of these extraordinary measures, I recommend strongly that you contact your county agent. Ask him to make a personal assessment of the problem and to give you his recommendation. A severe drainage problem requires the personal attention of an expert, and your county agent has the needed expertise in this area. Quite likely your drainage problem will be one which has been shared by some of your neighbors, and your county agent will be able to tell you how others have solved the problem in your area.

J. I. Rodale — founder of the
organic movement in America.

FERTILIZER — WHAT KIND? HOW MUCH?

In coming to the subject of fertilizer, we run into the first of
two great controversies. Will it be chemical — or organic? (The
second great controversy, met later on in this book, concerns insect control methods.)

My personal gardening approach is unabashedly organic, and
I will make no apologies for that because I think it is right. On the
other hand, I do not believe that chemical fertilizers are an insidi-
ous plot hatched by sinister forces out to destroy us. Chemical
fertilizers are, I believe, simply unnecessary in the home garden.
They become harmful only if applied to excess or if the gardener
comes to depend on them to the neglect of his soil. I have personally known hundreds of gardeners who get gratifying-to-
tremendous results year after year using no chemical fertilizer at
all. In twenty years of gardening, I have never used them myself,
and I have never missed them.

Chemical fertilization is scarcely a hundred years old. Gardening itself is thousands of years old. The use of chemicals began
with the great nineteenth century chemist, Justus von Liebig, who
discovered that certain mineral elements are necessary to the
growth of plants. Virtually singlehanded, von Liebig overthrew the
then-held theory that plants "ate" humus, and the age of scientific
agriculture was born. The distinguished and talented Englishman,
Sir Albert Howard, who ironically was born in the same year that

von Liebig died (1873), led the counterattack against the chemical
theory of soil treatment and crop fertilization some years later,
and became the father of the organic movement. Howard's thirty
years of agricultural research in India led him to doubt the wisdom of von Liebig's "fractionalized" approach to agriculture which
he saw as potentially or actually harmful to soil, plants, and man.
Howard died in 1947, but his work had by then been brought to
popular attention in America by the writings of J. I. Rodale.

Rodale, a New York accountant in his early years, became so
interested in Howard's work that in the 1930s he moved to a
run-down farm near Emmaus, Pennsylvania, and proceeded to
build it into a lush and productive showplace, using Howard's
organic method (which he refined and improved upon over the
years). Rodale founded a magazine, then called *Organic Farming
and Gardening*, in 1942, and subsidized it personally for many
years. Today, *Organic Gardening and Farming* claims nearly a
million subscribers, many of whom were drawn to organic methods
during the environmental movement which began in the 1960s.
Rodale died in 1971, and the magazine is now guided by his son
Robert Rodale.

The chemical side. Chemical fertilizers are generally formed by
the addition of chemicals to natural ground rock bases. These
fertilizers are soluble and immediately available to plants, as op-
posed to natural rock powders and the minerals found in all organic matter which become available more slowly, as they are
liberated in the soil through the actions of microorganisms. The
scientific application of chemical fertilizers will give plants a quick
"shot in the arm," and will improve production on a soil which
lacks those mineral elements supplied by the fertilizers. Chemical
fertilizers give quick results.

Most chemical fertilizers contain three elements — nitrogen
(N), phosphate (P_2O_5), and potash (K_2O). In grower's language, these
elements are referred to as N, P, and K. On the fertilizer bag, the
percentages of each are given in N-P-K order. A 5-10-5 fertilizer,
for instance, will contain 5 percent nitrogen, 10 percent phosphate,
and 5 percent potash. The common chemical form of nitrogen is
ammonium sulfate. Phosphate is usually supplied through super-
phosphate. And potash often comes in the form of muriate of
potash. Trace mineral supplements and lime are also supplied
through the chemical treatment of natural rock powders.

Nearly all government and university agricultural and horticultural experts are adherents of the chemical school of fertilization. They sometimes recommend some organic practices, such as
green manuring and the utilization of animal manures, but they
usually ignore other important organic practices such as composting and mulching. Many in the chemical school are convinced that,
if the organic people had their way, they would soon lead the
world to famine and death. The chemical people do not believe

that there is enough organic matter in the world to feed its population.

The organic side. Organic adherents claim that chemicals are not only unnecessary but harmful. Chemicals, they say, destroy soil texture; they inhibit or retard the growth of soil life, including earthworms and microorganisms; they alter the vitamin and protein content of certain crops; they make certain crops more vulnerable to disease by destroying the plants' natural biological controls; and they prevent plants from absorbing some needed minerals. Despite their short-term effects, they say, chemicals will eventually lead to poor yields and inferior crops because of their deleterious effects on the soil. Last, organic gardeners and farmers swear that organically-grown vegetables taste far better than their chemical counterparts.

The Secretary of Agriculture, on his visit to an organic garden, is disturbed by the presence of a bee.

(Courtesy, Jeff Cox, *Organic Gardening and Farming*.)

Organic soil feeding, on the other hand, is shown to be patterned after nature's own methods, which certainly have a good track record. Soil test results, since they are usually prepared by government or university agencies, will be accompanied by fertilizer recommendations in chemical terms. But the organic gardener will substitute compost, animal manures, green manure, or other forms of natural fertilizers for the recommended chemicals.

Further, organic gardeners and farmers place far more emphasis on year round soil building and feeding. They do not apply fertilizers just when a soil test indicates that a certain mineral is needed for a certain crop, but they carry on a continual program of feeding the soil, returning wastes, composting, mulching, and green manuring, so that the soil will be built into a peak of health and efficiency, capable of supporting lush growth and production of any common garden plant or farm crop. Again, we get back to the difference in philosophy between *feeding the plant* and *feeding the soil*, which distinguishes the approaches of these two schools.

This book, as I have said before, will concentrate on the organic approach to gardening. After twenty years of experience in organic gardening, I could not bring myself to recommend chemical fertilizers and pesticides. And any attempt at a middle-of-the-road course would be agonizing. If you are a chemical gardener, I maintain that you will find much in this book that will make your garden a better one. And, if you need recommendations for the application of chemical fertilizers or pesticides, your county agent can provide you with hundreds of pamphlets covering their every use.

Nitrogen supplies. Nitrogen is the nutrient most directly responsible for the healthy growth and dark green color of plants above the ground. Insufficient nitrogen will result in weak and stunted plant growth and a pale or yellow color in the foliage.

Nitrogen is supplied to plants from decaying organic matter through a complex chemical process that takes place in the soil. In brief, the protein from organic matter is broken down into its component amino acids from which ammonium compounds are formed. Certain bacteria then break down these compounds into nitrites, and different bacteria turn the nitrites into nitrates. It is only in the form of nitrates that plant roots can absorb nitrogen.

If your soil is now nitrogen-rich, you can keep it that way by annual applications of compost or manure. If, however, a soil test shows a serious lack, you can add large amounts in a hurry by growing *legume green manure crops*.

A green manure crop is one grown solely for the purpose of being turned under for soil enrichment, as I have said before. Legumes are members of the plant family *Leguminosae*, and include peas, beans, clover, and alfalfa as more prominent members of the family. The unique feature of legumes is their ability to draw huge amounts of nitrogen from the air, which is then stored in little lumps called *nodules*, which adhere to the roots of the plant. When the legumes are cut in fall, the nitrogen remains in the soil to aid next year's plantings. Further, the leafy parts of the plant, when plowed or tilled under, add other minerals and organic matter to the soil. It has been estimated that a single planting of a legume green manure crop will add as much nitrogen to one acre of soil as ten tons of manure, or 2,820 pounds of a 5-10-5 fertilizer. At today's prices, it would be worth well over $100, compared with the cost of a common 5 percent nitrogen chemical fertilizer.

In Wisconsin's climate, the best kinds of legume green manure crops are alfalfa and the clovers. Table 2 shows the results of legume tests carried out by researchers in Ames, Iowa.

You can see that Madrid sweetclover has done the best, by far, as a nitrogen-adding green manure legume. The sweetclover weevil, *Sitonia cylindricollis*, has caused many Wisconsin farmers to turn to other legumes less susceptible to the weevil; but the home gardener should not be bothered by this insect unless it is already in the area.

Growing legumes for green manure is not difficult. The soil

Table 2. Legume Production and Nitrogen Yield

Legume	Tons per Acre of Roots Plus Tops	Total Nitrogen Pounds per Acre
Madrid sweetclover	2.57	141
Grimm alfalfa	1.48	87
Southern common alfalfa	1.51	82
Ladino clover	1.30	74
Huban annual sweetclover	1.24	54
Medium red clover	.83	48

Source: Fribourg and Johnson, *Agronomy Journal* 47:73-76.

should be prepared as for any other crop, and the seed should be planted as directed when the soil warms up in the spring. Be sure that the soil is well supplied with phosphate and potassium for best results. (The incorporation of well-rotted manure or compost before planting will take care of this.) In addition, you should inoculate your seed with a *bacterial inoculant* for good nitrogen fixation. The inoculant is inexpensive and easy to use. It will appear as a dark brown or black powder, but actually it contains billions of beneficial bacteria that will enter the root hairs and form nodules on them. The nitrogen will be stored in these nodules, to the ultimate benefit of next year's plantings.

Since legumes are very deep-rooted plants, their nitrogen-giving benefits will extend way down to the subsoil, far beyond any that can be produced by spoon-feeding chemical forms of nitrogen. Last, remember that beans and peas are legumes, too, and will add significant amounts of nitrogen to the soil. Plant these crops in different parts of the garden each year, to help insure adequate nitrogen supplies for your entire garden plot. Also keep in mind that an early harvest of peas can be followed by another quick-growing vegetable crop in the same season — and the second crop will benefit from the nitrogen left in the soil by the peas.

Phosphorus. This mineral element is important for good root growth, for brighter color in all garden flowers, and for general plant health. Without sufficient phosphorus, the maturation of fruit (including that of vegetable plants) will be delayed, plants will be stunted, and the foliage may have a purplish tinge.

Many organic materials have substantial phosphorus content, but the best source naturally available is *phosphate rock*, which is actually about 30 percent pure phosphate — the other 70 percent being comprised of other minerals which are also beneficial to soil and plants. Again, a continuing program of organic soil feeding will add phosphorus — as well as other nutrients — to the soil throughout the year so that you should rarely have to worry about adding any single nutrient for any specific planting.

Potassium. This element is essential to plant growth, particularly in building strong stems, in aiding the plant to resist disease, in forming good fruit, and in reducing the moisture requirement of plants. If your plants are stunted in growth, if the fruit is small, and if the leaves turn brown, there is a chance of potassium deficiency.

Potassium, like all other plant nutrients, can be supplied through a general organic feeding program, using plenty of compost and manure. When large amounts are needed to correct a deficiency, however, it is best to turn to potash rock or to one of the other natural fertilizers high in potassium — granite dust, basalt rock, or greensand. Plant residues will also add potash to the soil, since much of the potash brought up by the plant roots is stored in the stems of the plant.

Calcium. This mineral element is important as a vital factor in chemical reactions of both soil and plants. It helps to neutralize toxic acids that might develop in plants, and it is important in preventing magnesium toxicity. Calcium is the principle element of limestone, and so it is inexorably a part of keeping the soil in the proper pH range. For more information on lime, see the section on acidity-alkalinity which follows.

Trace elements. The many so-called trace elements — including boron, cobalt, copper, iron, magnesium, manganese, molybdenum, and zinc — are vital to plants, but are needed in only very small amounts. A general organic soil-feeding program should be adequate insurance for the good supply of all these elements, without any further thought about them. But if you have been gardening chemically, or if you are working a plot which has been overworked in the past, shortages of any of them can cause problems. In this case, you should apply a mixture of rock powders, limestone, leaf mold (since trees bring up minerals from deep within the earth), and, if possible, some form of seaweed fertilizer. Milorganite, a commercially-available form of treated Milwaukee sewage sludge, is also very good as a source of trace minerals. The idea here is to get materials from outside your immediate area, since your own soil is already deficient in the minerals you are trying to introduce.

Acidity, alkalinity, and pH. The pH scale, which runs from 0 to 14, is used to indicate your soil's degree of acidity or alkalinity. The neutral point of the scale is 7. Soils that test out higher than 7 are alkaline; those that test out lower than 7 are acid. The entire matter of the pH scale, and how we have come to measure a soil in these terms, is involved in the general science of chemistry and is not worth going into fully here. You can, if you wish, find a full explanation in any good encyclopedia. Here, we will concern ourselves only with the effect of your own soil's pH on your garden plants, and how you can bring your soil into the pH range most favorable for the plants you want to grow.

Most garden plants — vegetables, fruits, and ornamentals —

like a slightly acid soil, perhaps in the pH range of 6.5 to 7.0. There
are significant exceptions, however, most involving bush and cane
berries. Among those plants that like a more acid soil (5.0 to 6.5)
are blackberries, blueberries, raspberries, and cranberries, as well
as marigolds, gardenias, and pink ladyslipper. Many other plants
like a soil only slightly less acid, while some plants prefer a soil
just slightly on the alkaline side. These include alyssum, iris,
phlox, asparagus, beans, beets, cabbage, cantaloupes, cauliflower,
celery, cucumbers, lettuce, onions, peas, rhubarb, and squash.
When cultivating instructions are given for specific plants in later
chapters, the pH preference of the plants will be mentioned if it
falls to the outside of the 6.5-7.0 range. Virtually no plant likes a
soil pH below 4.3 or above 7.4, however.

The soils of Wisconsin vary widely along the pH scale, although most are favorable for general plant growth. The northern
counties tend to have a neutral or slightly alkaline soil, although
the surface may be acid. Many of the north-central soils are sub-
stantially acid in nature, requiring correction before good garden
crops can be produced. The entire eastern third of the state has
predominantly neutral soil, as do the counties on the Minnesota
and Iowa borders. Finally, many soils of the southwest tend to be
mixed, running from the neutral range to fairly acid.

The best way to ascertain your soil's pH value is to have it

Table 3. POUNDS OF GROUND LIMESTONE NEEDED TO
RAISE pH IN SEVEN INCHES OF SOIL DEPTH

SOIL TYPE & AREA	pH 3.5 to 4.5	pH 4.5 to 5.5	pH 5.5 to 6.5
Sand & loamy sand:			
one acre	8000.0	1,000.0	1,200.0
100 sq. ft.	1.8	2.3	2.8
Sandy loam:			
one acre		1,600.0	2,600.0
100 sq. ft.		3.7	6.0
Loam:			
one acre		2,400.0	3,400.0
100 sq. ft.		5.5	7.8
Silt loam:			
one acre		3,000.0	4,000.0
100 sq. ft.		6.9	9.2
Clay loam:			
one acre		3,800.0	4,600.0
100 sq. ft.		8.8	10.6
Muck:			
one acre	5,800.0	7,600.0	8,600.0
100 sq. ft.	13.3	17.7	19.7

(Based on USDA agricultural tonnage figure recommendations.)

tested. The test is a simple one, and inexpensive to make. It will be a part of your basic soil test made by the State Soils Laboratory, or you can make it yourself using one of the little kits that many garden suppliers offer. In fact, you can tell immediately whether your soil is acid, alkaline, or neutral by exposing it to a piece of litmus paper. If the paper turns pink, the soil is acid. If it turns blue, it is alkaline. If it does not change color at all, the soil is neutral. You can also use the litmus paper to test the water you might use for your garden.

Correcting the soil's pH. As nearly every gardener knows, the way to correct an overly-acid soil is through the addition of lime. I believe that natural ground limestone is best, since there is no danger of poisoning the soil's life forms when the natural product is used. Limestone adds calcium to the soil, as well, thus serving double duty. (Note: If you want to add calcium to the soil without raising its pH, which is an unusual but conceivable situation, gypsum is the product generally recommended. Organic gardeners generally avoid it, since gypsum is a hydrated calcium sulfate, but it is difficult to find a substitute other than the lavish introduction of plant residues, which carry calcium in their leaves.)

The recommended amounts of lime to apply are given on the manufacturer's bag, or will be supplied with the return of your soil test. The recommended application will depend on your soil texture, but a normal application on loam, to move the pH up one point, is seventy-five pounds of limestone per 1,000 square feet of soil — more in heavy soils, and less in sandy soils.

Last, do not add lime to your soil each year as a routine matter. I do not know where the practice of annual and automatic "liming" got started, but I do know that plants are far more susceptible to an overly alkaline soil than to one that is acid — and that it is much more difficult to bring down the pH into the neutral range than to raise it from an acid condition.

If the soil is too alkaline, it can be brought down into the neutral range by the incorporation of organic matter with healthy helpings of peat moss, which is a naturally acid substance. Powdered sulfur is often recommended for this purpose, but the advantages of organic matter go far beyond the correction of pH, while the addition of sulfur provides few additional benefits.

The last word on pH is this: Do not take it too seriously. Do not get yourself in the position where you are trying to treat little patches of the garden differently because a pH of 6.5 is recommended for one crop and 7.0 for another. Nearly any garden plant will do well in the 6.5 to 7.0 range, no matter what the experts recommend. If, in your flower borders, you wish to incorporate peat to take down the pH for certain large plantings, fine. And if you want to do the same for your permanent berry patches, that's good. But if you try to put too fine a point on this pH business, you will soon find yourself tearing out your hair and cursing the day you ever heard of pH. A healthy soil, fed organically, seems to receive nearly all plants with equal grace. If, after a soil test, you want to correct the pH in a new garden plot, this is a wise thing to do. But after that, don't give it much thought. You will have better things to do.

One aker well compast is worth akers three.
—Thomas Tusser (1557)

Chapter Two

Composting and Mulching

The heart of the organic method of gardening and farming is *compost*. It is the keystone, the core, the pivotal activity of the natural method. To many organic gardeners, the compost heap is his chief source of pride. On a chilly autumn day, he will make a special trip behind the tool shed just to watch it steam. He will spend more time in investigating better composting methods than he will in looking for income tax deductions. And no wonder. Compost produces terrific results.

The subject of compost has received considerable attention from many experimenters. There is, in fact, a thousand-page book called *The Complete Book of Composting* (Rodale Press, 1960) which goes into the subject in as much fascinating detail as you could want. From that book, I will borrow a poem by Walt Whitman which gives full praises to compost (while saying something less laudatory about mankind):

Behold this compost! behold it well!
Perhaps every mite has once formed part of a sick person —
    yet behold!
The grass of spring covers the prairies,
The bean bursts noiselessly through the mould in the
    garden,
The delicate spear of the onion pierces upward,
The apple-buds cluster together on the apple-branches,
The resurrection of the wheat appears with pale visage out
    of its graves,
What chemistry!
That the winds are not really infectious,

That all is clean forever and forever,
That the cool drink from the well tastes so good,
That blackberries are so flavorous and juicy,
That the fruits of the apple-orchard and the orange-
      orchard, that melons, grapes, peaches, plums, will
      none of them poison me,
That when I recline on the grass I do not catch any disease,
Now I am terrified at the Earth, it is that calm and patient,
It grows such sweet things out of such corruptions,
It turns harmless and stainless on its axis, with such
      endless succession of diseased corpses,
It distils such exquisite winds out of such infused fetor,
It gives such divine materials to men, and accepts such
      leavings from them at last.

Compost! Wonderful stuff, indeed. But just what is it?

There are various definitions in different dictionaries, text-books, and agricultural bulletins, not all of which agree. My own definition of compost would be: *a mixture of different organic materials, air, and water, with the possible addition of soil and/or mineral products, which together have advanced so far in the process of decomposition as to be a valuable addition to soil for growing plants.*

That's quite a mouthful, but I do believe it is as short a definition as accuracy will allow. First, compost is a mixture — just as *fruit compote* is a mixture (both from the Latin *compositus*). Decomposed leaves alone are not compost, but they are *leaf mold*. Composted manure is not compost, but it is composted manure.

Second, compost is not compost until it has been composted! A pile of lawn clippings and garden refuse is not compost, and it will not be, until it is "finished" — sufficiently decomposed to be of immediate value in the soil to growing plants. The decomposition process requires both air and water, and so they are essential ingredients. On the other hand, both soil and mineral products (such as limestone) are valuable additions — but it is possible to make compost without them.

Is composting a fad? Composting has often been looked upon as a fad, especially by agricultural experts from government and university ranks. And, although these scientists have grudgingly come to accept composting in recent years (especially as fertilizer shortages occur), many of the "experts" still look upon compost making as some sort of mystic rite carried out by misguided organic zealots, perhaps during certain phases of the moon.

In truth, chemical fertilization can better be defined as a fad. It is a relatively recent deviation from the completely natural process of soil building that has been going on for millions of years, long before man ever rose up out of the primeval swamp. Composting is an essential part of nature's wheel of life, the never-ending process that brings new life from death. On the land, plant life springs from the soil, is fed by the sun and the rain, and, in death, returns to the soil to be composted and reborn. The marigold you grow today might contain a molecule (or one of Whitman's "mites") that has been the part of a thousand plants before, and traveled through the bellies of a hundred animals and birds. It may have ridden halfway around the world on the wind or the water. It may have formed part of a single cell of a small animal, or stayed for a hundred years in the trunk of a stately oak. It has died and been reborn countless times. So does nature conserve and recycle its resources, and so does compost play a vital role in this recycling process.

From raw plant wastes to rich, dark compost. Whether done in fourteen days or fourteen months, composting is the keystone of the organic method.

Composting is, then, an integral part of the wheel of life. It is nature's way of reducing raw organic materials (leaves, dead plants and animals, animal manure, etc.), mainly through the actions of soil organisms, to a crumbly brown humus which then becomes a vital part of the soil itself. All organic matter occurring naturally in the soil has gotten there by this composting process, which has been going on ever since the first crude plant life appeared and died on the face of the earth.

The gardener who composts his wastes is simply emulating nature's own methods. Of course, he has learned how to make certain refinements, to help along and speed the process, and he uses that compost where it will do his garden plants the most good. In this way, he works in harmony with nature, while achieving his own gardening ends in a most scientific and efficient way. To me, the practice of composting represents one of the best examples of man's using his mastery of empirical science to enhance his own life — and is far from any fad or antiscientific mystic rite, as I know the definitions of those terms. Composting is a sane application of the scientific method.

WHAT COMPOST DOES

Compost is a fertilizer. It contains nitrogen, phosphorous, potassium, calcium, the essential trace minerals — all the chemical nutrients that plants need for healthy growth. How much of these nutrients it contains depends, of course, on the ingredients that go into it. You can help determine its chemical composition by the materials you select.

Compost is a soil conditioner. It will lighten a heavy clay, add substance to a light sand, add porosity where it is lacking, improve water-holding capacity, aid soil structure, and enhance the physical environment for the growth of all plants.

Compost increases the population of the soil's life forms. It encourages the rapid multiplication of microorganisms and earthworms, both of which are vitally important to healthy plant growth.

Compost is a chemical catalyst for the release of mineral nutrients. The acids it forms during decomposition cause chemical changes which release those minerals so that plant roots can absorb and use them in the plant's natural growth processes. Other organisms which are encouraged by compost emit disease-resisting antibiotics to protect growing plants, while still others are able to fix nitrogen for plant absorption.

Last, many gardeners and farmers who have worked with compost for many years are convinced that it has some powers which we have not yet identified. This feeling comes about when composters look at the results of their efforts — the trees laden with sweet fruit, the vines heavy with robust vegetables, the large and brilliantly colored blossoms of their flowering plants, the rarity of disease and insect attack, and the vastly superior quality of everything they grow. It is a quality that they swear cannot be duplicated by any combination of chemical applications, and so they can attribute it only to some benefits imparted by compost, known to nature but unknown to men. This is not to infer that any mystical powers are involved, but merely to acknowledge that man has not yet learned all there is to know about the earth.

George Washington Carver, who was himself an agricultural chemical wizard, advised, "Make your own fertilizer on the farm. Buy as little as possible. A year-round compost pile is absolutely essential and can be had with little labor and practically no cash outlay."

Dr. Carver had plenty of experience with both compost and chemical fertilizers. He died in 1943 before the advocates of agribusiness had convinced most farmers that composting was "impractical."

HOW TO USE COMPOST

Compost will help all growing plants. You will screen it to use as a potting soil and to start seedlings and grow house plants. You will till it into the vegetable garden and the flower beds. You will side-dress your peonies with compost and you will make a "tea" of it to feed your roses in midsummer. You will spoon-feed it to your baby McIntosh apple tree, and you will rake it into the lawn in the spring. Your landscape plantings will gobble up tons of compost as the years go by, and you will be glad they did. You will use compost for everything you grow, after you have learned of its versatility and seen the results of its use. Compost is the nearest thing to a garden panacea that you are ever likely to see.

In the vegetable garden. Use all the compost you can in the vegetable garden. In the fall, spread a two-to-three-inch layer and till it in, along with the last of the plant wastes. When planting in spring, incorporate plenty of well-rotted compost with every seedling you transplant, and mix in plenty in the furrows where you plant seeds. During the growing season, apply compost as a top-dressing, hoeing it shallowly into the soil. It is virtually impossible to use too much compost, as you can see for yourself by sinking a tomato seedling into a well-advanced compost heap. The production of that plant will make your eyes pop.

Mulch window boxes with finished, sifted compost. The soil in the box will hold moisture longer, and each rainfall will wash nutrients down to hungry plant roots.

In the flower garden. The liberal use of compost will give you larger and healthier plants of all kinds, with larger and more brilliant blooms. When planting spring-flowering bulbs in the fall, work plenty of fully-matured compost directly under and around each bulb. When sowing annuals in the spring, treat the seedbed with compost just as you would for vegetable sowings. When perennials have come up in the spring, work generous amounts of compost into the beds after loosening the top several inches of soil. During the growing season, all flowers will benefit from feedings of "compost tea." Just fill a bucket one-third full of compost and fill the rest of the bucket with water. Stir well and let this stand for a day. Then stir again and pour the tea around your perennials and annuals. The good nutrients will soak down into the soil and feed the plant roots without disturbing them. You can use the same compost for several applications of tea, and afterwards you can work the remaining solid material into the soil for general enrichment purposes.

For the lawn. Compost will help you to establish a permanent and healthy lawn that will last a lifetime. The use of compost in building new lawns and renovating sick lawns is explained in Chapter 7, beginning on page 277. For regular lawn feeding, compost should be screened as fine as possible and scattered lightly over the lawn at regular intervals. In the spring, a major feeding may be made, using a spike tooth aerator. The holes that the aerator makes will catch screened compost and send it down to the roots, while rains will envelop surface compost and carry nutrients down slowly, thus providing nourishment throughout the season.

For trees and shrubs. No tree or shrub should be planted without incorporating a bushel or more of compost into the planting hole. The compost, mixed with topsoil, leaf mold, peat moss, limestone, and sand (or any combination of these, depending on soil requirements) will give a permanent planting a great send-off and will help it to get well-established in short order by providing an ideal root environment. Compost should also be used to keep tree and shrub roots well supplied with nutrients during the growing season. Again, full directions are given later on, in the chapter devoted to trees and shrubs.

For seedlings and houseplants. You will use your very best compost, well screened, as a potting soil for houseplants and for starting seeds in the early spring. You should use your most mature compost for this purpose, to avoid any chance of burning the tender young seedlings during their crucial first days.

Compost, then, is your all-around soil conditioner/fertilizer, more valuable than any commercial products you might buy. And you can make it yourself, right at home, for practically nothing or absolutely nothing. There is no greater bargain in the world.

HOW TO MAKE COMPOST

When you think about it, the term "making compost" is an arrogant one. We don't really *make* compost — we merely try to create the conditions that will encourage nature to make the compost herself. We are not following a dress pattern, here, or building a table — we are working with the very process of life itself. Neither are we working with a magic formula that will produce results with no understanding or effort on our part. I venture these thoughts not to air my personal philosophy, but because I think it can help us to work towards better compost and better gardens.

In March 1974, an interesting article appeared in the *Wall Street Journal*. The writer, Ralph E. Winter (an Ohioan who, the article tells us, was brought up on a Wisconsin dairy farm) was telling of his garden troubles and failures, including an unresponsive compost heap. He writes:

> That brings up the compost pile. It was supposed to solve the soil problem by providing virtually free fertilizer along with humus to condition the soil. We dutifully piled up the grass clippings all the previous summer and in the fall added a huge mound of leaves. We even drove around the community and picked up leaves the neighbors had bagged. We stirred it all together and left it to "compost" over winter.

> Well, something went wrong because when spring came we still had a pile of leaves, some wet and some dry but still perfectly sound leaves, instead of the expected decayed mulch. We dug it into the garden anyway rather than wait another year to see if the magical composting process would work.

Apparently, Mr. Winter received some bad advice, or, at best, incomplete advice on making compost. He followed bad directions with little understanding of the life processes he was dealing with, and then he sat back and waited for the "magical composting process" to perform for him. Just from his short description, I can count three major mistakes that he made:

1. He *"dutifully piled up grass clippings all the previous summer."* Instead, he should have been adding the clippings to a properly-constructed heap all summer long, and he should have included topsoil and at least some manure, which would have introduced essential microorganisms to the mixture.

2. *". . . and in the fall added a huge mound of leaves."* Leaves are perhaps the most difficult of all organic materials to compost (unless you choose to compost bones). They should be shredded, first, and in no case should they make up the bulk of any compost heap, unless you have all the time in the world.

3. *"We stirred it all together and left it to 'compost' over winter."*

Winter is the worst time for composting, because the cold temperatures inhibit the actions of the microorganisms that break down
organic materials. The compost heap should have been working
away all summer long.

In short, Mr. Winter did everything wrong, and then he
counted on the "magic" of composting to produce humus for his
garden. I think that no gardener will make mistakes like these if
he approaches composting with a realistic attitude — and that
attitude is, as I have said, one of *encouraging life processes*. A
compost heap must have water, because water is essential to all
life. It must have air because the essential microorganisms cannot
live without air. It must have soil from the garden because soil
contains the microorganisms that will multiply rapidly throughout
the heap, eagerly attacking the other materials and breaking them
down into humus. The compost heap must be large enough to
allow for its heating up, too — four by six feet is the smallest
generally recommended — because a heap that is too small will
lose too much heat from surface contact with the air. All these
factors — the basics of compost-making — are vitally important in
creating the composting life environment. Think about your composting project in these terms, and you will get better compost.

SIX COMPOSTING METHODS

The Indore method. There are quite a few ways to let nature
make compost for you — under the ground, above the ground, in
bins, boxes, bags, and garbage cans, in strips, in sheets, in
trenches, in fourteen months or in fourteen days, indoors or outdoors. But they all stem from the famous Indore method developed
by Sir Albert Howard during his agricultural research in India.
This is the basic method of composting, and the one that is still
used most widely today. Here is how to do it.

Select a good spot for the heap. The area should be fairly level,
at least four by six feet, preferably larger; six by ten would be
ideal for optimum heat conservation. Most people choose a spot at
the back of the garden, perhaps hidden by a small fence or a low
hedge. But remember that a compost heap does not have to be
unattractive, and it certainly shouldn't give off any offensive odors
or attract rodents — not if it is built right. Most people want to
contain the heap by constructing some sort of walls on three sides
of the designated area (leaving the fourth side open for working
room). These walls can be made of cinder blocks, wooden posts and
boards, or some other permanent construction — or, if you do not
want a permanent bin, you can use walls of sod or of posts and
wire fencing (which can be rolled up and moved after the heap is
finished), or an arrangement of boards that can be removed easily,
perhaps built upon the concept of the Lincoln Logs we used to
play with as kids. Or, you can have no walls at all — but in this

A compost bin can be quite attractive, if a little thought is put into it.

A split log compost bin allows air to enter for more efficient composting.

Wire fencing makes a good portable compost bin.

case, you should have plenty of room to work in, because the heap will tend to spread out as you add materials to it.

After you have selected the site, dig away the topsoil (twelve to eighteen inches) from the area and pile it to one side. You will use this to stimulate the heap from time to time, and you will be improving the subsoil which you have exposed.

Next, put a layer of brush over the area, perhaps a foot deep, to form a good base that will provide drainage. Now you are ready to begin to "sandwich" the layers of organic materials. (And the only reason for sandwiching layers is to be able to measure amounts of the different materials with some degree of accuracy.) Over the brush, put down a six-inch layer of green matter — weeds, grass clippings, plant wastes, leaves, etc. If you can shred these materials — with a compost shredder or by attacking a pile of them with your rotary lawn mower — they will decay much faster. (The microorganisms will have more surface area to work on.) After that, put down a two-inch layer of manure, followed by a sprinkling of topsoil mixed with powdered limestone. Repeat these layers — green matter, manure, topsoil/limestone — until the heap reaches about five feet in height. After that, keep the heap watered so that it is damp but not soggy, and wait for about six weeks. Then it will be time to turn it so that the materials on the

Keep the heap watered, making sure that it is always damp but never soggy. Bacteria cannot work without moisture.

outer edges of the heap get a chance to go into the inside, where all the action is. Turning the heap sounds like a back-breaking job, and if your back is weak, perhaps it is. But you need do it only twice a year at most, and a heap of the size I have just described can be turned in half an hour. If you shovel your own snow in winter, then turning the heap will present no problem. If not, then I suggest that you hire a husky boy for the job. Indore tradition specifies that you turn the heap a second time, in another six weeks, although some veteran gardeners have expressed doubts about the necessity of the second turning. Nevertheless, after three months, the heap should be finished and ready for use.

(A note on chemical fertilizers: Most government and university bulletins stress chemical fertilizer as an essential ingredient of the compost heap. I will flatly deny that they are essential, and I doubt very much whether they are beneficial to the final product. To me, chemical fertilizers are comparable to synthetic vitamin tablets. If your diet is a good one, rich in all the essential nutrients, you will not need synthetic vitamin supplements. And if your compost heap contains a variety of natural materials, rich in plant nutrients, you will certainly not need expensive chemical fertilizers. The only time I would resort to the practice, in fact, would be in a case where the soil is critically depleted of major nutrients and it is essential that it be built up quickly during the first season. At that, chemicals are a short-term answer, while natural compost will build your soil for the future.)

When compost is finished. How can you tell when the compost is finished? If it is crumbly, dark brown, and has that characteristic earthlike odor, it is finished. But if the materials are still easily recognizable, it is not. You can check the progress of your heap by plunging your hand into it and feeling the temperature. If it is "working" properly, the heap will be very hot inside — uncomfortable to the touch — because of the intense bacterial action. The heating process should begin during the first few days. After a number of days of heating, the heap will cool down slowly and, when it seems quite cool inside, the major composting action will be finished in that part of the heap.

Compost problems. If you detect a musty odor in the heap, like the one you get when you leave a sack of potatoes too long in the basement, that indicates that mold is forming because of a lack of air. Tear apart the heap, add some spoiled hay or straw to loosen it up, and put it back in the bin. On the other hand, if you detect an ammonia smell, it means that you are losing nitrogen through the formation of free ammonia. The problem may be too much fresh manure or too much lime. Cut down on these, tear apart the heap, add spoiled hay or straw and more green matter, and return the materials to the bin.

If the heap does nothing at all, it is usually a sign of a lack of nitrogen materials, or of microorganisms. Manure and topsoil are

Powdered limestone is a valuable addition to the heap.

The Indore method specifies that the heap be built in layers, so that measurement of materials is reasonably accurate. Here, a layer of green matter is being added.

This compost shredder will make the job faster and easier, because shredded materials give soil organisms more surface area to work on.

the remedies here. There are bacterial activators on the market, but they have never been proven more effective than topsoil, which has all the activators your heap can use.

The three-month estimate for finished compost is based on the following of directions for the traditional Indore heap. The amount of time it takes for your heap to complete its composting process will depend on several factors, including the weather (longer, if it is cool), the size of the heap (longer, if it small), and the particle size of the green matter you use (shorter, if you shred all materials).

When compost is crumbly, dark brown, and has that characteristic earth-like odor, you know it is finished and ready for use.

The Fourteen-Day method. When I worked as an editor for *Organic Gardening and Farming* magazine back in the 1950s, we ran experiments at the Rodale Organic Experimental Farm in Emmaus, Pennsylvania, to see in just how little time we could make finished compost. Scientists at the University of California had cut the minimum time to fourteen days, just by shredding all materials and turning the heap every two or three days. We followed the California recommendations and, after adding a few wrinkles of our own, got to the point where we could produce finished compost in *ten days*. Now you may have absolutely no desire to set any world records for composting — and neither did we, for that matter. But the lesson to be learned in such experimenting is just what factors are responsible for encouraging the composting process. Shredding of materials, of course, is the major factor. Another important one is the use of sufficient manure, which contains plenty of nitrogen and produces heat within the heap in the shortest possible time. The third factor of importance is moisture. Microorganisms cannot work in a bone-dry environment, nor in a constantly soggy one. Keep the heap *damp*, and provide good drainage. Aeration never presented a problem in our experiments, but it is doubtless a fourth important factor which you should consider carefully.

(Note: When shredding materials with a rotary mower, either use a grass-catcher attachment, or run the mower alongside a wall to catch the blowing material. Tip the mower onto its rear wheels and attack the pile of material gradually — and be sure to wear safety glasses and safety shoes.)

The anaerobic method. Anaerobic composting (composting without air) is a method that has led to some systems of municipal composting, the large-scale composting of urban wastes. The advantage of anaerobic composting is that it presents no problems with odor, which might be particularly important if you work with fresh manure on a small city lot. You can compost manure by piling it on the ground (not on grass or sod, which might discourage earthworms from coming up), soaking the manure heap with water, covering it with black plastic (to shut out the sun), sealing the edges with soil and rocks, and forgetting about it for a couple of months. When you lift the plastic, you should have crumbly, sweet-smelling, composted manure, the kind that you buy in bags at garden centers and seed stores. (I might say that I cannot personally guarantee the method, since I have never tried it myself, but others report great success with it.)

Other gardeners have reported success with anaerobic composting in dark-colored leaf bags or in garbage cans. Still, the method is not a very wide-spread one, and much research remains to be done in the area. I would not be surprised to see a commercially-made anaerobic composting bin offered to the public within the next several years — one that will produce finished compost in record time with no turning, no odor problems, and no possibility of nutrients leaching away into the earth.

The earthworm method. Still another composting method lets the earthworms do the work for you. Build wooden pits of any size, but probably no more than two feet high. Mix the materials in about the same proportions as recommended for the Indore method, and fill the pits to within a few inches of the top. Then moisten the mixture thoroughly and add earthworms. The more earthworms you add, the faster will be the composting process. About five hundred would be the absolute minimum for a pit three feet square. Then, put a lid on the box, since earthworms prefer to work in the dark, but do not make it too tight fitting. After that, let the earthworms go to work. At the end of a few months, you will have beautiful, crumbly compost, and about four times as many earthworms as you started with. Put about half of the earthworms into the garden (or let the kids sell some of them to fishermen), and start out again with more raw material.

Strip composting and sheet composting. Both of these methods were discussed briefly in Chapter 1 (page 16). Sheet composting is simply the process of spreading the raw materials over the soil and tilling them into the earth, thus allowing the composting process to take place right in the soil instead of in a heap or bin. The advantage of sheet composting is that there is very little work involved, and more of the material's nitrogen will be preserved (since some of a heap's nitrogen is inevitably vaporized and lost). The disadvantage is that you cannot plant anything in the garden during the month or two that the materials are working. The heat generated by the composting process would burn plants, especially if fresh manure is used.

Strip composting is identical to sheet composting, except that you divide the garden plot into wide strips, perhaps five feet each, and apply the compost materials to every other strip — or even every third strip — while you plant the other strips as usual. In the next growing season, you plant the strips you had composted the previous year, and compost the strips that you had planted the previous year. In this way, you take only part of your garden out of production each year, while enriching the remaining part for future years. Both strip and sheet composting are excellent methods of improving the soil for plants, but only if you are fortunate enough to have the garden space to spare.

GREAT MATERIALS FOR COMPOSTING: A BAKER'S DOZEN

By now you may be asking yourself, "Just where does he think I am going to get all this manure? How will I find enough green matter to build this glorious heap?" Perhaps the only material you really have in abundance is leaves, and you get those only once a year, in a whirl of autumn color.

Well, the gathering of composting materials can be a problem, but it is one you can solve. Begin in and around your own home, of course, with plant wastes, kitchen scraps, grass clippings, and any other organic materials you might come across. Then, if you need more, go out and scavenge. Need manure? Many farmers wouldn't part with  their manure under threat of death, but the operators of riding stables would, and so will many dairy farmers who keep large herds and till relatively little land. Is there a livestock feeding lot nearby? You can probably get all the manure you can use there. Or perhaps you have a farmer friend or relative. You probably can sweet-talk a friend out of enough manure to service your compost heap for a year. Investigate.

Then, for green matter and other materials, use your imagination and all the resources of your community. Get out the yellow pages and let your fingers do the walking. Call meat packing houses, mills, breweries, dairies, vegetable processing plants, etc. Call the city parks department to ask for lawn clippings and last

Bloodmeal is not only a good source of nitrogen, but an effective rabbit repellent, as well.

year's leaves. Live near the water? Aquatic plants are always in abundance — often a nuisance in the water, where they clog up boat propellers, but a blessing in the compost heap. With a little effort and a little ingenuity, you will find all the materials you want — and you might have some pleasant adventures along the way.

Here are a dozen and one materials that are great for composting. Most are fairly common, while others are harder to get but well worth going after. All are highly recommended for building the dark brown humus that makes plants grow.

Alfalfa hay. NPK (nitrogen-phosphorus-potash percentages) 2.45-0.50-2.10. A good source of both nitrogen and potash, alfalfa hay is available from many farmers in late August or September — or you might be able to buy a couple of bales of last year's crop at any time during the year, if the farmer has a surplus.

Bat guano. NPK 6.00-9.00-0.00. Here is a manure not available to everyone, but a great source of nitrogen and phosphorus, if you can get it. Large numbers of bats often roost in farmers' barns and in deserted outbuildings. Collect the guano during the day, when the bats will be sleeping high in the rafters. (It is best to keep out of their way during the evening feeding flight.)

Bloodmeal. NPK 15.00-1.30-0.70. A terrific nitrogen source, and also an effective rabbit repellent when sprinkled around the vegetable garden. Call meat packing houses to ask about bloodmeal. You can buy it by the pound in garden centers, but the price is apt to be high.

Bone meal. NPK 4.00-21.00-0.20. One of the highest sources of phosphorus available; most composters will have to buy it at the garden center, but some lucky ones can pick it up at bone mills.

Brewer's grains (wet). NPK 0.90-0.50-0.05. The golden hops that make Wisconsin's beer sparkle can make your compost heap absolutely glow! Brewers discard mounds of hops after they have been "spent", and will likely let you have all you can haul away.

Cattle manure (fresh). NPK 0.29-0.17-0.10. Manure is the greatest activator for your compost heap; it is very important for fast heating. Get some any way you can, but get some! (If the farmer is a real friend, he will lend his old Ford pickup truck to you for hauling it home.)

Duck manure (fresh). NPK 1.12-1.44-0.49. My waterfowling friends tell me that you can scrape copious amounts of wild duck manure off the ice of ponds in the early spring. But you will be luckier if you know a farmer who raises domestic ducks.

Horse manure (fresh). NPK 0.44-0.17-0.35. Find out on which days the stable hands clean out the stalls — and then get there before they do. One hour's volunteer effort will reward you with hundreds of pounds of the stuff — enough to last for months and months.

Kitchen scraps. The food scraps you discard end up either in

Twenty great organic soil builders. TOP ROW: (l. to r.) wood ashes, basic slag, leaves, sawdust, blood meal. SECOND ROW: raw phosphate, greensand, bone meal, peat moss, cottonseed meal. THIRD ROW: seaweed, dried manure, tankage, peanut shells, leaf mold. FOURTH ROW: wood chips, manure, cocoa bean shells, compost, grass clippings.

Wisconsin's waters, where they pollute, or in dumps or landfill sites. Why not put them into your garden, where they will do some good? Kitchen wastes can attract both domestic and wild animals (usually rodents), however, and you should be careful to bury them about a foot deep into the heap and cover with soil. In sheet or strip composting, just trench them into the earth at the end of each day.

Leaves are an especially important soil builder because of their abundance of trace minerals. Ask your local parks department where you can pick up leaves for garden use.

Oak leaves. NPK 0.65-0.13-0.52. Any kind of leaves are great, especially as a source of trace minerals, and oak leaves are given just as an example. But remember that they're tough and should be shredded before going into the heap.

Swine manure. NPK 0.60-0.41-0.13. You'll learn a new respect for the much-maligned swine, when you learn that his manure is more valuable than that of any other farm animal. Use it well!

Tobacco leaves. NPK 4.00-0.50-6.00. Residents of Wisconsin's tobacco-growing region should investigate the possibilities of picking up spoiled leaves from growers in the late summer and early fall. Shredding is essential for these giant leaves (and the stems, too), but the rewards in nutrients are well worth the effort expended.

Wood ashes. NPK 0.00-1.50-7.00. Potash is the big reward here. Save all the ashes from your fireplace, and urge your noncomposting neighbors to do the same. A single winter should produce a

Table 4. NUTRIENT CONTENT OF REPRESENTATIVE
WISCONSIN LEAF VARIETIES

Tree	Cal-cium	Magne-sium	Potas-sium	Phos-phorus	Nitro-gen	Ash	pH
Balsam fir	1.12	0.16	0.12	0.09	1.25	3.08	5.50
Red maple	1.29	0.40	0.40	0.09	0.52	10.97	4.70
Sugar maple	1.81	0.24	0.75	0.11	0.67	11.85	4.30
American beech	0.99	0.22	0.65	0.10	0.67	7.37	5.08
White ash	2.37	0.27	0.54	0.15	0.63	10.26	6.80
White oak	1.36	0.24	0.52	0.13	0.65	5.71	4.40
E. hemlock	0.68	0.14	0.27	0.07	1.05	--	5.50

Courtesy, *Organic Gardening and Farming*

twenty-gallon pail full of them if you use your fireplace a couple of
times a week. And with the price of commercial fertilizers, saving
your ashes is like getting a deposit back on your fireplace wood!

(Note: The NPK percentages given above for all manures assume that they are fresh, thus containing plenty of moisture.
Dried manure will contain up to four times the percentage of
nutrients, pound for pound.)

SECRETS OF MULCHING

The practice of mulching, like composting, is taken straight
from nature's textbook. In the wild, all soil is covered, either by
growing plants or by the plant wastes of years gone by. The forest
is covered constantly with a deep leaf mulch, and the prairie fields
are never bare, summer or winter. Nature's mulch is her one giant
step toward composting, for when any dead plant materials touch
the ground, they come into contact with soil microorganisms and
become intimately involved in the process of composting and soil
formation. Noting the success of Mother Nature in forest and field,
we do our best to emulate her in our gardens.

A mulch is simply any material — organic or inorganic —
placed on top of the soil to benefit growing plants. Most mulches
are organic, such as hay and sawdust, but others are inorganic,
including plastic sheets and rocks.

The benefits of mulches cannot be counted on two hands, so
valuable are they to garden success, especially here in Wisconsin's
cold climate. But here are the major rewards, any one of which
should be sufficient to send you on your way to gather up mulch
materials for every part of the garden:

1. Mulches conserve moisture, protecting your plants against
drought by slowing down evaporation. This is important for all
plants, but especially so for the shallow-rooted ones such as
blueberries. It is also essential for vegetable plantings in areas
where watering is difficult or impossible.

Spoiled hay is of little use to the farmer — but it is far and away the favorite mulch for the vegetable garden.

2. Mulches increase soil aeration by keeping the surface soil loose and preventing soil crusting.

3. Mulches check weeds, saving you hours of work and grumbling.

4. Mulches improve soil texture and fertility, and they encourage soil microorganisms and earthworms. Organic mulches break down slowly from the bottom up and can actually be regarded as a slow form of sheet composting. In the fall, many organic mulches can be plowed under for further soil enrichment.

5. Mulches moderate soil temperature. They reduce the possibility of root crops freezing in the late fall, and they protect young plants against late spring freezes, thus extending the growing season for many plants. During the summer, they also protect heat-sensitive crops (such as peas) from too much sun.

6. Mulches offer protection to small and tender plants from heavy winds, rain, and hail. A hay mulch can quickly be pulled up around young plants when bad weather threatens.

7. Mulches prevent the rotting and discoloration of those crops that ripen naturally on the ground, such as tomatoes, strawberries, cucumbers, and squash. They form a clean bed for these crops.

8. Mulches prevent root damage to perennials from winter heaving. The small feeder roots of perennials — especially the shallow-rooted ones — are often damaged by the heaving of the ground during alternate freezes and thaws, particularly during late fall and early spring. A heavy mulch helps to keep the soil temperature steady, thus preventing heaving and reducing root damage.

9. During heavy rains, mulches prevent mud from splashing on low-growing flowers, on sidewalks, on the siding of the house, on anything else that you would rather keep clean.

10. Mulches reduce the need for cultivation, sometimes eliminating it completely. Cultivating with a hoe kills weeds and keeps the soil loose and porous. A mulch does the same thing.

MATERIALS FOR MULCHING

A wide variety of materials are suitable for mulching, although some are more suitable than others. Here is a rundown of some of the more popular ones:

Buckwheat hulls. This is a very nice-looking mulch, effective against weeds and easy to handle, although a little light and subject to blowing for the first few days. Buckwheat hulls let water pass through easily, which is a big point in their favor. This is a mulch you will have to buy at the garden center unless you have access to a processing plant.

Cocoa bean hulls and shells. Both are attractive and effective mulches, suitable for your showy flower beds. For the first week, they will make your garden smell like one giant chocolate bar, which always delights the children. These must be purchased at the garden center, and the price is apt to be high enough for you to rake them up and store them in the autumn instead of tilling them under.

Lawn clippings. Here is an effective mulch that you can apply all season long. Clippings are effective against weeds, easy to handle, and they stay put. They do tend to heat up and decompose quickly, though, especially if they are very moist and the day is hot.

Leaves. Unshredded leaves tend to mat down like thousands of little ink blotters, excluding both air and moisture from reaching the soil. It is best to shred them and mix them with other materials, perhaps hay or sawdust.

Buckwheat hulls make an attractive mulch for the flower beds.

Paper and plastic. Both are sold commercially, in rolls. They are effective against weeds, but awfully unsightly, tear easily, blow away, and, in my opinion, ecologically offensive. They offer nothing for the soil after their use as a mulch has expired.

Peat moss. This is a good-looking material — rich, dark brown, and neat — that will really dress up flower beds. But weeds tend to grow up through peat, unless the peat is applied fairly heavily; and after it becomes dry it tends to shed water with all the facility of wax paper.

Pine needles. These are a good mulch for acid-loving plants such as berries, and, of course, young pine plantings.

Sawdust and wood chips. Both are effective mulches, although some experts believe there is some danger of sawdust robbing the soil of nitrogen. Sawdust is recommended for berries, especially, while the chips are rather attractive when used with landscape plantings.

Sawdust can often be picked up for the asking at lumber mills. It makes a great mulch for strawberries.

Spoiled hay. This is the most popular mulch for the vegetable garden. Buy or beg bales from a farmer. To place the mulch, cut the baling twine and just peel off six-to-eight inch slabs to place between the vegetable rows. The hay slabs go down fast, almost like putting carpet tile in your garden. Hay is effective against weeds, lets rain pass through easily, and keeps the soil moist and cool during summer. At the end of the season, just pick up the intact slabs and store them for next year. Any loose hay can be tilled under in the fall, used for winter protection of perennials, trees, and shrubs, or added to the compost heap.

Stones and rocks. If you have access to large, flat stones, try them as a mulch, especially on banks and steep slopes where they will help to prevent erosion most effectively. As a discourager of weeds, stones are obviously unbeatable. There are disadvantages, however. Stones are heavy to work with, and they do harbor some destructive insects.

Weeds. There is nothing wrong with using weeds for mulch, except that they are unattractive and capable of depositing unwanted seeds in the garden if they are added when the seeds are mature. For larger plantings of potatoes, squash, etc., however, they can be quite useful — although most gardeners prefer to relegate weeds to the compost heap.

Other materials. There are dozens of other materials you can use, including cornstalks and cobs, rotted pinewood, vegetable plant processing wastes, tree bark and sawmill scraps, leather tannery wastes, and other natural products and industrial wastes. If it isn't toxic and if it does the job, use it. Again, walk the yellow pages to find all the free and low-cost mulch materials you can use in every corner of your garden.

When to apply mulch. For annual flowers and vegetables, apply a spring mulch after the soil has warmed up fully and the seedlings and transplants are well established. If you apply mulch too early, the soil will not receive the full warming effects of the sun, and plant growth will be slowed. This is crucial here in Wisconsin where spring is slow enough, as it is.

Your prize landscape plants can be protected over the winter by the application of a heavy autumn mulch, preferably made after the soil has frozen. Remove the mulch after the last average spring frost date.

For your perennials, adopt the same policy. After the weather turns warm in the spring, remove the winter mulch and stack it near the beds. Cultivate lightly and then replace the mulch.

For all plants, the mulch should be applied after you have fertilized and incorporated any supplemental organic matter to the soil, just as a matter of convenience. This is true for both spring and fall mulch applications. If you apply more fertilizer during the season, the mulch can be pushed aside quite easily for the purpose, then replaced.

How much mulch? The amount of mulch you apply depends on how much is needed to do the job. You should apply enough so that the weeds do not grow through. In the case of hay, it might be eight inches or more — but only one inch of sawdust should do the same job. For materials such as cocoa bean shells, buckwheat

Mulch, mulch, and more mulch is the key to success for Ruth Stout, shown here working in her Connecticut garden.

hulls, pine needles, and lawn clippings, from two to three inches should be about right. As you experiment, you will quickly learn the right amounts of different mulches to use for all garden purposes.

The Ruth Stout no-work method. In 1955, Ruth Stout, an inveterate Connecticut gardener, published a book called *How to Have a Green Thumb Without an Aching Back* (Exposition Press). The book created a sensation in the gardening world because it advocated a deep, year-round hay mulch all over the garden. With the continuous mulch, Ruth Stout had eliminated all plowing, tilling, cultivating, composting, and several other time-honored pastimes of gardeners. Each spring, she simply pushed aside the mulch, dropped in the seeds or new plants, and returned to the back porch to watch another season of spectacular results.

Well, actually there is more to the method than that, and if you are interested in Miss Stout's revolutionary approach, I refer you to her books, which are certainly among the most delightful, entertaining, and informative in all garden literature. *How to Have a Green Thumb Without an Aching Back* is, I understand, now out in an inexpensive paperback edition (Cornerstone Library). And Miss Stout's sequel, *Gardening Without Work*, is still in print (Devin-Adair Co., 1961). Ruth Stout is fascinating, warm, and human, both in her books and in person. And her system works, at least for her. I have never been brave enough to adopt it, myself, but I do recommend that you look into her no-work system, especially if age or physical infirmity limits your activities. Ruth Stout is ninety years old now, and still maintains a large garden by applying her own labor-saving inventions.

At Christmas I no more desire a rose
Than wish a snow in May's new-fangled mirth;
But like of each thing that in season grows.
                    —Shakespeare
                         Love's Labour's Lost (1594-95)

Chapter Three

What To Do
About The Weather

Shakespeare apparently didn't foresee the age of the FTD florist truck, which can bring a rose at any old time — but he and his contemporaries must have kept a better sense of the natural order of things. In contrast, we have learned just enough to make ourselves dissatisfied with the weather, particularly in the early Wisconsin spring, when we feel that we just can't take any more snow and zero temperatures.

In Shakespeare's time, we would have learned to resign ourselves to the coming and going of the seasons. Now we fight. And the tools with which we fight are growing more numerous all the time.

If ever a way is found to make the weather perfect the year around, we Wisconsin gardeners would be a sorry lot. We love to complain about the weather. Some of us find it a handy scapegoat for many of our garden failures. Others hold up our harsh northern climate as a badge of courage, making our garden triumphs that much more satisfying. Most of us, though, usually just grumble or smile contentedly, depending on the weather of the day, and then we do the best we can.

In early April, when the books say we should be putting in our peas, we laugh bitterly as we grab our snow shovels, hopefully for the last time that season. Then, scarcely a month later, an early heat wave wilts our peas and sends our spinach bolting to seed. And no sooner do we pick the spinach when a cold and rainy week rots our lima beans cold in the ground, right where we planted them the week before.

Grumble as we may, though, we are more fortunate than many. Weather changes can come quickly, but not nearly so quickly as in the northern plain states to the west. Our growing season is short, but still long enough for us to grow almost all the vegetable crops we want (especially if we choose the right varieties) and enough different ornamental plants to afford ourselves an infinite variety of foliage and bloom for most of the year. And, perhaps most important, Wisconsin is blessed with one of the most favorable rainfall climates in the world, according to a fact-packed booklet called *Wisconsin Weather*.

In this chapter, we will not go into the volumes of climatological statistics for the state. For such statistics, as well as for much general and helpful information about Wisconsin's climate, I refer you to the aforementioned booklet, *Wisconsin Weather*, which is available free from your county Extension agent or by writing to Wisconsin Statistical Reporting Service, Post Office Box 5160, Madison, Wisconsin 53705. Instead, we will concentrate on the ways that weather affects your garden, and ways in which you can work with Wisconsin's climate to grow better gardens.

The growing season. The time between the last killing frost in spring and the first killing frost in autumn is the active growing season. That time, in Wisconsin, ranges from about 182 days down in Kenosha county in the extreme southeast, to 112 days up in Bayfield County, where the last spring frost can be expected on May 28, while the first frost of autumn comes around September 17, only sixteen weeks later.

Sixteen weeks seems an unmercifully short season, but most garden annuals — both flowers and vegetables — can be grown successfully in that time. When it comes to trees, shrubs, and perennials, varieties must be chosen with more care, since they must be winter hardy. But even gardeners in Wisconsin's coldest corners can stretch the season by the use of cold frames and hotbeds, by wise mulching methods, and by intelligent soil management. In Wisconsin, we do everything we can to start plants earlier in the spring, and to nurse along crops well into the fall. By applying season-stretching methods, we can form, for our own gardens, a microclimate nearly equivalent to the natural climate of any garden several hundred miles to the south.

CHOOSING VARIETIES FOR WISCONSIN

When buying seeds and plants, be sure to choose those varieties that will do well in Wisconsin's climate. You can play it safe by picking up the annual lists of recommended vegetable, fruit, and flower varieties from your county agent's office. These have been tested by state and university experts and have passed all tests. You can plant them with assurance. If you are adventurous, however, you will go beyond the official recommendations and try some varieties that have not been officially tested, but which sound interesting to you.

In selecting annuals, you can afford to be adventurous. Just remember that buying nonrecommended varieties is a gamble — and you should gamble only as much as you can afford to lose. Perhaps the best plan is to keep the bulk of your garden space to the recommended varieties and devote a smaller portion to experimental varieties. When choosing new permanent plantings, of course, the stakes are much higher. Few things are more discouraging than investing heavily in an attractive shrub or tree, nursing it along for three or four years, falling in love with it, only to have it winter-killed when it is approaching maturity.

If you choose varieties from the seed catalogs, look for the clues to northern hardiness. The first clue is the location of the seedsman or nursery. Generally, stock purchased from northern and local growers can be assumed to be fully hardy for our area. Local nurseries, in fact, would be foolish to sell you any other kind. However, the misconception is still common among northern gardeners that southern-grown stock is untrustworthy, that it will be tender and more susceptible to winter-kill than the same plant raised in a northern climate. This belief is effectively put to rest by Laurene Manning, head of the nationally-known Kelsey Nursery Service for many years, in his book *The How and Why of Better Gardening* (D. Van Nostrand Co., 1951):

> Now most nurseries, north and south alike, do not collect their own seed at all but buy it from seedsmen; hence the location of the nursery has nothing to do with the inherited hardiness of the plants grown there. Moreover, the named varieties of plants most commonly grown in nurseries never grow from seed, but only from grafts or cuttings and are identical in every respect, including hardiness, no matter where grown.

> How could such an erroneous idea get started? Probably because in early days most southern-grown roses and fruit trees died their first winter in the north. Northern gardeners damned southern stock, but the true villain was the calendar with its arbitrary divisions of the year. A woody plant is not safe until it has hardened off, no matter what the calendar says. The northerners wanted their shipments in October — the proper time for northern-grown plants — and southern nurserymen obliged. But in the south many plants do not harden off in October — it may be as late as early December — and unripened wood dies in the first freeze.

> As soon as the facts began to be known, scrupulous southern nurserymen refused early shipments. Sales were more difficult, for plants arrived north in December, rather

late for planting; they usually had to be stored carefully over the winter and not planted until spring. Incidentally, well-managed storage proved so safe and such an advantage for early spring shipments, that fall digging and winter storage are practiced more every year, both north and south, for such plants as can safely be handled that way. (Deciduous trees and shrubs can; evergreens usually cannot).

Southern-grown trees and shrubs, then, can be shipped north safely in early spring but not in autumn, unless you are willing to handle them in uncomfortably cold weather....

Look for other clues in the catalog, too. Look for the terms "winter hardy in the north," "extremely hardy," or "survived in winter trials at such and such below zero."

Hardiness, of course, refers to a plant's ability to withstand cold winters without being killed. A plant's hardiness will depend on its parentage, i.e., in what climate its predecessors originated. Modern plant breeding methods have attempted to encourage hardiness in trees, shrubs, and perennials, but their success has been limited. Unless you have a greenhouse, then, better take Shakespeare's advice. Don't look for roses at Christmas — or even for peas in May, for that matter.

In the catalogs, you will also see references to "half-hardy" plants. These are plants which are hardy under normal conditions, but which might be killed or severely injured by climatic abnormalities such as a prolonged cold snap out of season or an abnormal period of alternate freezing and thawing.

Protecting half-hardy plants. You can offer your half-hardy plants special protection, increasing greatly their chances for survival. Remember that these are plants teetering on the edge of their natural climates, and that you can do things to make them feel more at home. Here are the rules, as set down by Mr. Manning:

1. Plant half-hardy plants on a hill, where frosts will not settle. A north slope is better, since spring growth will be delayed until after late frosts have passed.

2. Ensure good drainage to encourage autumn ripening or "hardening off" of woody stems.

3. Protect plants from strong winds which might draw too much moisture from them. Wrap tree trunks with paper tape made for the purpose. Try to plant the half-hardies south of a windbreak — shrubs, trees, a hill, a building — anything that will break up sweeping fall and winter winds.

4. Mulch the plants after the ground has frozen. Soil moisture will be conserved and ground heaving will be minimized.

5. Keep plants well pruned to prevent wind damage.

6. Plant half-hardies in spring (not fall), so that they will have

a full growing season to become accustomed to their new environment and prepare for the winter.

7. Avoid pruning, watering, and feeding in late summer, to encourage hardening off and prevent new soft growth just before freezing temperatures set in. (In the case of evergreens, though, water heavily in the late autumn, since the roots must supply moisture to plants throughout the winter.)

8. For half-hardy perennial flowers, simply mulch heavily after the ground has frozen. The tops of perennials die back after the plant has bloomed, and the sap then retreats to the roots to await another spring. It is the roots that must be protected until warm weather returns. The mulch should be removed as soon as the sun begins to warm the ground, usually in May, sometimes earlier in the southern reaches of the state.

This sturdy, young tomato plant can be transplanted into the open as soon as all danger of frost has passed. But it still will not make any significant growth until the temperature gets into the 60s.

In growing annual flowers and vegetables, you need not be concerned about winter hardiness, since the plants will be expected to complete their growing cycle during a single growing season. Here, you should watch instead for the stated number of days to maturity. You can calculate your own growing season by checking the frost maps on pages 78-80. The spring map gives the *average* frost date for your locality (meaning that there is a 50 percent chance that frost will occur after that date) and an alternate date after which there is only a 10 percent chance of frost. The fall map gives similar percentages for chances of frost occurring *before* the dates indicated.

When calculating your growing season, remember that seeds do not germinate and plants do not grow when the temperature is below forty degrees, and that growth is slow among hot-weather plants until the thermometer gets into the sixties. An especially cold spring, even without frost, can retard plant development, and so can a long dry spell in summer. To be on the safe side, you should add about 20 percent to whatever figure the seed company gives as the days to maturity.

If you can find no clue to hardiness in the catalog or on the seed pack, check the lists of recommended varieties which are available from your county agent. If you still cannot find the plants you are interested in, do not hesitate to call your agent. He may not have the answer right at hand, since he would have to have a veritable computer for a brain to memorize the characteristics of hundreds of thousands of plants, but he can find out and call you back. (Suggestion: Make your plant selections in January and February and call your agent at that time; the demands on his time are enormous during the spring.)

Soil temperature. Plants respond to soil temperature just as they do to air temperature — sometimes, even more. Seeds will be retarded in germinating in a cold soil, and so will plant growth after those seeds have germinated. Soil temperature depends on air temperature, of course, but there are other factors. Heavy clay soils, for instance, warm up much more slowly in spring than sandy soils do. The number of hours of sunlight a soil receives has a great effect on its warming up, too, so that the soil temperature will be different in different parts of your garden. During the first really warm days of spring, mulches should be pulled aside so that the soil can receive the full warming effects of the sun.

Mulches are your best regulator of soil temperature. In general, they tend to keep soil temperatures in a moderate range, warming them in cold weather and keeping them cool in very hot weather. This is important not only for the physical protection of plants, but also as a conserver of water and an encourager of soil microorganisms. These microorganisms, which help to deliver plant nutrients, operate most efficiently in a moderate temperature — not below 41 degrees and not above 130 degrees, according to T. Bedfore Franklin, author of *Climates in Miniature* (Greenwood Press). Luxuriant growth of all plants depends on the delivery of nitrogen to the plant roots, and the soil bacteria will not deliver nitrogen efficiently when the soil is too cold. Again, remember that the "days to maturity" cited on the seed packet might be calculated for an ideal climate where the soil warms up early in the spring. Don't put full trust in these claims.

Before planting seeds directly in the garden, be sure to check the seed packets for any instructions pertaining to soil temperature. Some annuals, such as asters and lettuce, should be planted after danger of frost is past but while the soil is still cool. Others, including most flowers and vegetables, should be planted only after the soil has warmed up. And "warmed up" means warmed to at least sixty-five degrees at the depth to which the seeds will be planted.

There are several factors, aside from air temperature and sunlight, that affect soil temperature. Remember that a light, sandy soil will warm up more quickly in the spring than a heavy clay, and that the soil on a southern slope will warm up faster than soil on a northern slope, where the sun's rays are less direct. Shade from large trees or buildings will keep soil cooler in the spring and summer — but since the sun shifts in the sky as the season progresses, the shaded areas will shift, also. And remember, too, that the length of the summer days increases as you go northward. Wisconsin's northern residents can take solace in this gift of old sol, which compensates for the slightly lower summer temperatures. In fact, the compensation is ample, since the size of fruits and vegetables often depends more on the duration of daily sunlight than on the temperatures. (The difference in average August temperatures between Bayfield and Kenosha counties, incidentally, is a scant four degrees, despite their being in opposite corners of the state.)

Air temperature. Late spring and early fall frosts are banes of the Wisconsin gardener. Who has not been tempted to plant after a week of unseasonably warm April weather, only to remember the killing frosts of Aprils (and Mays, for that matter) of years past? Nevertheless, if the ground is sufficiently warm before the normal planting time, you can get an early start if you take proper precautions. Keep on hand an ample supply of hotcaps, mason jars, or other homemade or store-bought seedling protectors ("miniature greenhouses" they call them in the catalogs — at about ten cents each).

If your new plants are tender ones, keep your eye on the thermometer and on the weather reports, and cover all emerged seedlings if a heavy frost is predicted. You can cover them with a light, but thick, covering of hay or straw to ward off frost damage, by using the individual plant covers just mentioned, or by erecting simple structures of old storm windows supported by walls constructed of bales of hay. If your garden is small enough, you can get away with tricks like these. But if you are growing a half-acre or so, you would be foolish to plant before the recommended time.

Cool-weather gardening tips. It is an ill wind that blows no good at all, and Wisconsin's brisk spring winds do blow some good things our way. The same cool climate that rules out mangoes and artichokes makes it possible for us to grow the country's most luscious and flavorful peas, crisp garden lettuce, and tangy strawberries, not to mention firm and tasty potatoes, rutabagas, and other root crops. These plants do best in cool weather. You may have noticed for yourself that strawberries lose a great deal of their taste when they ripen in unseasonably hot weather. And peas grow little when the temperature rises above seventy-two degrees, reports Katherine C. Rhee, a Nova Scotia gardener writing in the December 1972 issue of *Organic Gardening and Farming*.

Ms. Rhee says a great deal about cool-weather gardening in that article. She notes that hot-weather crops stop growing when the temperature drops below fifty degrees or rises above one hundred-ten degrees. "Most plants need the lowest temperature for germination," she says, "a moderate level for leafy growth, and the highest temperature for blossoming and fruiting." Wisconsin's spring and summer climate certainly fills this bill. Take, for example, the growing of cucumbers in Dane County. In May, when seeds are germinating, the average temperature is a cool fifty-eight degrees. In June, when the main leafy growth takes place, it has warmed up to an average of sixty-eight degrees. And in July, when the first serious blossoming and fruiting is taking place, the temperature is at a year's high of seventy-three degrees. The same principle holds true in all parts of Wisconsin, for all hot-weather annual vegetables.

Remembering the above rule, it is not difficult to see why second plantings of vegetables made in July and August often do not do as well as initial spring plantings. Here, the order is reversed, the temperatures becoming progressively cooler as the plant germinates, leafs, and sets fruit. Still, second plantings produce enough for us to keep on making them year after year, and more will be said about them in another chapter.

Last, Ms. Rhee tells us of experiments in the USSR showing that a plant's resistance to cold is enhanced by ample supplies of the trace elements copper, zinc, aluminum, and molybdenum. These can be added to the soil by compost, but not by ordinary chemical fertilizers, giving just one more reason why compost is so vitally important to gardening success in Wisconsin!

Sunlight and plants. The effect of light on garden plants is a fascinating study in itself, worth your investigation. We won't have time to plunge deeply into the subject here, but some of the major principles should be set forth because they are important to gardening success.

Light is not only necessary for the plant's formation of carbon, hydrogen, and oxygen into plant tissue (photosynthesis), but it acts as a time clock for every plant, dictating its behavior to a large measure. In growing garden plants, this is important to remember. Many wild flower enthusiasts have made enough annual springtime trips to nearby woods to be able to anticipate the blooming of certain species, on certain days, at certain spots. These are native plants, almost fully predictable in their habits. Garden plants, often originating hundreds of miles away where light conditions are quite different, are something else again. Nevertheless, by close observation and some careful note taking, you can learn to predict the behavior of all your garden plants.

Dahlias and chrysanthemums are southern plants, which might come as a surprise to some people who think of them as fall bloomers. Because they are southern plants, their time clocks specify that blooming must take place when there is a certain amount of sunlight each day. Here in the north, the summer days are much longer. In effect, the sun tells the chrysanthemum and the dahlia not to bloom until they receive a precise amount of daylight — and this does not happen until late summer or autumn, when the days have begun to shorten. Commercial growers of potted plants can force chrysanthemums in pots at any time of the year, by regulating the amount of light they receive. I suppose we could force bloom in our gardens, too, although it would require an awful lot of careful attention. I just can't picture myself throwing huge black bags over my dahlias at a certain time every evening.

Some plants like full sun, some like partial shade, and others like fairly heavy shade or at least they will tolerate it. You should check the light requirements for every plant you choose, and plant accordingly. Use your shade trees to best advantage. Spring-flowering perennials, especially roses, will do well when planted just under the southern reaches of a shade tree. The plant will receive full sun in the spring, encouraging blooming, and then in midsummer when the sun is higher in the sky, the fully-leafed branches of the tree will offer good protection. But heat-loving plants, such as moss roses and marigolds, and most vegetables, should get full sun all day long.

You can make your own observations of the effect of light on garden plants if you will take the time to be observant. Moss roses (*portulacca*) will open at a definite time in the morning and close at a definite time in the afternoon, provided that the sun is shining. Some of your flowering plants that seem to be growing at unattractive angles may be reacting to the shade of a nearby tree, shrub, or building. By all means, keep a garden diary and record these observations. You will want to refer back to them at some date when you contemplate changes in your garden arrangement.

GETTING THE JUMP ON SPRING

If you want to put out large, robust tomato plants during late May or early June (when all danger of frost is past), there are two ways you can do it. You can either purchase large, robust plants

The cold frame — a simple and easily-built device — is almost essential
for complete gardening success.

at the local nursery or garden center, in which case you will pay
dearly and have little choice of varieties — or you can grow your
own plants from seed, starting them in the house, transferring
them to a cold frame in April, and setting them out at the usual
time. In this way, you can have your choice of many varieties —
and you can build a cold frame for about the same price you might
pay for a couple dozen robust tomato plants.

Cold frames and hotbeds (a hotbed is simply a cold frame with
the addition of a heating device) can push back the spring, enabling you to start many plants earlier than you otherwise could,
thus increasing your production for the season. But cold frames
and hotbeds have other uses, too. Cold frames can be used to grow
salad greens right up to Thanksgiving. You can use them for
propagating cuttings of perennials during the summer. You can, in
fact, use the cold frame or hotbed for any purpose requiring the
regulation of air and soil temperatures and protection of small
plants against frost in both spring and fall.

Cold frames and hotbeds can expand your gardening oppor-
tunities not only by lengthening the growing season for ordinary
plants, but by enabling you to experiment with exotic varieties
that would otherwise be difficult or impossible to grow here in
Wisconsin. Your local plant supplier, if he is typical, can afford to
offer only a relatively small selection of annual flowers and vegetables, those which he knows he won't be stuck with after "setting

out" time is past. But, if you are capable of starting your own plants from seeds, a whole new world of horticultural exploration is opened up for you. You can order seeds from any of dozens of specialty houses, and your cold frame or hotbed will enable you to start them successfully for transplanting when the weather turns warm. The cold frame or hotbed will, further, offer protection and breathing space for plants which arrive from mail-order nurseries too early for planting.

Directions for starting seeds in cold frames and hotbeds are given later on, in Chapter 4. Here we will concentrate on various ways of building cold frames and hotbeds.

Building the cold frame. The best site for a cold frame is the one that receives the most sun — in other words, a southern or southwestern exposure unshaded by large trees or buildings. Even on cold, raw days, the sun can heat a cold frame to thirty degrees or more above the outside air temperature.

The size and actual construction of the cold frame will vary according to your needs, the space available, and the materials you happen to have on hand. Many gardeners use waste lumber and old storm sashes for construction materials, while others prefer a more finished-looking job and are willing to pay for it. The choice is yours. You can spend as much as fifty dollars, or you can scrounge around for discarded materials and build it for practically nothing.

Whatever your actual construction decisions, however, there are certain basic rules that you should follow:

1. If possible, use two-inch thick lumber for all frames to provide good protection from swiftly changing temperatures.

2. If you use old storm sashes for lids, let their size determine the size of the frame.

3. The entire frame should be sunk two inches or more into the ground. It can be any length you choose, but the front of the frame should extend from six to ten inches above the ground (an eight to twelve inch board, in other words) and the back of the frame should be about six inches higher to allow for a back-to-front slope. The slope should be to the south, of course, to catch the maximum rays of the sun.

4. The depth of the frame can be any size you wish, although you will find it difficult to work within the frame if its depth is longer than your reach. And, if the depth is especially short, the difference in height between the back and the front boards can be less, while still retaining a proper slope of the lid.

5. Anchor the frame to the ground by driving two-by-four-inch stakes in all four corners, at least eighteen inches into the ground. Nail the planks of the frame securely to the stakes, and be sure to firm up the soil on all sides to prevent drafts. If you must affix one plank on top of another to gain the proper height, be sure that the fit is tight; use a wood filler if necessary.

6. The lid, which can be either a storm sash or a simple wood frame with tightly-anchored transparent plastic covers, should be hinged in the back, and provisions should be made for propping it open at various levels. (A notched stake is commonly used; dropping the lid to a lower notch will lower the lid.)

Soil for the bed. Since the cold frame will be crucial in growing many young seedlings, you should take care in establishing a good soil bed for it. Before putting together the frame, dig down at least ten inches and loosen the soil. If it is heavy, add sand and well-rotted compost to loosen it up and improve drainage. If the soil is far from ideal, remove the top eight inches and replace it with a mixture of 50 percent good garden loam, 25 percent sand, and 25 percent well-rotted leaf mold or compost. Do not add new compost or manure. The soil for seedlings should not be too rich in nitrogen, since this will stimulate growth too quickly and resulting in spindly and unhealthy plants.

Making a hotbed. There are two ways of making a cold frame into a hotbed. The first is the old traditional way: Dig out two feet of soil from the bed, then fill it with eighteen inches of fresh horse or chicken manure which has been thoroughly soaked and packed down firmly. Cover the manure with six inches of bedding soil. The manure will produce plenty of heat, even in the dead of winter, and will last for several weeks. This is the organic method.

The second method is strictly artificial: Arrange electric heating cables about five inches below the soil surface (or according to manufacturer's directions) and plug into the nearest outlet. This is the inorganic way. And if there is any point where I tip my hat and part company with the old organic way, this is it. The electric method produces a more even and controlled heat, is infinitely easier to set up, and will last for as long as the power plant survives. Nevertheless, if you do not have access to power in the area of your hotbed, or if you are more of a purist than I, the manure-heated bed works just fine — and it has the added benefit of producing composted manure all the while it is heating up the bed.

Controlling moisture, heat, and light. Cold frames form special microenvironments, very different from the outside environment when their lids are closed. Mother Nature will watch over your garden plants outside, but you must be responsible for the environment inside of your frame.

Moisture control is especially important when you are germinating seeds in a cold frame or hotbed. Very young seedlings are especially susceptible to damping-off, a fungus attack which causes them to wilt and die very quickly, often killing off entire flats. The fungus lives very near the soil surface and attacks the plant at the soil line. If you would prevent damping-off, you must prevent the conditions which enable the fungus to thrive and grow

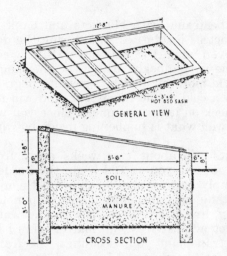

GENERAL VIEW

SOIL

MANURE

CROSS SECTION

Typical hotbed construction, showing placement of manure. Wood two inches thick is used for maximum insulation.

— and those conditions are (1) high humidity in both air and soil, and (2) lack of aeration.

Be sure to allow your germinating seeds at least some air movement by cracking the lid of the frame just a fraction of an inch whenever possible. If the weather is very cold, then let the air in just during the warmest part of the day. If you find a great deal of condensation on the glass in the morning, be sure to give the plants air as soon as temperatures permit. Last, avoid the most common (and fatal) error in germinating seeds — overwatering. The surface of the seedling soil should be dry, or very nearly dry, although there should be sufficient moisture under the surface. As an extra precaution, you might want to buy some vermiculite and spread a very thin layer of it over the top of the seeding bed. The seedlings will push up through it easily, and it will not support the killing fungus. Last, avoid overcrowding of young seedlings, because this, too, can encourage damping-off.

After your seedlings have established themselves into strong and healthy young plants, your problem might be the opposite — too little moisture. It is not difficult to forget about the moisture requirements of the cold frame, especially if you are preoccupied with chores out in the garden. Make it a habit to check into the cold frame every day. Do not overwater at any time, but avoid excessive dryness, too. Always give tepid water to plants in the cold frame — never cold water from the hose. It is a good idea to keep a sprinkling can filled and standing ready by the cold frame all during the growing season, so that the water inside will approximate the air temperature.

Heat control is also important. You should keep an outdoor thermometer in the cold frame at all times and watch it carefully, at least for the first year. Young seedlings should never be exposed to temperatures above eighty degrees or below fifty degrees.

If frost is predicted, cover the frame with blankets and bank up leaves around the frame to act as insulation. And during the day, remember that the sun — even when the air temperature is cool — can heat up the cold frame very quickly. Watch the thermometer and give the frame a little more air if it hits seventy degrees. After you have worked with a cold frame for a year, you will not have to keep such a close check on its environment, since you will have learned to judge fairly well what is happening inside by what is happening outside.

When your young plants are about two weeks away from transplanting into the open garden, you should begin the hardening-off process, which is simply the process of allowing them to become exposed to the outside environment slowly. Open the frame a little more each day, and cut back a little on the water during this time. (But protect against frost, no matter what.) By the time you are ready to transplant your seedlings, the frame should have been wide open for two or three days, and any transplanting shock should be absolutely minimized.

If you use electric cables to heat a hotbed, your control of temperature is obviously much finer. You will be able to plant earlier, and you will not have to worry so much about early morning frosts. Still, you must pay careful attention to moisture requirements — which can be very tricky if you cannot open the frame because of very cold weather. It would be best to begin with a cold frame, and then add heat after you have worked with it for a year or two.

Light is the third important factor, and the rules here are simple and few (unless you get into the forcing of blooms, which is another matter entirely). Germinating seeds should have very little light. You can lay boards over the frame lid until the seeds have germinated. After that, they should be exposed to light gradually. A couple of layers of cheesecloth will filter direct sun very effectively. As the plants grow, the layers can be removed, one by one, until the plants are able to take direct sunlight. Again, the object is to expose the young plants to the outside environment gradually, to prevent shock.

Other ways to challenge spring. The cold frame is by far your best ally in getting the jump on spring. But there are other ways of getting the best of an early start, too:

1. Keep a winter mulch on your vegetable garden and on your flower beds and borders. The mulch — applied in the fall after the ground has frozen — will prevent the frost line from going so deeply into the soil and will allow the soil to warm up more quickly in spring. Remove the mulch during the first warm days of spring.

2. If your soil is heavy, with a high percentage of clay, keep working to loosen it up and lighten it by incorporating plenty of compost and sand. Lighter soils warm up more quickly in the spring, and they provide better drainage, too.

3. Start seeds as early as possible indoors, and tend them with care. In April, you can transfer them to the cold frame where you can harden them off gradually until planting time. The earlier you start, the bigger your plants will be at planting time.

4. Plant cool-weather crops, such as peas and lettuce, as early as possible in your area. These can take a couple of light frosts without damage. You can lessen the effect of any frost, also, by sprinkling your young plants with cold water on the morning of the frost, before the sun has hit them. The water will dissipate the frost quickly.

5. Be prepared with hot caps, cloches, and other plant protectors for your early-planted vegetables. When frost threatens, cap the young plants in the early evening, before dark. Remove the caps the next day, when the sun has reached the garden patch.

Some gardeners will not want to go to the extra effort necessary to get plants into the open ground as early as possible — and some will maintain that later plantings will catch up sooner or later, anyway. I am somewhat sympathetic to this view — but on the other hand, I still can feel a sense of pride and accomplishment (or perhaps that good old American sense of competition) in getting in crops earlier than the recommended dates and having them thrive. The neighborhood garden hero is still the one who holds up the first ripe tomato.

EXTENDING THE SUMMER

Just as cold frames and hotbeds can push back the spring, they can extend the summer into fall, giving you salad greens right up to Thanksgiving and beyond. The usual crops grown for harvest in the cold frame are lettuce and endive, but you might wish to experiment with carrots, radishes, and other vegetables, as well. Just remember that any crops planted for this purpose must be low growing and should be tolerant to cool weather. In other words, bush beans and eggplants are *out*.

Check the seed packets of the vegetables you want to grow and note the days to maturity. Then, figuring backward in time, plant in order to harvest in early November. A forty-day leaf lettuce, for instance, should be planted about September 22 to be harvested about November 1. But you will probably want to begin several weeks sooner, making plantings every week or two, in order to have a continuous supply of greens throughout the fall. Remember, though, that lettuce does not germinate well in hot weather. Protect very young plants against direct sunlight when the weather is hot.

Along about November, when the first light snows have powdered the Wisconsin landscape, the fresh greens from the cold frame become an increasing source of pride. You might find yourself throwing dinner parties just to show off your fresh salads.

You will want to do everything you can to ward off frost and keep the greens coming for just another week. Again, throw blankets over the lid and bank up the frame with leaves on very cold nights. Go out in the morning and check the plants. If they have been frostbitten, sprinkle them gently with cold water. Generally, they will revive nicely — until that fateful morning when we will at last have to admit that Shakespeare had a point — at Christmas we should no more desire fresh endive than wish a snow in May's new-fangled mirth. Winter will be upon us.

Bales of hay and some old storm sashes can be used to protect tomato plants from early frosts. After the season is over, the same structure can be used to store root crops over the winter. In spring, use the hay for mulching.

WHEN ALL DANGER OF FROST IS PAST

The frost maps on pages 78 and 80 will enable you to find the average last frost date for spring and the average first frost date for fall, for your locality. The difference in days between these two dates, of course, is your average growing season.

In addition, the maps report data for several dozen scattered points of observation where long-term records have been kept. For each of these points of observation, there is given both the average date and a "10 percent validity" date. This latter date is the one at which there is only 10 percent chance of frost occurring, meaning that gardeners there can plant with a 90 percent assurance of safety from frost.

As an example, take the one point of observation in Lafayette County, in the southwest corner of the state. On the spring map, the average last frost there occurs on May 4. But the 10 percent validity date is May 23. There is only a 10 percent chance of frost occurring that late in the spring.

On the fall maps, the same information is given, except that we are now talking about the chances of frost occurring *before* the dates given. Again, taking Lafayette County, the first average frost occurs on September 30, and there is only a 10 percent chance that frost will occur as early as September 21.

The maps are very helpful to gardeners in all areas of the state. But you might wish to calculate your odds a little more closely. You might, for instance, be planting peas. You know that they can stand a nightly low of thirty-two degrees, which is an official frost, but you wouldn't like to see the temperature go down as low as twenty-eight degrees, and certainly not to twenty-four degrees, or below.

How do you calculate your odds? For complete information, I suggest that you ask your county agent to get for you a copy of a booklet called *Climate at the University of Wisconsin Experimental Farms*, prepared by the College of Agriculture in cooperation with the United States Weather Bureau. This booklet contains a wealth of climatological data for the nine experimental farms of the University of Wisconsin, spread throughout the state: Ashland, Spooner, Marshfield, Lancaster, Hancock, Sturgeon Bay, Valders, Arlington, and Madison (Charmany). You will find for each year of recording, monthly mean temperatures, highest and lowest temperatures for each month, precipitation totals and chances of precipitation, and much additional information, mostly in table form.

From that booklet, I will borrow Table 5 (a to e) of "critical temperatures," which give the percentage chances of freezes occurring before the official average dates.

Using these tables, you can find, for instance, that in Spooner, where the average last frost occurs on May 24, there is still a 20 percent chance of a freeze occurring up until June 3, and a 40 percent chance of the temperature dipping to twenty-four degrees or below on May 3.

To calculate the odds of frosts of varying severity occurring near your area, both spring and fall, consult the tables for the location nearest to your own.

74   WEATHER

Table 5.   Chances of Spring and Fall Frost Occurrences
Table 5-a.

ASHLAND
Location: four miles west of Ashland, near Chequamegon Bay in
northwestern Wisconsin
Last average spring frost: May 30
First average fall frost: September 16
Growing season: 109 days

Chances of Frost Occurring After Date in Spring

Temperature	20%	40%	60%	80%
32° or below	June 9	June 2	May 27	May 20
28° or below	May 29	May 22	May 16	May 9
24° or below	May 21	May 14	May 7	Apr. 30
20° or below	May 3	Apr. 25	Apr. 19	Apr. 11
16° or below	Apr. 21	Apr. 13	Apr. 7	Mar. 30

Chances of Frost Occurring Before Date in Fall

32° or below	Sept. 6	Sept. 13	Sept. 20	Sept. 27
28° or below	Sept. 17	Sept. 25	Oct. 1	Oct. 9
24° or below	Sept. 29	Oct. 7	Oct. 14	Oct. 21
20° or below	Oct. 14	Oct. 22	Oct. 28	Nov. 5
16° or below	Oct. 26	Nov. 3	Nov. 9	Nov. 17

Table 5-b.

HANCOCK
Location: two miles south of Hancock in Western Waushara
County in central Wisconsin
Last average spring frost: May 17
First average fall frost: September 30
Growing season: 135 days

Chances of Frost Occurring After Date in Spring

Temperature	20%	40%	60%	80%
32° or below	May 27	May 20	May 14	May 7
28° or below	May 16	May 9	May 3	Apr. 26
24° or below	May 6	Apr. 29	Apr. 22	Apr. 15
20° or below	Apr. 26	Apr. 18	Apr. 11	Apr. 3
16° or below	Apr. 13	Apr. 6	Mar. 31	Mar. 23

Chances of Frost Occurring Before Date in Fall

32° or below	Sept. 19	Sept. 26	Oct. 3	Oct. 10
28° or below	Sept. 26	Oct. 4	Oct. 10	Oct. 18
24° or below	Oct. 9	Oct. 16	Oct. 23	Oct. 31
20° or below	Oct. 20	Oct. 28	Nov. 3	Nov. 10
16° or below	Oct. 26	Nov. 3	Nov. 9	Nov. 17

Table 5-c

MARSHFIELD

Location: two miles southeast of Marshfield in Wood County on the central Wisconsin plains
Last average spring frost: May 17
First average fall frost: September 27
Growing season: 133 days

Chances of Frost Occurring After Date in Spring

Temperature	20%	40%	60%	80%
32° or below	May 27	May 20	May 14	May 7
28° or below	May 13	May 6	Apr. 30	Apr. 23
24° or below	May 1	Apr. 23	Apr. 17	Apr. 9
20° or below	Apr. 19	Apr. 12	Apr. 5	Mar. 28
16° or below	Apr. 8	Apr. 1	Mar. 25	Mar. 18

Chances of Frost Occurring Before Date in Fall

Temperature	20%	40%	60%	80%
32° or below	Sept. 17	Sept. 24	Sept. 30	Oct. 7
28° or below	Sept. 25	Oct. 2	Oct. 9	Oct. 17
24° or below	Oct. 7	Oct. 15	Oct. 22	Oct. 29
20° or below	Oct. 20	Oct. 27	Nov. 3	Nov. 10
16° or below	Oct. 30	Nov. 7	Nov. 13	Nov. 21

Table 5-d.

SPOONER

Location: two miles southeast of Spooner in Washburn County in northwestern Wisconsin
Last average spring frost: May 24
First average fall frost: September 20
Growing season: 120 days

Chances of Frost Occurring After Date in Spring

Temperature	20%	40%	60%	80%
32° or below	June 3	May 27	May 21	May 14
28° or below	May 20	May 13	May 7	Apr. 30
24° or below	May 11	May 3	Apr. 27	Apr. 20
20° or below	Apr. 29	Apr. 21	Apr. 14	Apr. 7
16° or below	Apr. 18	Apr. 11	Apr. 4	Mar. 28

Chances of Frost Occurring Before Date in Fall

Temperature	20%	40%	60%	80%
32° or below	Sept. 10	Sept. 17	Sept. 24	Oct. 1
28° or below	Sept. 19	Sept. 27	Oct. 4	Oct. 11
24° or below	Oct. 1	Oct. 9	Oct. 15	Oct. 23
20° or below	Oct. 12	Oct. 19	Oct. 26	Nov. 2
16° or below	Oct. 25	Nov. 2	Nov. 8	Nov. 16

Table 5-e.

STURGEON BAY

Location: two miles north of Sturgeon Bay on the Door Peninsula between Green Bay and Lake Michigan, in northeastern Wisconsin

Last average spring frost: May 17
First average fall frost: October 2
Growing season: 137 days

Chances of Frost Occurring After Date in Spring

Temperature	20%	40%	60%	80%
32° or below	May 27	May 20	May 14	May 8
28° or below	May 10	May 3	Apr. 27	Apr. 20
24° or below	Apr. 27	Apr. 20	Apr. 13	Apr. 6
20° or below	Apr. 15	Apr. 8	Apr. 1	Mar. 24
16° or below	Apr. 5	Mar. 29	Mar. 23	Mar. 15

Chances of Frost Occurring Before Date in Fall

32° or below	Sept. 22	Sept. 29	Oct. 5	Oct. 12
28° or below	Oct. 8	Oct. 15	Oct. 22	Oct. 29
24° or below	Oct. 22	Oct. 30	Nov. 5	Nov. 13
20° or below	Nov. 3	Nov. 11	Nov. 17	Nov. 25
16° or below	Nov. 14	Nov. 21	Nov. 28	Dec. 5

Source: *Climate at the University of Wisconsin Experimental Farms*, Research Report 17, Experiment Station, College of Agriculture, University of Wisconsin, U.S. Department of Commerce, Weather Bureau, Cooperating; December 1964.

WHEN IT RAINS — AND WHEN IT DOESN'T

Despite Wisconsin's favorable rainfall patterns, gardeners are not averse to grumbling when the rain does not fall exactly when they want it to, as gently as they would like it to, and in just the right amounts. Our springs are sometimes oddly dry. We carry buckets of water out to the young tomato plants, where the garden hose cannot reach, and we feel that the zucchini seeds must certainly have become desiccated in their parched little hills.

Then, in July, we go through a week or two when it seems to be raining all the time. The garden is a sea of mire, and we don't see how anything can escape either drowning or rot.

Still, we always seem to make it through the season — and so, usually, do our garden plants. And we have to admit that the weather hasn't been all that bad, after all.

There are things you can do to protect your plants against both dryness and prolonged rains, so that even our mini-droughts and rainy weeks will have minimal effects on your flowers and vegetables.

Fighting drought. For the small backyard garden, the garden hose offers surefire drought protection — if it is used properly.

Remember, though, that plants have built-in mechanisms to combat drought. They undergo definite physical and chemical changes in every cell, enabling them to survive fairly long periods of dryness. If you use the hose capriciously, watering once or twice and then neglecting the chore after that, you may be doing more harm than good, for you will have sent the plants back into their defenseless posture, meaning that continuing drought will hurt them more than if you had not watered at all. A tomato plant is like an expensive daughter — once she has been given the good things of life, she will continue to expect them in the future.

You should be aware, too, of the cost of watering your backyard garden with the hose. The USDA *Yearbook of Agriculture* for 1955 tells us that about twenty-seven hundred gallons of water will be used in thoroughly watering a 60' x 70' garden plot. This comes out to about sixty-four gallons per 100 square feet. You know the cost of water, whether you buy yours from the city or maintain your own well. Here in Madison, it is not difficult to see that liberal use of the garden hose on just an average city plot could raise the homeowner's water bill by as much as fifty dollars or more in a year. How much more simple, timesaving, and economical to adopt good mulching practices to conserve the water that your soil does receive!

Allies in drought. Your very best allies in drought are a good soil, a good mulch, and deep fertilizing.

The texture of your soil is vitally important to its water-holding capacity. The coarser the soil, the less is its ability to hold water. A sandy soil will hold only about .75 inch of water per foot; a fine sandy loam will hold 1.25 inches; and a silt loam, clay loam, or clay will hold from 2.5 to 3.0 inches per foot. If you live in one of Wisconsin's sand counties, then, you will do well to begin the soil-building program outlined in Chapter 1 (page 15), in order to build your soil's texture to the point where it will hold enough water to fight drought during the growing season.

And if you seem blessed with good garden loam, dig down two or three feet in the garden to see how your subsoil looks. You might find almost pure sand down there, meaning that many of your plant roots will be growing in sand, where the water drains quite rapidly. Your contractor, in building your home, might have blessed you with gravel fill under your topsoil. If so, you will have to assure your garden plants of the water they need, because they will not be able to bring it up from deep within the subsoil.

In a drought, the soil dries from the top down. A week of drought might dry out about two inches of soil — less each week, after that. And here is where your second ally comes in. A good mulch will reduce surface evaporation greatly, thus helping to conserve the moisture that your soil receives from normal rainfalls. An eight- to ten-inch hay mulch is my choice for the vegetable garden, while buckwheat hulls or cocoa bean shells (three

MAP 2

MAP SERIES SHOWING
CLIMATIC INFLUENCES ON SOILS
AND CROPS IN WISCONSIN

I. SPRING FROST (1925-1949)

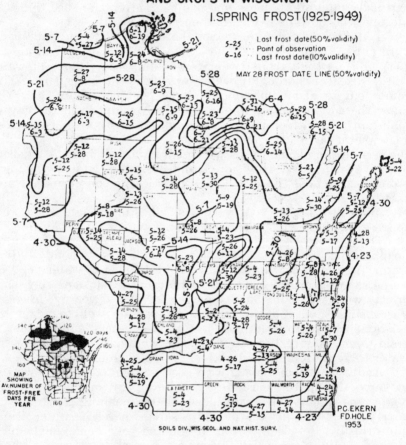

5-25   Last frost date (50% validity)
Point of observation
6-16   Last frost date (10% validity)

MAY 28 FROST DATE LINE (50% validity)

MAP
SHOWING
AV. NUMBER OF
FROST-FREE
DAYS PER
YEAR

P.C. EKERN
F.D. HOLE
1953

SOILS DIV., WIS. GEOL. AND NAT. HIST. SURV.

inches) look nice on the flower beds. All three are effective, in that they allow rainwater to pass through them easily, while still keeping the soil cool and preventing moisture escape.

Your third ally against drought is deep fertilizing. When drought strikes and the soil begins to dry out at the upper levels, plant roots begin to seek water at deeper levels. This means that they will draw their nutrients from those deeper levels, too, since nutrients are transported through the roots and to the plant system by water. If the soil is deficient in nutrients at those deeper levels, the plant will suffer accordingly. When a plant suffers during drought, it is not always because it cannot get water — it is because the water it receives contains very few nutrients. The answer is to carry on a year-round system of deep fertilization, including plenty of compost which is spaded or tilled as deeply into the soil as you can manage. Such a program will increase the soil's water-holding capacity, while providing a source of deep-lying, slow-releasing nutrients. You will be building up a veritable bank account of nutrients that your garden plants can call upon in time of need.

Too much rain. A problem less often encountered is that of too much rain, resulting in rot and strangulation of plants because of oxygen lack.

If your garden soil is still swimming in water more than a few hours after a heavy rain, look for the answer in the soil's texture, or, more often, in the subsoil. You may have a hardpan subsoil, which is impervious to water, thus preventing proper drainage. This is often a difficult and serious problem, sometimes requiring drastic steps for correction. Those steps are discussed in Chapter 1 (page 18).

Weather aids. The maps on the following pages, prepared by government and university agencies, will provide you with a wealth of useful data in greatly concentrated form. Aside from the frost maps, which we have already discussed, you will find maps giving average temperatures, rainfall, frost depths, snowfalls, hail storms, and even tornados, for different months of the year and in different parts of the state. You will want to refer to one or more of these maps when planning many of your garden operations throughout the year.

Finally, I would like to offer a little piece of advice for that inevitable Saturday in early May, the one you had reserved to till the garden because the weather had been so beautiful all that week. You arise at half-past seven, only to find outside your bedroom window what we charitably call "onion snow," this time mixed with both sleet and rain. At that time, it is perhaps best to take advice not from Shakespeare, who promised us newfangled mirth in May, but from Jonathan Swift, who some 265 years ago said —

"'Tis very warm weather when one's in bed."

MAP 3

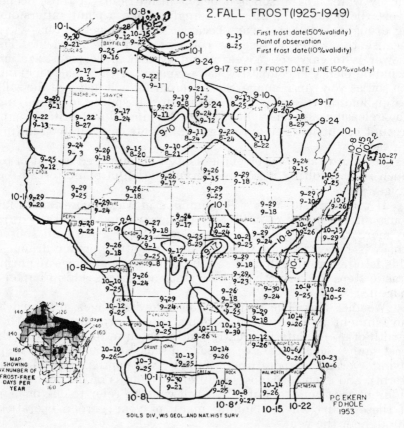

MAP SERIES SHOWING
CLIMATIC INFLUENCES ON SOILS
AND CROPS IN WISCONSIN
2. FALL FROST (1925-1949)

9-13 — First frost date (50% validity)
2 — Point of observation
8-25 — First frost date (10% validity)

9-17 SEPT 17 FROST DATE LINE (50% validity)

MAP SHOWING AV. NUMBER OF FROST-FREE DAYS PER YEAR

SOILS DIV., WIS. GEOL. AND NAT. HIST. SURV.

P.C. EKERN
F.D. HOLE
1953

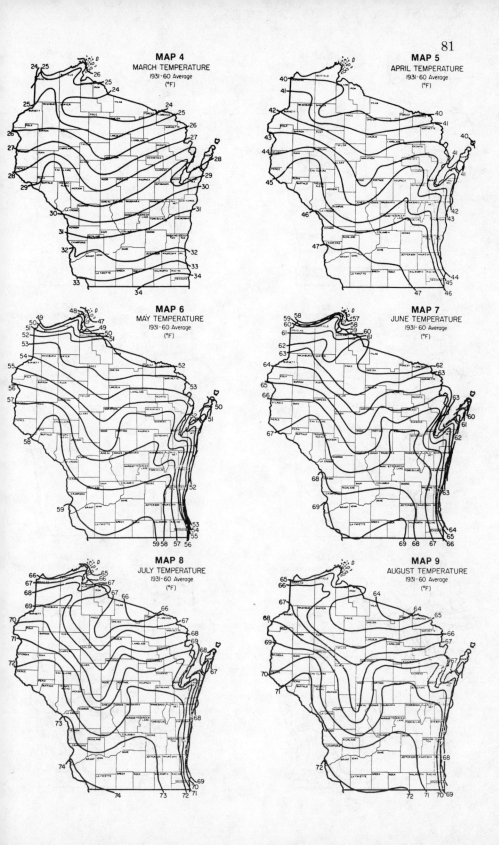

MAP 4
MARCH TEMPERATURE
1931-60 Average
(°F)

MAP 5
APRIL TEMPERATURE
1931-60 Average
(°F)

MAP 6
MAY TEMPERATURE
1931-60 Average
(°F)

MAP 7
JUNE TEMPERATURE
1931-60 Average
(°F)

MAP 8
JULY TEMPERATURE
1931-60 Average
(°F)

MAP 9
AUGUST TEMPERATURE
1931-60 Average
(°F)

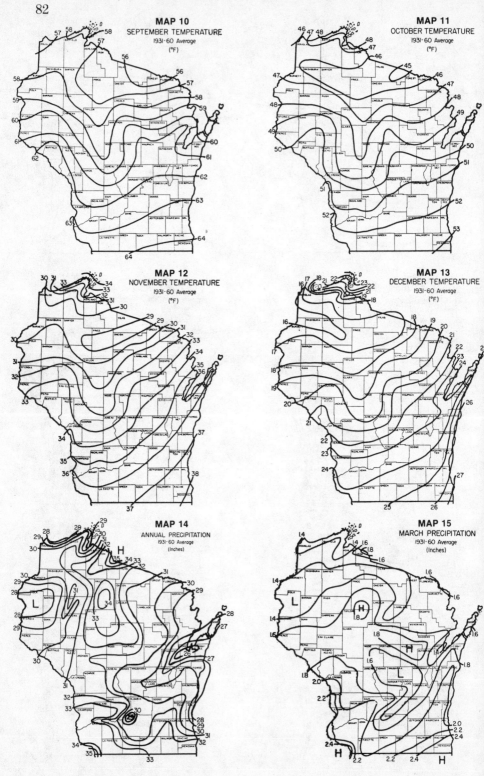

MAP 10
SEPTEMBER TEMPERATURE
1931-60 Average
(°F)

MAP 11
OCTOBER TEMPERATURE
1931-60 Average
(°F)

MAP 12
NOVEMBER TEMPERATURE
1931-60 Average
(°F)

MAP 13
DECEMBER TEMPERATURE
1931-60 Average
(°F)

MAP 14
ANNUAL PRECIPITATION
1931-60 Average
(Inches)

MAP 15
MARCH PRECIPITATION
1931-60 Average
(Inches)

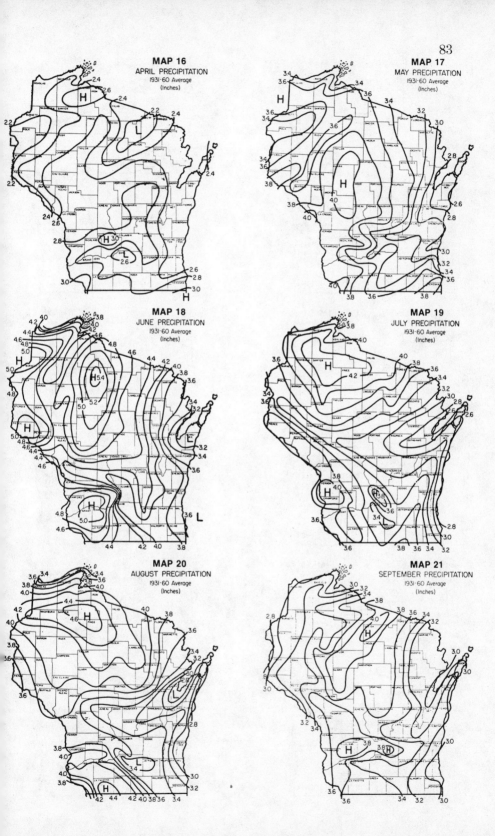

MAP 16
APRIL PRECIPITATION
1931-60 Average
(Inches)

MAP 17
MAY PRECIPITATION
1931-60 Average
(Inches)

MAP 18
JUNE PRECIPITATION
1931-60 Average
(Inches)

MAP 19
JULY PRECIPITATION
1931-60 Average
(Inches)

MAP 20
AUGUST PRECIPITATION
1931-60 Average
(Inches)

MAP 21
SEPTEMBER PRECIPITATION
1931-60 Average
(Inches)

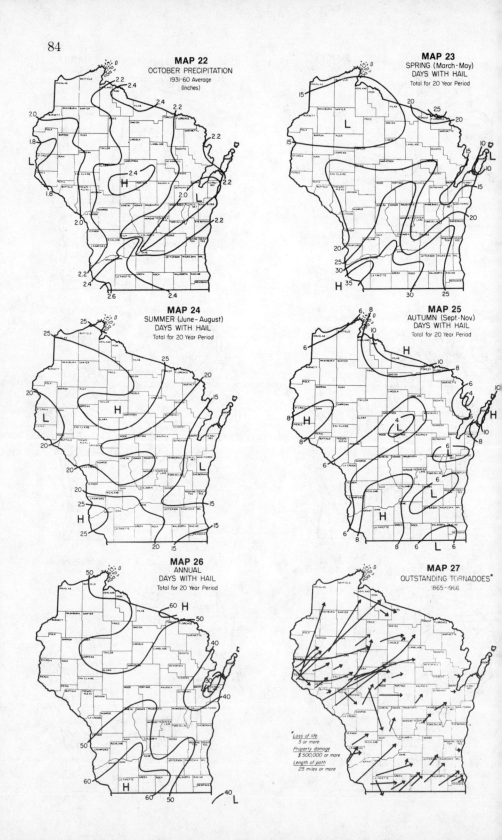

MAP 22
OCTOBER PRECIPITATION
1931-60 Average
(Inches)

MAP 23
SPRING (March-May)
DAYS WITH HAIL
Total for 20 Year Period

MAP 24
SUMMER (June-August)
DAYS WITH HAIL
Total for 20 Year Period

MAP 25
AUTUMN (Sept-Nov.)
DAYS WITH HAIL
Total for 20 Year Period

MAP 26
ANNUAL
DAYS WITH HAIL
Total for 20 Year Period

MAP 27
OUTSTANDING TORNADOES*
1865-1966

*Loss of life
5 or more
Property damage
$ 500,000 or more
Length of path
25 miles or more

Chapter Four

Vegetable Growing — Bounty For The Table

From the first tender asparagus tip of April until the last crisp carrot is dug in November, no gardening activity yields so much sheer satisfaction as vegetable growing. Flowers are beautiful to look at and to smell. Vegetables are beautiful to look at — and to eat!

If you have ever grown your own vegetables, you already know that there is absolutely no comparison between your homegrown varieties and those you buy at the supermarket. Peas are sweeter and more tender. Beets and potatoes are more solid, and they have *real taste*. Green beans are plump, flavorful, and plentiful. Onions are — well, wine-scented and poetic, actually. And tomatoes! To compare your first ripe, red tomato of the season to those pale and plastic imitations you have been buying at the supermarket is to know the whole reason for vegetable gardening.

But there are other rewards besides taste. Your homegrown vegetables are apt to be more nutritious. Processed vegetables inevitably lose some vitamins in the canning or freezing process.

Even "fresh" vegetables from the grocery produce bins have lost a good portion of their vitamin C in transit from distant farms. Commercially-grown varieties are chosen for their profitability — but your own vegetables are chosen and grown for taste and nutrition.

In your own vegetable garden, you can grow varieties that you never see in the supermarket: Chinese cabbage — Hungarian wax peppers — Swiss chard — purple pod bush beans — burpless cucumbers — ground cherries — Italian-style tomatoes — vegetable spaghetti — Dutch corn salad. Your options are limited only by your imagination, your daring, and the Wisconsin climate.

A vegetable garden can save you money, too — and with the price of food these days, this is reason enough for you to begin one this year. Every dollar invested in the early spring can yield many dollars in food for the rest of the year — particularly if you are cost conscious in planning your garden operation. If, on the other hand, you choose to spend hundreds of dollars on chemical fertilizers, unnecessary pesticides, and every garden gadget that you see in the garden center, then you might not come out ahead at all. To me, one of the challenges of gardening is to keep the cost low by using available materials and by going along with nature as closely as possible.

Last, I believe that the very act of growing one's own vegetables satisfies something deep within us — a desire for self-sufficiency in a world where we have been made increasingly dependent on the services of people we have never even met. If we can grow at least a part of our food to feed our family, then we can reaffirm our own sense of independence, in full spirit if not in total reality. For many of us, then, vegetable growing has a certain spiritual quality, one that every farmer has certainly felt at some time. And I think that quality makes better people of us.

CHOOSING THE SITE

If you are a city gardener, you may have only one available site for your vegetable garden — probably at the rear of the backyard. If it is an ideal spot — sunny, protected, and level — well and good. If not, then you must do anything within reason to bring it within specifications. You cannot, however, hope to grow a vegetable garden under a huge oak tree, or on the shady side of a garage. Sunlight is a most important consideration here, since you have little control over it (unless, of course, you choose to rip up the oak tree or knock down the garage).

If, on the other hand, you are fortunate enough to have a choice of garden sites, either on your own land or on a borrowed or rented plot, then your options might come into play.

Sunlight. A vegetable garden should be in a spot where it can receive full sun all day long. If obstacles make full sun impossible, the vegetable crops can still do well with sun for most of the day. But production will be decreased as the chances for sunlight are decreased. (Remember, if you are choosing a plot in winter, that the summer sun is much higher in the sky, thus shortening shadows from large trees and buildings.)

Soil. Next to sunlight, soil is the most important consideration. Look for well-drained soil of good texture, soil that is now perhaps supporting a healthy crop of weeds. Its nutrient content need not be high since you can correct that in a season or two, but texture and drainage are far more difficult to handle. Review Chapter 1 on soils, before exercising a choice of garden sites.

Trees. Large trees should not be too near the vegetable garden. A good rule of thumb is to keep the garden ten feet away from beneath the outermost reaches of any tree's branches. The problem is not only shade, but the competition of the tree's roots for your garden nutrients. In a battle like that, your garden plants will probably lose.

Slope. A moderate slope in any direction will not hurt the garden's performance. In fact, a southern slope will help it, since the rays of the sun will be more direct. But plants can do well even with a northern slope if it is not too severe. All vegetable rows should be at right angles to the slope to prevent soil runoff, erosion, and nutrient loss. If there is no slope, however, then it is better to run the rows north and south, since the sun's rays will be distributed more equally in passing from east to west.

Proximity to house. The vegetable garden should, if at all possible, be fairly close to the house. Not only will you be able to reach it with the garden hose when necessary, but you will be encouraged to spend odd moments in weeding, mulching, tying,

The enthusiasm of spring — will it give way to neglect in the heat of July?

and staking — those ten-minute jobs that you would not bother to
undertake if you had to walk or drive some distance to the garden.
Last, if you happen to live in the country, your garden will be less
susceptible to ravaging by racoons, rabbits, neighboring dogs, and
other marauders, if it is close to the house.

Size. The size of the vegetable garden should be determined by
the space available, the family's need, and the gardener's desire
and ability to maintain it properly. A 20' x 30' plot (600 square
feet) is a nice size for a family of four, capable of providing many
vegetables for the table from June through September, and quite a
few for canning and freezing, too.

A 20' x 50' plot (1000 square feet) is even better, since it will
provide copious amounts of a larger variety of vegetables, and
enough for canning and freezing to last through the winter. The
larger family, of course, will require a larger garden — but no
vegetable garden should be undertaken unless the family has the
desire to keep it free of weeds, stake and tie up those plants that
need support, carry and place mulching materials, occasionally
pick insects, and do the other chores that will encourage good
results. The enthusiasm of spring too often gives way to disin-
terest and neglect in the heat of July.

If garden space is limited, be sure to include as many vegetables as you can, even if you have to limit your selection to a couple
of tomato plants in large tubs on the patio, and cucumbers trained
to climb a trellis on the side of the garage.

The small-space gardener will use every trick in the book for maximum
yields — training plants upward, using movable tubs and other growing
containers, and ultra-careful selection of varieties.

WHICH VEGETABLES? WHICH VARIETIES?

Many so-called ideal vegetable garden plans are followed blindly by gardeners. But it would be foolish to plant a row of kale when nobody in the family cares a hoot for kale. And it would be equally foolish not to plant a double portion of acorn squash if your family really likes acorn squash. So, the first rule is a common sense rule: *Plant the vegetables you like.*

As for specific varieties, be guided by those that appear attractive to you, those that are recommended for Wisconsin's climate, and those that have been bred to be resistant to disease. In addition, if you plan to fill your freezer by the end of the year, choose varieties that are especially recommended for freezing. All these qualities are indicated in the listing of vegetables, beginning on page 110.

If your garden is a small one, you will also want to choose varieties that take up less space than others: (bantam corn, pole beans instead of bush beans, etc.) and vegetables that yield the most for the space that they take. Here are some of the more common garden vegetables, with the expected yield given for each per *100 feet of row:*

HEAVY YIELDERS

Cabbage (late) — 175 lbs.   Cucumbers — 150 lbs.
Carrots (late) — 150 lbs.   Rutabaga — 150 lbs.
Cauliflower — 45 heads   Tomatoes — 200 lbs.

MEDIUM YIELDERS

Beets — 100 lbs.   Parsnips — 100 lbs.
Cabbage (early) — 100 lbs.   Radishes — 1200 radishes
Carrots (early) — 100 lbs.   Sweet potatoes — 100 lbs.
Eggplant — 125 fruit   Turnips — 100 lbs.
Onions — 75-100 lbs.

LIGHT YIELDERS

Asparagus — 12-24 lbs.   Peas — 40 lbs.
Broccoli — 50 lbs.   Potatoes — 75 lbs.
Bush beans — 50 lbs.   Soybeans — 50 lbs.
Corn — 100 ears   Spinach — 50 lbs.
Lettuce (head or leaf) — 50 lbs.   Squash — 100 fruits
Lima beans — 60-75 lbs.

Another factor that you must take into consideration, in addition to the yield per row-foot, is the distance between rows. I have placed squash in the "light-yielder" category because it takes up so much room between rows (six to eight feet), while onions are counted as medium yielders because, although they yield only 75-100 pounds per 100 feet of row, their rows are only fifteen to eighteen inches apart. The recommended distances between rows for thirty-nine common garden vegetables are given in the Planting Guide on pages 98-103.

Succession planting can increase your garden yield by fully a third. Here, the soil is being
prepared in early July for a row
of carrots, in the same space
where spinach has just been
harvested.

Succession planting. Some plants can be harvested early, their
places taken by other crops which will yield before the first fall
frost sets in. This practice, called succession planting, is one that
the small-space gardener should study carefully, for it can enable
him to get the very most out of every precious square foot of
garden space. Early peas can be followed by any number of crops
— bush beans, tomatoes, late cabbage or carrots, corn, cucumbers,
and beets, to name a few. Other early crops in the succession
scheme are scallions, radishes, spinach, and leaf lettuce — all
fast-growing vegetables which like the cool weather of Wisconsin's
spring.

You can, in addition, follow late crops, such as corn and cabbage, with quick-growing vegetables such as lettuce (six weeks to
maturity) and radishes (four weeks). Conceivably, you could use
one section of the garden for as many as three crops, even during
Wisconsin's short growing season. Peas planted by April 15 can be
harvested by June 25. Cabbage plants can follow on June 26 and
be harvested by September 6, at which time radishes can go in, to
be harvested by October 6, well ahead of any serious frosts.

Intercropping. In addition to succession planting, you can plant
some vegetables in between the rows of others, harvesting the
quick growers while the others are just beginning to make good
progress. O. B. Combs and John A. Schoenemann, professors of
horticulture at the University of Wisconsin-Madison, give some

good examples in their popular booklet *The Vegetable Garden* (available from your county Extension agent):

> Early radish and spinach, for example, may be planted in the same row before late beet, late carrot, Chinese cabbage, cucumber or tomato. When you grow tomatoes this way, the plants are often set in the row before the early crop is all harvested. Cucumbers, if transplanted or seeded in hills, may be planted in the same way.
>
> Early, quick-growing crops like radish and spinach, as well as early beet, carrot, pea and leaf lettuce also may be planted between rows of cucumber, pumpkin, squash, tomato or late planted sweet corn. Likewise, head lettuce plants may be set between plants of early cabbage, early cauliflower, or tomato or ahead of late cabbage plants.

The main thing to remember when practicing succession planting and intercropping is to keep your soil well supplied with nutrients. After harvesting an early crop, return all plant wastes to the compost heap and then dig in some well-rotted compost before planting the succession crop. A few applications of compost tea during the growing season will do no harm, either. And, after the last crop in autumn has been harvested, dig in some half-finished compost and let it finish its job over the winter and into the following spring.

Marigolds are good companions for many garden vegetables, because their strong aroma repels some harmful garden insects.

Companion planting. A relatively new wrinkle in vegetable gardening is the study and practice of companion planting, which is simply the planting together of vegetables, herbs, and flowers that appear to like each other, or at least do better in each other's presence.

The basis for companionship may exist in light relationships — one plant providing a filtered light suitable for another plant. Or, a deep-rooted plant may break up soil that can better feed a shallow-rooted plant. There are slow and fast growers that can live happily side by side, as explained earlier in discussing intercropping. Or, one plant can offer support for another, such as corn supporting pole beans. Certain flowers and herbs also seem to emit odors that repel some harmful insects. The Herb Society of America, in a release entitled "Try Herbs Instead of Sprays", tells us that mint drives away the white cabbage butterfly, thus making cabbage and mint good companions.

Or, if we wish to believe the startling research that Peter Tompkins and Christopher Bird report in their equally startling book, *The Secret Life of Plants* (Harper & Row, 1973), plants may even like each other for purely emotional, intellectual, or social reasons. I am not prepared to explain the workings of companion planting — but I do know that a garden is an ecosystem, where every plant has a certain effect upon every other plant, however slight, and I know just as well that the horticultural experts have not even begun to sort out these interrelationships.

As our old Vermont friend Sam Ogden says, "There are mysteries that keep turning up in the garden, and of this I'm certain, that I've never solved any of them."

So, companion planting is presented here as a mystery, an avenue that you might wish to explore. It is probably the last remaining avenue that hasn't already been staked out by the experts, and so you might wish to have some fun with your own experiments.

Table 6, then, is a list of common garden vegetables, their companions and their antagonists, as reported to the editors of *Organic Gardening and Farming* by subscribers and other researchers.

"If we can grow at least a part of our food to feed our family, then we can reaffirm our own sense of independence . . . ."

Table 6.   GARDEN COMPANIONS

Vegetable	Likes	Dislikes
Asparagus	Tomatoes, parsley, basil	
Beans	Potatoes, carrots, cucumbers, cauliflower, cabbage, summer savory, most vegetables and herbs	Onions, garlic, gladiolus
Pole beans	Corn, summer savory	Onions, beets, kohlrabi, sunflowers
Bush beans	Potatoes, cucumbers, corn, strawberries, celery, summer savory	Onions
Beets	Onions, kohlrabi	Pole beans
Cabbage family (cabbage, cauliflower, kale, kohlrabi, broccoli, Brussels sprouts)	Aromatic plants, potatoes, celery, dill, camomile, sage, peppermint, mint, rosemary, beets, onions	Strawberries, tomatoes, pole beans
Carrots	Peas, leaf lettuce, chives, onions, leek, rosemary, sage, tomatoes	Dill
Celery	Leek, tomatoes, bush beans, cauliflower, cabbage	
Chives	Carrots	Peas, beans
Corn	Potatoes, peas, beans, cucumbers, pumpkin, squash	
Cucumbers	Beans, corn, peas, radishes, sunflowers	Potatoes, aromatic herbs

Tomatoes	Chives, onion, parsley, asparagus, marigold, nasturtium, carrot	Kohlrabi, potato, fennel, cabbage
Eggplant	Beans	
Peas	Carrots, turnips, radishes, cucumbers, corn, beans, most vegetables and herbs	Onions, garlic, gladiolus, potatoes
Squash	Nasturtium, corn	
Onion (including garlic)	Beets, strawberries, tomatoes, lettuce, summer savory, camomile	Peas, beans
Leek	Onions, celery, carrots	
Lettuce	Carrots and radishes (lettuce, carrots and radishes make a strong team when grown together), strawberries, cucumbers	
Radishes	Peas, nasturtium, lettuce, cucumbers	
Potatoes	Beans, corn, cabbage, horseradish (should be planted at corners of patch), marigold, eggplant (as a lure for Colorado potato beetle)	Pumpkin, squash, cucumber, sunflowers, tomatoes, raspberries
Pumpkin	Corn	Potatoes
Soybeans	Grows with anything, helps everything	
Strawberries	Bush beans, spinach, borage, lettuce (as a border)	Cabbage
Spinach	Strawberries	
Sunflowers	Cucumbers	
Turnips	Peas	Potatoes

Courtesy, Organic Gardening and Farming

Table 7. PLANTING GUIDE FOR WISCONSIN VEGETABLES

| | — PLANTING TIME — | | — SEEDS OR PLANTS — | |
VEGETABLE	Indoors at Madison*	Outdoors at Madison*	For 1 foot of row	For 100 feet of row
ASPARAGUS		April 15	½ plant	50 plants
BEAN, bush, lima		May 25	6 to 8	8 oz.
BEAN, bush, green & wax		May 10	6 to 8	8 oz.
BEAN, pole		May 10	4 to 6	6 oz.
BEET		April 15	10 to 15	1 to 1¼ oz.
BROCCOLI	March 15	May 1 (plants)		40 to 50 plants
BRUSSELS SPROUTS		May 15 (seeds)	2 to 4 seeds	⅛ oz.
CABBAGE, early	March 15	May 1 (plants)		50 to 67 plants
CABBAGE, late		May 15 (seeds)		40 to 50 plants
CARROT		April 15	30 to 40	¼ oz.
CAULI-FLOWER	March 15	May 1 (plants)		50 to 70 plants
CELERIAC	March 1	April 15	2 plants	200 plants
CELERY	March 15	May 20	2 plants	200 plants
CHARD		April 15	10 to 15	1 to 1¼ oz.
CHINESE CABBAGE		June 20 (seeds)	15 to 20	⅛ oz.
CHIVES		April 15	2 clusters	1 packet
COLLARDS		May 15		1 packet
CORN SALAD		April 15		1 packet
CUCUMBER		May 20	4 to 6	1/3 oz.
EGGPLANT	March 15	June 1 (plants)		40 to 50
ENDIVE	March 1	April 15		1 packet
FINOCCHIO		May 15		1 packet

Depth to Plant (inches)	—SPACING— Between Rows (inches)	Between Plants (inches)	Amount for One Person	Days to Harvest
6 to 8	36 to 40	24	30 to 40 ft.	2 years
1 to 1½	24 to 30	3 to 4	30 to 40 ft.	70 to 80
1 to 1½	24 to 30	2 to 3	50 to 60 ft.	50 to 60
1 to 1½	30 to 36	4 to 6	20 to 30 ft.	60 to 65
¾ to 1	15 to 18	2 to 3	24 ft.	50 to 60
3 to 4	36 to 42	24 to 30	2 plants	60 to 70
¾ to 1	24 to 30	12 to 18	2 plants	90 to 100
3 to 4	24 to 30	12 to 18	5 plants	60 to 70
3 to 4	30 to 36	18 to 24	12 plants	90 to 100
½ to ¾	15 to 18	1 to 2	48 ft.	60 to 70
3 to 4	24 to 30	12 to 18	4 to 6 plants	50 to 60
⅛	18 to 24	4 to 6	3 plants	115
2 to 2½	36 to 42	4 to 6	5 to 6 plants	100 to 100
¾ to 1	15 to 18	2 to 4	3 ft.	40 to 50
¾ to 1	24 to 30	6 to 10	3 ft.	90 to 100
½	14 to 16	6 to 10	3 plants	60 to 90
½	18 to 24	18 to 24	12 ft.	75
½	14 to 16	12	6 ft.	35 to 45
1 to 1½	42 to 48	4 to 6	12 ft.	50 to 60
3 to 4	36 to 42	24 to 30	2 to 3 plants	70 to 80
½	18 to 24	12	6 ft.	70
½	18 to 24	4 to 6	6 ft.	90

Table 7. PLANTING GUIDE FOR WISCONSIN VEGETABLES

| VEGETABLE | —PLANTING TIME— | | —SEEDS OR PLANTS— | |
	Indoors at Madison*	Outdoors at Madison*	For 1 foot of row	For 100 feet of row
GARLIC		April 15	4 to 6 cloves	1 lb. cloves
GROUND CHERRY	March 15	May 10		1 packet
HORSERADISH		April 15		50 to 75 cuttings
JERUSALEM ARTICHOKE		May 1		120 tubers
KALE		April 15		1 packet
KOHLRABI		April 15	10 to 15	⅛ oz.
LEEK		April 15		1 packet
LETTUCE, head	March 15	May 1 (plants)	1 plant	100 plants
LETTUCE, leaf		April 15	25 to 30	¼ oz.
MUSKMELON	May 1	May 20	4 to 6	⅓ oz.
MUSTARD		April 15		1 packet
OKRA	April 1	May 15		2 oz.
ONION, plants	February 20	May 1 (plants)	3 to 4	300 to 400
ONION, sets		April 15	6 to 12	3 to 4 lbs.
PARSLEY	March 15	May 1 (plants)	1 plant	100 plants
PARSNIP		April 15	20 to 25	½ oz.
PEA		April 15	12 to 15	1 lb.
PEPPER	March 15	June 1 (plants)		50 to 70
POTATO, early		April 15	1 piece	9 lbs.
POTATO, late		April 15	1 piece	9 lbs.

Depth to Plant (inches)	—SPACING— Between Rows (inches)	Between Plants (inches)	Amount for One Person	Days to Harvest
1 to 2	14 to 16	2 to 3	1 to 2 ft.	60 to 90
½	18 to 24	12 to 18	6 ft.	65 to 80
2	24 to 30	18 to 24	8 ft.	75 to 100
4 to 6	30 to 36	10	6 ft.	100
½	18 to 24	12 to 15	8 ft.	70
¾ to 1	15 to 18	3 to 4	5 to 6 ft.	50 to 60
½ to 1	14 to 16	2 to 3	6 ft.	100
2 to 2½	18 to 24	8 to 10	3 to 4 plants	60 to 70
¼ to ½	15 to 18	2 to 3	12 ft.	40 to 50
¾ to 1	42 to 48	6 to 8	10 to 12 plants	80 to 90
½	14 to 16	12	6 ft.	30 to 45
1 to 1½	36 to 42	24	10 ft.	90
2 to 2½	15 to 18	2 to 3	12 ft.	110 to 120
2 to 3	15 to 18	1 to 2	12 ft.	40 to 50
2 to 3	18 to 24	6 to 8	1 plant	30 to 40
½ to ¾	24 to 30	2 to 3	12 ft.	1000 to 120
1½ to 2	15 to 18	1 to 2	145 ft.	60 to 70
3 to 4	30 to 36	12 to 18	2 plants	60 to 70
3 to 4	30 to 36	12	100 ft.	80 to 100
4 to 6	36 to 42	12	300 ft.	130 to 140

Table 7. PLANTING GUIDE FOR WISCONSIN VEGETABLES

VEGETABLE	—PLANTING TIME—		—SEEDS OR PLANTS—	
	Indoors at Madison*	Outdoors at Madison*	For 1 foot of row	For 100 feet of row
PUMPKIN, pie	May 1	May 20 (plants)	2 to 4	½ oz.
RADISH		April 15	20 to 25	1 oz.
RHUBARB		April 15		35 plants
RUTABAGA		June 15†	15 to 20	⅛ oz.
SALSIFY		April 15		1 oz.
SHALLOT		April 15		1 lb. cloves
SORREL		April 15		1 packet
SOYBEAN		May 10		8 to 16 oz.
SPINACH		April 15	20 to 25	1 oz.
SQUASH, summer		May 20	2 to 4 seeds	2 oz.
SQUASH, winter		May 20 (plants)	2 to 4 seeds	2 oz.
SWEET CORN		May 10	3 to 4 seeds	4 oz.
TOMATO	March 15	May 20 (plants)		28 to 34 plants
TURNIP		April 15	20 to 30	¼ oz.
WATERMELON	April 1	May 10		1 packet

Depth to Plant (inches)	—SPACING— Between Rows (inches)	Between Plants (inches)	Amount for One Person	Days to Harvest
1 to 1½	48 to 60	15 to 18	4 ft.	90 to 110
½ to ¾	15 to 18	1	36 ft.	25 to 30
6 to 8	48 to 54	36	2 plants	2 years
¾ to 1	24 to 30	6 to 8	12 ft.	100 to 110
½	18 to 26	2 to 3	6 ft.	120 to 140
1 to 2	12 to 18	2 to 3	8 ft.	90
½	18 to 24	5 to 8	6 ft.	60
1 to 1½	24 to 30	3	12 ft.	50 to 65
½ to ¾	15 to 18	1 to 2	24 ft.	40 to 50
1 to 1½	48 to 60	15 to 18	2 plants	50 to 60
1 to 1½	72 to 84	15 to 18	12 ft.	90 to 120
1 to 1½	30 to 36	8 to 10	84 ft.	65 to 90
3 to 4	36 to 42	24 to 36	12 plants	65 to 80
½ to ¾	18 to 24	2 to 3	10 to 15 ft.	60 to 70
1 to 2	96 to 120	8 ft. (hills)	1 hill	110 to 120

SOURCE: O. B. Combs, *Vegetable Varieties and Planting Guide for Gardens, 1974.*
Additions by the author.
*Plant about one week later in central Wisconsin, two weeks later in northern Wisconsin. Consult spring frost map for your area.
†Plant about one week earlier in central Wisconsin, two weeks earlier in northern Wisconsin, in order that roots may mature during early autumn frosts.

CHARTING THE GARDEN

After you have determined the size of your garden and which vegetables you want to plant, and after you have taken into consideration the benefits of succession planting, intercropping, and companion planting, you will want to draw up a vegetable chart to plan out your entire garden. This is great fun for one of those cold days in mid-March, when the winter has really gotten the best of you. Use quarter-inch graph paper, if you have it, or any ruled paper that you can block off into equal squares. Let each square represent one foot of garden space. That way, a standard 8½-by-11-inch sheet of quarter-inch graph paper will represent a thirty-four by forty-four-foot garden.

Then, use the Planting Guide (Table 7) to help you to devise your own garden scheme. The guide will give you the approximate earliest planting dates, number of seeds or plants to a foot of row, planting depth, distance between rows, distance between plants in the row, the amount to plant to feed one person, and the number of days to harvest — all you need to know to draw up a workable plan.

Nearly every book on vegetable gardening gives one or more "ideal" plans, and I do not like these very much because they are so filled with vegetables my family doesn't like — and they lack many of the vegetables we do like — that by the time I have made substitutions, I have so disturbed the general plan that I tear it up and start from scratch. Nevertheless, I will borrow one here to present to you (Table 8) so that you can see how it works. This particular plan is for a moderate-size garden, twenty-by-fifty feet, and it comes from Profs. Combs and Schoenemann's booklet, *The Vegetable Garden*. It is the best that I could present as an example, not only because it makes eminent sense, but also because all the vegetables were selected to suit the Wisconsin climate.

Table 8.   A TYPICAL 20' x 50' VEGETABLE GARDEN PLAN
           FOR WISCONSIN.

Distance from end of Garden	Crop	Planting Date*	Suggestions for Planting
Row 1 1'6"	Parlsey	April 15 (seed) or	First 2 feet of row
	Chard	April 15	Next 3 feet of row
	Cavalier Radish and Parsnip	April 15	Seed together 7 feet
	Pepper	June 1	3 plants
Row 2 3'6"	Spinach	May 1	
	Late Carrot	July 1	Carrots follow Spinach
Row 3 5'0"	Cavalier Radish	May 10	
	Late Carrot	July 1	Carrots follow radishes
Row 4 6'3"	Onion	April 15 (seed) or May 1 (plants)	
Row 5 8'3"	Cauliflower	May 1	Cauliflower interplanted with lettuce and followed by Chinese cabbage
	Buttercrunch Head Letuce (plants)	May 1	
	Chinese Cabbage	July 10	
Row 6 10'3"	Buttercrunch Head Lettuce (plants)	May 1	Lettuce interplanted with cabbage
	Late Cabbage (plants)	July 1	

Row 7	12'3"	Early Cabbage	May 1	Cabbage interplanted with lettuce plants and followed by turnip
		Head Lettuce (plants)	May 1	
		Turnip	August 1	
Row 8	14'0"	Pea	April 15	Two rows, 6 in. apart
Row 9	15'9"	Cavalier Radish	April 15	Radishes followed by cucumbers
		Cucumber	June 1	
Row 10	17'6"	Pea	April 15	Two rows, 6 in. apart
Row 11	19'9"	Spinach	April 15	Spinach followed by tomatoes
		Tomato (seed) or	April 15	Sow seeds in hills when spinach is planted
		Tomato (plants)	May 20	Set plants in spinach row, 2 ft. apart if staked; 3 ft. unstaked
Row 12	22'0"	Pea	May 10	Two rows, 6 in. apart
Row 13	24'3"	Spinach	April 15	Spinach followed by tomatoes as in row 11
Row 14	26'6"	Pea	May 10	Two rows 6 in. apart
Row 15 Radish	28'0"	White Icicle April 15		Radishes followed by beans
		Kentucky Wonder Pole Bean	June 15	

Row 16 Radish	29'0"	Scarlet Globe April 15		Radishes followed by beans
		Kentucky Wonder Pole Bean	June 15	
Row 17	31'0"	Spinach	May 1	Spinach followed by beans
		Green Bush Bean	July 1	
Row 18	32'6"	Wax Bush Bean	May 10	
Row 19	34'0"	Green Bush Bean	May 10	
Row 20	35'6"	Early Beet	April 15	Beets followed by turnips
		Turnip	August 1	
Row 21	36'9"	Cavalier Radish	May 1	Radishes followed by corn
		Sweet Corn	June 10	
Row 22	38'0"	Early Carrot	April 15	
Row 23	39'3"	White Icicle Radishes	May 1	Radishes followed by corn
		Sweet Corn	June 10	
Row 24	40'6"	Onion (sets)	April 15	
Row 25	41'9"	Sweet Corn	May 10	Corn followed by radishes
		Scarlet Globe Radish	August 10	
Row 26	43'0"	Leaf Lettuce	April 15	Lettuce followed by radishes
		Scarlet Globe Radish	August 10	
Row 27	44'3"	Sweet Corn	May 10	Corn followed by radishes
		Scarlet Globe Radish	August 20	

Row 28	45'6"	Spinach	May 10	Spinach followed by lettuce
		Fall Leaf Lettuce	August 10	
Row 29	46'9"	Sweet Corn	May 10	Corn followed by lettuce
		Fall Leaf Lettuce	August 10	
Row 30	48'6"	White Icicle Radish	May 10	
		Late Beet	July 10	
	50'0"	End of Garden		

SOURCE: O. B. Combs and John A. Schoenemann, *The Vegetable Garden*, University of Wisconsin-Extension Special Circular 117.
*NOTE: Planting dates given are for Madison; plant about one week later in central Wisconsin, two weeks later in northern Wisconsin.

SIXTY-TWO VEGETABLES FOR WISCONSIN

Here are sixty-two vegetables, some common and some uncommon, that will grow in Wisconsin. I have grown many of them personally, but I certainly have not grown all of them, and I imagine it would be difficult to find anyone who ever has. The information given for these sixty-two vegetables, then, is necessarily drawn from a variety of sources — from my own experience, yes, but mainly from government and university reports, from the works of other garden writers, from the pages of *Organic Gardening and Farming* magazine, from the personal advice of gardening friends and Extension agents, and even from newspaper articles.

To the best of my knowledge, all the information given here is accurate, or at least as accurate as such a compilation can be. Because of space restrictions, the cultural directions are brief. Remember, though, that these directions should be supplemented by the information given in the Planting Guide, which will give you the space between plants, space between rows, approximate planting dates, number of days to harvest, and other valuable data. If you would like still more information about any of these varieties, check your library or bookstore for a good vegetable encyclopedia, or ask your county agent for information on the vegetables that interest you. He might have a pamphlet giving full cultural directions.

Then, a word about the recommended varieties given for each vegetable: Those followed by an asterisk (*) are those recommended for growing in Wisconsin in the pamphlet *Vegetable Varieties and Planting Guide for Gardens*, prepared by Prof. O. B. Combs of the University of Wisconsin-Madison.

This pamphlet is revised annually to include new varieties, and is available from your county agent at no charge. Those without an asterisk have not been so recommended, but they give every indication of being suitable for Wisconsin growing.

Varieties particularly recommended for freezing appear in italics and these recommendations come either from the pamphlet mentioned earlier or from the seed growers or nurserymen who breed these varieties (in the case of those not followed by an asterisk).

Last, those followed by a dagger (†) are especially recommended for growing in northern Wisconsin by Eugene E. Anderson, Area Community Development Agent, University of Wisconsin-Extension.

ASPARAGUS

It takes several years to establish a producing asparagus bed, even when roots instead of seeds are planted. But, properly cared for, an asparagus bed will last a lifetime. Asparagus is the first vegetable to be brought to the table in spring, usually in late April or early May, and it will continue to produce up until July 1.

Soil. Asparagus prefers a sandy loam, but will do well even in heavier soils, if they are well drained.

pH. 6.0 - 7.0

Culture. Select a sunny corner of the garden, one with rich, deep, well-drained soil. In early spring, as soon as the ground can be worked, dig a trench ten inches deep and ten inches wide. (A rotary tiller can be used for easier trench digging.) Line the bottom of the trench with three inches of well-rotted compost, including plenty of old manure. Dig this into the bottom of the trench to a depth of at least six inches. Set one-year-old crowns two feet apart in the row and cover with two inches of well-rotted and screened compost. Water well. Fill the trench very gradually throughout the summer with a mixture of screened compost and good topsoil, until it is full by September 15. A bed prepared in this careful manner will give roots a good start and will support the plants for many years to come.

Do not cut any spears the first year, but let them grow into the ferny brush that will establish the planting for future years. In the second year, you may cut spears for the first several weeks,

but not after that. During the third year, you may cut spears up until the middle of June, after which you should leave them alone. After the third year, you may make a full harvest, cutting up until July 1 — but not after.

Asparagus does not need much fertilizing, since its roots are so deep and vigorous, drawing nutrients from six feet in any direction. But you might adopt the practice of hilling the rows in spring and side dressing with a mixture of compost and either limestone or wood ashes.

Do not remove the ferny brush in fall, but let it die down naturally, cutting it only in the following spring. A winter mulch of hay will prevent frost from damaging the roots, and it will prevent heaving, which tends to bring the roots slowly to the surface.

Special tips. If you maintain a fairly large bed, sow a cover crop of cowpeas or soybeans after the cutting season has ended. Sow between the asparagus rows and till under the cover crop in fall for soil enrichment.

Varieties. *Mary Washington**†, *Waltham Washington** (both tolerant to rust).

BEAN (bush, green)

Bush beans (also called snap beans) are a most rewarding crop, easy to grow, productive, simple to harvest, and suitable for both canning and freezing. They are a good source of vitamin A.

Soil. Bush beans thrive in almost any soil, from light sand to heavy clay.

pH. 6.0 - 7.5

Culture. Inoculate seeds with a nitrogen inoculant before planting, to give them a faster start. After the young plants have grown to about three inches high, thin until they are four to six inches apart. Cultivate lightly with a hoe during the season, being careful not to disturb the shallow roots. A light mulch may be applied after the plants are established and thriving. Beans should be picked before they have matured, when the pods are fairly small and the tips soft. Regular picking is important, since the plant will stop producing if the seeds are allowed to mature.

Special tips. Instead of making one large planting of bush beans, make several plantings, separated by two-week intervals. This practice will assure a continuous supply of beans throughout the summer and early fall.

Varieties. Tendergreen*†, *Earligreen**, *Tendercrop*†*, *Gardengreen*†* (mosaic resistant), *Bush Blue Lake 274**.

These yellow-podded wax beans will be cleaner because of the heavy straw mulch placed under them.

BEAN (bush, wax)

Wax beans are yellow podded instead of green, but otherwise there is little difference in their use or taste. Culture is the same as for green bush beans.

Varieties. Pencil Pod*†, *Kinghorn*†*, *Cherokee*†* (mosaic resistant), *Midas** (mosaic resistant), *Eastern Butterwax, Gold Crop* (1974 All America Winner), *Honey Gold* (mosaic tolerant).

BEAN (pole, green)

Pole beans have the same general taste as bush beans. They generally require a longer time to mature, but the gardener who is pinched for space will certainly want to include them, since their yield is higher.

Soil. Pole beans have the same general soil and climatic requirements as bush beans, except that they seem able to thrive in heavier soils.

Culture. The traditional method of planting pole beans is to drive seven-foot stakes into the ground, hilling up some soil around the base and planting six seeds (inoculated) in the hill around each pole. The hills should be eighteen to twenty-four inches apart, although some gardeners plant much more closely. Rows are three feet apart. After the seeds have produced young plants, thin to three per hill, and be sure that the vines get a good start up the pole. Some gardeners erect the poles in tepee fashion, building veritable cones of pole beans. Others stretch washline horizontally between vertical poles, to provide even more climbing room for the vigorous vines. Begin with traditional poles, and then experiment with your own devices.

Special tips. All beans fix nitrogen in the soil, and thus are valuable soil builders. When clearing garden wastes after the last harvest, cut the bean stalks at ground level, but do not tear up their roots. It is the roots that hold the nitrogen. In the following season, plant a nitrogen-loving vegetable where the beans stood — early beets or cabbage, cauliflower, spinach, or white potatoes. All will benefit from the bean's legacy of nitrogen.

Varieties. *Kentucky Wonder**†, *Blue Lake**†, *Romano**†, Kentucky Wonder Wax.

BEAN (bush, lima)

Lima beans are native to warmer regions and are not always easy to grow here in Wisconsin. They require a slightly more acid soil than snap beans, and long, warm days. They generally take from ten to twenty days more to mature than bush or pole beans.

Soil. Limas do well in a light, but rich, garden loam.

pH. 5.5 - 6.5

Culture. Select the sunniest spot in the garden for limas. Plant seeds (inoculated) only when the soil has warmed up thoroughly, or else the seeds might well rot in the ground. The soil surface cannot be hard and crusty or the young seedlings might be unable to push the large seed halves through the surface. After the plants have bloomed and the tiny pods have been set, be careful not to disturb the plants for about a week, for the young pods drop off easily. A large dog running through the lima bean row at the wrong time can decimate your crop in seconds. The plants also need extra moisture after they have bloomed, but it should be applied by irrigating the rows or hand watering along the roots with care — never by training the hose on the plants or dragging the hose between the rows where it might brush up against the plants.

Special tips. Even when you do everything right with limas, they might respond with luxuriant leafy growth and a scant crop of beans, especially if the soil is too rich. This is a difficult crop for most gardeners, and many in Wisconsin will not want to assume the high risk of failure.

Varieties. *Fordhook 242**†, *Thorogreen**†, *Thaxter* (baby limas), *Baby Potato*, Burpee's Improved Bush.

BEET

Beets are a rewarding garden crop, relatively easy to grow, fast developing, and requiring little space. They do especially well in the cooler regions of the state. We grow them for the red roots which are good sources of vitamins B_1 and C, but the beet tops are good, too, as a source of vitamins A and C, and iron.

Soil. Beets do well on nearly any well-composted soil, so long as it is rich in nutrients. Beets are notorious consumers of potash, and for this reason you should incorporate either hardwood ashes or potash rock in that part of the garden you have reserved for beets, before planting in the early spring.

pH. 5.8 - 7.0

Culture. Seeds can go into the open ground very early, at the same time as peas. You can thin the young plants by picking the baby beets to use in salads. Sowings made every few weeks during the season will give you a continuous crop throughout the summer and into fall's heavy frosts — but very hot weather might force them into bolting and woodiness.

Special tips. Late-planted beets can be harvested just before the first severe frost of the autumn. Packed in sand and kept barely moist at a temperature of thirty-five to forty degrees, they will last for several months, probably into January.

Varieties. *Early Wonder**†, *Perfected Detroit**, *Detroit Red†*, *Ruby Queen**†, Vermilion, Cylindra†, Spring Red (slow to bolt), Early Red Ball, Crosby Egyptian, Red Pak (good for canning), Detroit Dark Red, Garnet, Crosby Green Top, Long Season (eighty days).

BROCCOLI

Broccoli is regarded as a delicacy by some, and as a punishment by others. It is not difficult to grow in Wisconsin, and the mature plant will be quite resistant to the first fall frosts, thus extending the growing season beyond that of many other vegetables. Broccoli is one of the few vegetables that we grow for their flowers, for it is the bunches of flowering buds and their tender branches that we pick to eat.

Soil. Broccoli needs a fertile and well-drained soil, rich in organic matter and lime.

pH. 6.0 - 7.0

Culture. The broccoli plant will grow quickly during hot weather, but once the heads begin to form, the plant prefers cool nights. This preference makes broccoli a good succession crop, perhaps following a planting of early spinach. You can buy plants

Broccoli frequently flourishes well into November in Wisconsin, since it is seldom bothered by night temperatures even as low as twenty-six degrees.

from most nurseries and local garden centers, or you may start seeds indoors about six weeks before transplanting time. When the heads begin to form, you might side-dress the plants with a strong compost tea. A mulch should be kept around the plants once they have become well established (spoiled hay is good for these large plants), and if the weather becomes particularly hot and dry, extra water should be given to them.

Special tips. The leaves of the broccoli plant are particularly susceptible to attack by the cabbageworm. The worm doesn't attack the edible portions of the plant, however, and therefore doesn't cause much concern. The cabbageworms can be picked off by hand, or, if the infestation is great, you can control them with rotenone. If plant lice or aphids get into the heads, it is best to cut the heads into small pieces and drop them into a fairly strong solution of salt water for a few minutes. The insects will float to the top and the broccoli, after having been washed, will be perfectly good to eat.

Varieties. *Spartan Early**†, *Green Comet**† (hybrid), *Waltham 29**, *Royal Purple "Cauliflower,"** *Cleopatra,* Italian Sprouting, Green Mountain (recommended for short-season areas where nights are cold), Bravo, Green Hornet, Green Comet, *Early Purple Head.*

BRUSSELS SPROUTS

Brussels sprouts have been a prized vegetable in America for more than a hundred years and in Europe for several hundred. They do well in Wisconsin, like other members of the cabbage family, because of our cool nights. Excessive heat, however, might force growth to the point where the heads will become loose and leafy instead of tight and firm, as they should be.

Soil. Brussels sprouts like a fairly heavy soil, well drained and well supplied with compost and lime. On sandy soils great care must be given to heavy fertilization and extra water.

pH. 6.0 - 7.0

Culture. Sow seeds in the open garden after the danger of heavy frost has passed. Or, sow seeds later in the season for a fall crop. When the young plants are about three inches high, they should be thinned and transplanted to the recommended distances. A mulch will help to moderate the soil temperature, keeping growth at just the right pace. When the little heads begin to form on the axils of the leaves, give the plants an application of compost tea. When the heads begin to mature, cut off the lower leaves (below the heads) to facilitate cutting.

Varieties. *Jade Cross* (hybrid)*†, Jade Cross E (slightly taller than Jade Cross), Early Morn, Long Island Improved, Green Pearl (120 days).

Wisconsin's cool climate is perfect for these Brussels sprouts.

Cabbage plants are heavy feeders and heavy drinkers of water. Be sure that you give yours enough of both, for best results.

CABBAGE

The rightful head of the cabbage family is cabbage itself, an old Wisconsin favorite. At the turn of the century, when traveling photographers made their rounds of Wisconsin rural areas, one of the favorite late summer pictures was the one of the entire family gathered around a display of their garden's harvest. And the picture was never complete without at least one mammoth cabbage head, often set directly in front of the proud and dour head of the family. Cabbage is, indeed, a garden product you can be justly pround of. In the home garden, you can produce heads that weigh twenty pounds or more by giving the plants plenty of compost and plenty of water. And few vegetables are more versatile then cabbage. Cooked with pork roast or corned beef, cut up into crisp slaw, made into sauerkraut, or just eaten raw in chunks, cabbage returns all the effort put into raising it, many times over.

Soil. Like other members of its family, cabbage prefers a rather heavy loam, rich in nutrient matter. Few plants feed more heavily, and so generous applications of compost, including plenty of manure, are essential. If the soil is sandy, care must be taken to keep it well supplied with water during the growing season, for cabbages are heavy drinkers as well as eaters.

pH. 6.0 - 7.0

Culture. Start seeds indoors about six weeks before transplanting time, or buy plants at your garden center. Set them out when
danger of heavy frost has passed. The early varieties are smaller
than the late ones, and they must be picked as soon as they are
firm, or else the heat of midsummer will force a seed head to form,
destroying the quality of the head. The late varieties, which are
larger and require considerably more time to mature, do not demand early picking, since they will mature as the weather turns
cool. The late varieties can stand a couple of light frosts. Like
Brussels sprouts, in fact, the flavor of cabbage is enhanced by an
early frost or two.

When planting cabbage, work aged compost at least eight
inches into the ground for best results. The roots will go down
three feet or more, if they can, to draw moisture to quench their
heavy thirst. When you do apply water during dry spells, soak the
ground thoroughly — never sprinkle. During the growing season,
give plants a couple of applications of compost tea, fortified with
dried blood. The dried blood, which is rich in nitrogen, will give the
plants an extra boost when they need it most. It is also a good
idea to plant cabbages where last year's peas or beans stood, since
the nitrogen that these legumes leave in the soil will be eagerly
received by the cabbage plants.

Special tips. Those pretty yellow and white butterflies that you
see darting around your young cabbage plants are up to no good.
They are laying eggs that will hatch the dread cabbageworm. This
is a good time to get the children interested in collecting butterflies — providing that the kids are old enough to avoid stepping on
the young plants. After the worms have appeared and have begun
to eat huge, gaping holes in the leaves, they can be controlled with
rotenone if there are too many to pick by hand. But do not be too
concerned when holes appear on the outer leaves. The cabbage
head grows from the inside out, and the head will be good even
when the outer leaves look ragged. The other major attacker of
early cabbage is the root maggot, which can be controlled by
placing tarpaper discs around the stems of the young plants at the
soil surface. The discs are inexpensive and can be purchased at
most garden centers.

Cabbages can be stored for a short time in a cool cellar, by
pulling out the head, getting as much of the root as possible, tying
a paper sack around the head, and hanging it up by the root. Or,
you may store them underground, covering them with layers of
soil and straw to protect them against freezing. Further storage
hints are given in the table on page 185.

Varieties. Jersey Queen*, Stonehead†, Market Dawn*, Wisconsin Golden Acre*†, Badger Market*†, Market Topper* (hybrid),
King Cole*, Market Prize* (hybrid), Red Acre*† (shows insect resistance), Greenback*†, TBR Globe*†, Little Rock*, Sanibel* (all
resistant to yellows and listed in order of earliness), Vangard*

(Savoy), Savoy King* (hybrid, shows insect resistance).

(Note: There are so many varieties of cabbage commercially available — more than fifty are offered in the Stokes catalog alone — that I have listed only those recommended specifically for Wisconsin.)

CARROT

Carrots have a long and distinguished heritage, going back to the time of the ancient Greeks. They are a rich source of vitamin A and have long been a popular garden vegetable. It is not difficult to grow carrots, but it is considerably more difficult to grow good-looking carrots. They require far more personal attention than most garden vegetables, although many gardeners think that the final product is worth the extra effort.

Soil. Carrots will grow in most soils, but they prefer a sandy loam that is free from stones and lumps. These obstructions will inhibit the growth of the carrot (which is a taproot) and will cause it to be misshapen. If your soil is heavy, you had better choose among the half-long varieties. The long varieties require about a foot of well-prepared soil of fine texture. In any case, the soil should be well supplied with compost and should be given an application of limestone, well worked in, before planting.

pH. 5.5 - 6.5

Culture. Carrots can be planted as soon as the soil can be worked in spring. They are slow to germinate and must be thinned so that the individual plants are one or two inches apart, depending on the variety. This is a slow and tedious job which, once done, will prompt you to sow carrots more thinly next time. In order to avoid having all the carrots mature at once, successive plantings can be made up until about July 15 in Wisconsin. After the initial thinning, made when the young seedlings are about two inches tall, the plants may be further thinned throughout the season. (Use the young carrots in salads.) In fall, the last of the mature carrots should be dug and stored just before the first hard frost. They are particularly suitable for storage in an underground root barrel.

Special tips. Try interplanting radishes with your carrots. Sow the radishes *very thinly* (perhaps two seeds to the inch), right in with the carrot seeds. The radishes will germinate first, and will be picked before they begin to crowd the carrots. The early-germinating radishes serve another purpose, in that they will mark the row until the carrots show their foliage later on.

Half-long varieties. *Nantes*, Red Cored Chantenay*†, Scarlet Nantes†, Spartan Bonus** (hybrid), *Danvers 126*, Coreless Amsterdam†, Baby-Finger Nantes, Touchon Deluxe, Pioneer, Oxhart†.*

Long varieties. *Imperator*†, Gold Spike*, Gold Pak*†, Spartan Sweet†, Canuck, Spartan Fancy, Gold Pak, Ultra Pak, Waltham Hicolor.*

To bleach the heads of cauliflower, tie the outer leaves
loosely over the heads, to
shield them from the sun.

CAULIFLOWER

Cauliflower is an interesting plant to grow, both challenging and rewarding. It should not be attempted unless you are pre-pared to give it the special attention it requires, and its needs are quite specific. Like broccoli, it is the flower of the plant which we covet. Many gardeners are willing to spend the time to grow perfect blooms for both the eye and the palate.

Soil. Cauliflower is perhaps the heaviest feeder of the garden, even hungrier than cabbage. Be sure that the soil is well supplied with all nutrients, particularly nitrogen. Cauliflower will do well where beans or peas grew in the previous year, since these legumes leave nitrogen stores behind. Lime should be incorporated deeply before planting.

pH. 6.0 - 7.0

Culture. The plant does best during cool and moist weather, and is a voracious drinker of water. Apply a mulch as soon as the young plants are set out, and never let the soil become dry. Do not disturb the roots in cultivating, or else the heads will grow un-evenly and become fuzzy. Either a late spring frost or a lack of nitrogen can cause premature heading, in which case the plants should be pulled out and discarded.

Special tips. When the heads are about 2½-inches in diameter, take the outside leaves and tie them loosely over the heads to shade them from the sun. This will result in the pure white heads that are prized by growers. This bleaching process may be started later, depending on which expert you listen to, even as late as a week before harvesting.

Succession plantings may be made, although late plantings must be given even more water than early ones. The keys to good cauliflower are heavy composting and heavy mulching.

Varieties. *Early Snowball**†, *Snowdrift**†, *Super Snowball**†, *Snow Kind** (hybrid), *Snowball Imperial**, *Extra Early Snowball*, Super Junior, Snowmound (developed for fall crops), Idol Original, Perfected Snowball, Clou, Snowball-Y, *Igloo*, Self-Blance (no tying needed), Early Purple-Head†, Royal Purple.

Celeriac is an unusual but rewarding root crop, long popular in Europe but just making itself known in Wisconsin.

CELERIAC

This vegetable, sometimes called "knob celery," is more popular in Europe than in America, but it has caught the fancy of some Wisconsin gardeners to the point where it can now be found in some garden centers. It is related to celery and it has a similar taste. The difference is that we grow celeriac for its enlarged root crown, which the Europeans prize for soups and stews. The sliced root can also be used in salads.

Soil. Celeriac likes a fertile, well-limed, and rather heavy loam. (The heavier soils provide ample supplies of water, which are needed for the plant's success.)

pH. 6.0 - 7.0

Culture. Celeriac requires less care than celery, and it is easier to grow. If your local seedsman or nursery cannot supply seed, it may be ordered from one of the larger mail order seed houses such as Olds, Stokes, or Harris. Seed is sown about eight weeks before transplanting time, which is about May 15 in Madison, June 1 in Superior. It is a slow-grower, requiring 110-120 days, but it can take a few light fall frosts without apparent damage. Set three- to four-inch seedlings six to eight inches apart in rows two feet apart, and apply a light mulch to conserve moisture. Roots can be harvested when they have reached two inches in diameter. After the first light frosts in fall, and before a really hard frost, the remaining roots can be dug and stored either in an underground root barrel or in a cool basement, where they should be packed in moist sand.

Varieties. Alabaster (120 days), Large Smooth Prague (110 days), New Giant Prague (115 days).

CELERY

The ancestors of modern garden celery come from the marshes of Western Europe and Northern Africa, and celery still grows best in a marshy soil which supplies plenty of water and plenty of lime. However, it may be grown successfully in any soil, if moisture and fertilization requirements are met. There are two common types — golden (or yellow), which was much preferred until recent years, and the green variety, which we see most often in supermarkets under the label of Pascal celery.

Soil. Celery likes a fertile soil, rich in all elements, and plenty of available water. A generous application of well-rotted manure before planting will virtually assure a good crop.

pH. 6.0 - 7.0

Culture. Seeds are slow to germinate and to grow, so that indoor sowings should be made a full nine weeks before setting out the plants in May or June. If you have a cold frame, seeds may be started even earlier, indoors, and set into the frame to harden off along about April, giving you larger plants with which to start the outdoor growing season. Be careful not to break the taproot when transplanting, for this can injure the plant, perhaps fatally. It is best to sow seeds in peat pots, which can be put into the ground, pot and all, thus eliminating any possibility of root injury. The surface of the seeding soil should be kept damp at all times. (Since a damp surface is one of the major causes of damping-off disease,

A side-dressing of wood ashes will supply the potash these young celery plants need for vigorous growth.

you may now wonder how to prevent the problem with celery. The answer is to apply a light sprinkling of washed sand on the bedding surface. The seeds can germinate through the sand, and the damping-off disease cannot function in this medium.) Water the peat pots by placing them in a shallow tray of water until the surface becomes damp. In the garden, keep a light mulch around the plants and do not let the soil become dry. During hot spells, water the soil around the plants, but do not direct water on the plants themselves. The foliage should not be wet unnecessarily.

Special tips. Celery is a heavy potash feeder, but will react badly to excessive nitrogen supplies. The potash can be supplied by sprinkling hardwood ashes alongside of the plants several times during the growing season. The rains will wash the ashes down to the shallow roots. You can bleach the stems if you wish, by sliding a four-inch drain tile down over the plant, or by staking up boards on each side, or simply by wrapping the stems loosely with several layers of newspaper. Care must be taken not to suffocate the foliage with the bleaching material that you use. Begin the bleaching process when the plants are fully mature. About a week of cover should do the job.

Golden varieties. Golden Self-Blanching*†, Golden Plume, Cornell 619.

Green varieties. Summer Pascal*†, Utah 52-70*, Utah Early Green, Florida 683, Slow Bolt, Tendercrisp, Beacon, Florimart.

CHARD

Chard, often called Swiss chard, was described by Aristotle as early as 350 B.C. It is an ancestor of the beet, to which it is closely related, although it is grown for its large and tender leaves which are cooked and eaten much like spinach. (The tender stems may also be cooked and served like asparagus.)

Soil. Chard will grow well in any good garden soil so long as it is planted in a sunny and open place, and it will repay your efforts by aerating your subsoil. The vigorous roots go as far down as six feet, breaking up the subsoil and improving drainage wherever they grow.

pH. 5.8 - 7.0

Culture. Few plants are easier to grow. Sow seed in the open garden as soon as the soil has warmed. Rows should be eighteen to twenty-four inches apart, and later the plants should be thinned to ten inches apart in the row. Chard may be picked as soon as the leaves are large enough to make the picking worth your while, and it will continue to grow even after being cut.

Varieties. *Large White Ribbed**†, *Fordhook Giant**†, *Rhubarb**†, Dark Green White Ribbed, Lucullus†, White King, Burgendy Swiss Chard.

CHICORY

Chicory might as well be three plants instead of one, because different varieties are grown for entirely different purposes. Early varieties are grown and eaten like lettuce. Other varieties are picked in fall, stored, and sprouted in the basement for "winter greens." Still other varieties are grown for their roots, which are prized as a coffee additive or substitute. Depending on its use, chicory is sometimes called French endive or coffee weed. It is an interesting and easy plant to grow — so easy, in fact, that it can easily become a bothersome weed if it is not checked.

Soil. Any deeply prepared, reasonably fertile, and loose garden soil is fine for chicory.

pH. 6.0 - 7.0

Culture. The handling of chicory varies widely, depending on the variety grown. The asparagus type is sown in early spring, and grown, picked, and eaten much like leaf lettuce. The Witloof variety, which we know as French endive, is the one that provides winter salads, and for cultural directions I turn to the Harris seed catalog:

> Witloof Chicory (usually called "French Endive" but more properly "Belgian Endive") makes an appetizing and delicious salad and is easy to grow. Sow seed outdoors in May or June and dig the roots in the fall. Trim tops and place in sand in a warm dark place in winter. The roots produce large tender white sprouts . . . and they have an unusual and delightful flavor.

When growing varieties for use as a coffee additive or substitute, dig the large roots before the first really hard frost. The plant is very tolerant to frost, however, and you need not rush to rescue roots at the first warning from the weatherman. The roots are dried thoroughly, ground, and stored in jars for later use.

Spacing requirements are not given here, because they vary so widely, depending on the variety grown. Instructions are on every seed packet, however.

Varieties. Witloof Improved (French endive, 110 days), Magdeburgh Improved (for coffee, 100 days), Cicoria Catalogna (asparagus type, 65 days), Cicoria San Pasquale (salad type, 70 days).

CHINESE CABBAGE

Chinese cabbage does indeed come from China, where it has been grown for several thousand years. Its thin and tender leaves fold together and grow upward in a cylindrical shape, and they are good either in salads or cooked as greens. The taste is fresh and delicate.

Soil. A rich, light loam, well supplied with compost, is best for Chinese cabbage.

pH. 6.0 - 7.0

Culture. This is definitely a cool-weather crop. In Wisconsin, which is apt to have several prolonged hot spells during any summer, it is best to sow seeds during the latter part of June, so that the plant will mature during the cooler days of August and September. When the young plants are thinned, the rejects may be used in salads. Give the plants a good mulch and make certain that the soil does not become dry during rainless periods.

Since it is important to force quick and tender growth, an application of well-rotted and screeened manure or compost tea will be beneficial during the growing season. The manure should be worked in very lightly at the sides of the plants, taking great care not to injure the roots.

When the plants reach maturity, they may be cut and used as needed. After the first light frost, all plants may be dug up by their roots and stored in a cool cellar or in the cold frame. Remove the outer leaves, pack the plants in layers separated by straw, and cover with soil.

Varieties. Early Hybrid G*, Michihli*†, Springtime, Summertime, Wintertime the last three, hybrids).

CHIVES

Chives are ridiculously easy to grow and are welcome additions to soups, sauces, salads, omelets, and hundreds of other dishes.

Soil. Chives like a rich, coarse soil, with plenty of small pebbles and plenty of compost. They may not do well in heavier soils, but you can easily cater to their needs, since they take up so little space.

pH. 6.0 - 7.0

Culture. The easiest way to grow chives is to buy a couple of pots of the growing plants, which are offered in most large supermarkets. In winter, keep the pot in a sunny window, keep it watered (but not soggy), and cut the tops of the slender onion-like leaves as you need them. In spring, divide the small bulbs and plant them outside in a sunny location. The plant is a perennial, producing very attractive blue flowers, and is not at all out of place in the perennial flower bed. Throw a mulch over the plants after they have died down in winter, and they will reappear in the following spring and every spring thereafter. Or, you may wish to dig up a potful of the plants after the first light frost, for kitchen use.

Varieties. The Olds catalog offers chives, if you wish to plant from seed (like onions). There are no varieties to speak of.

COLLARDS

Collards are generally ignored in the North, for reasons unknown to me. They are regarded as a southerner's substitute for cabbage, which cannot grow well in the heat of the South, but actually the flavors of the two are quite different. Collards are heavy producers, and they are easy to grow. They are usually boiled like other greens, often with ham hocks. They are rich in vitamins B and C, and in minerals.

Soil. Give collards a deeply-tilled, rich soil with plenty of moisture and nitrogen for fast, tender growth.

pH. 6.0 - 7.0

Culture. Collards are large plants, growing to thirty inches or more in height. Rows should be three feet apart, with plants two feet apart in the row. Plant them in the space where early peas were harvested, or (at the same time as cabbage) in another part of the garden where they will get full sun all day long. They are heat loving, of course, but they are tolerant to light frosts in the autumn, too. Quick and tender growth is important, here, and so a mid-season application of nitrogen-rich compost tea, or a side-dressing of compost, will spur them along. Harvest the whole young plants, or, with older plants, cut the outer and lower leaves first, before they become tough.

Varieties. Georgia or Southern† (seventy-five days), Vates† (eighty days).

CORN SALAD

This is a quick-growing salad green (forty-five days) that is favored by a special few. It has a mild taste, and goes well in salads with stronger-tasting greens such as watercress. It resembles spinach in appearance.

Soil. A good garden loam, well supplied with compost and lime, will suit corn salad just fine.

pH. 6.5 - 7.0

Culture. Corn salad is a fast grower and is fairly hardy, but it cannot stand summer heat. Therefore, it is best to plant it either with the earliest crops (April 15 in Madison) or in late August for an early October crop. A light covering of straw will protect fall plantings from frosts, so long as the frosts are not too severe. Rows should be sixteen to eighteen inches apart, and plants should be four to six inches apart in the row. The leaves should be harvested before the seed stalk forms, or else the leaves will become tough.

Varieties. There is no choice of varieties.

CRESS

Cress (also called *peppergrass* or *winter cress*) is a name given rather loosely to several members of the mustard family. All are valued as greens, because of their tangy flavor, and many are worth growing for this reason. Cress is especially rewarding because it is about the only garden plant that grows faster than the weeds — as little as ten days to maturity! This will be the first salad green you will harvest in the early spring.

Soil. Any fertile, well-drained garden soil will be fine for cress.

pH. 6.0 - 7.0

Culture. Sow thickly, in rows one foot apart, as soon as the soil can be worked in early spring. Cress runs to seed quickly, and so it must be harvested when ready, but you can keep a constant supply by sowing a few more feet of row every three or four days, for at least a month. Fall sowings of the quick-growing variety may be made as close as three weeks from the date of the first average killing frost in your locality. If you like cress particularly, you may make sowings in the cold frame as late as October, harvesting into November.

Varieties. Fine Curled (Peppergrass, ten days), Extra Fine Curled (forty-five days), Curled (forty-five days).

(See also *water cress*.)

CUCUMBER

Cucumbers are fun to grow because there have been so many new varieties introduced in the past several years. One of the most interesting is the new hybrid burpless, a slicing cucumber that does (or, rather, *doesn't* do) just what it says. Cucumber varieties are grouped into those recommended for slicing and eating fresh, and those intended for pickling. Wisconsin's warm summer days and breezy nights are perfect for cucumbers, which have most trouble flourishing in hot, humid, and still weather.

Soil. Cucumbers do well on a well-drained sandy loam that is well supplied with compost, lime, and moisture.

pH. 6.0 - 8.0

Culture. These are tropical plants, very sensitive to frost in either spring or fall. They are one of the last plants to go in, after all danger of frost is past. Cucumbers are generally planted in hills or mounds, spaced according to directions for the particular variety. A mulch should be placed between the hills and can be drawn in closer to the hills after the young plants have established themselves. This will give the vigorous vines a soft bed on which to rest their fruit and will keep down weeds and conserve moisture. It is difficult to cultivate cucumbers without injuring the shallow roots or cutting into the vines, hence the special value of the mulch.

Special tips. Bees are necessary to cucumber production, since they must carry the pollen from the male to the female flowers in order for fertilization to occur. The female flower must be pollinated on the first day that it is ready, in order for perfect fruit to form. Otherwise, the cucumbers will be misshapen and wasplike in shape, or will not form at all.

It is vitally important that cucumbers be picked every day. They form their fruits very rapidly, and if the fruits are allowed to ripen on the vine, the plant will wither and die, for it will have completed its life cycle. But, if you keep picking before the fruits reach maturity, the plant will continue to produce right up until frost.

Pickling varieties. Wisconsin SMR 18*, Crusader*, Wisconsin SMR 58*, Pioneer* (all resistant to mosaic and scab), Spartan Salad* (resistant to scab, mosaic, powdery mildew, beetles; nonbitter), Improved Chicago Pickling, Spartan Dawn, Triple Purpose (scab, mosaic, and powdery mildew tolerant), Salty (highly tolerant to scab, mosaic, powdery and downy mildew), Wisconsin SMR 12, Double Yield Pickling.

Slicing varieties. Meridian*, Gemini*†, Spartan Valor*†, Marketmore*† (all resistant to mosaic and scab), Burpless*, Burpee F-1 Hybrid*, Challenger F-1 Hybrid, Marketer, Longfellow, Triumph F-1 Hybrid, Straight 8, Long Marketer, Windermoor Wonder, Tablegreen, Palomar.

EGGPLANT

The eggplant traces its ancestry back to Asia, where it is grown as a perennial in tropical regions. Our climate dictates that we grow this handsome vegetable as an annual, to be set out among the latest of our garden plants. The purple varieties are the ones we are used to, because they are the ones we see in supermarkets, but the Europeans have long preferred the white varieties for their better taste. (White varieties are, in fact, hard to come by in America, but one — White Beauty — is offered by the Farmer Seed and Nursery Company.)

Soil. Eggplant is related to both tomatoes and peppers, and its requirements are similar. It likes a medium or sandy loam, well drained and rich in nutrients. It is a heavy feeder.

pH. 6.0 - 7.0

Culture. Young plants of the purple varieties may be purchased at nurseries and garden centers at planting time, or seeds may be started in flats or peat pots about ten weeks before planting time. Because of their extreme sensitivity to cold weather (even several degrees above the frost level) it is a good idea to provide some kind of covering for the young plants for the first week or two outdoors. After the young plants have become well established, put down a thick mulch in order to preserve valuable moisture and keep a constant soil temperature. Along about the end of July or the beginning of August, the plants will benefit from a side-dressing of compost or compost tea. They need not be fully ripe in order to be picked. In fact, they are best used before fully ripening (during which time they begin to turn from purple to brown). In September, keep your eye on the weather forecasts and pick all remaining fruits before the first frost. They will keep for some time if stored in a cool and dark place.

Varieties. Early Beauty*, Mission Bell*, Black Magic*, Black Oval* (all hybrids), Black Beauty*†, Modern Midget (early variety), Faribo Hybrid, Applegreen, Royal Knight, Blacknite, Jersey King (hybrid), Burpee Hybrid, White Beauty.

ENDIVE

This plant is similar to lettuce both in its appearance and culture, but its taste is far stronger. It is sometimes called *escarole*, but it should not be confused with *French endive*, which is actually chicory.

Soil. Any good garden soil will support endive, so long as its nutrient content is fairly high.

pH. 6.0 - 7.0

Culture. Endive is grown much like lettuce, with seeds sown in the open ground as soon as the soil can be worked. Unlike leaf lettuce, however, endive requires eighty-five to ninety-five days to mature. Some gardeners follow early lettuce with endive, although in this case care must be taken to shade the young plants from excessive sun and heat. Successful culture depends on forcing quick and succulent growth, and thus plenty of moisture and feeding are necessary. If the soil is well composted to begin with, extra feeding will not be necessary. Otherwise, apply a side-dressing of compost six weeks after planting. The heads may be picked as soon as they are large enough to make picking worthwhile.

Special tips. Many gardeners prefer to blanch the heads about two or three weeks before picking them for use. The blanching makes the leaves more tender and less pungent, but it also reduces the vitamin C content. To blanch the heads, pull up the outer leaves and tie loosely over the top, just enough to exclude light, but not enough to exclude air. The same effect may be promoted by placing large flower pots over the heads.

Varieties. Green Curled†, Full Heart Batavian†, Florida Deep Heart.

FINOCCHIO

Finocchio, fairly popular in Europe but little known here, has a pleasant anise-like flavor and is used either as a cooked vegetable or fresh, in salads. It is related to fennel, and in fact it is sometimes called *sweet fennel* or Florence fennel, although it grows and is used quite differently from true fennel, which is an herb. It grows from a large bulblike structure, looking much like celery, and it is this base structure which is most highly prized, although the stalks can be eaten also. Finocchio is difficult to find locally. Harris, however, offers the seeds in its catalog.

Soil. Plants do best on a well-drained, average loam, well composted and well supplied with lime.

pH. 6.0 - 7.0

Culture. Sow in rows 1½ to 2 feet apart and, later, thin the young plants to a distance of six to eight inches apart in the row. About three weeks before harvesting, the soil should be drawn up around the plants to blanch the bulbs.

Varieties. Mammoth.

GARLIC

Every garlic-loving family should plant at least a few sets each year. Garlic does not take up much room, and it is easy to grow. Fresh garlic from the garden — plump, juicy, and flavorful — is entirely different from the dried bulbs purchased in supermarkets. And, of course, your own bulbs can be dried, braided, and hung in the kitchen for year-round use.

Soil. Any soil that is good for onions will support garlic. This means a good, loose loam, well drained and well supplied with moisture. Even sandy soils can support garlic if enough organic matter is incorporated into the soil.

pH. 6.0 - 7.0

Culture. Garlic can be grown from seed, but the home gardener will find it easier to plant sets, which are the cloves that together comprise the bulb. Every clove will grow an entire bulb. The sets are planted at the same time and in the same way as onions. The plant should mature in about ninety days. After the tops have turned yellow and begun to die down, the bulbs may be pulled, dried in a shady place, and stored like onions or braided and hung indoors.

Varieties. There is seldom a choice of varieties. However, Nichols Garden Nursery does offer an interesting *Elephant Garlic*, which is said to produce bulbs weighing one pound or more, milder in taste than ordinary garlic.

GOURD

Few varieties of gourds are edible, but we often include them in the vegetable garden for their unusual, decorative, and sometimes useful fruits. Every children's garden should include gourds, since they are easy to grow and fun to dry and use afterwards. There are dozens of varieties, too many to list and describe here, but some large seed companies list a wide array in their catalogs. The Stokes catalog, for instance, lists fourteen individual varieties, and most seedsmen offer mixed packets of both large and small gourds. One variety I will mention is *Luffa cylindrica* or *Lagenaria leucanthe*, otherwise known as the *dishcloth gourd*. The cellulose of this gourd is similar to that of cotton, and the inner mass, carefully removed, can be used just as any ordinary household sponge. Bath shops sell luffa sponges for about two dollars each, but you can grow your own for practically nothing. Luffa seed is offered by Henry Field, Gurney, and R. H. Shumway, among others.

Soil. Gourds do best on a well drained loam, but will grow in most soils except heavy clays.

pH. 6.0 - 7.0

Culture. Gourds need full sunlight and about a hundred growing days. Given these requirements, they are vigorous growers when planted nearly anywhere. Most varieties are good climbers, and are often used to screen in the southern sides of porches, offering cooling shade during August's hot days. Others plant gourds in bare, ugly spots, since they are fairly attractive ground covers.

Seeds can be started indoors, about April 15 in Madison, and transplanted outdoors whenever it is safe to put out tomato plants. Or, the seed may be planted directly into the open ground around June 10. If the vines are to grow along the ground, be sure to apply a hay mulch, so that the fruits will not be flat and discolored from lying on the ground. Better still, tie up soft washline for them to climb, or plant beneath a trellis that receives plenty of sun. Northern Wisconsin residents may have trouble growing gourds in any case, because of the short season, but they are certainly worth a try.

Special tips. From the Stokes catalog, we get drying instructions: "Pick fruit carefully from the vines when completely ripe. [The rind should be hard when your fingernail presses into it — J. M.] It is most important not to injure or bruise the fruit when handling. Wash each gourd with a strong disinfectant, to remove dirt and fungi that might cause rotting. Spread the fruit out evenly, so that they do not touch each other, in a dry, well-ventilated place. Turn the fruit regularly during the drying period, which usually takes three to four weeks. When completely dry, wax with ordinary floor wax and polish with a soft cloth."

Small varieties. Alladins Turban, Bicolour Pear, Miniature Bottle, Minature Ball, Crown of Thorns, Flat Striped, Spoon, Striped Pear, White Pear, Orange Warted.

Large varieties. Cave Man's Club, Dipper or Birdhouse, Large Turk's Turban, Wild Cucumber, Luffa.

Edible variety. Italian Edible.

GROUND CHERRY

The ground cherry, also called *husk tomato* or *strawberry tomato*, is closely related to the Chinese lantern plant. Both are members of the *Physalis* family. The edible variety offers small cherry-like fruit encased in a husk, and is used extensively in pies. Ground cherries are hardly the most popular of garden crops, but they have long been treasured by some, and they are an interesting plant to grow. Stokes offers seed.

Soil. Like tomatoes, ground cherries like an open, well-drained soil. They do best on a sandy loam which is well supplied with nutrients.

pH. 6.0 - 7.0

Culture. Start the seeds indoors towards the end of March and transplant to the open garden after all danger of frost is past. Space according to directions on the seed packet. The fruits may be picked when they have turned yellow.

Varieties. True Yellow*.

HORSERADISH

When I was a boy, the horseradish man used to come through the alleys with horse and cart every Saturday morning. He would grind the roots from the back of the wagon — fifteen cents for a half-pint jar. And, if you were daring enough to take a good sniff from the jar while carrying it home, your sinuses took an instant and jolting cleaning that no modern-day cold remedy can hope to match. Fresh horseradish is difficult to come by these days — the commercial products seem so tame — but you can bring back the old days in your own garden, if you reserve a little corner of it for horseradish.

Soil. Horseradish needs a deeply-prepared and rich sandy loam, with plenty of room to grow long, straight roots. It will be worth your while to prepare the soil well, for the plant is a perennial and you will not have to do it again. Your main problem, in fact, will be in containing the plant to the corner you have chosen.

pH. 6.0 - 8.0

Culture. Horseradish is grown from roots or crowns, and is established much like asparagus. The roots are usually set out in early spring, in rows two to three feet apart, with the roots ten to eighteen inches apart in the row. The top of the cutting should be placed from two to five inches below the soil surface, and the soil should be packed carefully around the roots, to bring them into good contact with the soil for fast growth. Apply liquid fertilizer or compost tea late in August and into September, for this is when the plant makes its most important growth.

The roots spread by extending lateral branches across the uppermost twelve inches of soil. You can keep the planting going from year to year, by digging only a few roots at a time (which is all you really will need).

Special tips. To prepare horseradish, clean the roots well, remove the brown outer skins with a vegetable peeler, and grind the white roots thoroughly with a meat grinder or food chopper. For every cup of granted horseradish, add ½ cup of white vinegar and ¼ teaspoon of salt. Mix well and store in jars in the refrigerator.

Your next corned beef and cabbage dinner should be one to remember!

Varieties. Bohemian (offered by J. W. Jung).

JERUSALEM ARTICHOKE

The Jerusalem artichoke does not come from Jerusalem, and it is not an artichoke. The word Jerusalem, used here, is actually a corruption of the Italian word *girasole*, meaning "turning toward the sun," and the word "artichoke" was tacked on because someone apparently thought that this vegetable tasted like globe artichokes. (It doesn't.) Were I to rename the plant, I would call it the "sunflower potato" because it is a member of the sunflower family (producing attractive yellow blossoms in summer), and because the food part of the plant is the brown tuber, which resembles a potato. The plants are amazingly prolific, once established, and they will come up year after year. They are cooked and eaten just like potatoes, and their flavor is mild and slightly nut-sweet.

Soil. Jerusalem artichoke will do well on nearly any kind of soil except very heavy clays. They do better, in fact, on poor soils lacking nutrients, since too much nitrogen forces great top growth and small tubers.

pH. 6.0 - 8.0

Culture. Select a sunny, out-of-the-way spot for Jerusalem artichokes, for they spread rapidly and will gladly take over the garden if you let them. They grow six to eight feet high, and can be used as a rather attractive screen. Or, plant them in soil that won't grow much of anything else. The tubers are planted much like potatoes, one eye to a cutting, and are set a foot apart in rows two to three feet apart. Planting should be done at the same time as potatoes — April 15 in Madison — and you should never have to plant them again. They are best dug after the first frost in fall. Harvest up to half of the crop without worrying about depleting next year's supply. They can be stored like potatoes or left right in the ground and dug when needed, right up until the ground is too hard for digging.

Special tips. Jerusalem artichokes are a good potato substitute for those on diets, or for those who must restrict their intake of carbohydrates. There are virtually no carbohydrates in the tubers, since this plant stores its carbohydrates in the form of insulin, and there is little sugar. There are virtually no calories, either — as few as 22 in a full pound of freshly-dug tubers. As the tubers are stored, however, the insulin is gradually converted into sugar, and the tubers then may contain as many as 235 calories in a pound — which still makes it a low-calorie vegetable. The Jerusalem artichoke is a good source of both potassium and thiamine in the diet.

Varieties. There is no choice of varieties. (If you have trouble locating seed tubers, contact Nichols Garden Nursery.)

Jerusalem artichokes will brighten your garden with attractive yellow flowers during the summer . . .

. . . and will offer their crisp and tasty tubers in the fall!

KALE

Kale is the richest in vitamins of all the potherbs. A member of the cabbage family, it is easy to grow if given proper conditions, and it is a heavy yielder. We grow it for the large leaves, which can be used in salads when they are very young and tender, or, more commonly, boiled with ham.

Soil. Since quick and succulent growth is essential for high quality leaves, the soil should be rich and loamy. A liberal application of compost before planting will pay rich dividends.

pH. 6.0 - 7.0

Culture. The growing directions given for collards can be used in growing kale, since the two are so closely related. Kale is highly resistant to both heat and cold, so that it can be planted any time from early spring right up to eight weeks before frost. It matures in about fifty-five to seventy days, and is especially good as a succession crop, perhaps following peas, since a couple of early autumn frosts improve the quality and taste of the leaves. The roots are shallow and widespread, making it chancy to work the soil with a hoe. Instead, apply a heavy mulch to protect those shallow-lying roots from drying out. A couple of midsummer applications of compost tea will spur along the rapid and tender growth you seek.

Varieties. *Dwarf Green Curled**†, Tall Green Curled Scotch (tender after exposure to frost), Dwarf Curled Scotch†, Dwarf Blue Curled, Green Curled Scotch.

KOHLRABI

Kohlrabi has been described as a "turnip growing on a cabbage root," and that seems to be an apt description of this unusual member of the cabbage family. It grows well in Wisconsin, for it likes cool weather, and it is one of the few vegetables that gardeners like to grow and then, for some reason, don't like to eat. The problem, perhaps, is that we don't pick and eat them early enough. The bulbs and roots should be harvested while they are still young and succulent — not after the plant has attained full maturity and has become tough and woody. Harvest when the bulbs are no more than two inches in diameter, or even when they are as small as golf balls. Slice both bulbs and roots for raw salads, or boil them as a cooked vegetable.

Soil. Like other members of the cabbage family, kohlrabi likes a richly-prepared loam, well supplied with moisture, for quick and tender growth.

pH. 6.0 - 7.0

Culture. Seed is sown into the open ground in early spring, at the same time as onions and carrots. Successful growth must be quick growth, and so ample nutrients and water are essential. Apply a good mulch as soon as the young plants are established, to conserve moisture and also to protect the young and shallow-lying roots. Cultivation can easily injure these roots, which spread laterally just under the soil surface, but a good mulch will make cultivation unnecessary. If the plants seem to be slow in growing, stimulate them with a few mid-season applications of a strong manure tea. The two big kohlrabi cautions: Don't let them grow slowly, and don't harvest them too late!

Special tips. If the kohlrabi are growing faster then you can use them, pick them anyway and store them in a cool basement. Or, store them underground, surrounded by straw. They will keep cool underground during summer, and they will not freeze there during winter. Late-harvested kohlrabi can also be stored in a cold frame up until December.

Varieties. *White Vienna**†, *Purple Vienna**†.

LEEK

If you like to use cooked onions in recipes but the onions don't like you, leeks might be just the thing you are looking for. They are very onionlike, but milder in taste and effect. Many French recipes call for leeks, too, for their subtle enhancement of stews and other dishes.

Soil. Any good garden soil, well composted, will grow leeks successfully.

pH. 6.0 - 7.0

Culture. Leeks are planted from seed instead of sets, but otherwise culture is the same as that for onions. Sow seed sparingly in early spring, in a fully sunny place. Make rows twenty inches apart and thin the young plants to three or four to a foot of row. During the growing season, continue to hill the soil up around the growing stems, to blanch them. We grow leeks not for a bulb, but for the thick and tender stems. A few side-dressings of rich compost during the season will help along the growth of this rather slow-growing plant. Harvest when they are large enough to make the harvesting worth your while. They can take a few good frosts in autumn, and can be stored in a root cellar.

Special tips. If your growing season is too short for leeks, you can cut down the growing time by starting the seeds inside and transplanting them. Sow seeds six weeks before transplanting time (April 15 in Madison). When setting the young plants into the open ground, trim off one-half of their roots and one-third of the tops. Then set them in a shallow trench well lined with aged compost.

Varieties. American Flag*, Giant Musselburg* (ninety days), Titan (early, seventy days), Elephant (eighty-five days), Swiss Special, Conqueror.

LETTUCE

Lettuce is certainly our most popular salad green. There are four major groups: *loose-leaf* or nonheading; *butterhead*; *crisp-head* or cabbagehead; and *cos* or Romaine. All are easy to grow in Wisconsin except crisp-head, which is difficult to grow almost anywhere except in the mountains of the western United States.

Soil. Lettuce needs a well-drained soil, well supplied with compost. It will grow well in either sandy or clay loams, but either must be kept well supplied with moisture for the quick and succulent growth needed for successful production.

pH. 6.0 - 7.0

Culture. Lettuce needs warm days and cool nights for optimum growth. Crisp-head lettuce is especially particular in this respect, often failing to form heads if the weather turns hot at heading time. All lettuce can be grown best in an area where the sunlight is filtered for at least part of the day, or on a northern or western slope where the sun's rays are indirect. If part of your garden lies in the afternoon shadow of a large tree, use this spot for lettuce.

Loose-leaf culture. This is the easiest and fastest to grow. Sow seed in the open ground in early spring, spaced according to directions. Thin the rows by cutting leaves for salads as you need them. Make successive plantings for as long as a month, but do not expect to get good results when the weather turns hot.

Butterhead culture. This lettuce forms a soft and loose head. Plant seeds thinly in the row and later thin out the plants to the distances recommended for the particular variety. To avoid the danger of midsummer heat, you can start plants indoors, in the cold frame, or in peat pots, transplanting them into the open garden as soon as the weather permits.

Crisp-head culture. The secret of growing head lettuce lies in getting a very early start, and then praying for cool weather when the plant gets ready to head-up. Sow seeds in flats indoors, in a cool but sunny window, about the middle of March. Thin the plants carefully, so that no plant touches another. Keep the soil damp, but not soggy, and do not let the young plants suffer from dry household air. When the first true leaves have formed, transplant the seedlings to flats or peat pots, being careful not to disturb the roots any more than is necessary.

Transplant the young plants into the open garden as early as possible — no later than April 15 in southern Wisconsin, May 1 in the north. Lettuce may appear to be extremely tender, when in reality it is fairly hardy and will not be bothered by a few light frosts. Cover with hot caps if a heavy frost threatens. (Note: If you have a cold frame, you may begin plants indoors as much as a month earlier, transplanting to the frame about a month before setting them into the open garden. Harden off the plants by admitting air to the frame on mild afternoons.) Once in the garden, planted in well composted rows, lettuce needs plenty of moisture. And, even after all your early work and special care, you still must worry about damaging hot spells. As a precaution, you might construct a light wooden frame along the row, over which you can stretch cheesecloth or open lath to act as a sun filter. Build the frame early in the season, and add the shading material only when you need it.

Cos culture. Cos or Romaine lettuce is a tall-growing type, with long spoon-shaped leaves that fold gracefully in toward the center of the plant, naturally bleaching the inner leaves. It is highly prized in French restaurants as a crisp salad lettuce, and is not too difficult to grow. Its culture is the same as for the butterhead varieties. The seed is sown thinly in early spring, and plants are thinned out to stand about eight inches apart in the row. The plant takes sixty-six to seventy-five days to mature, but may be harvested before maturity, if you so choose.

Loose-leaf varieties. Black Seeded Simpson*†, Oakleaf*†, Salad Bowl*†, Domineer, Grand Rapids, Waldmann's Dark Green, Red Salad Bowl, Green Salad Bowl, Slobolt.

Butterhead varieties. Buttercrunch*†, Summer Bibb*†, Butter King*†, White Boston, Dark Green Boston, Bibb, Tom Thumb Midget.

Crisp-head varieties. Great Lakes 659*†, Fulton*, Pennlake†, Minilake, Ithaca, Minetto, Imperial (recommended for muckland), Fairton, Evergreen (frost-resistant late variety).

Cos varieties. Paris White, Paris Island, Valmaine, Sweet Midget.

MUSHROOMS

Mushroom culture, which is undertaken indoors under very exacting conditions, will not be treated in this outdoor gardening book. However, Stokes does offer a variety, called *Lambert's*, which is grown outdoors, under the lawn. The technique involves rolling back a piece of sod four inches deep, in a shady area, sprinkling the mushroom spawn on the soil surface, and then replacing the sod. The mushrooms grow through the sod and can be harvested in about seven weeks.

Stokes also offers a book for those interested in indoor mushroom culture. It is called *Practical & Scientific Mushroom Culture*, seventy pages, and is listed in their catalog for $2.25. Several other books are available on the commercial market.

MUSKMELONS

There are many varieties of muskmelons that will grow well in Wisconsin. Some are similar to the cantaloupe, and may even be sold under that name in stores, but the true cantaloupe is native to warmer regions and is not widely grown in the United States. Most supermarket "cantaloupes" are actually *nutmeg melons*.

Soil. Muskmelons grow best in a light, well-drained soil, rich in nutrients. They will not do well in clays.

pH. 6.0 - 7.0

Culture. All melons need full sunshine and a long number of warm days to reach sweet maturity. They might not do well in Wisconsin's northern areas, particularly where long stretches of cool and sunless days will retard their growth. Most varieties require eighty-five days or more, and this period can be extended if the weather does not cooperate.

Melons are very sensitive to frost, and plants should not be put into the open garden until all danger of frost is past. The long maturity period, then, dictates that seeds be started indoors, in plant bands or peat pots. In southern Wisconsin, start seeds indoors around May 1 (they germinate only at temperatures above sixty-five degrees) and transplant into the open garden around May 20. Apply compost liberally to the outdoor planting area before setting in plants. The best method is to put a layer of compost or rotted manure about six inches under the soil, covering this with a three-inch layer of good garden loam. Firm the plants in well, and the roots will soon find the nourishing compost with no chance of "burning." Apply a good mulch, to conserve moisture and to provide a soft bed for the fruit, and be sure to give the plants plenty of moisture after the flowers have dried and the fruit begins to form.

Special tips. How can you tell when a melon is ripe? Thumping is the traditional method, but it is unreliable. A better way is to apply gentle pressure with the thumb between the fruit and the base of the stem. If the fruit separates easily from the stem, the fruit is ripe. Chill the melons and eat them the same day they are picked. The difference between your own vine-ripened melons and the supermarket kinds — which are picked green and shipped from distant states — is tremendous.

Varieties. *Mainrock**, *Gold Star**, *Supermarket**, *Delicious 51*†*, *Harvest Queen*†*, Iroquois*†, *Saticoy**, *Harper**, *Spartan Rock†*, Pride of Wisconsin, Honey or Sugar Rock, Early Delicious, Sungold Casaba, Hales Best Jumbo, Milwaukee Market, New Yorker, Burpee, Samson, Canada Gem. (Most of these are hybrids, and all marked with an asterisk are resistant to fusarium.)

MUSTARD

Mustard is grown in the home garden for its leaves, which are used as potherbs, much as are collards and kale. They are quick-growing plants and very heavy yielders. There are quite a few devotees of mustard greens in Wisconsin, although the crop is not so popular as kale. The home gardener can also harvest the seeds, which are widely used as a pickling spice. We use so little of this condiment, however, that harvesting our own seeds is rarely worth the trouble.

Soil. Because of the quick-growing nature of the plant, it likes a heavy loam, well drained and well supplied with nutrients. Tender growth depends on a large supply of available nutrients.

pH. 6.0 - 7.0

Culture. Seed is sown in the open ground in the early spring — April 15 in Madison. Thin the plants by harvesting some of the leaves for table use. The plants will mature in forty-five to sixty days. They can stand dry weather, but particularly hot weather may send them bolting to seed, destroying the quality of the leaves. Harvest the greens while they are young and tender. Cut off any flower buds that might appear.

Varieties. Giant Long Standing Southern Curled†, Mustard Spinach or Tender Green, Green Wave†, Giant Curled.

OKRA

Okra is a southern plant, a tropical requiring long, warm, sunny days to come to maturity. By book logic, it should not do well in Wisconsin, and yet it does. I have seen a beautiful stand of okra in the garden of Marvin Raney, near Stoughton in Dane County. Mr. Raney pickles the young and tender pods for use as condiments the year-round, but okra is good also in gumbo soups and even served as a table vegetable. If you have never eaten okra, you might find it difficult to become accustomed to its consistency, which is somewhat mucilaginous, but there are many okra devotees who will be willing to reserve parts of their gardens for this unusual vegetable.

Soil. Okra will thrive in a variety of soils, but only if they are well drained. Drainage is, by far, the most important soil consideration.

pH. 6.0 - 7.0

Culture. Okra is a rapid-growing plant, maturing in less than two months. It is a heavy feeder, however, and should be planted in a fully sunny place that has been well composted and manured. Plenty of available nutrients will give you a faster-growing and more successful crop. Sow seeds lightly in rows or plant in hills after all danger of frost is past — at the same time as beans. A rainy week immediately after planting may well rot the seeds, for they do rot easily, and will necessitate your replanting. After the plants are several inches tall, thin them to stand eighteen to twenty inches apart, choosing the healthiest and most robust for your permanent finalists.

Pick the pods when they are young — one to four inches — and use them as quickly after picking as possible. Even if you do not plan to use the pods, pick them every day. If the pods are allowed to remain on the plant, they will mature and the plant will stop producing for the season. Okra can be canned, frozen, or dried for later use.

Varieties. *Emerald*†*, *Clemson Spineless*†*, Perkins Mammoth Long Pod.

ONION

Onions have been cultivated, treasured, and savored since ancient times. They are Robert Louis Stevenson's "rose among roots," and even if they don't remind you much of roses, you will have to admit that life would be mighty dull without them.

Wisconsin gardeners can grow onions from sets, plants, or seeds. It is most difficult to grow them from seed in most parts of the state, but if you master the technique you will have increased

These sweet Spanish onions will grow much more quickly if they are mulched and kept free of weeds during the season.

your options to include dozens of varieties that are simply not offered in set or plant form. Summer onions are usually grown from sets. Those for late fall use and winter storage are usually grown from plants or seeds.

Soils. Onions need a deeply-prepared, fertile, rather loose, and well-drained soil for best results. They will not do well in heavy clays that turn to hardpan in the absence of rain.

pH. 6.0 - 7.0

Set culture. Sets are little pickling onions that are used to produce either scallions (when picked while they are young) or cooking onions (later in the season). The sets traditionally offered in supermarkets and garden centers are those of the Ebenezer type (white or yellow) that are perhaps the easiest of all onions to grow. The first thing to remember is to avoid particularly large sets when buying them. The large ones may look good, but they tend to produce seedstalks, big necks, and undersized onions. Avoid also the very small, shriveled-up sets that obviously lack vigor. Instead, look for plump, medium-sized sets that have not yet sent out shoots. They will produce the best onions.

Plant the sets carefully, in their natural position (root end down). There are differences of opinion on planting depth, some advising to plant two to three inches deep, others preferring to let just the top of the set protrude above the soil. I have always covered them with about a half-inch of loose soil, with good success, but you might experiment by planting different rows to different depths and comparing harvests. Give them ample moisture and keep the onion patch entirely free of weeds. In five weeks or so, the onions can be pulled and used as scallions. Or, you may leave them in to use as white or yellow cooking onions later on in the season.

Plant culture. Plant onions are bought in bunches, usually 50 to 100 slender plants in a bunch. Red slicer onions of the Bermuda type are grown from plants, and so are the large yellow and white sweet Spanish varieties. Like sets, they are planted early in the spring to their natural depth. They can be thinned out by picking every other one after fifty to sixty days, giving the remaining plants room to expand. You do, however, run the risk of disturbing the roots of the remaining plants by adopting this procedure. Thin very carefully and gently. Planted April 15, the onions should be fully mature by the middle of August or the beginning of September. A few light frosts will not hurt them.

Seed culture. Few home gardeners have much luck in planting onions from seed, but you might be the happy exception. In Wisconsin's muck regions, on the other hand, onions grown from seed are the rule rather than the exception. The seed is sown thickly in rows in early spring, and the young plants are thinned to stand two to three inches apart. From that point, they are treated just as sets or plants, keeping the rows free from weeds and insuring ample moisture. The rows should be cultivated frequently, to keep the soil loose and to allow air to reach the roots, and those large-growing bulbs that threaten to "pop out" of the soil should be hilled-in so that just the tops of the bulbs show.

Special tips. Pinch off the flower buds from all onions as soon as you see them. If you can recognize the seed stalk coming from the neck of the onion, in fact, it is better to cut the stalk right then, to prevent the neck from becoming large and stunting the bulb. When the tops begin to wither and fall over, the onions are mature. When most of them have reached this stage, you can knock down the others. Pull the onions a few days later and leave them on top of the ground for a few days, so that they can be cured naturally by the sun and the wind. Then, gather them up, cut off the tops to within an inch from the bulbs, and spread them out on a large table, under cover, in an outdoor and airy place. They can stay there to complete their curing until a heavy frost is forecast. On that day, take them indoors and store them for the winter in a cool and dry basement, or perhaps in a well-ventilated attic. They should be stored in open containers. Orange crates are perfect, or, you can hang them from the rafters in netting.

Set varieties. Ebenezer*† (white or yellow), Stuttgarter.

Plant varieties. Sweet Spanish*†, Early Harvest*, White Bermuda† (all hybrids, for late summer and early fall use only; do not store well), Red Slicer or Hamburger.

Seed varieties. Early Harvest*, Abundance*†, Hickory*, Nugget* (all are fusarium wilt-resistance hybrids), Early Yellow Globe, Southport White Globe, Southport Red Globe, Downing Yellow Globe, Autumn Spice (a hybrid good for storage), Crystal White Wax (Bermuda variety), White Spanish Green Bunching (forms clusters of small onions), Yellow Globe Danvers, Sweet Spanish, Yellow Spanish (hybrid), many other varieties in various seed house catalogs.

PARSLEY

If you occasionally buy parsley in the supermarket, then plant some, by all means. Parsley can be grown with ease in the vegetable garden, or it can form an attractive border in the herb garden, or even in flower borders. It does not take up much room, but it is slow-growing and requires patience. One packet of seed will supply all you will need for the year.

Soil. Any average garden soil will support parsley, although a good nitrogen supply will increase the yield.

pH. 5.0 - 7.0

Culture. Since seed is slow to germinate, it is best to soak it in lukewarm water for twenty-four hours before planting. Sow rather thickly, so that you can thin out the young plants, using the thinnings in the kitchen. Seed should be sown in early spring, as soon as the soil can be worked, and you still will not see anything come up for about four weeks. It makes good progress after that, however, and should produce from June until frost.

Special tips. When heavy frost threatens, carefully dig up the parsley, getting all the roots, and pot it. Bring it indoors and cut all the foliage down to the crowns. Freeze the foliage for future use. Then, place the pots in a sunny window and provide periodic watering. New growth should begin, and should provide fresh parsley for the family all winter long.

Varieties. *Moss Curled**†, *Perfection**, Hamburg (edible roots, similar to a small parsnip), Banquet, Plain Italian Dark Green, Deep Green, Bravour, Darki, Extra Triple Curled, Champion Moss Curled.

PARSNIP

The lowly parsnip may not be the world's favorite vegetable, but it has one thing going for it: The parsnip is the only vegetable that actually likes Wisconsin's autumn freezes! The flavor of this root vegetable is greatly improved by a couple of hard freezes, and in fact you can leave parsnips in the ground until just before the ground freezes too hard to allow them to be dug. If the Badger State ever adopts an official state vegetable, it just might have to be the parsnip.

Soil. Like all deeply-growing root crops, parsnips prefer a deeply-prepared, loose, and somewhat sandy loam. Heavy clays will inhibit root growth. As a slow-grower, the parsnip is not a particularly heavy feeder, but its progress will be aided by a good application of aged manure, made before planting time.

pH. 6. 0 - 8.0

The parsnip — should it become Wisconsin's official state vegetable?

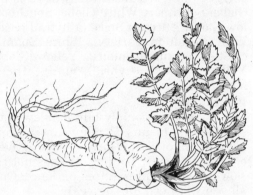

Culture. The seed is slow to germinate and will be aided by soaking it overnight in cool water. Sow thickly in rows as soon as the ground can be worked in early spring, and scatter a few radish seeds in the row to act as a marker. (You will harvest the radishes just as the parsnips are making some good progress.) Apply a light mulch in order to conserve soil moisture, since the seed must remain damp in order to germinate at all. Thin the young plants to two to three inches apart in the rows, and then increase the thickness of the mulch, to avoid weeding for the rest of the season. Parsnip is a long-season crop — 100 to 120 days — but you will never have to worry about fall frosts. Begin to harvest after the first hard freeze, and continue for as long as possible.

Varieties. Model*†, All-America*†, Hollow Crown, Harris Model.

PEA

Few garden crops are as highly prized as peas, which are one of the earliest vegetables to appear on the table, usually in June. Peas take up a lot of garden space, and they do not yield heavily for the space they take. Therefore — unless you have all the garden space in the world — it is best to use them as a succession crop (first in line) or a companion crop. As a succession crop, peas can be followed by any heat-loving, quick-growing crop, such as beans. In fact, runner beans can use the same trellises you have erected for peas. Or, peas can go in between the rows of tomatoes, corn, or squash, as a companion crop, and they will be harvested before the other plants need much growing room. (The old pea vines, in fact, can be cut and used as a mulch for the long-season plants.) Peas must go in early, however, to take advantage of these techniques. If you wait until the middle of May to plant, the peas will not have matured in time for you to plant most succession crops, and they will have interfered with the growth of companions.

Soil. Peas like a loose, sandy loam, well supplied with compost and manure for fast growth.

pH. 6.0 - 8.0

Culture. Plant peas in the early spring, as soon as the ground can be worked. A few light frosts will not hurt them. Inoculate the seeds with a bacterial inoculant (available at all garden centers) before planting. If you want really fast germination, spread the seeds out in a shallow pan in a dark place and line the bottom of the pan with water, so that the peas are just half-covered. Just as sprouts begin to show, plant them in the open garden. (Inoculate just before planting.)

The garden pea is a trailing plant, and will appreciate a trellis to climb on. The trellis will afford the plants optimum sun and air, and will also make harvesting easier. (Not necessary with dwarf varieties.) Mulch the plants after they have become established, to keep the soil cool.

It might take some experience in order to tell just when to pick peas for optimum quality. They should be picked as soon as the pods are filled, but before they become really hard. Edible-podded peas (snow peas) should be picked just as the peas become visible, forming little bumps on the pods.

Dwarf varieties. Alaska*†, *Little Marvel*†, *Frezonian*†, WR Surprise* (the last two are fusarium wilt resistant), Frosty†, *Wando*†, *Thomas Laxton*†, *Lincoln.* (Many gardeners report success with Lincoln after failure with other varieties.)

Tall-growing varieties. Alderman*†, Perfection (wilt-resistant), Alaska (wilt resistant).

Edible-podded varieties. Dwarf Gray Sugar*†, Mammoth Melting Sugar*† (tall-growing), Little Sweetie (dwarf), Super Sweetpod (tall-growing).

PEANUT

Peanut country is in Virginia, not Wisconsin. Nevertheless, gardeners in the southern half of our state may dabble in peanuts with some expectations of success, if they follow the rules.

Soil. Peanuts have traditionally been a poor-soil crop, grown in areas unsuited for nitrogen-loving plants. An excess of nitrogen, in fact, will lead to too much top growth and a poor crop of peanuts. They do, however, respond to an application of compost made before planting time. In Wisconsin, plant peanuts only on a loose and sandy loam, with a southern exposure, in full sun.

pH. 6.0 - 7.0

Culture. Peanuts require a 120-day growing season. If yours is much shorter, your chances for success are reduced proportionally.

Peanuts in Wisconsin? Choose the right varieties and follow the rules, and you might reward yourself with a bumper crop for roasting and storing.

Prepare the soil deeply, keeping it loose, after the sun has warmed it thoroughly in May (around May 10 in Madison). Plant the peanuts in mounds, as you would squash, four kernels to a mound, about 1½ inches deep. Keep the mounds 18 to 24 inches apart, in rows two to three feet apart. (You may add several weeks to your growing season if you start seeds in peat pots and transplant in early May — but be very careful not to disturb the roots.)

Germination of seed planted outdoors may be slow — up to two weeks, if the weather is cool and rainy. When the plants are about six inches tall, begin to cultivate the soil, to knock out weeds and keep it loose. After the plants are about a foot high, begin to hill up the plants as you would potatoes, bringing the soil up high around each plant, to the base of the bottom branches. Lay a loose mulch around the plants after they have been hilled. Small flowers will soon appear in the axils of the leaves. These inconspicuous flowers will soon bend toward the soil, fade, and bury themselves in it. New seeds will be formed underground which, of course, are the new peanut crop.

From the point of mulching, you should not disturb the plants until harvest, which will be after the first hard frost has killed the tops of the plants in October. Then, lift out each plant from the soil with a garden fork, shake the soil loose, and pick off the peanuts. Look in the hole for any that may have dropped. The peanuts should be placed in shallow trays and stored in a cool and *dry* place — perhaps in the attic — to cure. After about two months, they will be ready for roasting. Place them, one-deep, in a shallow pan or on a cookie sheet and roast in a 300-degree oven for twenty minutes. Then place them on wooden trays to cool. For peanut butter, simply add a little salt and run them through the meat grinder a couple of times.

Varieties. Early Spanish (earliest variety to mature), Mammoth Virginia (the type usually seen in stores), Early Virginia.

PEPPER

The garden pepper is a long-season crop that needs warm and sunny days. The secret of success in Wisconsin is in setting out large plants in the spring, and giving the plants the sun and nourishment they need to come to maturity. There are two general types — the sweet pepper, usually represented by the bells, and the hot or pungent pepper, of which there are many varieties. Because peppers react so sensitively to differences and variations in soil, climatic, and weather conditions, it is especially important that only tried varieties be planted in Wisconsin, if you hold high hopes for success. The foliage of the plants is bright and attractive, so they may be included in flower borders or among landscape plantings.

Soil. Peppers will grow in most good garden soils, but they prefer a loose and sandy loam that provides good drainage and good aeration. A generous application of compost before planting will benefit the crop. Magnesium and phosphorus are particularly important.

pH. 6.0 - 7.0

Culture. Seeds may be started inside, about ten weeks before transplanting time, or established plants may be purchased at any garden center in May or early June. Set plants outside as soon as all danger of frost has passed in a location where they will receive full sun. Mulch the plants immediately, to keep the soil moist and the weeds down. The first peppers should be ready for harvest in August.

Sweet varieties. *Early Calwonder**, Bell Boy*† (hybrid), *Yolo Wonder "B"**†, *Midway** (the last three are mosaic resistant).

Pungent varieties. Goldspike*, Hungarian Wax*†, Long Red Cayenne*†, Hot Portugal*.

POPCORN

Popcorn is a fun crop to grow, even though it cannot possibly be justified on a dollars-and-cents basis since the commercial variety is so inexpensive. But the kids will love to see their very own popcorn growing in the garden. If nothing else, it will demonstrate to them that their favorite snack foods are not really born in a plastic bag in the supermarket, but, like all life, come from the sun and the soil.

What makes popcorn pop? It does so because the corneous endosperm (the shell) is hard and rigid, unlike sweet corn and most field corn. When heated, this endosperm (which becomes hard only after the corn has dried) confines the steam which is formed from the moisture inside the kernel, until the pressure becomes great enough to explode the kernel. If popcorn does not pop well, it may be either because the kernels are immature and not hard enough, or because they have been stored in warm temperatures where they have lost moisture. (Do not store popcorn in a cabinet above a stove or oven.)

Soil. Wisconsin is good popcorn country, along with the entire Mississippi Valley. Any good loam or sandy loam will grow popcorn, and its nutrient demands are not particularly high.

pH. 6.0 - 7.0

Culture. Popcorn is grown just as sweet corn, the seed sown in the open garden after danger of frost has passed. Some authorities advise earlier planting, since the seed is so slow to germinate. However, University of Wisconsin horticulturists specify May 10 in the southern part of the state, May 24 in the north. Keep the corn patch free of weeds — mulch it, if the area is not too large, or run the rotary tiller between rows — and hope for bright and not-too-wet weather, which produces the best popcorn.

Do not harvest the ears until they have dried out well in the fall. Then, pick the ears, shuck them, and store them in a dry place where air can circulate around them. A table in a well-ventilated attic is good; or, tie them up with strings and hang them in any room in the house. After a month or so, give one ear a trial popping. If results are unsatisfactory, wait for a few weeks and try again. After the corn has proved suitable for popping, it may be shelled and stored in jars.

Varieties. Minhybrid 250 White Hulless, Faribo, Fireside, Hybrid Gold, Snow Cloud (hybrid), Tom Thumb, Purdue 202 Yellow Hybrid (long-season; not suitable for north), Strawberry Popcorn, White Cloud.

POTATO

Potatoes have not traditionally been very popular in the urban home garden, because they take up so much room and because they always have been so cheap in the stores. In recent years, however, the spiraling price of potatoes has edged them toward the gourmet food aisle, and now many home gardeners are planting all they can. If you can borrow a spare piece of land from a farmer friend, you can grow all the potatoes your family can use from autumn through the following spring. Suppose that you want to plant 300 linear feet of potatoes. Preparing the soil, planting, and mulching will take nearly a full day of labor for two people on some cool Saturday in April. After that effort, however, there is

A good harvest of potatoes in the cellar is like money in the bank. Beg, borrow, or rent space for potatoes this year. (Shown above are Katahdins, a good late variety for Wisconsin.)

little work that will be necessary. You should visit the patch every fortnight, to check for insects or disease and perhaps to rearrange the mulch. But your work is essentially finished until harvest time. Your 300 feet of row should provide from ten to twenty bushels of potatoes, which can easily be stored in a cool and dark cellar at no expense. The larger family can easily save fifty to a hundred dollars in food costs each year, by finding, begging, renting, or borrowing space for a family potato patch.

Soil. Potatoes will grow on nearly any average garden soil, even soils that are too poor in nutrients to grow other crops. In Wisconsin, they will thrive on sands, loams, and muck soils. An ideal soil, however, will be one that is rich in nutrients, well drained and well supplied with air pockets. As with other root and tuber crops, a hard clay will make tough going for potatoes. Last, professional growers much prefer an acid soil for potatoes, not necessarily because alkalinity decreases yields, but because it encourages scab. The scab does not hurt the quality of the potato, but it does blight the skin, making it unattractive to the eye and rendering the potato unsuitable for baking. The easiest way to lower your soil's pH is to grow a green manure crop of soybeans, plowing them under in the fall. Plant potatoes there in the following spring. (Other ways to lower the soil's pH are given on page 26.)

pH. 4.8 - 6.5

Culture. Potatoes should never be planted in the same place two years in a row, or following tomatoes (which are members of the same family and carry some of the same diseases). Be sure to buy certified disease-free seed potatoes for planting — not those that have begun to sprout under your kitchen sink.

The day before you plan to plant, cut the seed potatoes so that there is at least one eye to each cutting and plenty of flesh around the eye (which the sprout will use as food). Let these dry overnight. The next day, till the soil well and make rows at the recommended distances. Well-aged compost can be incorporated at this time, but never fresh manure, which can easily burn the seed potatoes. (Ideally, the manure should have been tilled under the previous fall.) Dig very shallow trenches, with the tiller or with a hoe, and lay the potatoes in, eyes up. Cover the potatoes with soil, and then hill up the soil along the rows slightly, so that the seed potatoes are about four inches beneath the soil. (Later, weeds may be killed easily by leveling the rows with a hoe, being careful not to break the potato sprouts.) Mulch this area deeply, with ten to twelve inches of hay, but keep the mulch very loose directly above the rows where the sprouts will emerge. The mulch will eliminate weeding and will keep the soil moist and cool, which is very important to successful potato production.

When the majority of the tops have withered and turned brown in the late season, the potatoes are mature and ready for harvest. Dig them with a garden fork or spade, and dry them in a cool and airy place, out of the sun. A day or two of drying should do the job. Then, clean them and store them in a cool and dark place. They will keep well for several months, since this is their natural rest period, but after that the storage conditions are critical. A temperature of thirty-four to forty-one degrees is necessary to prevent sprouting during the winter.

Special tips. A novel way of growing potatoes — well worth trying — is outlined by Mrs. Lois Hebble of Decatur, Indiana, in *The Complete Book of Composting:*

> In the fall I choose a very wide strip of garden where I want my potato patch to be the next year. Leaves are piled all over this spot almost three feet deep.
>
> By spring they have packed down and already the earthworms are hungrily working up through them. When the time is right, I plant the potatoes by laying them in long rows right on top of the leaves. The potatoes are then covered with twelve or fourteen inches of straw. Sometimes I have to put a little more on later on if I see any potato tubers sticking through.
>
> When it is time to dig the potatoes, I just pull the mulch aside and harvest. The potatoes are the best-tasting, smoothest and largest I have ever grown. I might add that so far I have never seen a *single* potato bug on the potatoes I grow this way.

Early varieties. Early Gem*† (scab-resistant), Norland*† (tolerant to scab), Irish Cobbler, New Norgold Russet, Anoka.

Midseason varieties. Superior*†, Haig (both scab resistant), Chippewa.

Late varieties. Katahdin*, Red LaSoda*, Red Pontiac*†, Kennebec*†, Sebago*† (white or russet; russet is scab resistant). (Late varieties may be questionable in northern Wisconsin.)

PUMPKIN

Horticulturally and botanically speaking, pumpkins include a lot of vegetables that most of us would call *squash*. It just so happens that the pumpkin family includes acorn squash, crooknecks, zucchini, white scallops, and other squashlike varieties. We won't bother with horticultural distinctions here, but we will call pumpkins those big yellow-orange globe-shaped things that we use either for pies or jack-o'-lanterns. We will include all the other horticulturists' "pumpkins" where they, through common usage, properly belong — under the heading of "squash."

That done, I will make a plea for pumpkin growing, which is both fun and rewarding. No crisp Wisconsin autumn would be complete without its share of pumpkin pies, and of course no Halloween could pass without its glowing jack-o'-lantern. Both will be more satisfying when the pumpkins come from your own garden. They do take up a lot of room, but you might be able to grow some, using no extra room at all. (See "special tips" below.)

Soil. Pumpkins will do well in a variety of soils, but they like best a sandy loam that is well supplied with rotted manure.

pH. 6.0 - 8.0

Culture. Plant pumpkins after all danger of frost has passed. They are traditionally planted in hills, spaced according to directions for the particular variety. Add a few shovelsful of rotted manure to each hill and mix it in well, to give the plants a vigorous start. In a few weeks, the plants should be thinned out, again according to directions on the seed packet. After that, they need very little additional care, since they grow vigorously and are not bothered by weeds to any great extent.

If you are shooting for a champion-sized jack-o'-lantern, you will do well to allow only one or two pumpkins to grow from any plant. Otherwise, nature will take its course and produce more, but smaller, pumpkins. A midseason application of compost tea will also spur growth. And, if you want to avoid having a flat and mottled side to the jack-o'-lantern, provide it with a soft bed of hay mulch and place it upright when it is very young (being careful not to strain its connection to the vine).

Special tips. Many gardeners with space limitations use sweet corn and pumpkins as companion plants. Plant pumpkins in every third row of corn, spaced eight to ten feet apart in the rows. As soon as the corn is picked in July or August, knock down the stalks so that the pumpkins can have full exposure to the sun. This method will not produce results equal to those of a separate pumpkin patch, but good success can still be attained, and at a great saving in space.

Pie varieties. Small sugar*†, Cinderella*, Spookie*.

Jack-o'-lantern varieties. Halloween*† (hybrid), Connecticut Field, Big Max (largest variety).

RADISH

Radishes are said to be the easiest of all garden vegetables to grow, and yet many gardeners have trouble with them. If you do, the trouble may lie in one of three areas: (1) *Timing.* Radishes must be planted as early as possible in the spring. Hot weather will make the roots pithy, misshapen, and generally worthless. Their ideal growing temperature is around forty-five degrees. (2) *Nutrient supply.* Radish soil should be well composted and moist, so that the plants can grow quickly and tenderly. Slow-growing radishes become hot and woody. (3) *Spacing.* Too many gardeners sow the seed too thickly, and then fail to thin the plants properly. Crowded seedlings will not develop at all. Avoid these three pitfalls, and radish production should be as simple as everyone says it is.

Soil. Radishes do best on a loose and fertile soil of any kind — one that will not bake hard in the absence of rain. Do not add extra nitrogen; it will only increase top growth.

pH. 6.0 - 8.0

Culture. As early in spring as the soil can be worked, sow seeds *thinly* in the row. The experts recommend twenty to twenty-five seeds to a foot of row, but I think that this is too many. The seeds will germinate within a couple of days, and if some areas don't show any plants after a week, it is a simple matter to bring out the seed packet and reseed those areas. After the plants have developed their first true leaves, thin the plants so that they are one to two inches apart in the row. Then no more care is needed, except that you will want to cultivate with a hoe between rows to keep out weeds. Sow new seed every week for a month for a continuous supply. After that, the weather will turn hot, making it unsuitable for radish growing.

Red varieties. Cavalier*†, Cherry Belle*†, Early Scarlet Globe*†, Red Prince* (fusarium wilt resistant), Crimson Giant, French Breakfast, Red Boy, Stop Lite, Comet.

White varieties. White Icicle*†, Burpee White, White Globe Hailstone.

(**Note:** There are also several varieties of so-called "winter radishes," which are recommended for planting in July and August for a fall crop. These are quite a bit larger than the early varieties. They include Round Black Spanish*, New White Chinese, China Rose Winter, Chinese Rose, and Chinese White. They mature in about fifty-five days.)

RHUBARB

Every garden should have a little corner reserved for rhubarb. This hardy perennial, once planted and established, needs virtually no care at all. It will continue to come up year after year, producing tender stalks that you can turn into tart and juicy pies in the middle of spring. Later in the season, you can enjoy strawberry pies — but we depend on rhubarb to initiate the fresh pie-baking season. (One caution: Do not let the kids nibble on the leaves, which contain large concentrations of poisonous calcium oxylate.)

Soil. Rhubarb will grow on almost any soil, but really prefers a sandy loam.

pH. 6.0 - 7.0

Culture. You can probably get some root divisions from a friend who has plenty of rhubarb. Explain to him that your taking some of his roots will benefit his plants, since all rhubarb should be dug up and the roots divided and replanted every five years, anyway. The plant should be dug up in early spring, before growth starts. Break apart the roots so that each division will have one bud on the crown and a root — or, if you can't identify a bud, simply divide into several good-sized clumps. Replant the divisions, so that the bud is just covered with soil. When you replant your share, prepare a generous hole, twelve inches deep, and incorporate plenty of aged compost into the soil. This will give the plant a good start and will feed it for several years. You may begin to harvest two years after planting, and every year thereafter.

Commercial growers have traditionally spread a few forksful of rotted manure over the plants each fall, letting it seep into the ground over the winter and into the following spring. The home gardener should adopt this practice, and he may work any remaining manure into the soil in the early spring.

Varieties. *McDonald*†, Canada Red*†, Valentine**, Chipman's Red.

RICE, WILD

Wild rice is the last crop that the average home gardener would want to attempt to grow — even if he could. Traditionally, wild rice has been gathered, by canoe, in the shallow and pure waters of northern Minnesota and Wisconsin. It was not cultivated. But now — in Minnesota at least — there are serious efforts to domesticate this wild grain to boost sagging rural economies in those areas where wild rice will grow (*Science News*, Vol. 104, No. 3). A nonshattering variety has now been developed (more dependable and easier to harvest) by the Monomin Development Company, Deer River, Minnesota. The rice is being planted in paddies, which also serve as nesting and feeding grounds for wildfowl and spawning areas for northern pike. If you happen to have a piece of land in northern Wisconsin that you think might be suitable for wild rice cultivation, write to Monomin for more detailed information. You might be able to develop a most unusual and desirable garden vegetable.

RUTABAGA

The rutabaga is similar to the turnip both in taste and in culture. The rutabaga usually grows larger, and its flesh is more dense. Rutabagas are also planted later in the season in order to enable them to be harvested as a fall crop. They mature best in nippy weather, explaining the late planting date (June 15 in southern Wisconsin, one to two weeks earlier in the north). Rutabagas are a good crop for winter storage. They may be stored just as potatoes are, or they may be packed in moist sand and kept in a cool basement. They are also suitable for pit storage outdoors. The rutabaga is not the most popular of vegetables, but it is favored by some, and its nutrient content is quite high.

Soil. Rutabagas prefer a loam or a rather heavy sandy loam, well composted and well drained.

pH. 6.0 - 8.0

Culture. Rutabagas should be planted from June 1 to June 15 in Wisconsin, in order for them to mature when the first autumn frosts arrive. Sow the seeds in the open ground and keep the area free of weeds, at least until the plants have established themselves. The quality of the roots will be better if they are harvested after a few frosts — but do not allow the roots to freeze in the ground, or else their keeping qualities will be impaired.

Varieties. Laurentian*† (ninety days), American Purple Top Yellow (eighty-five days), Altasweet (ninety-two days), American Purple Top, Macomber.

SALSIFY

Salsify (also called *oyster plant*, for its oysterlike flavor) is a root crop, similar to parsnip but not quite as large. It is not a popular vegetable in Wisconsin, although our climate is well suited to its production. Salsify is used in the kitchen much as turnips and parsnips. If you favor these two vegetables, you might give salsify a whirl.

Soil. Salsify likes a well-drained and loose soil, such as a sandy loam, well composted and well aerated. Since the roots grow six to eight inches long, the soil should be prepared deeply.

pH. 6.0 - 8.0

Culture. Sow seed in the open garden in the early spring, as soon as the soil can be worked. Make the rows twenty inches apart and thin the plants to stand four or five inches apart. Mulch the rows after the plants have established themselves, in order to keep the soil moist and cool and to discourage weeds. The roots can be dug for use anytime that they have grown large enough to make the digging worthwhile. Like many root crops, however, their flavor will be improved by a few brisk autumn frosts. They may be stored in moist sand in the cellar, or in an outdoor root pit.

Varieties. Mammoth Sandwich Island*†.

SHALLOT

Shallots are large, sweet, and mild-flavored onions that are often called for in French recipes. Some seed houses and nurseries offer them under the name of *multiplier onions*. They grow much as garlic does, each plant producing several cloves which eventually form a bulb. The plants may be pulled at any time, and the cloves may be separated and used as bunching onions (scallions).

Their soil requirements and culture are the same as for other onions. Stokes offer sets for planting under the name of multiplier onions.

Soybeans are a vegetable of the future, but many Wisconsin gardeners are learning of their versatility right now.

SOYBEAN

Soybeans are probably the most underrated vegetable crop of all, deserving far more garden space than they have been given up until now — not only in Wisconsin, but in all parts of the country. Here is a crop that grows easily in almost any kind of soil, requires almost no care during the season, and produces very heavy yields. The beans can be cooked and eaten fresh, much like lima beans. They can be sprouted and eaten in salads. They can be frozen. Or they can be dried and stored for use anytime during the year. They are unequalled in the vegetable world for their nutritional value, offering high levels of complete and usable protein (one cup of cooked soybeans equalling the protein content of one-quarter pound of meat), the B vitamins, calcium, phosphorus, and iron.

When sprouted, soybeans even offer significant levels of vitamin C, making this bean a complete nutritional package. And after the plant has offered all this to us, it continues to serve. Plowed under in the fall, the plants add their precious nitrogen stores to the soil, improving the garden for the season to come. Soybeans are, in fact, often grown for a green manure crop alone — but considering the quality of the harvest, it seems a shame not to use all those power-packed little beans. The Chinese have depended on soybeans for centuries, as a meat substitute. I have no doubt that they will continue to grow in popularity here and all across America.

Soil. Soybeans prefer a well-drained and sandy soil, but will grow well on nearly all soils except heavy clays that do not offer good drainage. The plant's nutrient demands are not high. It will return more nutrient matter to the soil than it removes.

pH. 6.0 - 7.0

Culture. Sow seed in a composted area after all danger of spring frost has passed — about the same time as bush beans. Allow three feet between rows and thin plants to stand one foot apart in the rows. They are vigorous growers and need plenty of room. The plants will mature in about 100 days. If you are going to dry the beans, let them mature on the vines until the pods have turned yellow. For freezing or eating fresh, pick them while the pods are still tender and green, but well-rounded. Freeze them like peas. To dry the mature beans, spread them on pans and put them in the oven for thirty to sixty minutes at 135 degrees. Cool them and place in bags or jars for storage. They can be used for your favorite baked bean recipes.

Varieties. *Bansei, Kanrich*, Giant Green Soy†. (If you have trouble ordering seed, try Burpee or Burgess.)

SPINACH

Spinach is one of Wisconsin's favorite cool-weather crops. The idea is to give spinach plenty of water and nitrogen, grow it fast, and harvest it before hot weather comes along. The heat will send it bolting to seed, destroying the tender quality of the leaves. It can be followed by a fast-growing and heat-loving succession crop, such as bush beans.

Soil. Spinach will grow well in a wide variety of soils. The most important factor is the pH level. Spinach cannot tolerate an acid soil, and so enough limestone should be incorporated into the area to bring the soil up to the recommended level. (A soil test will tell you the current pH level.) The soil should be prepared deeply, and should be well composted. Nitrogen is especially important to fast and tender growth.

pH. 6.5 - 7.0

Culture. Sow seed in the open ground as soon as the soil can be worked. Thin plants in the row according to recommendations, and then begin to pick for table use by cutting every other plant in the row, giving the others a chance to spread out. A mulch is especially important for keeping the soil cool, and also in keeping down weeds. Spinach planted on April 15 should be completely harvested by June 1, when hot weather begins to set in.

Varieties. *Long Standing Bloomsdale**†, *King of Denmark**†, *Wisconsin Bloomsdale**† (downy mildew resistant), New Zealand*† (summer "spinach"), America, Gold Resistant Savory, Hybrid USDA Number 7, Giant Nobel.

There are many varieties of squash, but nearly all of them require plenty of room to spread out and grow.

SQUASH

Most of our popular squashes are actually *pumpkins*, botanically speaking. These include most summer varieties, including zucchini and the scalloped varieties, and fall squashes such as the acorn. True squashes include the hubbards and butternuts. Here we will treat all these as squashes, since they are thought of as such, despite botanical differences.

Squashes have been popular in Wisconsin since the time of the pioneers. The great conservationist John Muir speaks enthusiastically of squashes in his uncompleted autobiography, *The Story of My Boyhood and Youth* (University of Wisconsin Press, 1965). As a boy living on a Columbia County farm in the 1840s, he recalls the amazement he felt upon planting a few seeds in a sandy corner of the farm, and later harvesting wagonloads of huge and sumptuous squash. The common nineteenth century photo of the family's garden harvest nearly always included a mammoth hubbard, which was both a source of pride and a good winter keeper.

There are many varieties to choose from, and these are usually divided into summer and winter groups (those picked and eaten during the summer, and those stored for winter use). If you have the space (squash are greedy consumers of ground), it is a good idea to plant at least one summer and one winter squash.

Soil. Squash prefer a sandy loam, well aerated and well drained, but they also need rich amounts of nutrients for their vigorous growth. The soil should be well composted before planting.

pH. 6.0 - 8.0

Culture. Squash, which is thought to be a native of tropical America, can be planted only when the ground has warmed up and all danger of frost has passed. The seeds are planted in hills three to four feet apart in both directions. Eight to ten seeds are planted in each hill, and later the plants are thinned out to three or four per hill. The strong runner vines will soon spread and crowd out most weeds, and the plants will need no more of your care after they have established themselves.

Summer varieties. Greyzini*†, Chiefini*†, Diplomat, Black Jack, Zucchini Select, Caserta, Black Beauty (all zucchini types; the first two, hybrids), Saint Pat Scallop*, Seneca Butterbar* (these two, hybrids), Early Summer Crookneck (resistant to squash bug), Delicious Green, Mammoth White Bush Scallop, Vegetable Marrow Bush, Cocozelle, (and many others).

Winter varieties. Table Queen*† (acorn, resistant to squash bug), Bush Ebony* (bush-type plant), Special Butternut, *Waltham Butternut*†, *Buttercup*† (bush type), *Mooregold*†, Gold Nugget*, *Kindred*, Hungarian Mammoth (giant variety, 120 days), Baby Hubbard, Warted Hubbard (110 days), Golden Hubbard, New England Blue Hubbard (110 days), Perfection, Delicata ("sweet potato" squash), Ebony Acorn, Blue Hubbard (110 days), True Hubbard, Butternut (resistant to squash bug), Hercules (butternut type). (See also *pumpkin*.)

SUNFLOWER

Sunflowers (*Helianthus*) are attractive, in a rugged sort of way, and productive, too. Their seeds are rich in protein, calcium, phosphorus, and the B vitamins. They were grown for their seed by the American Indians, and also by many European peoples. Sunflowers make an effective screen in the late summer, and they will provide bird seed for the winter. There are several varieties of edible sunflowers suited to Wisconsin, some growing to a height of twelve feet or more.

Soil. Sunflowers will grow in most soils, but they prefer a loose and sandy loam, well fertilized and well supplied with water.

pH. 6.0 - 8.0

Culture. Plant seed one foot apart, in rows three feet apart, around the middle of May. (They can tolerate a few light spring frosts.) When the plants have become established, thin them so that the plants are three feet apart in the row. If the soil has been composted before planting, the plants will grow quickly and vigorously and should come to maturity in about 120 days. When the birds begin to eat the seeds, you know they are ready for harvesting. Cut off the heads with enough stalk attached to enable them to be tied into bunches. Hang the bunches in an airy place to dry. In a month or so the seeds should come loose quite easily, and they may then be placed in jars or plastic bags for storage.

Varieties. Mammoth Russian (available from Olds), Mingren (from Jung).

SWEET CORN

Sweet corn brought home from the roadside stand is good, but it cannot compare to the ears that are picked from your own garden, husked, and wisked away to the cooking pot without delay — and here is why: The sugars in sweet corn are very delicately balanced. As soon as the ear is separated from the stalk, chemical changes begin which quickly reduce the quality of the kernels. Corn which is as little as three hours old has already lost a significant amount of its quality, and if it is a day old, you might as well buy canned or frozen corn in the supermarket. The trick is to get the corn from the stalk to the cooking pot as quickly as possible. And if you can't use yours immediately, be sure to store it in the refrigerator, unhusked, until cooking time. Follow the same "rush" rule when freezing corn.

Varieties are placed into one of three groups — early, second early, and main crop. Some gardeners plant all three, so that the supply lasts from midsummer right up until frost.

Soil. Corn will grow well in most soils, although it prefers a loose, well-drained loam. If your soil is heavy, stay with the late varieties. In any case, work plenty of compost into the soil before planting, for corn is a heavy nitrogen consumer.

pH. 6.0 - 7.0

Culture. Sweet corn can be planted about the time of the last killing frost. It is better to plan your corn patch to occupy a block of the garden, rather than one or two long rows. The plants should be in close proximity with each other, to aid pollination, and a long, single row makes pollination particularly difficult. (Without pollination, of course, no corn is produced.)

Plant in rows according to spacing directions for the specific variety. Right after planting, lay a mulch between the rows, but not right on top of them. As soon as the plants are six to eight inches high, gently mulch between the plants. This is a lot of work, especially for a good-sized patch, but it will eliminate hours of weeding and cultivating during the super-hot days of July and August. A good mulch will also eliminate the danger of injuring the shallow roots in cultivating. If the roots are disturbed at any time during the growing season, the development of the ears can be affected. Corn, which appears to be so rugged, is in many ways a very delicate plant.

If you do not want your corn to come in all at once, plant one-fourth of it every week for four weeks. You will then assure yourself of a continuous crop. Even when doing this, however, divide the corn patch into four quarters instead of four long strips, to aid pollination.

Special tips. Many gardeners have been disappointed to harvest ears that are stunted, only half-filled, or not filled at all. Here are some of the causes of such failure: (1) *Too-close planting.* Corn needs room to develop properly. Do not plant closer than the distances recommended for the variety. If you are pinched for space, grow one of the midget varieties. (2) *Insects.* The corn earworm is hatched on the corn silk and feeds on it, while it works its way into the ear. One strand of silk is attached to each embryo kernel, and each kernel must be pollinated in order to develop. If the worm eats the silk strand before it has received pollen, its kernel will not develop. For control, go through the corn patch every fourth day and cut off all the silks that have been out for more than a day, and apply a few drops of mineral oil into the top of the ear. These silks will already have done their pollinating job, and the worms will be dumped along with the silks you cut off. (3) *Excess rain.* A rainy day may make the pollen sticky, preventing it from being released from the tassels. This is often the cause of incompletely-filled ears, but there is not much you can do about it. (4) *Acid soil.* Check yours; add lime if necessary. (5) *Lack of nutrients or moisture.* Compost thoroughly before planting; apply a good mulch.

Early varieties. Early Sunglow*†, Seneca 60*, Improved Spancross*†, Golden Rocket*, Sprite*, Butter and Sugar* (these last two, white and yellow kernels mixed), Golden Miniature, Earlivee, Spancross, Garden Treat, Sunny Vee, (many others).

Second early varieties. Golden Beauty*†, Early King*†, Gold Rush*†, Honey and Cream* (white and yellow kernels mixed), Extra Early Super Sweet, (many others).

Main crop varieties. *Wisconsin 900*†, *Wisconsin 909*, *Jubilee*†, *Foremost*, *Mellogold*, *Sugar Daddy*, *Sugar King*, *Target*, *Pacer*, *Midway*, *Golden Cross Bantam*†, *Sweet Sue* (white and yellow kernels mixed), *Super Sweet Illinichief* (extra high sugar), Summer Treat, *Barbecue*, Gold Rush, Morning Sun, Marcross, *Improved Carmelcross*, (and many others).

SWEET POTATO

Sweet potatoes are rich in both vitamins A and C — a nutritious addition to any vegetable garden. Although sweet potatoes are a southern crop, they have enjoyed commercial success in central Wisconsin, and they have become popular additions to many home gardens in recent years. The secret of success lies in choosing the right varieties for Wisconsin, and in treating the soil properly.

Soil. The sweet potato, a native of hot and often dry climates, has learned to send its roots deep into the soil to bring up both moisture and food. Large yields, then, depend on a subsoil in good condition. Compost applied to the topsoil will help to increase yields, also, but sweet potatoes have traditionally been grown on poor soil. Excess nitrogen will promote luxuriant top growth, but will reduce yields. Often, the best crops have sparse and stunted-looking vines.

pH. 5.5 - 7.0

Three-pound sweet potatoes? Yes, the Judson Wrights of Beloit, Wisconsin, raise them each year, using lots of compost, manure, wood ashes, bone meal, lime, and rock dust — the full organic treatment.

Culture. Sweet potatoes are grown from plants which are set fifteen inches apart in rows thirty to thirty-six inches apart. Plants are not set out until the weather has actually become warm — the first week of June, in southern Wisconsin. Make a shallow furrow for each row, and line it with compost or aged manure. Then, pull up the soil with a hoe or rake so that there is a ten-or-twelve-inch ridge of loose soil running all along the row. Set the plants in the ridge, with the roots four or five inches under the soil. (If you are wondering why this special treatment, it is to enable the tubers to be harvested with ease later in the season.) Keep the sweet potato patch free of weeds until the vines are vigorous enough to take care of themselves, and then do not disturb the plants until harvest time. They will never need water.

Do not harvest the sweet potatoes until the first frost is forecast. Then, before frost hits, dig them with a spade or garden fork, leave them them to cure on the ground for an afternoon, and then take them in and store them in a warm room for ten days to three weeks. After that, move them to a cooler spot (fifty to sixty degrees) where the humidity is relatively high (up to 75 percent) for the winter. They should receive good ventilation all during the curing and storage periods.

Varieties. Centennial*, All Gold*, Gold Rush*.

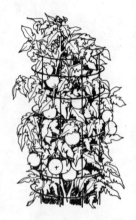

Wire cylinders for tomatoes will conserve garden space, keep the fruit off the ground, and hold mulch snugly around the plants.

TOMATO

Surely no vegetable crop is more popular in the Wisconsin home garden than tomatoes. And why not? Garden-fresh tomatoes are delicious, easy to grow, heavy yielding, and can be preserved in dozens of different ways. You can grow any of scores of different varieties in Wisconsin — pear-shaped, heart-shaped, apple-shaped, plum-shaped — red, pink, yellow, or white — cantaloupe-sized or cherry-sized. You can put them in salads, in stews, in sandwiches, on hamburgers, in a thousand casseroles. You can "put them by" by the dozens of quarts, to help you make all the chili and spaghetti you will want from now until next tomato season. You can make tomato juice, tomato paste, tomato sauce, tomato preserves, chili sauce, catsup, pickled tomatoes, and chutney. You can fry them green in butter. You can make them into tomato aspic, tomato surprise, tomato soup, stewed tomatoes, stuffed tomatoes. You can use them in countless recipes, and you can take the extras to friends when you visit.

Perhaps best of all, you can simply sit down in the garden by your favorite Big Boy plant, and just eat a tomato right off the vine. No other experience will better bring home the real reason why we dig, hoe, rake, and sweat in the sun from April until

A heavy straw mulch pays rich dividends with tomatoes.

October of each year. That first ripe tomato is the answer, pure and simple and sweet.

Soil. Tomatoes will grow on a variety of garden soils, although they do best on a sandy loam. Two things they will require are good drainage and good aeration. The soil should be loose.

pH. 6.0 - 7.0

Culture. Tomatoes can be planted indoors from seed, then transplanted about eight weeks later. In this way you will have your choice of scores of varieties. And, if your seedlings do not develop as you had hoped, you can always buy plants at the garden center or nursery at planting time, choosing among the tried and true varieties that are offered there. Early varieties should be planted three feet apart in either directions; later varieties need more room, and should be planted from four to five feet apart. If you are cramped for space, you will want to train your tomatoes on poles or trellises, in which case you may plant more closely — eighteen to twenty-four inches apart in rows two to four feet apart. Midget varieties can be planted more closely.

Tomatoes should be planted in an open place, for they need full sun for maximum growth and production. The soil should be well composted in advance of planting, and an extra handful of well-aged compost may be thrown into the planting hole before you set in the plant. Never plant tomatoes in a spot where puddles form, for this indicates poor drainage and a great possibility of bacterial wilt, stunting, and fruit rot. Good air circulation is equally important, since this will help to prevent leaf-blighting fungus diseases and fruit decay.

Set healthy plants in the open garden after all danger of frost has passed. If you plan to stake the plants, drive in the stake at planting time and tie the young plant to the stake (tightly around the stake, but loosely around the plant). After that, allow just two main shoots to grow, pinching off any side shoots, until the plants have reached about two feet in height. Then you may allow more side shoots to develop. Keep the shoots tied to the stake as they grow. In this way, you will get larger tomatoes with less chance of the fruit cracking.

Mulching is a good idea in any case, but it is especially important if you do not stake your tomatoes. (Your total yield, if you do not stake, will be more for each plant but less from a given area of ground.) A bed of clean straw mulch will keep the fruits out of direct contact with the ground and will prevent much fruit damage.

Your tomato harvest should last from late July or early August right up until hard frost hits. You can protect the fruit from light frosts by covering the plants with burlap during the night. But before that first hard, killing frost hits, go out and harvest all the green tomatoes, large and small, and bring them in. The small ones can be used for pickling and for relish. The larger green tomatoes can be wrapped in newspaper, stored in shallow, open boxes, and will ripen in the dark for several weeks. The larger green ones can also be covered with salt and flour, and fried in butter. They are delicious that way.

Early varieties. Springset*, Spring Giant* (both hybrids; both resistant to fusarium and verticillium wilts), Wayahead*†, Earliana, Fireball, Burgess' F1 Hybrid Number 1, Burgess' F1Hybrid Number 2.

Main crop. Patio* (hybrid; small growing, for tubs), Glamour*†, Heinz 1350 (resistant to fusarium and verticillium wilts), Campbell 1327 (resistant to fusarium and verticillium wilts), Cardinal* (hybrid), Jet Star* (hybrid, resistant to fusarium and verticillium wilts), Better Boy* (hybrid, resistant to fusarium and verticillium wilts and nematodes), Supersonic* (hybrid; resistant to fusarium and verticillium wilts), Big Boy*† (hybrid), Beefeater* (hybrid; resistant to fusarium and verticillium wilts and nematodes), Wisconsin Chief, Wisconsin 55, Glamour, Bonny Best, Oxheart, Burgess Trip-L-Crop Climbing (grows ten to twenty feet high when staked), Crackproof, Marglobe (wilt and rust resistant), Rutgers (wilt and rust resistant), (and many others).

Paste varieties. Roma* (resistant to fusarium and verticillium wilts), San Marzano, Nova, Red top.

Yellow varieties. Golden Delight* (early), Jubilee*†, Sunray*†.

Small-fruited varieties. Pixie* (hybrid), Small Fry*† (hybrid; resistant to fusarium and verticillium wilts), Presto* (hybrid), Tiny Tim†, Burgess Early Salad Hybrid, Yellow Plum, Red Cherry.

Greenhouse forcing varieties. Ohio MR12 Pink Forcing (TMV), Ohio WR7 Pink Forcing, Ohio WR25 Pink Forcing (wilt tolerant).

White variety. White Beauty (low acid content).

TURNIP

Turnips are best grown fast and eaten young. The larger they get, and the warmer the weather gets, the more unpalatable they become. Tender, young turnips, however, have a zesty flavor all their own, and they make a welcome addition to the dining table in June and July.

Soil. Turnips are not particular when it comes to soil types, but they do like a loose soil, well drained and well composted. A large supply of available nutrients will spur the quick growth that is essential to producing tender roots. The soil should be deeply prepared, as with any root crop.

pH. 6.0 - 8.0

Culture. The culture of turnips is similar to that of rutabagas. Plant in early spring, as soon as the ground can be worked. Thin plants when they have grown their first true leaves, and then apply a good mulch in order to keep the ground moist and cool. Harvest the roots before hot weather sets in, and follow with a planting of bush beans.

Varieties. *Purple Top White Globe**†, Purple Top Strap Leaf (earliest variety), Cow Horn, Tokyo Cross Hybrid.

VEGETABLE SPAGHETTI

Vegetable spaghetti is actually a pumpkin with a novel twist. The squashlike fruit is cooked whole, then split in half. The pulp, which is in long strings like spaghetti (but tastes like squash) is then removed and eaten. Served either hot or cold, it is said to be delicious. It has been used in the Orient for many years.

Soil. Vegetable spaghetti, like squash, likes a sandy loam, well drained, well aerated, and well composted.

pH. 6.0 - 8.0

Culture. The culture for vegetable spaghetti is the same as that for winter squash (see *squash*).

Varieties. There is no choice of varieties. Nichols offers seeds.

WATER CRESS

I had always assumed that water cress would grow only along the banks of streams, shaded by overhanging trees. I was greatly surprised, then, to see our friends, David and Carole Vetter, growing water cress right in their backyard in New York City! They planted it next to the house, where it would receive a good amount of shade from the house itself and from a nearby tree, and they watered it thoroughly every day. With no other special treatment, it thrived with vigor. You might try water cress in your own garden, or somewhere else around the house, especially if you love it as much as I do.

Soil. Water cress has no particular soil requirements.

Culture. Experiment with conditions around your home. Remember that water cress will grow where there is plenty of clean and cool water, and where there is plenty of shade. Some people sink pots of water cress in tubs of water, changing the water daily by running the hose in the tub for several minutes. If you have a stream running through your place, of course, the task should be easier.

Start seeds in a mixture of garden loam, a little ground limestone, and some sifted wood humus. (Wild water cress uses wood humus from nearby trees.) Keep the soil moist at all times, keep it cool, and give it only partial sun. When the young plants have grown large enough to handle, they may be placed outdoors. If you are planting them in a stream, choose a protected place close to the bank where they will not wash out. May is a good time for planting outdoors in Wisconsin. You might have trouble in getting the bed established in a stream, but keep on trying, for once water cress is established, it will provide cuttings each spring and fall thereafter.

(Note: If you can find wild water cress, remember that the plants can also be propagated by rooting the cuttings in water.)

Varieties. There is no choice of varieties. Harris and Stokes offer seed.

WATERMELON

In our grandfathers' time, watermelons were difficult or impossible to grow well in Wisconsin. Now, thanks to the new short-season varieties, we can grow all the melons we want — smaller than the Georgia varieties, perhaps, but just as cool and sweet on a hot summer day.

Soil. Watermelons are a warm-weather plant, no matter what the variety, and they prefer a sandy soil that warms up quickly and stays warm. Nutrient content of the soil is not too important — and, in fact, an excess of nitrogen will grow luxuriant vines and small fruits. More important is the number of hot and sunny days in the growing season.

pH. 6.0 - 7.0

Culture. The culture of watermelons is the same as that of muskmelons. Plant them on a southern slope, if possible, and certainly in full sun.

Varieties. Top Yield*, Summer Festival* (these two, hybrids), Sugar Baby*†, Black Daimond*, Charleston Gray†, Crimson Sweet*†, Petite Sweet* (the last three, resistant to anthracnose and fusarium wilt), Wilt-Resistant Klondike, Congo, Wilt-Resistant Dixie Queen†, Dixie Queen F1 Hybrid, Family Fun F-1 Hybrid, Winter or Xmas, Northern Sweet, New Hampshire Midget†. (All mature in less than 100 days.)

HERBS

Every garden should include some herbs. Most are not difficult to grow, and together they offer a variety of rewards, both practical and pleasing. Herbs can be used to add zesty or delicate flavorings to nearly all recipes. They can be used in sachets for imparting delicate odors to drawers and closets, and many people use herbs for medicinal purposes. Here, we will focus on culinary herbs, not the medicinals or "simples," as they were once known. A good book on the latter, however, is Margaret B. Kreig's *Green Medicine* (Rand McNally, 1964; Bantam, 1966).

History. For most of recorded history, herbs served a place of great importance — as medicines and cosmetics, first, and as condiments only secondarily. Until the present century, in fact, herbs served as perfumes, salves, deodorants, magic potents, holy objects, and both curative and preventive medicines. Every civilization depended on herbs for most or all of these purposes. Even today, many of our modern medicines are derived from herbs, and these plants still function in some of their older roles. In Italy, for instance, an herb still serves as a lover's signal. If an Italian maiden places a pot of basil in her window, it is a sign to her lover that he is expected.

Where to plant herbs. Most herbs are attractive and low-growing, and thus suited for inclusion in many garden areas. They can be planted in the vegetable garden, in a special herb garden (formal, as in the grand gardens of seventeenth and eighteenth century Europe, or informal), in hanging pots on the patio, in tubs on the rooftop, in among the flower borders, in rock gardens, or simply in small and odd spaces anywhere on the home grounds. They do require full or nearly-full sun (except for a few, which are noted in the listings that follow) and their mature heights should be checked before they are interplanted among flowers or vegetables. Some herbs, such as fennel, commonly grow to five feet or more in height.

Herb culture. The nature of herbs varies as widely as that of vegetables. Some are annual, some biennial, and many are perennials. Some are planted from seed, others from nursery plants or divisions of roots. Some are grown for their seeds or flowers, but most are grown for their leaves, which are rich in essential oils. Generally, herbs favor a well-drained soil, not too acid and not too rich. The oils of these plants develop slowly, and a soil that is too rich in nutrients may well spur rank growth and diminished quality. Herbs should be nursed along slowly, as they are in their natural settings. For the same reason, they do not require frequent watering. This, too, will spur too-rapid growth and a lowering of leaf quality. Last, the perennial herbs should be planted together, so that they will not be disturbed during the spring planting of the annuals.

Harvesting herbs. Herbs should be harvested when their essential oils are at a peak of concentration in the leaves. For most herbs, this point is reached just before the flower of the plant has opened. Tradition dictates that the plants be cut after the dew has dried on a day that promises to be hot. You can follow this advice or ignore it, and probably you will be pleased with the results in either case. When it comes to herbs, a veritable mountain of tradition surrounds every step of growing, harvesting, storing, and using.

After you have cut the plants, bring them indoors to dry. Some experts suggest that they be washed, while others do not wash them unless they happen to be mud stained. A quick rinsing in cool water is probably a good idea in any case. The plants then should be blotted dry, placed on trays of wire mesh or netting, and allowed to remain in an airy place for three or four days, until they are thoroughly dry. (Some experts tell us to strip the leaves before setting them out to dry; others recommend stripping after they have dried. Again, I do not think it makes much difference.)

Another drying method involves the use of small, brown, paper bags, the kind sold in stores for school lunches. These will be clean and odorless. After the plants have been dried for a day on wire mesh or netting, they are tied together at the bottom stems and hung upsidedown in the bag. The top of the bag is tied shut around the stems, so that the leaves do not touch the sides, and the bags are then hung in an attic or another little-used room. In this way, the essential oils are not allowed to dissipate in the air, the plants are kept free of dust, and yet they receive enough air to dry thoroughly. After a month or two in the bag, they should be thoroughly dry. Roll the bag in your hands in order to free the leaves from the stem, and then open the bag and empty the crushed leaves into clean and dry jars for permanent storage.

Traditionalists may find some horror in this method, but I have found it to be quite satisfactory for a number of years. It was first introduced to me by the late Dorothy Franz of Coopersburg, Pennsylvania, who had a way not only with herbs, but with all food plants she touched, from the garden right to the kitchen table.

TWENTY-FIVE HERBS FOR WISCONSIN

The following twenty-five herbs are nearly all of the culinary variety. They include some of the most popular herbs for growing in this part of the country, but they certainly do not represent a comprehensive list. Taylor's *Encyclopedia of Gardening*, for instance, lists fifty-eight culinary herbs, and *their* list is far from comprehensive. Most of the data used to compile this list comes either from Charlotte Dunn's pamphlet (Special Circular 132, *Herbs*) distributed by the University of Wisconsin-Extension Programs (available from your county agent), and from listings compiled by the editors of *Organic Gardening and Farming* magazine. If you would like more information on herbs of any kind, I recommend that you write to the Herb Society of America, 300 Massachusetts Avenue, Horticultural Hall, Boston, Massachusetts 02115. Ask for a list of publications.

ANISE

Characteristics. Slow-growing annual; grows to eighteen inches; white flowers.

Culture. Plant from seed in moderately-rich, well-drained, sandy soil. Thin plants to stand six to eight inches apart. Plant in sunny place.

Harvest. Gather on dry summer day after seeds develop. Place seed heads on frames of stretched cheesecloth or netting for air circulation. Place in cool shed or room. When dry, remove seeds from stems and seal in bottles.

Uses. Green leaves and seeds can be used in salads, beverages, soups, chowders, meats, game and poultry, breads and cakes. In Holland, seeds are steeped in hot milk as a sleep inducer.

BASIL (SWEET)

Characteristics. Annual; dark green leaves with clove-pepper odor and taste. Grows to twenty-four inches; white flowers. Good border plant.

Culture. Plant in well-drained, medium-rich soil. Likes sunny, sheltered location. Space mature plants twelve inches apart. Give plants some protection from the wind. Several shearings from top three to four inches of plant can be made during the season.

Harvest. Cut plant when starting to flower. Hang for drying in warm, dry, dark room. Crush flowering tops and pack in closed containers.

Basil likes a sunny and sheltered location.

Uses. Superb for tomatoes and tomato dishes, in soups, and with meat, fish, and vegetables. Use in salads and in egg, cheese, rice, and spaghetti dishes.

Borage is a fast grower, great for salads and summer drinks.

BORAGE
Characteristics. Attractive annual; grows to fifteen inches or more; white or blue flowers.

Culture. Plant seeds and thin young plants to stand fifteen inches apart. Likes medium-rich soil, full sun. This plant matures in six weeks, and so several sowings should be made for season-long supply.

Harvest. The leaves are usually used while still green, when their oils are in high concentration.

Uses. Adds piquent cucumberlike flavor to salads and drinks. Blossoms are used as garnish for drinks.

BURNET, SALAD

Characteristics. Hardy, sprawling perennial; grows twelve to eighteen inches high; white or rose flowers.

Culture. Sow seed as an annual, in full sun, and later thin plants to stand twelve inches apart. Likes a poor and dry soil.

Harvest. Use younger leaves fresh, for flavoring in salads. Harvest plants when flower buds have formed.

Uses. Adds a cucumberlike flavor to salads. Good also for herb teas.

CARAWAY

Characteristics. Biennial; feathery foliage and creamy white flowers; grows twenty-four to thirty-six inches high.

Culture. Plant seeds in light soil in full sun. Later, thin plants to stand six inches apart. Seeds will not be produced the first year; however, if seeds are sown in fall, the plant will produce seeds the following year.

Harvest. Same as for anise.

Uses. Seeds are used in breads, cakes, cookies, potato salad, and baked fruit; add to ragouts and homemade cheese.

CHERVIL

Characteristics. Annual; resembles fine-leaved parsley. Tastes like parsley and fennel combined. Grows to eighteen inches; white flowers.

Culture. Plant seeds in early spring in moderately-rich soil. Needs some shade. Space mature plants nine inches apart.

Harvest. Pick leaves for fresh use, or dry them late in season. Flavor of leaves is captured best, however, when they are frozen.

Uses. Add leaves fresh or dry to salads, salad dressings, meats, soups, omelets, and stews. Combine with butter sauce when basting chicken for broiling.

CHIVES

(See page 125.)

CORIANDER

Characteristics. A biennial which must be grown as an annual in Wisconsin. Plants grow to two feet in height; pinkish-white flowers; disagreeable odor.

Culture. Plant seed in light, medium-rich soil, in full sun. Space mature plants to stand ten inches apart.

Harvest. Seeds should be harvested as soon as they are ripe. Flavor develops when seeds are dry. See *anise* for drying directions.

Uses. Seeds taste and smell like orange. Use in baking, poultry dressings, and French salad dressing.

COSTMARY

Characteristics. A tall-growing perennial which will spread rapidly if not checked. Grows to five feet; yellow flowers.

Culture. Plant seeds in spring, and thin plants to stand twelve inches apart. After the first year, root divisions may be made to propagate the plant. Likes sun, but will tolerate some shade.

Harvest. Gather and dry leaves when flower buds have formed in late season.

Uses. Has strong aniselike flavor. Use sparingly in green salads, poultry dishes, some jellies. Some people use it for herb teas.

DILL

Characteristics. Annual; grows two to three feet tall, with feathery foliage and yellow flowers.

Culture. Plant seed in sandy, well-drained soil, in full sun. Needs wind protection. Space mature plants eight to ten inches apart.

Harvest. Seed should be harvested as soon as it is ripe. Cut entire plant and hang to dry, or dry on screens.

Uses. Fresh plant, flower heads, and/or seeds are used for vinegar and pickling. Leaves can flavor soups, sauces, fish, and lamb. Cook with beans, sauerkraut, cabbage, cauliflower. Mix into potato salad, macaroni, coleslaw.

FENNEL

Characteristics. A tall-growing perennial (treated as an annual in Wisconsin). Grows to five feet; yellow flowers.

Culture. Sow seed in early spring and thin mature plants to stand eighteen inches apart. Needs full sun and good soil. The heavy flower heads will need support.

Harvest. Cut leaves at any time for fresh use. Harvest plants in late season.

Uses. The thick stems can be used like celery. Seeds and leaves give a licorice tang to fish sauces, chowders, soups, and pickles. Use seeds for breads and tea.

LAVENDER

Characteristics. A tall-growing perennial raised almost exclusively for its fragrance.

Culture. Can be grown from seed, but more successfully from plants or cuttings. Plant in gravel or sandy, well-limed soil, in full sun. Must be grown in poor soil to produce optimum fragrance. Needs winter protection.

Harvest. Same as for anise.

Uses. Place in small cloth bags for scenting linen and clothes closets.

LEMON BALM

Characteristics. A perennial growing to twenty-four inches, with white flowers. Has a sweet, aromatic, lemonlike odor and flavor.

Culture. Plant seed in early spring in partial shade. Likes a moist and moderately-rich soil. Thin plants to stand eighteen inches apart.

Lemon balm adds lemony zest
to iced tea, and is excellent
when used with fish.

    Harvest. Use fresh leaves at any time; harvest plant in late season.

    Uses. Use fresh leaves as you would mint, in salads, beverages, and teas. Good for iced tea. Use also with fish, lamb, and beef. Leaves can be dried and used in tea.

MARJORAM (SWEET)

    Characteristics. An annual, growing into a small (twelve-inch) bush, producing white flowers.

    Culture. Sow seed in early spring, in medium-rich and dry soil. Seedlings require shade until well started, then full sun. Space mature plants six to ten inches apart.

    Harvest. Same as for basil.

    Uses. Leaves can be used with poultry, meats, egg dishes, poultry stuffings, soups, potato salad, creamed potatoes, and strong beans. Rub leaves on meats before roasting.

MINT (SPEARMINT)

    Characteristics. A perennial with a refreshing odor and purple flowers. Grows to twelve inches.

    Culture. A friend may part with some young plants for transplanting, or you might find them growing wild in heavy soils. Plant these in rich and moist soil, twelve inches apart. Thin beds and renew every three or four years. Do not allow stalks to go to seed before using the aromatic leaves.

    Harvest. Use fresh leaves at any time. Gather in the morning after dew is gone, but before hot sun dries flavoring oils. Dry as recommended for basil.

    Uses. A perennial favorite for iced tea. Adds flavor to jellies. Use as a garnish to fruit cups and salads. Excellent with lamb, peas, and cream of pea soup. Use to make mint sauce. Dried, it can be sprinkled on fresh fruits, peas, or squash. Combine with lemon balm for delightful "lemint" vinegar. Crush fresh leaves before using.

OREGANO

Characteristics. A perennial growing to twenty inches, with pink flowers.

Culture. Plant seed (or, preferably, root divisions) in early spring, in fairly dry soil, in full sun. Space mature plants to stand twelve inches apart.

Harvest. Use leaves fresh at any time; harvest plants as flowers begin to open.

Uses. A favorite in Spanish, Mexican, and Italian dishes. Rub fresh leaves on veal and lamb before roasting. Add to goulash, stews, sauces, and soups. The dried leaves of oregano can be used in a variety of recipes calling for it.

PARSLEY

(See page 143.)

ROSEMARY

Characteristics. A tender, slow-growing perennial with pale blue flowers, grown as an annual in Wisconsin. Leaves have spicy odor.

Culture. Plant seeds in early spring, in well-drained and highly-limed soil. Seeds are slow to germinate, but may be started indoors in March. Needs full sun and wind shelter. Space mature plants eighteen to thirty-six inches apart, or so that they do not crowd each other. If the plant is potted in the garden, it can easily be taken indoors for the winter.

Harvest. Same as for basil.

Uses. Fresh or dried leaves should be used sparingly in cream soups, poultry, stews, and sauces. Blend with parsley and butter and spread on chicken breasts and thighs when roasting. Add to water when cooking peas, potatoes, turnips. Sprinkle dried and crushed leaves on meats before roasting or broiling.

SAFFRON (FALL-BLOOMING CROCUS)

Characteristics. Annual; low-growing; lilac-colored flowers.

Culture. Best to buy bulbs. Plant in well-drained soil in sheltered spot. Space mature plants six inches apart.

Harvest. Same as for basil.

Uses. Add very small amounts of dried flower stamens to sauces, cookies, rice, chicken, cakes, gravies, and biscuits.

SAGE, GARDEN

Characteristics. Perennial shrub growing to twenty-four inches; gray leaves and blue flowers.

Culture. Soak seeds for a few hours to aid germination. Plant in full sun, in sandy or well-drained soil. Space mature plants to stand two to three inches apart.

Harvest. Cut when just starting to flower, then handle according to directions given for basil.

Uses. Mix with onions for stuffing pork, ducks, and geese; use with fish. Rub powdered leaves on ham and pork loins. Good in soups and salads. Use with egg and cheese dishes. Some people use sage tea for relieving sore throats.

SAVORY (SUMMER)

Characteristics. Annual; grows twelve to eighteen inches; pink flowers; weak stems might need support.

Culture. Plant seeds in moderately-rich, rather dry soil, in full sun. Make several sowings three weeks apart. Space mature plants to stand six inches apart. Does not transplant well.

Harvest. Same as for basil.

Uses. Fresh or dried leaves are used in meat loaf, hamburger, beef stew, biscuit and dumpling batters, egg dishes, pea and bean soups. Use on fish and pork, and in cooking beans, peas, cabbage, and sauerkraut. Good for stuffings, salads, and sauces for veal and poultry.

SESAME

Characteristics. Annual growing eighteen to seventy-two inches, depending on the variety. (The best probably is Renner Number 1, a nonshattering commercial variety.) Lavender flowers.

Culture. Sow seed in medium soil, in full sun. Space mature plants to stand six inches apart.

Harvest. Seeds cannot be sown until all danger of frost has passed, and crop takes 90-100 days to mature, making it a risky venture for any but southern Wisconsin gardeners. Harvest pods when seeds are ripe. Dry in airy place, shake seeds loose, and store in jars.

Uses. Add seeds to breads and cakes. Grind and mix with nuts, figs, poppy seed or honey to make a healthful candy.

SHALLOTS

(See page 155.)

TARRAGON, FRENCH

Characteristics. A hardy perennial, treated as an annual in Wisconsin. Grows to twenty-four inches; yellow flowers. The French variety is far superior to Russian tarragon.

Culture. Start root cuttings indoors or transplant root divisions twelve inches apart in full sun. Likes medium soil and some protection from wind.

Harvest. Use fresh leaves at any time. Harvest plant when the small flower heads begin to open. Dry for storage.

Uses. Many French recipes call for tarragon. Use fresh or dried leaves with egg and cheese dishes, poultry, steak, and fish. Add to green salad and salad dressings, and to tartar and lemon-butter sauces. Rub roasting bird inside and outside with fresh leaves.

THYME

Characteristics. Perennial; grows to twelve inches; lavender flowers.

Culture. Plant seed, cuttings, or divisions in sandy or well-drained and well-limed soil, in full sun. Space mature plants to stand eight inches apart. Clip back each spring for bushy growth.

Harvest. Cut leafy tops and flower clusters when plants are in bloom. Then dry according to directions given for basil.

Uses. Probably the most versatile of herbs. Often blended with other herbs. Leaves can be used in meats, poultry stuffing, gravies, soups, egg dishes, cheese, and clam chowder. Good with tomatoes and cheese canapes, and many other recipes.

A final word on herbs. The world of herbs is a rich one, full of tradition, challenges, surprises, rewards, and — sometimes — disappointments. You can probably hold the disappointments to a minimum, if you set out plants instead of starting seeds, at least until you have gained some experience in this area. It is sometimes difficult to find the herb plants you want at your local nursery, but there are some smaller outlets in various areas of the state. A herb-loving housewife in your area might raise plants to sell, or you might find some at a local gift shop. Ask the best gardeners you know for any private sources they might have. (Here in Dane County, probably the best source is McFarland House, 5923 Exchange Street, McFarland, Wisconsin 53558. They have a very interesting herb pamphlet that is free upon request.)

You can also get herbs — especially the perennials — simply by finding other growers in your area and then swapping. Perennials spread naturally, and the beds usually must be trimmed back each year anyway. Be there with flowerpots in hand!

STARTING SEEDS INDOORS

Probably the one area of gardening that is most often heart-rending, fraught with peril, and subject to general failure is the starting of seeds indoors. If you have received past disappointments in this area, you might look for the errors of your ways and seek to correct them. Just remember that seeds are made by nature to *grow*, and that it is your job to give those seeds the environment they need to fulfill their natural potential.

Seed-starting failure can usually be traced to one or more of the following factors:

1. **Improper starting medium.** The starting medium must be low in fertility and light in texture. A nutrient-rich medium will encourage spindly growth and weak plants, while a heavy-textured medium will hold too much moisture and exclude air that the young seeds and roots need desperately.

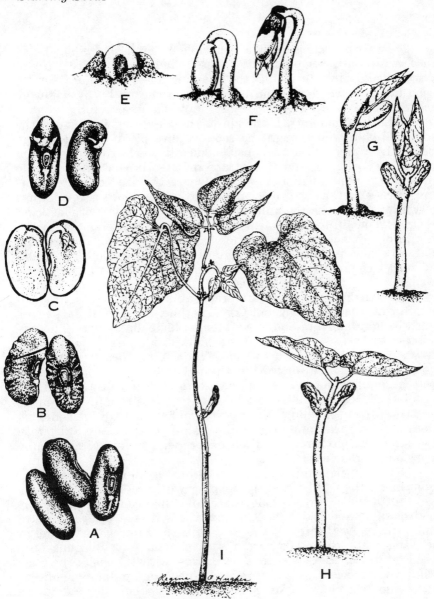

DEVELOPMENT OF A BEAN

A, dry seeds of beans; B, the seeds have imbibed water, the seedcoats are wrinkled; C, the seed opened to show the embryo; D, the radicle appears; E, the seedling is pushing up through the soil; F, the seedlings are up, part of the seedcoat still adheres to the one on the right; G, the seedlings are straightening up, the primary leaves are unfolding, and the seedling on the right shows how the two leaves are fitted together; H, the primary leaves are open and the stem has elongated; I, the trifoliate leaves have appeared.

2. **Disease organisms.** The principle killer is *damping-off disease*, which attacks plants at the soil line. You can be sure to discourage it by sterilizing the starting medium before sowing seed (an hour in a medium oven will do the trick), by watering moderately and properly, and by thinning plants promptly.

3. **Lack of humidity.** If the air surrounding seedlings is dry, the tops will wilt even though the roots receive plenty of water from below. In March, most Wisconsin homes have closed windows and operating furnaces, and this means dryness in the air. If you do not have a humidifier in the room where the seedlings are growing, then make other provisions. Some people place several trays of water among the flats and cover them with sheets of plastic on a light frame, in tentlike fashion. This method will promote humidity, although adequate circulation must be provided. For a small flat, an otherwise unemployed aquarium will serve well. There are, of course, commercial "miniature greenhouses" that will do the job well, but they tend to be expensive.

The starting medium. Start preparations for spring seed starting during the preceding fall. At that time, fill several flats heaping with garden loam and leave them outside, undisturbed, for the winter. In early spring, take these flats inside and allow them to thaw, but do not disturb the soil. When it has dried thoroughly, you can pulverize it (or work it through a fine screen) and mix it with an equal amount of sand and a little lime (about a cup of lime to a bushel of soil-sand should be enough). This mixture will make a good starting medium. Many nurserymen use various combinations of sand, peat, and vermiculite, using no soil at all. Start with the standard mixture, and then experiment to find the combination that works best for you.

Sowing in flats. Line the bottom third of the flat with sphagnum moss, then fill it slightly heaping with the starting medium. Level off the soil with a long board and then compress it slightly with a short and wide board so that the soil is at a level about a half-inch below the top of the flat. Make furrows with a dowel or rod and place the seeds carefully in the furrows. Sprinkle pure sand on top of the seeds to a level even with the soil. (The sand will prevent excessive moisture from encouraging damping-off disease, and will allow air to reach the seeds.) Sink the flat into a wash basin or tub of water, so that the water comes about two-thirds of the way up the sides of the flat. As soon as the surface of the soil has become moist, take the flats out of the water and place them in any room of the house, out of direct sunlight. To conserve moisture, you may cover the flats with clear plastic or glass, so long as you remove the covering for at least fifteen minutes daily to assure adequate ventilation. (Remove the covering permanently if fungus appears.)

There are many variations of this procedure, although this one is close to the standard and is fairly reliable. You can also plant in

Furrows in the flat should be made the proper depth for the seeds. Check the seed package directions carefully.

peat pots or peat cubes, or in plant bands, to make things a little easier, but again these cost money. Try them yourself to see if results justify the extra expense.

Germinating. When the first of the seeds have begun to germinate, remove any covering and place the flat in a sunny — preferably a southern — window. At this time, reduce the amount of water (still watering from the bottom — never by pouring water on the soil surface), so that the roots will be encouraged to go seeking their own water, and thus grow strong. But never allow the flat to become completely dry. *Moistness* — not wetness or dryness — is the key.

Begin to thin the young seedlings almost immediately. If they touch each other, they need thinning. Do this job slowly and tenderly, using a pair of tweezers. (Better still, do not sow seed too thickly to begin with.)

Temperature. Most seeds need cool temperatures to germinate well. Cool-weather crops, such as lettuce, onions, and members of the cabbage family do best when night temperatures are not above 50 degrees. Warm-weather vegetables such as tomatoes, eggplants, and peppers can take a warmer temperature — up to 60 degrees at night. During the day, temperatures may be up to 20 degrees warmer. Keep a thermometer next to the seedlings and make adjustments as necessary in the room's heating device.

Transplanting. Seeds, as we have said, do not need a nutrient-rich soil to germinate. In fact, a starting medium that is too rich will be detrimental to the germination process — especially of tomatoes. The seedlings are not able to use soil nutrients until their first *true leaves* appear. The first "leaves" you will see are actually the *cotyledons* that come from the seed structure. They cannot perform photosynthesis and cannot take advantage of soil fertility in any case.

When the first true leaves appear, however (the second set you will see coming from the center of the plant) it is time to transplant the seedlings to a richer soil mixture, for they will then be able to operate as true plants. There are two ways in which you can avoid this operation: (1) Add compost tea to the original starting medium after the first true leaves have appeared, thus introducing nutrients to the mixture; or (2) make the top half-inch layer of the original medium a mixture of peat and sand, overlaying a more fertile mixture. The seeds will germinate in the infertile mixture, and the roots will penetrate to the fertile layer as the first true leaves are showing. You may experiment with either of these methods, but remember that most professionals still transplant when the first true leaves have appeared.

Transplanting to flats. The soil mixture for the transplanting flat should be the same as for the starting flat, except that a little well-screened compost should be added and mixed in thoroughly. The mixture should still be kept lean, however, so a slight handful of compost for each flat should be plenty. The idea here is to encourage the roots to search for food, and thus grow large and strong. If the mixture is too rich, the roots will not develop well, the stems will grow tall, spindly, and weak, and the chances of ultimate failure will increase drastically.

Dampen the soil before transplanting, in both the starting flat and the transplanting flat. Remove the seedlings very carefully from the starting flat, keeping as much soil around the roots as possible. Reset the seedlings in the transplanting flats containing the new soil mixture, keeping the seedlings two inches apart in both directions. Plant them to the original depth, in holes that you have poked with a small stick, and firm the soil carefully around the young roots. Keep the transplants out of direct sun until they show signs of active growth. Most plants will not be bothered by the transplanting process, although some may wilt from shock, but they will recover in a day or two. There are some plants which seemingly cannot take transplanting at all, however, and I have tried to identify these when discussing the individual vegetables earlier in this chapter. Generally, you will want to start indoors the seeds of tender varieties which take a long time to mature, such as cabbage, head lettuce, broccoli, eggplants, tomatoes, and peppers, while there is not much sense in spending this time with leaf lettuce, radishes, beans, peas, and other vegetables that can either be planted very early in spring, or that come to maturity in sixty or seventy days or less. Those varieties which should be started indoors, but do not take well to transplanting, should be started in peat pots, peat cubes, or plant bands, so that they can be moved without disturbing their roots.

Young cabbage seedlings might look limp, wilted, and near death for the first few days after transplanting. Generally, however, they recover nicely and grow with amazing speed after the weather turns hot.

Transplanting outdoors. For each vegetable, plan carefully the date on which you will transplant it into its final garden location. It is best not to crowd this date, for your seedlings can still make good progress indoors if all conditions are right, while a late spring frost can quickly undo all your efforts should you set them out too quickly.

About two weeks before the setting-out date, begin the hardening-off process. This is simply the practice of exposing the young plants gradually to the outside environment, in order to avoid as much shock as possible. Begin by setting the flats outside in the midday filtered sun, protected from the wind, for a half-hour. Gradually expand this time outdoors until, on the day before transplanting, they remain outside until dark, only then being brought inside. (If you have a cold frame, you should use this for the hardening-off process, keeping the lid closed at night and opening it for longer and wider periods each day.)

On the day of final transplanting, remember to protect the young plants against direct sun, strong wind, and excessive cold. The ideal day should be cool and cloudy. If you cannot find a day such as this, then do the best you can to protect the plants. Never let the sun shine directly on the exposed roots. Prepare the beds carefully. The top several inches of the garden bed should be raked as finely as possible, and the soil should be loose. Keep the rows straight, using pegs and strings as guides, if necessary, not only for the sake of neatness but to retain the proper planting distances. Pay strict attention to the recommended distances both in the rows and between rows. It may look as if you have all the room in the world when you are putting in new plants, and the temptation to crowd in a few more plants is strong. Along about

Both newly-planted seeds and seedlings should be watered with a fine mist from a sprinkler hose. Gentleness and thoroughness are the keys.

August, however, you will be sorry if you had yielded to temptation in May. Crowded plants do not produce well.

Dampen the beds with the fine spray of a garden hose several hours before transplanting, in order to give the water a chance to penetrate fully and to avoid any sogginess on top. Set in the transplants a little lower than they were in the flats. In the case of tomatoes, you can sink them in quite a bit lower — especially if the transplants are spindly — and the below-earth stem portions will form vigorous root systems. Again, be sure to firm the soil all around the roots. Any roots that do not come into contact with soil will probably wither and die, and so it is important to avoid any air pockets.

After transplanting, water the plants thoroughly and — if possible — provide some protection against both sun and wind, at least for a few days. If you have not used all your seedlings, return them to the house. If any of your outdoor-planted seedlings do not make it, they can be replaced. If you mulch the plants, pile it high around each plant for the first few days. A straw mulch can be set very lightly to cover the plants, offering good protection from the wind while filtering the strong sunlight. The mulch can be pulled back gradually over a period of a week. After that, the plants can be treated normally. Keep a good mulch and keep the garden reasonably free of weeds.

LAST YEAR'S SEEDS

Should you throw away last year's packaged seeds? Probably not. If they have been kept in a spot free from excessive heat, there is every chance that they are still viable and capable of producing good crops. Here are the reasonable viability periods of some common garden vegetable seeds:

Two years: Corn, onion, parsnip, soy bean, salsify.
Three years: Bean, leek, parsley, pea.
Four years: Carrot, mustard, pepper, tomato.
Five years: Broccoli, cabbage, cauliflower, kohlrabi, lettuce, okra, pumpkin, radish, spinach, turnip.
Six years: Beet, eggplant, melon, squash.
Eight years: Celery.
Ten years: Cucumber, endive.

Many seeds will last for considerably longer periods of time. If you have any doubts about your seeds' viability, try a germination test. Count out twenty seeds or so, and place them on a layer of sterilized cotton in a saucer. Put another layer of cotton on top, and soak both layers with water. Pour off any excess. Keep the cotton damp throughout the test. Some seeds take only a day to germinate, others take several weeks. Lift the top layer of cotton every day to check for sprouting and to let some air in. If mold appears, take off the top layer permanently, but keep the bottom layer moist and in a dim or dark place. If all, or nearly all, of the seeds sprout within a reasonable time, you can count on the viability of the rest. If only half germinate, you may still use the seed if you sow twice as thickly as recommended. If less than 25 percent germinate, do not use that seed.

Dan Miller of Madison grew these enormous sunflower plants for fun and as a source of winter bird feed.

Table 9. ENERGY-SAVING STORAGE OF FRUITS AND VEGETABLES

Commodity	Place to Store[1]	Storage Period	Temperature[2]	Humidity
VEGETABLES:				
DRY BEANS AND PEAS	Any cool, dry place	As long as desired	Cool	Dry
LATE CABBAGE	Pit, trench, or outdoor cellar	Through late fall and winter	"	Moderately moist
CAULIFLOWER AND BROCCOLI	Any cold place	2 to 3 weeks	32°	"
LATE CELERY	Pit or trench; roots in soil in storage cellar	Through late fall and winter	Cool	Moist
ENDIVE	Roots in soil in storage cellar	2 to 3 months	"	"
ONIONS	Any cool, dry place	Through fall and winter	"	Dry
PARSNIPS	Where they grew, or in storage cellar	"	Cold; freezing in soil does not injure.	Moist
VARIOUS ROOT CROPS	Pit or in storage cellar	"	Cool	"
POTATOES	"	"	See text.	"
PUMPKINS AND SQUASHES	Moderately dry cellar or basement	"	50° to 60° F	Moderately dry
SWEET POTATOES	"	"	55° to 60° F	"
TOMATOES (mature green)	"	4 to 6 weeks	"	"
FRUITS:				
APPLES	Storage cellar, pit, or basement	Through fall and winter	Cool	Moderately moist
PEARS	Storage cellar	Depending on variety	"	"
GRAPES	Basement or storage cellar	1 to 2 months	"	"
PEACHES	"	2 to 4 weeks	31° to 32° F	"
PLUMS	"	4 to 6 weeks	Cool	"

SOURCE: USDA data.
NOTE: 1. Always avoid contact with free water that may condense and drip from ceilings.
2. Cool indicates a temperature of 32° to 40°; avoid freezing.

My faith is all a doubtful thing,
  Wove on a doubtful loom, –
Until there comes, each showery spring,
  A cherry-tree in bloom.
                    — David Morton

Chapter Five

Fruits, Berries, and Nuts — Perennial Providers

Who has to be convinced of the value of a cherry tree? In spring, it thrills our senses with a flood of delicate, white blossoms. All summer long it provides cooling shade and green beauty. And then, as if that were not enough, in late July or early August it offers us all the bright and succulent fruits of its boughs, which we can preserve to enjoy throughout the year.

Granted, here in Wisconsin that cherry tree is likely to be a sour cherry, for our winters are too severe to play a proper host to the sweet varieties. Similarly, most of us can virtually rule out peaches, apricots, many pear and apple varieties, and scores of other fruits that can be grown only by our southern neighbors. Only in Wisconsin's extreme southeast corner, in Zone 1 (map 28), is the choice of fruit trees really a wide one.

What does that leave for the rest of us? It leaves a tempting variety of fruits to satisfy nearly any home gardener. We have apples aplenty — tangy Courtlands and McIntoshes, the most popular, but including more than a dozen other varieties that will do well even in the coldest reaches of our state. We have pears — not suited to commercial production, but some varieties — including the popular Bartlett — that are fine for the home garden.

MAP 28

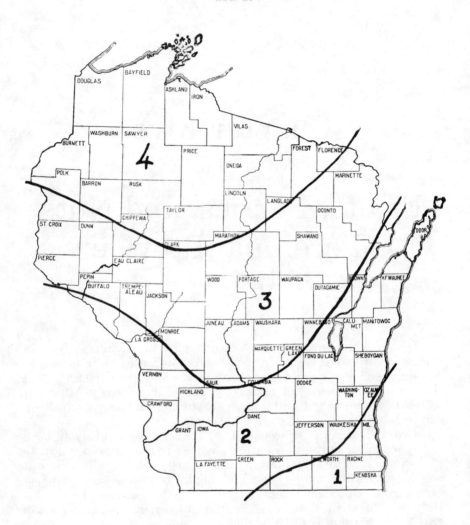

University of Wisconsin-Extension

Plums are not difficult to grow here, and some of us can even try a few apricot varieties with a good expectation of success.

Then there are berries and grapes, many of which respond to the zest of Wisconsin's climate with a pure and tangy flavor produced in few other sections of the country. Strawberries are by far the most popular of these. In June, it is difficult to take a country drive without being invited by a sign to "pick your own" at a nearby farm or orchard. As good as these are, your own will taste even better. Not far behind are grapes, which also respond well to the Wisconsin climate. The varieties that do well here are generally those that have been developed in the cooler sections of the northeast, in New York and Massachusetts. Raspberries are so easy to grow that gardeners have difficulty in keeping them in check. And then there are currants, trouble-free and great for jellies — and gooseberries, which make a pie that is beyond comparison, reserved for the special few who are wise enough to include this fruit in their garden plans.

Last among the perennial providers are the nut trees. You can harvest nuts in the wild every autumn, looking for butternuts, hazelnuts, hickories, black walnuts, and — if you are lucky — a few remaining American chestnuts. These wild-growing trees are native to Wisconsin, and they may be cultivated on your own land with relative ease. In addition, the Chinese chestnut, which found sudden popularity in America after the blight wiped out nearly all of our native chestnuts, can be grown in most areas of the state. The advantage of growing nut trees is that they generally grow much larger than fruit trees, and thus serve much the same purpose as shade trees, but are bothered far less by insects and diseases than fruit trees.

PLANNING FOR MATURITY

Size is important. Most fruits and nuts are not very particular about soil requirements, and so the paramount consideration in planning its *site and size*. A full-sized apple tree will require up to forty feet of room in both directions — sixteen hundred square feet in all. You can grow a generous family garden in this space and, if you are pinched for space, you had best think in terms of the smaller berries or dwarf varieties of fruit trees. When planning, think ahead twenty years.

Nut trees grow to enormous sizes. A full-sized, mature apple tree will grow to 30 feet or more in height, but a good hickory will grow to 100 feet. Chestnuts, on the other hand, are lower and bushier, and will require less room. The general rule is to plant all nut trees 50 feet apart from each other, except for chestnuts, which can be planted 30 feet apart.

Berries and grapes, of course, require less room. Strawberries can fit nicely into the vegetable garden, in a patch of their own, or

Table 10. PLANTING DISTANCES AND BEARING TIMES
          FOR FRUIT TREES

	Planting Distance, Each Way	Years to First Crop	Years of Bearing
Apple	40 ft.	3-10	50-100
Apple, dwarf	10-15 ft.	1-3	25-50
Apricot	20 ft.	3-4	10-25
Cherry, sour	20 ft.	3-4	15-25
Peach	20-25 ft.	3-4	20-25
Peach, dwarf	10-13 ft.	1-3	10-15
Pear	20-25 ft.	3-5	25-75
Pear, dwarf	12-16 ft.	1-3	15-40
Plum	20 ft.	3-4	30-40
Plum, dwarf	10-12 ft.	1-3	15-20

even in a colorful strawberry barrel or "pyramid patch," a space-saving arrangement of progressively elevated and diminishing circles of soil, raised by the use of circular aluminum strips. The strawberries are planted on the "steps" of the pyramid. Raspberries, currants, and gooseberries are cane and bush fruits, and should be planted on the edges of the garden where they will be out of the way. The foliage of raspberries is not particularly attractive, but currants can serve ornamental purposes in many places on the home grounds. Grapes are attractive plants, also. Their vines can be used to cover arbors, climb up over porches on trellises, or form pleasant screens for backyard privacy. Both bush fruits and grapes, however, should not be planted right up to your neighbor's lot line, unless you have some sort of an arrangement with him whereby he will not resent the spreading plants.

Effect of trees on plants. Remember that trees will cast significant shadows after a few years, and that they should not be planted where they will reduce the amount of sunlight to the vegetable garden or to flower plantings. Another major consideration is the great expanse of the root structure of all trees. The roots will spread far beyond the drip line of the branches, and can easily compete for nutrients with your less-robust garden plants, both vegetables and flowers.

Insects and disease. Last, remember that the highly-developed commercial varieties of most fruit trees are generally very susceptible to attack by both insects and disease. There are methods to assure good harvests of healthy fruit without resorting to chemical pesticides, but these natural control methods are often time-consuming to apply and sometimes not fully effective. Your choices, then, often come down to either spraying heavily and often, or remaining organic and spending the time to research and apply natural control methods. If you have both the will and the time, the latter choice is a practicable one.

Soil and site. Since the roots of trees drive deeply into the earth to bring up both nutrients and moisture, the condition of the topsoil is not particularly crucial, except perhaps during the first few years when the tree is becoming established. If you are working for maximum fruit production, however, there are some rules you should observe:

1. Plant trees in a well-drained soil, to enable you to feed them more effectively. Compost will wash down to the roots, if the soil is well drained.

2. Avoid low-lying frost pockets, which can lead to both fruit damage in early autumn and the winter-killing of buds. Avoid equally the planting of fruit trees on the top of a hill, unprotected from the wind. They can dry out quickly here, and strong spring winds can strip the tree of blossoms (and the possibility of fruit) in a short time.

3. Plant on hillsides, if you can — preferably on a northern or eastern slope — to avoid winter damage and late spring frost injury.

4. Give the tree maximum sunlight. Sunlight is very important to production, and a site that offers full sun is also likely to offer good air circulation, which is also important.

5. The soil should be slightly on the acid side for best production.

HOW TO BUY A GOOD TREE

Any tree you buy should be vigorous, showing good signs of growth. It should be young and stocky — not spindly and overly tall — and it should be entirely free of disease and injury. Choose a variety that you know is resistant to disease, insofar as possible, and be absolutely sure that yours is a *self-fertilizing* tree, unless you plan to plant two or more of compatable varieties in close proximity. If you plant a single, self-sterile tree, you will get no fruit.

The safest way to buy a good fruit tree is to know a good nurseryman and to trust his judgment. Mail order trees may appear attractive in the catalogs — and there is a good chance of success with these — but any young tree will suffer some shock in being transported, most of the damage coming from dryness. You might pay a little more in buying locally, but you will be able to examine your tree, see it growing, and be assured that it was raised in the area where you will plant it. When you consider that you are planting a tree to last for several generations, the difference of a few dollars does not seem very significant.

Choosing the proper variety of any tree, bush, or other permanent planting depends greatly on where you live. There are four distinct climate zones in Wisconsin, indicated by the map on page 188. Many varieties recommended for Zones 1 and 2 are not suitable for more northern areas. This chapter will offer guides to selection among different varieties. Before making a final selection and purchase of any tree, however, you should check with your nurseryman and, if you feel that you should, ask your county Extension agent to confirm his recommendation. If, for instance, you live in a low-lying lake area, you might discover that you can plant more varieties than are indicated in the following general recommendations. The warmer air on the leeward side of a large body of water often creates a narrow "fruit belt" which simulates the climate of an area many miles to the south.

DWARF TREES AND ESPALIERS

Dwarf fruit trees are a boon for the home gardener. They take up far less room than their full-sized counterparts, and yet they yield fruit of fully equal size and quality. They are easier to care for, simply because they are smaller, and they begin to bear at a much earlier age (although their life span is shorter).

Dwarf trees are nothing new. The Europeans have bred and cultivated them for hundreds of years, for the same reasons of space conservation that we grow them today. Modern plant breeders have, furthermore, now developed semidwarf varieties to fill in the gap between dwarfs and the full-sized trees. While dwarfs may grow to a mature height of five to ten feet, and full-sized fruit trees to thirty feet or more, the semidwarfs grow in the twelve-to-fifteen-foot range. They are large enough to produce significant amounts of fruit, but not so tall as to frighten you when you are picking from the upper limbs.

A dwarf tree is developed by grafting the bud of a standard variety onto the rootstock of a dwarf variety that bears imperfect fruit. Because it is the rootstock that determines the size of the tree, and the bud which determines the character of the fruit, plant breeders have combined these two to get the best of both worlds.

Espaliers. Espaliers, which also have been popular in European gardens for hundreds of years, are fruit trees whose branches are especially trained to predetermined shapes. They are grown against walls, or against trellises or some other structure, so that they virtually have only two dimensions — height and width — instead of a rounded three. They are grown from dwarf rootstock especially chosen for the purpose, and the grafting of the bud is done to assure the proper shape and number of the branches. After they are planted, they must be carefully trained, pruned, and supported. The shape of the espalier can be modified, but not much beyond the basic shape for which its initial grafting has prepared it.

Henry Leuthardt, the owner of a nursery in Long Island, New

Espalier trees trained against a building.

York, and a leading American prioneer of both dwarf and espalier trees, gives this good advice on the care of espaliers:

Espaliers will grow wherever other fruit trees will grow. They need about six hours of intense sun per day in order to grow well and bear a good crop of fruit. If trees get sun from 10 a.m. on, it is sufficient — but, do not plant a tree in a location that receives sun until 10 a.m. only, for it is not enough. However, if you desire the espalier for decorative purposes only, or if you do not care about the quantities of fruit the tree will bear, you may plant the trees where they receive less sun.

A tree that has been espaliered attains its permanent pattern and the owner should refrain from bending the main structure into his own design. Vertical-type espaliers will not expand in spread, but will continue to grow in height. Horizontal types will continue their spread, but making additional height depends upon the nature of the tree. Fan-shaped espaliers will grow in spread and height but desirable size may be obtained by pruning.

Planting dwarf varieties. The soil and site for dwarf varieties should be about the same as for their big half-brothers, although a little more attention might be paid to the site selection. They should be planted in an open and sunny place, and yet in one that offers at least some protection from strong north winds. Avoid both frost pockets and the tops of hills. City-lot gardeners should not have to worry much about these factors, since surrounding buildings and trees will offer good protection, but country gardeners might have to give the matter considerable thought.

The actual planting should be done according to the recommendations given for planting other trees (page 194), although the dimensions of the hole should be proportionally smaller.

For the first few years, you might wish to wrap the trunk in order to offer winter protection, using special elastic wrap available at nurseries and garden centers. And, you might wish to wrap a fine wire mesh around the base of the trunk to protect it from rodents, especially if you live in the country. Dwarf varieties require very little pruning, although crossing limbs and competing limbs should be eliminated at an early stage. All dwarf trees will appreciate a good straw mulch, and otherwise will require the standard care recommended for other fruit trees.

When planting dwarfs and espaliers, a vitally important thing to remember is to *plant with the graft-union above the ground*. The graft-union is the point at the bottom of the trunk where the bud of the standard variety has been grafted to the dwarf rootstock. You will recognize it easily by noticing the differences between the two woods. Also, there is a noticeable knob at that point. If you plant the graft-union below the ground, the standard bud will form its own roots, and you will end up with a full-sized tree.

WHEN TO PLANT

All fruit trees, including dwarfs and espaliers, are best planted in the spring in Wisconsin. Further south, fall-planted trees can withstand the ensuing winter, but our winters are not so kind. Plant early in the spring, soon after the last average frost date in your area.

POLLINATION

Plan also for pollination. Unless you are assured that the trees you buy are self-fertilizing, you must plant two or more compatable varieties, or two of the same variety, in reasonably close proximity. Apples and pears are usually not self-fertilizing, while sour cherries are. To be sure, ask your nurseryman.

HOW TO PLANT A TREE

"It is better to plant a one-dollar tree in a five-dollar hole, than to plant a five-dollar tree in a one-dollar hole."

I don't remember who said that, but it must have been said a long time ago, considering the price of trees today. Nevertheless, those words should be remembered. The scrawniest and barest sapling can be made to grow, if provided with a good root environment, while the hardiest of nursery trees can wither and die because of improper planting. *Take the time to do the job right*.

The hole should be dug about three feet deep, and wide enough to accommodate the tree's roots easily when they are spread out naturally on the ground. Most roots are cut back at the nursery, and so the diameter of the hole will probably be from three to five feet.

It should be emphasized that this will require a lot of digging, not easily accomplished. In planting a tree, you can expect to move forty bushels or more of soil, and then you will have to move it back. Doing the job properly will take at least three hours, and you should have a helper after you are ready to set the tree into the hole.

After the hole has been dug, take a crowbar and break up the subsoil at the bottom of the hole and around the sides. This is especially important if the soil is packed and hard. Your service here will make it much easier for the young roots to push into the soil and get themselves established. Work aged compost into the loosened subsoil, adding a few good handfuls of bone meal. Then, line the bottom of the hole with four inches of good garden loam. If the loam is not particularly rich, you may add some aged compost to it. Never use fresh manure.

You are now ready to set in the tree. If the tree's roots are encased in a burlap ball, simply make a mound of soil in the bottom of the hole and set in the tree, well centered. If the tree has come in a tub or container, remove the tree from the container

A crowbar is a handy tool for breaking up the subsoil at the bottom of the hole.

as gently as possible, trying not to disturb the roots, and set it into the hole. If the tree's roots are bare, trim back any broken ones past the point of the break, spread out all the roots in their natural positions, and set the tree in as gently as possible on a mound of soil, so that the roots may dip downward naturally.

At this point, you should call for your helper. Someone has to hold the tree upright while the other works with the roots in the hole. If you are going to stake the tree, now is the time to drive in two supporting stakes at opposite ends of the hole. Drive them about one foot into the bottom of the hole and allow five feet of stake above the soil line. (Adding the three-foot depth of the hole, this means a nine-foot stake.)

Check the tree now, to see whether it will be at its proper planting depth when the hole is filled in. If it is too low in the ground, mound soil under the roots until it is at the proper height. Remember, though, that it will settle just a little as you fill in around the roots. Now, begin to pack the soil around the roots. One person holds the tree steady, while the other fills in good garden loam, very gently and very carefully, around the roots. Allow no air pockets, for they will injure the roots. During the filling operation, flood the hole with water several times while the other person gently rocks the tree just slightly, so that the movement of soil around the roots will fill in any air pockets.

When the hole is finally filled, soak it very thoroughly. Then come back in an hour and work the soil around the tree into a

Work plenty of compost into the loosened subsoil, to give the young tree a running start on life.

slight basin or saucer, so that rainwater will be directed toward the trunk. Now is the time, also, to wrap the trunk with tree wrap, which will help to prevent summer sun scald and winter drying, and to place wire mesh around the base of the trunk to foil rodents who otherwise might nibble the tender bark during the winter. After you have finished these wrappings, you may attach the trunk of the tree to the supporting stakes, using hose-covered wire.

You are finished.

In a few days, mulch the tree with hay or aged compost, clear out to the drip line. (If you are planting the tree in a lawn, of course, you will not want to do this.) Keep the mulch two feet away from the trunk, however, to remove rodent nesting places.

FERTILIZING

Unless your soil is particularly poor, you should not have to fertilize your fruit trees to obtain normal production. You will, however, increase production if you do provide additional nutrients. Manure is the traditional fertilizer for fruit trees, but you may substitute good compost if you cannot obtain manure. In the orchard or field, the manure is simply spread beneath the tree, out to the drip line, and allowed to seep into the soil with the rains. This method has obvious disadvantages on a city lot. Here, dig small holes (about eighteen inches deep) around the tree, spacing them fairly evenly out to the drip line. Save the sod for replacement later. Nearly fill the holes with manure or compost, cover this with a two-inch layer of topsoil, and replace the sod. This is a two-hour job, per tree, but it does not have to be done more than once a year. The only disadvantage is that the grass on top of the holes might well turn emerald green and grow twice as fast as the surrounding grass — which should tell you something about manure. Dig next year's holes in different spots.

Many gardeners with small orchards also grow cover crops to help provide nutrients for the trees. Plant a winter cover of vetch or clover, and turn it under with a rotary tiller in the spring. (More information about cover crops is given on page 16.) Never fertilize in late summer or fall, since this practice will stimulate new and tender growth going into winter, when the new wood can be destroyed by subzero winds.

Work compost into the soil out to the tree's drip line; only in this way will you be sure to get nutrients down to the active, outer roots.

PRUNING FRUIT TREES

Many gardeners approach pruning with trepidation, fearing that they will injure or kill the tree, or at least deform it irreversibly. Actually, if a tree needs pruning, even a rather bad job of it is likely to result in more benefit than had the tree not been pruned at all. Far from injuring a tree, pruning rejuvenates it. The removal of the more undesirable limbs will stimulate the growth of the others, since they will receive a proportionately larger share of moisture from the roots. Too-heavy branches will be cut back, thus lessening the danger of breakage and real injury. More light will filter down to the tree's leaves and fruit, improving production and aiding the health of the entire tree. You should be no more afraid to prune your fruit tree than you are to prune your lawn, which in fact you do, every time you mow it.

The one danger you must guard against is infection. You can help to prevent it by sterilizing your tools before pruning, by making your cuts sharp, clean, and close to the trunk of the tree, by painting the exposed wood of large cuts (over two inches) with one of the products designed for this purpose, and by pruning in very early spring, before the leaves have come out and before there are disease spores in the air. (The other advantage of early spring pruning is that you can see the branches in far greater detail than you can after leafing has occurred.)

Fruit trees should be pruned every year, to remove dead wood, to eliminate weak and broken branches, to train the tree into a pleasing and productive form, to eliminate crossing or competing branches, to control the height and width of the tree, and, by all of these, to increase fruit production.

For the first few years of your tree's life, pruning should be directed mainly toward establishing a good framework that will make the tree strong in maturity. Lateral branches should be allowed to grow from the main leader (nurseryman's term for the young trunk) only insofar as they are spaced evenly, both above and below each other, and around the tree's main leader. The lateral branches should, in general, be well-balanced, and you can control this balance by careful and early pruning.

Elminate, also, those branches that form a small angle with the trunk. The crotches of these branches will be weak and subject to injury. Favor those branches that form a wide angle (sixty to ninety degrees) with the trunk, since these will be the strongest.

Never allow any branch to compete with the main leader, or the tree might develop a forked leader, or trunk, that will be subject to splitting in later years. Encourage the development of one clearly-defined trunk. If such a competing branch has already developed, prune it just above the first good lateral branch, so that the branch will be trained outward instead of upward.

If several branches develop very close together on a limb, prune out all but the strongest one.

Once you have decided upon the main lateral limbs you wish to encourage, do not prune the growth that comes from these limbs, for the fruit will form on this new and tender growth. Prune only if any of these small branches threaten to disrupt the general form of the tree, or if they grow so numerous as to exclude sunlight and impede air passage.

Pruning is an art, one that will come with practice and with a great deal more detailed information than can be offered in these pages. There are several good books on the subject, and there are illustrated pamphlets at your county Extension agent's office. Your interest in pruning will, of course, depend on the number of trees you grow. But no matter how inexperienced you may be, do not neglect this important job because of fear of hurting the tree. Make your plans and do the job as well as you can.

WHEN TREES WON'T BEAR

If your fruit tree is of bearing age and shows no signs of bearing, the trouble might lie in one or more of several areas:

1. **Lack of pollination.** If the tree is not self-fruiting, it will need another tree of the same variety, or a compatable variety, planted near it. Check with your nurseryman.

2. **Lack of nutrients.** Apply compost in one of the two methods described earlier in this section.

3. **Nitrogen excess.** An overabundance of nitrogen forces luxuriant leaf growth, and discourages fruit development. It is unlikely if organic fertilizing methods are used.

4. **Severe pruning.** If lateral branches are stripped of all spur growth in spring pruning, neither blossoms nor fruit will develop.

5. **Frost damage.** A very heavy frost after trees have blossomed in spring can result in the destruction of many or all blossoms, depending upon the severity of the frost and the hardiness of the tree.

6. **Lack of hardiness.** Blossom buds of fruit trees form during the season preceding their blooming. If the tree variety is not hardy in your area, severe winter temepratures can kill the embryo and the pistil in the flower bud. Even though the bud might open the following spring, it will not set fruit. Do not count on trees that are not hardy in your area.

CONTROLLING INSECTS AND DISEASE

Commercial fruit growers employ a continuing program of chemical control for the insects, fungi, bacteria, and viruses that commonly attack trees and plants. Apple trees are sprayed as many as sixteen times in a season. For commercial production of fruit, chemical control is probably necessary, at least at the present time and under the present market structure, since we lack the full technical capability to meet the threats of insects and disease by natural means. Not that commercial growers could not raise good market fruit without chemicals — they could — but natural control methods require far more time to apply, and the commercial grower could not turn to them and still compete in the present market structure.

My organic friends (those more organic than I, that is) might dispute the foregoing statement — and they would have ample fodder for their counterattack, for there are commercial fruit growers today who are operating organically and making a living at it. Most of these pioneer orchard men, however, sell to small specialty markets — stores that advertise and sell organically-grown products, and the significantly higher prices that organic fruits bring are testimony enough to the high costs of raising them.

The home gardener, however, is in a completely different boat. He will have only a few fruit trees, perhaps a dozen, perhaps only one. He can afford to forgo chemical poisons in favor of natural controls, and he can produce beautiful fruit in so doing. The difference is that the home gardener does not count his time as an expense of producing food, as a commercial grower must. He raises fruit trees because he likes to raise fruit trees, and the time he spends in working with his trees is rewarded — both immediately, in the outdoor activity and reflective solitude he gains for himself, and later on, when he enjoys the fruits of his harvest. And, because he is an organic gardener, he has the further consolation of the conservationist. He has produced food without contributing to the poisoning of the earth, sky, and waters.

PRINCIPLES OF PREVENTION

Before turning to specific insects and diseases, there are some general principles of prevention that should be learned well and followed rigorously. Their application might well reduce insect and disease problems by half.

1. **Disease-resistant varieties.** Diseases of fruit are most difficult to control, even with chemicals. That is why it is vitally important to buy disease-resistant varieties at all times. Resistance characteristics are detailed in the listings of individual fruits, beginning on page 210.

2. **Clean cultivation and proper pruning.** It is extremely important to keep a clean garden, in order to remove the nesting and breeding places of many harmful insects and other pests. All diseased plants should be sunk immediately into the hot center of the compost pile, to destroy the disease organisms. If there are too many, they should be burned or discarded in a place where they will not affect other trees. Cankers (lesions of the bark) and diseased limbs should be cut away promptly, before the disease spreads, and open wounds in trees should be painted immediately. Fungus on trees must be removed early. Pruning must be carried out regularly, to open the tree to air and lessen the chances of

moisture-loving fungus propagation. Loose bark must be scraped off, to remove hiding places of insects.

Weeds should be eliminated, since they harbor many destructive insects such as the tree hopper. In fall, gather up leaves and put them into the compost pile. Apple scab fungi live through the winter in the leaves you fail to collect. Keep the garden free of all debris, containers that will collect water, old boards lying on the ground, fallen fruit, and brush piles.

3. **Birds and toads.** Do everything you can to attract birds to your garden. The amount of fruit they eat is small in comparison to the quantities of harmful insects they devour. Feed the birds during the winter, build houses or nesting shelves for them, provide water, and go so far as to leave out bits of string and hair in the spring, to encourage the birds to build nests in your yard.

Equally effective, if you can get them, are toads. A toad will eat up to ten thousand insects over a summer. Most of these are garden insects, such as slugs and cutworms, but toads eat caterpillars, too, some of which can find their way to your fruit trees. You would do well to put some of the neighborhood kids to work in rounding up toads for your garden. A toad house can be built by overturning a flower pot, knocking out a door in it, and screwing it slightly into the ground. Keep a sunken pan of water nearby (the toad must sit in it to drink, since he drinks through his skin) and be sure to put both the toad house and the water under a protective bush. If you treat your toads right, they might decide to like your place and stay around for a while. If so, you will have gained valuable new allies.

4. **Beneficial insects.** There are also beneficial insects that, although they do no harm to your trees and plants, will wreak havoc on those insects which do. Chief among these is the ladybug or lady beetle, which feasts voraciously on aphids, scales, and other soft-bodied attackers of plants. Ladybugs can be purchased by mail order, as can praying mantids. These large and formidable-looking insects exists solely on a diet of insects — aphids, caterpillars, and a large assortment of other destructive insects, both large and small. Among other helpful insects are wasps, aphid lions, grasshopper maggots, assassin bugs, dragonflies and damselflies, ground beetles, minute pirate bugs, spiders, and syrphid flies. Learn to identify these insects, and recognize them as friends.

GENERAL CONTROL MEASURES

In addition to specific control measures for specific insects (which are covered in Chapter 8), there are some general measures that you can carry out on a regular basis, to keep down the populations of many insects which attack fruits. These general controls will help to stop trouble before it begins.

1. **Sticky bands.** Some worms and insects are unable to fly, and therefore they crawl up the trunk of the tree to do their damage. Chief among these are the female inch worm moth and the tent caterpillar. Ants also carry aphids up the trunk into trees. You can control these vertical migrations by the use of bands of sticky material, going under the names *Tanglefoot, Stickem,* and perhaps others. The insects which attempt to cross the bands become stuck to them and are destroyed.

Other insects will be induced to hide in a band of corrugated cardboard, the kind that ordinary cartons are made from. Staple a band of cardboard around the trunk of your tree, inspect it regularly, and then remove and destroy it when necessary.

2. **Traps.** Night-flying moths can be killed in large numbers by the use of light traps and insect electrocutors, both commercially available. These traps tend to be expensive, and are not particularly pleasant to have around (the electrocutor, for instance, makes a chilling "ZAP" sound every time it disposes of a victim), but they do trap thousands of moths which otherwise would lay eggs and breed hundreds of thousands of hungry caterpillars.

3. **Dormant oil spray.** An annual application of dormant oil spray on fruit trees is perhaps the most dramatically effective of the perfectly-safe insect control measures. The oil does not poison the insects on contact, but alters their immediate environment so that it is impossible for them to survive. It is harmless to humans and other warm-blooded animals while it is being used, and it will not affect the leaves or fruit of the tree.

Organic gardeners in various parts of the country have reported success in using a 3 percent miscible oil dormant spray to control a broad spectrum of chewing, sucking, and scale insects, including aphids, red spiders, thrips, mealybugs, pear psylla, mites, and the eggs of codling moth, Oriental fruit moth, various leaf rollers, and cankerworms. Most of these insects are troublesome in Wisconsin.

The time to apply dormant oil spray is in the early spring, before leafing has occurred, perhaps at the same time that you prune your trees. The oil forms a light film over insect eggs and the coverings of scales, and literally suffocates the hatching insects. Since the oil is harmless, you will not have to worry about putting on too much — but when you buy dormant oil spray, be sure it is not mixed with Bordeaux mixture, arsenate of lead, or other deadly chemicals that can be potentially hazardous to the person who sprays the trees.

4. **Safe insecticides.** Dormant oil spray can be termed an insecticide, because it does kill insects. Two other safe insecticides for occasional use in the fruit orchard are derivatives of plants — *Ryania,* a powder made from the roots of the South American plant *Ryania speciosa,* and *rotenone,* made from a combination of several tropical plants. Both are "natural" insecticides. Ryania is

effective against cranberry fruitworm, codling moth, Oriental fruit moth, and some other insects that injure fruit trees. Rotenone is used mainly against pests in the vegetable garden and is of little use in the orchard.

Still another safe insecticide is based on a natural, microbial agent, *Bacillus thuringiensis*, which is effective against oakmoth larvae, cankerworm, and tent caterpillars on all trees. (Brand names include Biotrol, Bio-Guard, and Thuricide.) All of these safe insecticides may be used without fear of poisoning people or pets, or even birds, but none should be used except when real insect troubles appear and cannot be controlled by the general methods previously mentioned.

MAJOR INSECT PESTS OF FRUIT

Listed below are the insects that are most likely to attack your fruit trees, vines, canes, shrubs, and plants. Actually, there are literally hundreds of potentially harmful insects, any of which can do damage from time to time — but these are the major attackers whose presence might call for special measures. Suggestions for the control of many of them will be found in the chapter devoted to insect control, beginning on page 299.

Apples: Rose chafer, picnic beetle, apple maggot, curculio, tent caterpillar, scales, codling moth, red-banded leaf roller, apple aphid, eye-spotted bud moth, fruit tree roller, oystershell scale, European red mite.

Blueberries: Rose chafer, picnic beetle, apple maggot, curculio, tent caterpillar, some scales.

Cherries: Aphids, buffalo treehopper, plum curculio, tent caterpillar.

Currants: Currant aphid (leaf louse), currant borer, currant worm.

Grapes: Grape berry moth, grape cane girdler, grape leafhopper, rose chafer beetle.

Pears: Codling moth, New York weevil, pear leaf blister mite, pear psylla, San Jose scale.

Plums: San Jose scale, plum curculio.

Raspberries: Raspberry cane borer, raspberry root borer.

Strawberries: Slugs, strawberry crown borer, strawberry leafroller, strawberry weevil.

MAJOR FRUIT DISEASES

Many of the fungi, bacteria, and viruses that produce disease in fruit can be controlled by the same methods recommended for the control of insects. This means the selection of disease-resistant varieties whenever possible, clean cultivation throughout the garden, regular and proper pruning, annual dormant oil spraying, the prompt removal of fallen fruit, and — only as a last resort when all other methods have been exhausted — chemical spraying.

Full directions for the chemical control of fruit diseases are readily available at the office of your county Extension agent. Here we will list some of the major diseases of fruits, keys to their recognition, and some nonchemical means of specific control. Using these control methods, in addition to the general controls previously listed, the home gardener will seldom have to resort to chemical controls.

APPLES

Apple powdery mildew. This is a fungus that overwinters in the bud of the apple blossom. It becomes active in the spring, when leaves appear, spreading a gray, powdery mildew over the leaves and twigs. Fruit may be stunted and cracked, showing fine russet-colored lines.

Prune out the twigs that appear to be heavily infested and dispose of them immediately. McIntosh is a favorite Wisconsin variety that is somewhat resistant to apple powdery mildew.

Apple scab. This disease is caused by the fungus *Venturia inaequalis*, which overwinters in leaves that lie on the ground. Spores are released into the air in spring, affecting the new growth. Brown spots appear on the fruit, and the fruit may be stunted and cracked. Leaves will show the same brown spots.

The major method of control is the clean removal of fallen leaves in autumn, and the pruning out of heavily-infested twigs during regular spring pruning. No Wisconsin varieties show any great resistance, but damage may be kept to a minimum by practicing clean cultivation.

Fire blight. See under *pears*.

BLUEBERRIES

There are few diseases of blueberries that have proved troublesome in the home garden. Any which might begin to appear should be eliminated by the prompt cutting out of the affected branches and twigs.

Sour cherries — the pride of Door County.

A pair of sour cherry trees in the backyard will give any family more than enough fruit to can or freeze for year-round use.

CHERRIES, SOUR

Diseases are rarely a major problem with sour cherries grown in the home garden. The one which might prove bothersome is *brown rot*, a fungus which attacks and rots the fruit thoroughly. Keep a close watch on the developing fruit and remove any which show signs of rot. The fungus can work clear thjough the fruit and into the twig, and so the twig should be removed also. Be sure to pick up all fruit and leaves which have fallen prematurely, for these are likely to be diseased.

CURRANTS AND GOOSEBERRIES

Anthracnose. Although currants and gooseberries are virtually trouble-free, they may be subject to occasional attack by any one of several diseases, among them *anthracnose*, which is characterized by dark, brown, and sunken spots on the fruit. Control rests in pruning out and removing affected branches promptly.

Crown gall. This disease attacks the plants at the soil level. It will not usually kill the plant or interfere greatly with its production. If it does, the plant should be uprooted and replaced.

Mildew. This fungus might prove bothersome if the weather is particularly cool and wet, and if the bushes are planted under large trees. Control *mildew* by removing the cobweblike substance from the top surfaces of the leaves, and by opening up the plant to greater sun and air by judicious pruning.

Cane blight. This is a fungus disease that attacks when the bushes are heavy with fruit, causing the entire cane to wilt. Again, the affected canes should be removed promptly, so that the disease does not spread. Clean cultivation and conscientious pruning are especially important to the prevention of this fungus disease.

GRAPES

Black rot. This fungus disease affects both the leaves and the fruit, as well as the blossoms. Light spots appear on the grapes when they are half-grown, and the fruit gradually turns black and shrivels up.

Remove any affected fruit during the season, and be sure to remove all plant wastes after the season is over. The fungus overwinters in the parts of the plant it has affected. By removing all these wastes, you will drastically reduce next year's spore population.

Downy mildew. This fungus is particularly bothersome in wet seasons, since it requires plenty of moisture in order to flourish. The first sign of infestation is the appearance of pale, yellow blotches on the upper surfaces of the leaves. The blotches will grow in size and will eventually turn brown. The fruit will be affected, too, being covered with a white mildew. Older fruit will turn brown if the disease is not checked.

Remove affected plant parts promptly, and prune vines properly each year in order to promote plenty of sun and good air circulation. The varieties Fredonia, Niagara, and Delaware are very susceptible to downy mildew.

PEARS

Fire blight. This bacterial disease, also called *pear blight*, can affect apples as well as pears. As its name implies, the affected portions of the tree look as if they have been burned black, including the leaves, flowers, twigs, and fruit. The infection enters the blossoms at pollinating time, often being carried by bees.

It is crucial to keep an eye out for *fire blight*, and to cut away the diseased parts of the tree well below the infection. Burn the waste promptly. Pears are rarely grown commercially in Wisconsin because of *fire blight*, which can wipe out an orchard in short order. One or two trees in the home garden, however, are far less likely to be affected. Nevertheless, constant checks and, if needed, immediate surgery are the best answers to *fire blight*.

Pear scab. Similar to *apple scab* in appearance, effect, and control, is *pear scab*. There are resistant pear varieties, some of which are suitable for growing in Wisconsin. Check with your nurseryman to see which are recommended for your area.

PLUMS

Brown rot and **black knot.** These diseases, which rot and destroy the fruit, can most easily be controlled by clean cultivation, prompt removal of fallen fruit and leaves, and, especially, careful and proper pruning. Prune away all branches very close to the trunk or larger branch from which they grew, and paint even small cuts on plum trees to prevent infestation. Remove all diseased material promptly and burn it.

RASPBERRIES

The United States Department of Agriculture gives these six steps for the general control and prevention of all raspberry diseases. All six make very good sense:

1. Choose disease-resistant varieties.
2. Plant only healthy stock.

3. Plant black or purple varieties in fields that have not recently been used for tomatoes, potatoes, or eggplant. (Note: These vegetables are subject to many of the same diseases, and may spread them to raspberries.)

4. Remove old canes after harvest.

5. Keep the field clean of weeds and fallen leaves.

6. Destroy seriously diseased plants. Use pesticides when needed.

These measures alone will probably make others unnecessary. Nevertheless, there are some specific diseases of raspberries that you should watch out for:

Anthracnose. See under *currants and gooseberries.*

Cane blight. See under *currants and gooseberries.*

Mosaic. This is a virus disease, and a serious attacker of raspberries. You can recognize it in the young leaves by the mottled yellow and green patches. Later in the spring, green blisters will appear on the leaves, surrounded with yellowish tissue. The entire plant is stunted, and the fruit will be ruined by a severe attack.

Check the plants often and dig out any that are diseased. Burn the waste immediately, to prevent spread of the disease. Latham is the standard variety of red raspberry in Wisconsin, and fortunately it is fairly resistant to *mosaic.* Newburg, a variety suited to southern Wisconsin, is also fairly resistant. All black raspberries are very susceptible to disease, including *mosaic,* and are planted only at the gardener's peril.

Raspberry leaf curl. This virus disease is usually confined to wild raspberries and black raspberries, but it can spread to the red varieties. Canes become stunted, leaves curl, turn yellowish, and eventually become stiff and brittle. For control, remove and burn all affected plants. More important, never plant red raspberries near black or wild varieties.

Spur blight. A fungus disease that attacks red raspberries, *spur blight* can be spotted by infestation appearing first on the buds nearer the ground. Brown or purple spots will appear at the buds. Soon, the buds shrivel and become inactive. For control, remove infected canes promptly and destroy them.

STRAWBERRIES

Black root rot. This is a disease that seems to affect roots that are not healthy in the first place. Roots turn black, rot, and die, killing the plant.

The best answer to *black root rot* is to buy healthy plants, and then to plant them in good soil, well drained and well composted. Premier and Catskill, two varieties that do well in Wisconsin, show resistance to this disease.

Fruit rot. This is a fungus that attacks the ripening fruit during rainy periods.

For control, keep the plants mulched with straw, to keep the fruit off the wet ground, and pick all ripe fruit after a rain, to prevent the spores of the disease from spreading to the green fruit.

Leaf scorch. Small reddish-brown or purple spots are the clue to this disease. Heavy clay soils that remain wet after rain will produce susceptible plants, and so the best prevention is to insure good drainage before planting strawberries.

Leafspot. This is a fungus disease characterized by spots on the plant's leaves. The spots begin as purple ones, gradually changing to tan, and then to white. Wet weather and frequent rains will help to spread the spores of this disease.

The best prevention is to choose resistant plants. In Wisconsin one of the most popular of the resistant varieties is Premier, although there are others.

FRUIT TREE VARIETIES FOR WISCONSIN

When choosing a fruit tree, you should be guided by two major considerations: First, choose a variety that is hardy in your area; and second, choose — among those hardy varieties — one that bears fruit that your family really likes. It is surprising how many people actually plant fruit trees when they have little or no idea of the actual characteristics of the fruit.

When it comes to hardiness, there are no hard and fast lines to be found. There are varieties that are definitely hardy in your area, there are those that don't stand a chance, and there are many in that gray area in between. Peaches, for instance, are not recommended for growing in Wisconsin because they are supposedly not hardy here. Nevertheless, many Wisconsin gardeners have grown peach trees for years, and they harvest beautiful fruit annually. The fact is that the official recommendations, which come from university research centers and which are published in the pamphlets distributed by your county agent, are usually geared not to the home gardener but to the commercial fruit grower. Of course, it would be foolish for a farmer in Stevens Point to plant an acre of peach trees and hope thereby to establish a successful commercial enterprise. At the same time, the home gardener in Wisconsin's milder areas (Zones 1 and 2, and perhaps part of Zone 3) can plant peach trees with a good expectation of success. He must choose the very hardiest of peach varieties, of course, and he must not gamble more than he can afford to lose. Chances are, however, that the extent of his loss will be irregular fruiting, smaller size of fruit than could be obtained further south, and occasional winter or spring killing of blossoms and resultant loss of fruit for that season. The trees, though, will have an excellent chance to survive, grow to maturity, and produce enough peaches to make any family proud and happy.

The fruit variety recommendations which follow are on the

conservative side, nearly all based on the publications *Fruit Varieties for Wisconsin*, by G. C. Klingbeil and M. N. Dana of the University of Wisconsin, and *Fruit Cultivars for Northern Wisconsin*, by E. E. Anderson (Northern Area Horticultural Agent at Washburn) and Professor Klingbeil. Their recommendations, all of which are followed by an asterisk (*), are solid ones, based on years of experience, research, and observations made in many parts of the state. To these, I have added other varieties that, according to reports from other growers both here and in other states, appear to stand an excellent chance of thriving in Wisconsin. These varieties will increase your options, but remember that they have not necessarily been proven hardy in Wisconsin. Don't gamble more than you can afford to lose.

APPLES

Although Wisconsin is known throughout the nation for its sour cherry production, there are more apple trees than cherry trees here, and a large part of the reason is that apple trees are so popular in home gardens. The choice of varieties is a wide one.

Manet*. Originated in Canada. Fruit medium in size, skin creamy yellow and striped lightly with crimson; flesh fine grained, tender, juicy, and aromatic. Eating quality excellent. Ripens before Wealthy. Tree upright and hardy. Zones 1, 2, 3, and 4.

Beacon.* Originated in Minnesota. Fruit attractive red color, flesh yellowish, medium tough, juicy, subacid. Tree productive. Not a good keeper. Ripens with Wealthy. Fair flesh, good for baking. Zones 2, 3, and 4.

Red Melba.* Originated in Canada. Skin crimson blush over waxy yellow with light bluish bloom. Large, mildly subacid, and pleasantly aromatic. Bruises easily. Annual bearer. Good fresh and for sauce. Does not keep long. Late summer apple. Tree is hardy. Zones 1, 2, 3, and 4.

Wealthy.* Originated in Minnesota. Fruit medium, skin greenish yellow, blushed and striped with red. Flesh white, tender, and crisp. Tree is hardy. Fruit must be thinned heavily. Tends to bear on alternate years. Ripens about two weeks before McIntosh. Good fresh and for sauce. Poor keeper.

McIntosh.* Originated in Canada, from a chance seedling on the McIntosh homestead. A handsome red, large apple with tender, juicy, aromatic flesh. A heavy, annual bearer that comes into bearing quite young. Variety is subject to scab and drops badly at maturity. Good all-purpose apple. Good keeper. Ripens in mid-September in the Madison area. Zones 1, 2, 3, and 4.

Courtland.* Originated in New York. Resembles McIntosh with lighter red skin color and firmer flesh that discolors slowly on exposure to air. Early annual bearer. Good all-purpose apple. Generally ripens just after McIntosh. Good keeper. Zones 1, 2, and 3.

Northwestern Greening.* Originated in Waupaca County from a chance seedling. A large and smooth-skinned fruit, waxy yellow or greenish. Flesh yellowish, firm, juicy, with slight aroma. Good keeper. Tree hardy, bears annually if thinned. One of the best baking and cooking apples. A good winter apple. Zones 1, 2, 3, and 4.

Red Delicious.* Originated in Iowa. Red striped with yellow flesh. A high quality dessert apple. Often a shy bearer. The red sports of the variety are often more highly colored. A good keeper. Zones 1 and 2.

Secor.* Originated in Iowa. Fruit red striped, with red blush. Juicy and sprightly flavored. A high quality apple. Keeps well in storage. Ripens late. Zones 1, 2, and 3.

Whitney Crab*. Originated in Illinois. Most popular of the larger crabs. Skin lemon yellow, splashed with dull red. Flesh yellow, crisp. Commonly used for pickling but is often used fresh. Tends to get mealy at maturity. A hardy tree that generally produces annually. Ripens in early fall. Zones 1, 2, 3, and 4.

Golden Delicious. Good for cooking, baking, canning, jelly, and apple butter. A favorite for making into baby food. Zone 1.

Winesap. Medium-sized fruit, crisp texture, tart and tangy taste. Excellent for eating and baking. Apples ripen in October. Zones 1 and 2.

Rome Beauty. Large, red fruit, best for baking but good for eating fresh, too. Fruit ripens in October. Zones 1 and 2.

Stark Earliest. A very early bearer, fully hardy. Medium-sized, scarlet fruit, ripening in midsummer. Mild taste, good for baking. Offered by Stark Brothers. Zones 1, 2, 3, and 4.

APRICOTS

There are several varieties of apricots which can be grown with good chances of success in Wisconsin's warmer regions — Zone 1 and the milder parts of Zone 2.

Wilson Delicious. Perhaps the hardiest of the apricots. Large, excellent-tasting fruit. Good for eating fresh, canning, cooking, freezing, and drying.

Stark Earli-Orange. An early freestone variety with firm and juicy fruits. The tree is handsome and makes a nice ornamental. Offered by Stark Brothers.

Sungold and Moongold. Both developed at the University of Minnesota, and both available from Farmer Seed and Nursery. Sungold ripens in early August, bears golden, freestone fruit, is attractive both in spring bloom and autumn color. Moongold has a sweeter flavor, is good for jam and sauce, and bears slightly earlier. Each needs cross-pollination, which can be supplied by each other.

CHERRIES, SOUR

Sour cherries are the pride of Wisconsin's Door Peninsula, but they can be grown in most parts of Wisconsin, the chances for success increasing with the mildness of the winters. Although sour cherries are generally considered fit only for pies and baking, many people love to eat them fresh, with a bit of sugar sprinkled over them. They freeze and can beautifully.

Montmorency*. Originated in France. Medium-red, large fruit; tart and rather firm flesh. Trees generally uniformly productive annually. Leading sour cherry in Wisconsin. Zones 1 and 2.

North Star*. Originated in Minnesota. Tree small, very hardy in wood and fruit bud. Can be grown in areas too cold for Montmorency. Zones 1, 2, and 3.

Meteor*. A large cherry with a light red skin. Originated in Minnesota. Tree is both hardy and attractive. Zones 1, 2, and 3.

Early Richmond. Medium-sized fruit, bright red color. A good producer which bears at an early age. Fruit ripens early. Zones 1, 2, and 3.

CHERRIES, SWEET

There are a few sweet cherry varieties that might be tried, with no guarantee of success, in Wisconsin's Zone 1 and the warmer parts of Zone 2. For the adventurous:

Schmidt's Biggareau. Similar to the popular Bing, which is less hardy. Large, very dark red fruit. Excellent for eating fresh.

Venus. A relatively new variety. Deep, glossy red fruit, highly resistant to cracking. Good-quality flesh. Tree is medium sized, spreads freely and openly, needs little pruning.

Van. Similar to Bing in color, flavor, form, and firmness. One of the hardiest of the sweet cherries.

Emperor Francis. Large, high-quality, medium-red fruit. Resists cracking during wet seasons. Tree is medium sized. Good producer.

English Morello*. Zones 1 and 2.

PEACHES

All the peaches are not down in Georgia. Most Wisconsin gardeners can grow peaches of excellent quality. This was not true in years past, but modern breeders have discovered and developed varieties that stand an excellent chance of producing in all but the coldest parts of the state.

Wisconsin. This variety was developed from a chance seedling found growing in central Wisconsin, where it had survived many severe winters without injury. It is a large, firm, freestone variety with yellow flesh. Olds and Henry Field offer trees.

Marquette. This tree originated in Michigan's northern peninsula, where winters are pretty severe, too. Olds, which offers the variety, describes the fruit as a freestone of medium size, white flesh, and excellent quality

Reliance. Perhaps the hardiest peach variety of all, Reliance was developed at the University of New Hampshire, where winters equal our own in severity. This variety has survived winters of twenty-five degrees below zero, and has produced full crops in the following season. Stark, Emlong's, and J. E. Miller offer this variety.

Polly or **Eskimo.** Developed at Iowa State University, this variety has survived winters of fifteen below. It might be the hardiest of the white-fleshed varieties. Gurney and Interstate list it in their catalogs.

(Other varieties that show some evidence of hardiness include Goldray, Golden Jubilee, Cresthaven, Kalhaven, New Sun Haven, Champion, Sunapee, and Frost King.)

PEARS

As mentioned previously in this chapter, pears are not often grown commercially in Wisconsin because of the danger of fire blight. They are, however, popular in many home gardens, where the investment is smaller and where the trees can receive close and regular attention. Most pears are not self-fruiting, and so you must either plant two trees, or be certain that a single tree has been specially grafted to be self-pollinating.

Parker*. Originated in Minnesota. Tree upright, fairly hardy. Susceptible to fire blight. Fruit large, roundish, yellow-blushed red; flesh whitish and juicy. Quality fair. Season mid-to-late September. Needs cross-pollination. Zones 1 and 2.

Felmish Beauty*. Originated in Belgium. Tree vigorous, often spreading, quite hardy. Fruit medium in size, roundish; flesh yellowish white, firm, juicy, and sweet. Quality very good. Season late September. Needs cross-pollination for best results, and is an excellent pollinator for other varieties. Zones 1 and 2.

Clapp Favorite*. Originated in Massachusetts. Tree large, upright, generally productive and hardy. Very susceptible to fire blight. Fruit much like Bartlett, but ripens at least a week earlier than Bartlett. Chief fault of the fruit is that it softens at the center when ripening on the tree. Must be picked about ten days before it ripens. Needs cross-pollination. Zones 1 and 2.

Bartlett*. Originated in England. Tree medium in size, upright, fairly hardy and productive. Is susceptible to fire blight. Probably the most commonly-grown variety. Fruit matures in September, is large, clear yellow, and smooth. Flesh is white, juicy, and of good quality. Needs cross-pollination. Zones 1 and 2.

Winter Nells*. Originated in Belgium. Tree slow growing and not attractive in shape, but fairly hardy and heavy bearing annually. Fairly resistant to fire blight. Fruit small and unattractive. Flesh tender, sweet, with aromatic flavor. One of the finest in quality. Ripens late and keeps well in storage. Needs cross-pollination. Zone 1.

Other varieties. *Bosc,* Zone 1. *Seekel,* Zones 1 and 2. *Anjou,* Zones 1 and 2. *Kieffer,* Zones 1 and 2. *Patten,* Zones 1 and 2. *Lincoln,* Zones 1 and 2.

PLUMS

Plums are perhaps the easiest of tree fruits to grow in Wisconsin. Many are hardy throughout the state. They are not particular about soil type, and they require relatively little pruning. Further, varieties such as Mount Royal, Stanley, and Wisconsin Prune are excellent for canning. There are two groups — red and blue.

RED VARIETIES:

Superior*. An apricot-plum cross which originated in Minnesota. Fruit red, early, large, firm, with very good quality. Tree vigorous, fairly heavy bearer. Needs cross-pollination. Zones 1, 2, and 3.

South Dakota (S.D. 27)*. Fruit red, medium size, freestone, good quality. Tree very hardy and productive. Should be planted as a pollinator. Zones 1, 2, 3, and 4.

Fiebing*. Originated in Minnesota. Fruit large, fairly early, and of good quality. Tree very hardy and spreading. Needs cross-pollination. Zones 1, 2, 3, and 4.

Other red varieties. *Underwood**, Zones 1, 2, and 3. *Monitor**, Zones 1, 2, 3, and 4. *Ember**, Zones 1, 2, and 3.

BLUE VARIETIES:

Mount Royal*. Originated near Montreal. Fruit medium size, blue, juicy, mild, excellent quality, excellent for canning. Tree of medium vigor, hardy, and generally productive annually. Zones 1, 2, and 3.

Other blue varieties. *Krikon Damson**, Zones 1, 2, and 3. *Wisconsin Prune**, Zones 1 and 2.

Cherry plum hybrids:

These trees are bushlike in shape, small and hardy. Their fruit is slightly astringent when fresh, but excellent when canned or preserved. Susceptible to brown rot. Varieties incluse *Opata**, *Sapa**, and *Sapalta**, all for Zones 1, 2, 3, and 4. The *Campass** variety is recommended as a pollenizer for these varieties.

GROWING SMALL FRUITS

Small fruits can fit into many spots around the home grounds. Grapes, blueberries, currants, and gooseberries are often planted near lot lines in city gardens, where they provide some privacy as well as food. Strawberries are usually worked into the vegetable garden, although they can occupy their own spot in nearly any sunny place. Rhubarb, watermelons, and muskmelons are considered fruit by those who eat them, although growers usually treat them as vegetables. In this book, you will find cultural directions for all three in the chapter devoted to vegetables.

BLUEBERRIES

Blueberries have long been native to Wisconsin, especially in the northern and central regions of the state, and there is no reason why nursery-bred stock will not do well in our home gardens. There are a few precautions, of course, but if you pay attention to these, there is no reason why you cannot harvest quarts of the luscious berries each year.

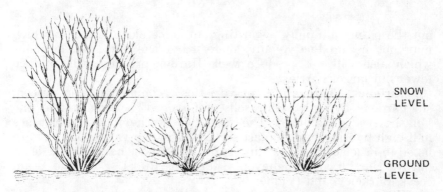

SNOW
LEVEL

GROUND
LEVEL

Highbush and half-high hybrid varieties rise above the usual Wisconsin snow level and may be damaged by low winter temperatures.

University of Wisconsin-Extension.

There are three general types of blueberries — lowbush, high-bush, and half-high hybrids. Of the three, the last is perhaps best suited to home production in our climate. Blueberries will tolerate winter temperatures to about twenty-below-zero without much problem. Much below that, the fruit buds (which are formed dur-ing the previous season) will begin to die off and the crop will be diminished. A high snowbank, however, will protect plants from severe temperatures. You can create this bank easily, with a snowblower, but be careful not to break the branches by piling on wet, heavy snow.

Blueberries ripen in from 60 to 90 days after blossoming, de-pending on the variety. If the growing season is under 100 days, the earlier lowbush or half-high hybrids should be planted.

Soil. Blueberries will grow in most good garden soils, so long as they are loose and well drained. The one important soil re-quirement is acidity. Blueberries need a pH of 4.2 to 5.5 to produce normally. If your soil is on the alkaline side, it can be corrected for blueberries by incorporating plenty of leaf mold to a depth of fifteen inches. Choose the more acid leaves for this purpose, such as sugar maple, white oak, or red maple. White ash leaves should not be used, since their pH is about 6.8. (See page 26 for more complete directions on correcting soil pH.)

Culture. Plant the bushes in late April or early May in a fully sunny place. The soil should be well composted and the compost should include peat and sawdust, but no lime. Set the plants about four feet apart in both directions, and then mulch them with an acid material such as sawdust or peat. They should need no fer-tilizer after that, although they will respond to an annual applica-tion of compost tea. In the first year, give them an application about four weeks after planting, and another when the blossoms have faded.

Pruning. Prune away only dead or broken branches for the first two or three years. Then, to maintain productive plants, thin out the plants annually by cutting out some older branches which may not be productive any longer, and the very slender ones which also will not produce well. Harder pruning will produce fewer but larger berries.

Varieties. There are eight varieties recommended for Wisconsin gardens by G. C. Klingbeil, professor of horticulture at the University of Wisconsin. The first two in the following list are half-high hybrids, and the last six are highbush varieties. They are listed in order of their hardiness, from the most hardy to the least hardy: Northland, Bluehaven, Bluecrop, Rubel, Earliblue, Rancocas, Berkeley, and Pemberton.

Here are the same eight varieties, this time listed in order of their ripening (from earliest to latest): Earliblue, Northland, Bluehaven, Rancocas, Bluecrop, Berkeley, Pemberton, and Rubel.

Finally, here are the same eight again, this time listed in order of the size of their fruit, from largest to smallest: Berkeley, Bluecrop, Earliblue, Bluehaven, Pemberton, Northland, Rancocas, and Rubel.

A little scanning will indicate that perhaps Bluecrop — a highbush variety — might be the best bet for Wisconsin. It has the second largest fruits of the eight, is third in the hardiness category, and ripens in a time only slightly longer than the average.

Bluecrop and Berkeley are available from Rayner Brothers. Earl Ferris offers Bluecrop. Farmer Seed and Nursery has Berkeley. Earliblue, Berkeley, and Bluecrop are listed by Zikle Brothers.

CURRANTS AND GOOSEBERRIES

Currants and gooseberries are listed and discussed together because the culture of these two plants is identical, as are their insect and disease problems (which are few). The uses of the fruit are similar, as well. They are both used extensively for jellies and jams. Some people love the tart taste of fully-ripe currants, eaten fresh with a little sugar sprinkled on them, while almost everyone likes gooseberry pie.

These are easy fruits to grow. They will do well even in partial shade, and they respond well to Wisconsin's cool climate. They are little bothered by insects and disease, and they make attractive foliage plants and hedges.

(Note: There are control zones in Wisconsin in which currants and gooseberries have been eradicated. Check with your county agent before planting either, or write to the Plant Industry Division, Department of Agriculture, 801 West Badger Road, Madison, Wisconsin 53713.)

Soil. Currants and gooseberries will grow in any average garden soil. They will respond nicely to an annual application of compost tea or manure tea, although they are not particular in this respect.

Culture. Plants can be propagated by making cuttings from one-year-old canes in the fall, or by setting out nursery plants in the spring. The plants should be set four feet apart in rows six feet apart, in late April or early May. The roots of these plants are shallow and easily injured by cultivation. It is best to keep them mulched with hay or straw, to keep down weeds without cultivation.

Currants turn red early in the season, but are best when they turn dead ripe (mid- to-late August in southern Wisconsin). They are at their sweetest, then, and perfectly suitable for eating fresh.

Pruning. Annual pruning in the early spring or midfall is a good practice for both currants and gooseberries. The best fruit is produced by canes two, three, or four years old. Prune away the older ones, in order to direct the plant's energy to the producing canes. Also prune out very slender, broken, or diseased canes.

Currant varieties. Red Lake, Cherry.

Gooseberry varieties. Welcome, Pixwell.

GRAPES

If you are planting grapes in a new location, it will be worth your while to do the job well, for you are planting for future generations. A good grape arbor, well cared for, will last for fifty or sixty years, and possibly more. And, if you have inherited an older planting, it will again be worth your while to take good care of it. Even an ancient, unproductive vine can usually be rejuvenated, using proper pruning and fertilizing methods.

The blue varieties have long been the most popular in Wisconsin, possibly because they are the easiest to grow here. But there are some green and red grapes that will do well here, too, in Zones 1, 2, and 3. Grape growers in Zone 4 will find the going hard, except in those isolated areas of mildness along lakes Michigan and Superior. Even in the coldest reaches of Zone 4, however, there are three blue varieties — Moores Early, Fredonia, and Van Buren — which may be grown successfully. Production might not be so high as in more southerly areas, but these varieties are certainly worth trying on a small scale.

Soil. Grapes will thrive in any average garden loam. They will not do well in very light sands or heavy clays. Sandy loams and gravelly or clay loams are especially recommended.

Culture. Vigorous two-year-old vines are best for planting, although one-year-olds are entirely satisfactory. You may also start your own plants by either layering or rooting hardwood cuttings. Both methods are explained in *Growing Grapes in Wisconsin*, an informative publication available free from your county Extension agent.

Spring planting is recommended in Wisconsin. Choose a sunny location, preferably on a gentle, southern slope. Plants may be set in as soon as the ground can be worked. Holes twelve to fourteen inches deep and sixteen inches in diameter should be dug eight feet apart (ten feet for Worden, Concord, and Niagara varieties).

Mix in some aged compost (including bone meal or ground granite rock, if you have it) into the soil at the bottom of each hole. Trim back the top of the plant until only one strong cane remains. Then trim that cane back so that only two buds remain. Apply a mulch of hay or straw.

You will need no permanent support for the vines during the first year. In the second year, some sort of trellis will be necessary. Unless you are using an ornamental trellis (such as might be constructed at the side of a porch), support stakes should be driven in, and two wires strung between the posts. The posts should be eight feet long, driven a little more than two feet into the ground. Considering that the grape planting is a fifty-year proposition, the posts might well be metal ones, with metal wire stretched between them.

Pruning. The real key to growing grapes is pruning. Unpruned grapes will produce so much fruit that it will not ripen well. The fruit will be of poor quality, and the growth of the canes will be impeded. Proper pruning, however, will maintain the balance between cane growth and fruit production that is necessary for good production.

There are several traditional methods of pruning grapes. Here we will consider only one — the Kniffin system — which is the most popular system used east of the Rocky Mountains, and certainly the most popular in Wisconsin. We are indebted to Professors G. C. Klingbeil, E. K. Wade, and C. F. Koval, for the following explanation of the Kniffin system:

First year. After planting, cut back the strongest cane to two buds and remove all other canes. Shoots will arise from the buds. Select the most vigorous shoot and tie it loosely to a temporary, five-foot stake set next to the plant. Remove other shoots. The selected shoot will become the permanent trunk of the vine.

Before the second spring, erect a permanent trellis. Set durable wood or steel posts sixteen to twenty feet apart in the row and run two strands of No. 10 galvanized wire between the posts. Run one wire thirty to thirty-six inches above the ground and a second about two feet above the first wire. Fasten the wires so they can be tightened each spring.

Second year. How much pruning you do the second year depends on how the vine grew the first year. If the cane is long enough, tie it to the top wire of the trellis and cut it off just above the wire. If the cane will not reach the top wire, cut it back just above the lower wire and tie it.

If the growth doesn't reach the lower wire, or appears weak, cut the cane back to two buds as you did at planting time. Vigorous growth will generally follow.

After tying the vines to the permanent trellis, remove the temporary stakes.

Third year. Third year pruning depends on the training the vines got during the second year. Canes which were tied to the top wire should have developed side branches during the growing season. Select four of these canes, two for each wire, and cut them back to four or five buds. Remove all other canes. Tie two canes to each wire, one to the right and one to the left of the trunk.

Canes cut back at the lower wire should have produced several canes. Extend one cane, tie it to the top wire and cut if off at that height. Select two canes for the lower wire. Cut them back to four or five buds and tie them loosely to the wire — one to the right and one to the left of the trunk. Remove all other canes.

Canes that were cut back to two buds should have produced enough to reach the top wire. Prune them the same as a vigorous second season plant.

Fourth year prune for fruiting. By the fourth year the vine should be well established and producing a considerable fruit crop. Prune now with fruit production in mind.

Grapes are borne on shoots from buds produced the previous year. High production of good-quality fruit depends on balancing the fruit load with the productive potential of the vine and providing for new fruiting canes for the following year. The fruiting shoots arise from selected canes left on each wire. The potential canes for the following year's fruiting shoots should arise from spurs on the arm of the vine.

For fruiting, select canes arising on an arm or as near the trunk as possible. Choose four canes, one on or near each arm if possible. The ideal fruiting cane is about the size of a pencil. Leave five to ten buds on each cane (depending on the vigor of the vine) and remove the remaining growth. Tie each cane loosely to the trellis.

Also leave one or two "renewal spurs" (canes cut back to two buds) near each fruiting cane. The shoot growth from the renewal spurs becomes the fruiting canes for the following year. After you select fruiting canes and renewal spurs, cut out all other growth and deadwood.

Prune the mature vines in this way every year before growth starts. This insures you of new fruiting wood as near the trunk as possible.

Pruning neglected vines. Generally, neglected vines have too much deadwood, and the fruiting wood is too far from the main stem. Old vines don't produce many grapes. But they can be rapidly rejuvenated by pruning. Quite often there are young canes arising from the roots. Select a single cane, tie it to the top wire, and treat it as a vigorous, second-year cane. Remove all the remaining parts of the vine.

If complete renewal isn't desirable, remove as much as possible of the old, nonfruiting wood to encourage new growth near the main stems or trunk. You can select several fruiting canes even though they are some distance from the main trunk. Old vines generally have large root systems and are able to support about twice as many buds as young vines.

BLUE VARIETIES:

Concord*. Fruit large and good quality when mature. Generally ripens too late in Wisconsin to obtain best fruit quality. Vines are vigorous and productive. Zone 1.

Worden*. Good quality, large berries. Ripens about seven to ten days earlier than Concord. Crop improved if pollinated by another variety. Vines of medium vigor. Zones 1 and 2.

Fredonia*. Ripens about three weeks before Concord. Vigorous and hardy, but susceptible to mildew. Zones 1 and 2.

Van Buren*. Berries smaller than Concord, good quality. About as early as Fredonia. Vines fairly vigorous. Zones 1 and 2.

Moore's Early*. Berries often drop early. Fair quality. May be just slightly earlier than Fredonia. Vines medium vigor but hardy. Zones 1, 2, and 3.

Beta*. Fruit small with only fair quality. Hardy, vigorous, and productive. Used mainly for jelly. Zones 2 and 3.

Blue Jay*. Fruit about size of Concord, fair quality. Vine vigorous and hardy. Zones 2 and 3.

AMBER (GREEN) VARIETIES:

Portland*. Fruit fair quality. Ripens with Moore's early. Zone 1.

Niagara*. Fruit fair quality. Ripens just before Concord. Vine vigorous but moderately hardy; susceptible to diseases. Zone 1.

Moonbeam*. Fruit quite large, fair quality, bland. Vine vigorous and hardy. Zones 2 and 3.

RED VARIETIES:

Delaware*. Fruit small, excellent quality. Ripens with Worden. Vine tender and lacks vigor. Requires heavy pruning. Zone 1.

Brighton*. Fruit tender and attractive. Ripens with Worden. Vine fairly hardy and vigorous. Requires cross-pollination to set fruit. Zone 1.

Red Amber*. Fruit smaller than Concord, sweet, good quality. Vine hardy and moderately vigorous. Zones 1, 2, and 3.

RASPBERRIES

Raspberries are very popular in Wisconsin, both because their fruit is so luscious, and because they are easy to grow in all corners of the state. All you need for raspberries are average growing conditions and a fair amount of room for the spreading canes.

Black raspberries can be grown in Wisconsin, but they are not recommended because they are so very susceptible to disease. Red varieties are the only kind cultivated extensively in the state.

There are some yellow varieties, which really are variations of the red berries, and which have all their characteristics.

Soil. Raspberries will grow well in any average garden soil, from sandy loam to clay. In fact, the subsoil is more important, since the plants send their roots deep into the subsoil to bring up moisture. If raspberries are planted over hardpan, the roots will be prevented from getting the necessary moisture to combat drought.

Culture. There is no need to buy nursery plants if you have a friend who owns a raspberry patch. The plants are simple to propagate by suckering. Red raspberries send up suckers — new shoots — from the underground stems or roots. These suckers may be dug up at anytime during the season. Try to hold on to as much of the root as you can, take the suckers home, and transplant them into your garden. They may either be transplanted into a nursery, where they will build up strength before being trans-planted into permanent locations the following year, or they may be set into their permanent locations at once. It is easier to propa-gate red raspberries than nearly any other fruit, and the removal of the suckers will not harm the parent plants in any way.

Suckers may be planted at any time. Nursery plants are usu-ally planted in the spring, as soon as the ground can be worked. Choose a sloping area and avoid frost pockets when choosing a site, particularly if winters are especially severe in your area. The ground should be tilled to a depth of six inches, and plenty of aged compost should be worked into the soil at the bottom of the holes. Holes should be dug two to three feet apart, and as wide as necessary to accommodate the spread-out roots with ease. Apply a mulch of hay or straw after planting.

Thinning. Raspberries are thinned, rather than pruned. The roots and crowns of this plant are perennial — but the canes are biennial, i.e., they grow one year but do not produce; they produce fruit the second year; and they die soon after fruiting. The first group of canes to be pruned away, then, are those which have just

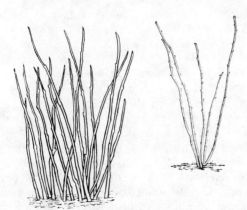

Left: Red raspberry plant be-fore thinning and pruning. Right: The same plant after thinning and pruning.

USDA

produced fruit. Their job is done, and their continued presence will just impede the development of the plant. You can prune away year-old canes anytime after they have fruited, from midsummer right up into fall, or even during the following spring. It will be easiest right after fruiting, however, since they will be easier to identify at that time.

The second group of canes to be pruned away are those which must be pruned in order to thin the plant. Ideally, after fall pruning, each plant should have only four to eight canes, and they should be spaced four to six inches apart. To attain this ideal, prune away first the broken or diseased canes. Then prune away the most slender canes, which will not bear well in any case. Then, prune away any that are growing too close to your most robust new canes.

All cuts should be made as close to the crown as possible (without cutting into the crown, of course) and as cleanly as possible. Clean cuts are important to the prevention of disease. A small pruning shears will do the job, but a sharp pocket knife will probably do a better job.

RED VARIETIES:

June*. Fruit bright red, medium-sized, round, attractive, of fair quality. Fruit requires careful handling. Begins to ripen about ten days before Latham. Plants fairly hardy and often slow to produce suckers. Zones 1 and 2.

Latham*. The standard variety for all of Wisconsin. Originated in Minnesota. Fruit attractive light red but turns dark when over-ripe; large, roundish, and quite firm, but inclined to crumble; mildly flavored. Good quality, ripens late. Plants vigorous, upright, productive, and hardy. Will grow in a wide range of soils and climate. Zones 1, 2, 3, and 4.

Other red varieties. *Newburg**, Zones 1 and 2. *Viking**, Zones 1, 2, 3, and 4. *Willamette**, Zones 1 and 2. *Durham**, fall-bearing, Zones 1 and 2.

YELLOW VARIETIES:

Golden Queen*, Zones 1, 2, and 3. *Amber**, Zones 1, 2, and 3.

PURPLE VARIETIES:

Sodus*, Zones 1 and 2. *Marion**, Zones 1 and 2.

BLACK VARIETIES:

Cumberland*, Zones 1 and 2. *Black Hawk**, Zones 1, 2, and 3.

ROSE HIPS

Rose hips are not commonly grown in Wisconsin, or anywhere else in the United States for that matter. They are well worth mentioning, however, for one very important reason: They are among nature's richest sources of vitamin C — forty to sixty times richer, for instance, than oranges. They are grown commonly in the Scandinavian countries, where long winters increase the human body's need for vitamin C, and where short summers rule out many other natural sources of this vitamin. Rose hips can be made into jams and jellies, into tart and delicious teas and juices, or they can be dried for winter use. They can be combined with other fruits to make healthful pies, and their extract can be added to many drinks as a vitamin C booster.

All roses produce hips, which are actually the seed pods or fruits produced after the blossom dies, but the best variety for producing edible hips is *Rosa rugosa*. This variety's foliage is not attractive, and so it will not serve well as an ornamental. However, it can make a fast-growing and effective hedge. Set plants of *Rosa rugosa* two feet apart, for making a hedge, but remember that individual plants will spread to five feet in diameter and more than ten feet in height. Plants are set out in spring. *Rosa rugosa* is hardy and is seldom bothered by insects or disease. Plants are offered by Farmer Seed and Nursery and by Wayside Gardens.

STRAWBERRIES

Strawberries are unquestionably the most popular small fruit grown in Wisconsin. And, in terms of the number of people who grow strawberries, they are the most popular fruit of any kind.

The reasons for the strawberry's popularity are obvious. They are easy to grow in every part of Wisconsin. Our cool climate is well suited to this fruit, which responds with firm and flavorful berries. There are scores of varieties to choose from, for every taste and climate. They are the first fruit of the season to be brought to the table (if you discount rhubarb), and for that kindness they are doubly treasured.

Soil. Strawberries will do well in most good garden soils, so long as they are well drained. They do not require much fertilizer — and, in fact, an excess of nitrogen will produce luxuriant foliage and scant fruit. Spring-planted berries will benefit by soil that had been well manured the previous fall, but further fertilization during the season is unnecessary. The exception will be those strawberries that are grown on very sandy soil. Since light sand cannot hold nutrients well, several applications of compost tea or manure tea during the season will be appreciated by the plants.

Culture. Strawberries should be planted in early spring, as soon as the soil can be worked. Depth of planting is vitally important. The plants should be set deep enough to bring the soil up to the crown, but not over the crown or the young leaves that should then be growing from it. Dig the hole to the proper depth, and wide enough to accommodate the roots easily when they are spread out naturally. Put a small mound of soil in the center of the hole and set the plant on this mound, so that the roots drop down naturally. Then, fill in soil around the roots, packing it gently but firmly so that all the roots come into contact with soil. Water the plants thoroughly after they have been set in.

The spacing of plants depends on the variety and the cultivation method chosen. Strawberry plants send out runners that root and produce "daughter" plants. These daughters grow into full-sized plants that will bear in the future. Since each plant remains viable for only a few years, it is important to cultivate these daughter plants, in order to keep the bed fresh and productive year after year. The space that you allow between plants and between rows, then, depends upon the mature size of the mother plants and the number of runners that you will permit to develop. The average variety can be planted twelve to eighteen inches apart in rows eighteen inches apart. Runners are then permitted to the extent that they do not crowd each other or the mother plants. An overcrowded bed will cut production severely.

A straw mulch under strawberries will keep the fruit clean and rot-free.

Although strawberries do not require heavy fertilization, they do require soil moisture throughout the growing season, and especially during their entire fruiting period. As for all garden plants, any water applied should be given in occasional, long, soaking doses — never in frequent sprinkles. More important, plants should be mulched as soon as they have been put into the ground. Hay or sawdust are the recommended mulching materials for strawberries.

Harvest the berries as soon as they are ripe, even the undersized or overripe ones that you will not use. Only in this way will the plants continue to produce to the limit of their capacity.

Varieties. There are two groups of strawberries — June bearers and everbearers. As their name implies, the June varieties —

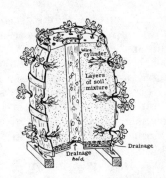

A strawberry barrel is one way to grow strawberries when you have no room for strawberries.

which are more popular — produce their crop starting in mid-June and lasting for about three weeks. (The season is from two to three weeks later in central and northern Wisconsin.) The ever-bearers, however, set and produce fruit from June up until the first snows fly. These everbearing varieties yield larger crops during the season, but the June bearers have nevertheless retained their popularity — perhaps because of habit (everbearers are a relatively recent innovation) or perhaps gardeners want quantities of berries early in the season, when other fruits are unavailable, rather than a steady supply throughout the summer and fall.

Because there are so many varieties suitable for Wisconsin's climate, I will list here only those June bearers recommended by our University of Wisconsin horticulturists. But I do suggest that you look into the wide world of strawberries by requesting the catalogs of one or more of the mail-order nurseries that specialize in berries. These include Conner, Brittingham's, W. F. Allen, and Rayner Brothers. In addition, you should see what your local nursery or garden center has to offer. But remember that those varieties recommended in catalogs "for home gardens only" are likely to be far better than those suitable for commercial production. What the commercial grower gains in shipping qualities, he loses in succulence and eating quality. The berries you grow at home should be head and shoulders above the supermarket varieties.

EARLY JUNE BEARERS:

Sunrise*. The fruit is medium-sized, orange red, firm, subacid in flavor, but not good for freezing. Plants are vigorous and produce many runners. Sunrise is resistant to verticillium wilt, leaf scorch, and some races of red stele, but is susceptible to leaf spot. Zones 1, 2, 3, and 4.

Premier*. A good plant maker with fair vigor. Generally a good producer of bright, moderately-firm fruit. It is widely grown in Wisconsin as a standard early variety. Zones 1, 2, 3, and 4.

EARLY-MIDSEASON JUNE BEARERS:

Cyclone*. Fruit is medium but variable in size, of good quality, but somewhat soft in wet seasons and subject to mold. It is fairly good for freezing. Cyclone is somewhat resistant to leaf spot and scorch under Wisconsin conditions. Zones 1, 2, 3, and 4.

Redglow*. Maintains fair fruit size during the season. Fruit is moderately firm, deep red and very glossy, and above average for freezing. Plants are vigorous and produce many runners. They do best in eighteen-inch-wide rows. Susceptible to leaf spot and red mites, but resistant to red stele. Zones 1, 2, 3, and 4.

Robinson*. A vigorous grower and plant maker. Yields are high. Fruit is large in size and of fair quality. Ripens about one week later than Premier. It is adapted to a wide range of conditions and is widely grown in Wisconsin. Not recommended for shipping or freezing. Zones 1, 2, 3, and 4.

Wisconsin 537*. A vigorous grower and good plant producer, generally a good berry producer. Fruit is medium to large in size and of good quality. Ripens about a week later than Premier. This variety is rated high for quick freezing. It has a history of being susceptible to the "yellows," but this can be controlled in the home garden by routing those plants showing the disease. Zones 1, 2, 3, and 4.

MIDSEASON JUNE BEARERS:

Catskill*. Fruit is large, irregular, moderately firm, bright red, and glossy. It is mildly subacid, of good quality, and fairly good for freezing. Catskill is very vigorous and productive, but susceptible to leaf spot and virus diseases. Zones 1, 2, 3, and 4.

Midway*. Fruit is medium-sized, firm, deep red, and glossy. It is subacid, of good quality, and satisfactory for freezing. Plants are moderately vigorous, fairly productive, and prolific runner producers. Midway is resistant to common races of red stele and moderately resistant to scorch and leaf spot. Zones 1, 2, 3, and 4.

LATE JUNE BEARERS:

Badgerbelle*. Fruit is large, moderately firm, and medium glossy red with prominent yellow seeds. It is of fair to good quality and is satisfactory for freezing. Plants are vigorous, hardy, produce many runners, and yield good crops. Badgerbelle has some resistance to leaf spot. Zones 1, 2, 3, and 4.

Sparkle*. Fruit is medium-sized, becoming smaller in late season, and dark red. It has excellent flavor and is above average for freezing. Plants are vigorous, productive, hardy, and have many runners. Sparkle is fairly resistant to leaf spot and red stele, but susceptible to virus diseases and cyclamen mite. Zones 1, 2, 3, and 4.

EVERBEARING VARIETIES:

Superfection*, **Gem***, or **Brilliant***. These varieties are virtually identical. Fruit is large and of good quality. Plant is vigorous and quite hardy. Does best in sandy loam soils. Zones 2, 3, and 4.

Ozark Beauty. Fruit is large, sweet, firm, and has good flavor. Plants are good yielders, with fair runner production. A good freezer. Zones 1, 2, 3, and 4.

Such a starved bank of moss
  Till, that May-morn,
Blue ran the flash across:
  Violets were born!
          —Robert Browning
          The Two Poets of Croisic (1878)

Chapter Six

Flowers for Wisconsin — Nine Months of Glory

As vegetables provide food for the body, so do flowers offer food for the spirit. And, even though many gardeners will concentrate on vegetables and other food plants, it is inconceivable that any garden should be without its ornamental flowering plants.

Here in Wisconsin, we are fortunate to have the beauty of outdoor bloom for as many as nine months of the year. In the southern parts of the state, at least, we can look forward to the first spring crocus blooms by the middle of March. These welcome harbingers are followed in quick succession by the other spring-flowering bulbs—tulips, daffodils, hyacinths, and more—and by a host of wild flowers which, with just a little persuasion, will become willing volunteers in our gardens. These spring-blooming plants are quickly followed by the early-blooming perennials, including peonies, poppies, alyssum, geraniums, phlox, and scores of others. By midsummer, the annuals which you planted earlier will have created a profusion of bloom, and these—along with many long-blooming perennials and summer-flowering bulbs—can be counted on to serve right up until the first killing frost. After that, there are still the hardy and half-hardy autumn-flowering plants—notably the asters and chrysanthemums—that will fill your life with color right into October and even early November, if the season is favorable.

Even though "nine months of bloom" might be a slight exaggeration, then, it is true that only during December, January, and

The first crocus blooms signify the approach of spring in Wisconsin.

February are all of us denied completely the companionship of outdoor bloom.

WHAT IS A FLOWER?

The flower which we cultivate to delight our senses has a completely different purpose for the plant that produces it. For the plant, the flower contains the reproductive organs which enable it to perpetuate its species. Thus, every plant must produce flowers in order for the species to survive. Often these flowers are so small that they escape our attention. Other times we look at them without being more than dimly aware that they are flowers at all—such as in the case of cauliflower and broccoli, two flowers which we grow with scant recognition of their biological status.

Since every plant produces flowers, our choice of ornamental flowering plants for the home garden is enormous. Out of the thousands and thousands of varieties available to us, however, we have narrowed down our choices to several hundred—perhaps a thousand—which include those plants which produce blossoms large enough, showy enough, and colorful enough to capture our attention and affection. The most attractive of these have been captured by plant breeders, who have improved them by generations of breeding and crossbreeding, until the most desirable characteristics of each variety are accentuated to the fullest extent possible.

Perhaps the most outstanding example of this breeding process are the hybrid tea roses, while at the other end of the scale are the many native wild flowers of Wisconsin. But there are disadvantages as well as advantages in growing the highly bred varieties. Hybrid tea roses, for instance, have been so finely bred that they have lost most of their natural resistance to insects and diseases. It is virtually impossible to grow them successfully without spraying, dusting, meticulous pruning, and special winter care. A common wild flower such as the blue wood violet (*Viola papilonacea*, our official state flower), however, will grow freely and without care, once we have provided it with a suitable environment in which it can carry out its natural cycle.

In between hybrid tea roses and wood violets, there are hundreds and hundreds of flowering plants of all shapes and sizes, and with blooms of every imaginable color and form, from which we can choose to complete our garden schemes. If you do not want to devote the bulk of your gardening time to growing flowers, then you will pick those varieties that require relatively little care and which are fairly resistant to insects and diseases. Probably, you already have some experience in flower gardening, and you have some old favorites which you call upon each year. You might wish to expand upon this group by adding one or two new varieties annually. But, if you have never grown flowers before, it will be

A well-planned flower garden will bring color, beauty, and fragrance to your home from early spring until the first hard frosts of autumn.

In the flower beds, a cocoa bean shell mulch is both attractive and practical. The shells can be lifted and stored in the fall.

best for you to begin with some of the easier-grown plants—spring-flowering bulbs, of course, marigolds, petunias, and zinnias among the annuals, peonies, phlox, and lilies among the perennials, and perhaps chrysanthemums and asters for fall bloom. This small sampling will provide color from early spring until the first hard frosts of fall, and these plants can be grown with little trouble from insects and diseases. There are, of course, many more which will fit into the easily-grown category, and you have only to study a few of the nursery and seed catalogs to get some idea of the huge array of offerings. Most are well suited to Wisconsin's soil and climate, especially if they are offered by a northern nursery.

LATIN CLASSIFICATIONS

In dealing with vegetable varieties, there are not so many as to require us to call upon their Latin names. When it comes to flowering ornamentals, however, the Latin nomenclature is sometimes useful, especially since many flowering plants have more than one common name and since so many varieties are often found within a single species which goes by a single name. The home flower gardener will sometimes use Latin names to get exactly what he wants, and it will do us no harm to understand the very fundamentals of the game. A good and concise explanation of the Latin classification system appears in Norman C. Fassett's *Spring Flora of Wisconsin* (University of Wisconsin Press, 4th ed., 1975):

> Plants are grouped into species. A species is composed of all the individuals in existence which resemble each other closely enough to be considered of one kind. Species are grouped into genera, and the name of a plant is composed of the generic name followed by the specific name. Thus we have grouped under the genus *Cypripedium* the various species, or kinds, of Lady's Slipper: *Cypripedium arietinum*, the Ram's Head Lady's Slipper; *Cypripedium candidum*, the White Lady's Slipper; *Cypripedium acaule*, the Stemless Lady's Slipper. Genera are grouped into families; *Cypripedium*, *Habenaria*, *Orchis*, and various others are included in the *Orchidaceae*, or Orchid Family. Family names, with a few exceptions, end in *-aceae*.

In addition, we must deal with the term *variety*. None is used more loosely in discussing horticultural matters. It can be used to refer to nearly any classification of plants, but botanically speaking, it denotes a group of plants within a species which are different from other members of the species, but not different enough to have earned individual species names. *Parthenocissus tricuspidata veitchii*, for instance, is a climbing plant of the genus *Parthenocissus* (the grape family), the species *tricuspidata* (meaning, literally, "with three sharp, stiff points"), and the variety *veitchii*, which finally identifies the plant as Boston ivy.

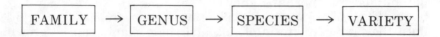

That done, we will do our best to avoid Latin classifications for the rest of this chapter, preferring to stay with the common names. Boston ivy will remain Boston ivy, and *Parthenocissus tricuspidata veitchii* will be given back to the botanists.

Spider plant or cleome (foreground) is only one of many spectacular annuals that can brighten Wisconsin gardens.

PLANNING THE FLOWER GARDEN

There can be no recommended flower garden plan for your home, because any plan will necessarily depend on variables that only you can identify: the size and location of your house, the contour of your ground, the nature of your permanent landscape plantings, the patterns of sunlight and shade on your grounds, your soil and climate, and—most important— your individual preferences.

There are, nevertheless, a few general rules—suggestions, really—which might be considered in making any garden plan. Some are so obvious that I hesitate to even list them—and yet I have seen twelve-inch marigolds struggling behind five-foot dahlias, and I have seen large tulip beds in front of houses, breathtakingly beautiful in May, but creating a large brown and lifeless patch for the rest of the summer. The following rules, then, are presented both with apologies and with the hope that at least one or two of them might improve your own individual plan:

1. **Plan for season-long bloom.** Don't concentrate solely on spring-flowering plants, but do plant annuals among the spring bulbs as soon as they have finished blooming. The fast-growing annuals will soon hide the brown foliage of the tulips and daffodils. Don't plant masses of chrysanthemums and dahlias without some shorter-growing and earlier-blooming flowers in front of them. Marigolds, for instance, will keep dahlias colorful company until the end of August or the beginning of September, when the dahlias come into bloom, and the short-growing marigolds will not interfere with the development of the dahlias.

2. **Don't scatter plants too thinly.** Mass groupings of flowering plants are far more effective than single plants scattered here and there, and your garden space is conserved in this way, too. This does not mean that a grouping must comprise only one variety or species, but simply that flower beds are more pleasing than scattered flowering lants.

3. **Don't be afraid to mix annuals and perennials in the same bed.** You may plan a perennial bed, but do not be afraid to add annuals if they will serve the desired aesthetic purposes.

4. **Plan your flower garden to suit the character of your home and grounds.** Follow natural contours of the ground. Soften harsh lines of the house with tall-growing and graceful plants, but do not make your flowers compete with the more ornate features of the house. Try to visualize each plant growing and blooming in its place. Go so far as to take a color print of the house and sketch in, with oils, the flowering plants you are considering.

5. **Avoid rectangular or other stiffly formal flower beds,** unless you are certain that they will fit best into your scheme. Generally, gracefully curved beds are more pleasing to the eye. You can form these curves by laying down the garden hose and moving it around until you have come upon the shape that seems right. Then cut away the sod to make the bed.

6. **Do not plant short plants behind tall plants.** Know the varieties of the plants you buy, and know their expected heights at maturity.

7. **Don't plant a monocolor garden.** A "blue bed" or a "pink bed" might seem to be a delightful idea in conception, but in reality it will probably bore you stiff. There are few colors that nature cannot mix with grace. Generally, you will achieve gratifying results by using old favorites as the core of your collection, mixing colors freely.

8. **Consider the family's use of the yard when planning flower beds.** It won't make much sense, for instance, to plant your prize hybrid teas where your kids have traditionally played baseball, or to make the yard off-limits for family enjoyment of outdoor activities. Fit flower beds into the total scheme of home use and enjoyment.

ANNUALS FOR WISCONSIN

Annuals are probably the most popular flowering plants, and for several very good reasons. They are easy to grow. They are inexpensive to buy. They require relatively little care. They produce results quickly, often blooming within a few weeks after germinating. They offer a huge variety of colors, shapes, and sizes. And many of them bloom continually from midspring until the first hard frosts of autumn. Annuals are hard to beat—but, as their name suggests, they complete their life cycle in one short season. Next year, they must be planted all over again.

Soil. Annuals will grow well in most good garden soils, although most prefer a loose and well-drained sandy loam that has been well supplied with compost. Annuals are plants in a hurry, since they must complete their life cycle—from their own germination to the final production of seed—in one short Wisconsin season. And, because of their urgency, they need relatively large amounts of nutrients. It will be best to dig copious amounts of compost into the annual beds during the autumn preceding spring planting. If you have not done this, however, you may dig in well-aged compost in the early spring, as soon as the ground can be worked—but in this case, it should be screened compost that will not impede the germination of seeds. Feeding during the season should be made in the form of compost tea, if it is made at all. The roots of most annuals are shallow and easily disturbed by cultivation, and so side dressings of compost are not recommended.

Location. Most annuals do best in a sunny and open location. None will do well in total shade, but some will bloom quite well in partial shade, including the following: sweet alyssum, snapdragon, sweet-sultan, cornflower, China aster, clarkia, cynoglossum, California poppy, godetia, balsam, lupine, mimulus, forget-me-not, nemophelia, flowering tobacco, pansy, petunia, schizanthus, ageratum, calendula, nocotiana, zinnia, cleome, cornflower, lobelia, nasturtium, wishbone-flower (*Torenia fournieri*), and impatiens.

If you have an area with very little sun, there are a few other considerations you should heed. First, try to remove some of the sources of the shade, if at all possible. A tree might be pruned judiciously, in order to let more light come through, or an old board fence might come down and be replaced by a wire fence. Soil drainage should be checked carefully, too, since the soil in dim places tends to stagnate and become heavy and waterlogged. Last, some authorities remind us that the white varieties of any species will do better in shade than those of different colors.

If you are faced with total shade, however, you will be better off in planting ground covers and certain perennials recommended for deep shade.

Culture. Nearly all common garden vegetables are annual plants, and are grown in much the same way as are flowering annuals. And, since we have covered the culture of garden vegetables extensively in Chapter 4, it would serve no point here in going over the same material for a second time. I refer you, then, to Chapter 4 for directions and suggestions for starting seeds, preparing seed beds, transplanting young plants and thinning them, and on weed control, watering, and general care during the growing season. In addition, the principles that were set down in the chapters on soil, on composting and mulching, and on climate and weather, apply to flower growing as well as vegetable growing, and should be studied carefully.

Plants or seeds? Your best chance for success with annuals lies in buying young plants from a local nursery or garden center in the spring. These are usually popular varieties which are placed on sale at the proper planting time, and they are varieties that will grow in your area. Of course, your choice of varieties will grow tremendously if you buy seeds by mail order—but, then, your chances for success will not be so high. If you do choose to buy seeds, chances for success will be greater if you sow them directly into the garden at the proper time in spring. You can, of course,

Table 11. GERMINATION TIME FOR GARDEN
          FLOWER SEEDS

Plant	Days	Plant	Days
Ageratum	5-8	Godetia	12-15
Alyssum	4-5	Heliotrope	15-18
Anchusa	18-20	Hollyhock	15-18
Arctotis	12-15	Larkspur (annual)	15-18
Baby's breath	18-20	Lobelia	8-10
Balsam	5-8	Marigold	5-8
Butterfly weed	10-12	Mignonette	8-10
Calendula	8-10	Morning glory	8-10
Candytuft	5-8	Nasturtium	8-10
Canterbury bells	12-15	Nicotiana	18-20
Clarkia	7-10	Nigella	8-10
Cockscomb	5-8	Pansy	10-12
Columbine	15-18	Pea, sweet	15-18
Coreopsis	15-20	Penstemon	18-20
Cornflower	5-8	Periwinkle	15-18
Cosmos	5-8	Petunia	10-18
Dahlia	8-10	Phlox (annual)	15-18
Delphinium	10-15	Poppy (Iceland)	18-20
Dianthus	8-10	Portulaca	15-18
English daisy	5-8	Sage, blue	12-15
Forget-me-not	12-15	Shasta daisy	18-21
Four-o'clock	5-8	Strawflower	5-8
Gaillardia	15-20	Zinnia	5-8

Courtesy, *Organic Gardening and Farming*

start plants from seed indoors or in a hotbed or cold frame. You will gain several weeks in doing so, but there is a lot of work connected with the process which does not seem—at least to many people—to balance the results to be expected. Unless you plan to spend a great amount of time in experimenting with different annual varieties, then, you can probably achieve easiest success by spending a few dollars to buy started plants at the local nursery or garden center.

Planting times. Started plants or seeds of most annuals should not be set outside until all danger of frost has passed. The ideal soil temperature for the germination and early growth of these half-hardy and tender annuals is sixty to seventy degrees. If the soil is much cooler than that, the seeds will simply not germinate and started plants will not grow larger.

Exceptions to the rule are these hardy annuals that can be set out in the early spring, as soon as the soil can be worked: babys-breath, cornflower, gaillardia, globe-amaranth, phlox, poppy, sal-piglossia, cleome, stock, strawflower, summer-cypress, sweet alys-sum, and sweetpea. Recommendations for planting times are given on the backs of most seed packets.

Removing wilted flowers. One important rule to observe in growing annuals is to remove wilted and dried flowers almost daily. If the flowers are allowed to produce seeds, the plant will have completed the final stage of its life cycle and will stop produc-ing new blossoms. In order to keep each plant producing blossoms, then, you must remove the old flowers before they have begun to produce seed pods.

Sixty-four annuals for Wisconsin. Table 12 lists sixty-four an-nual flowering plants that will grow well in Wisconsin's climate. This list is by no means exhaustive, but it will give you an idea of the range of annuals that is open to you. You can learn much more about the characteristics of different annuals by sending for several seed catalogs during the late winter and early spring. Particularly recommended for showing various annuals in color are Burpee's and Wayside Gardens', both of which have, for the past several years, been printed in full or nearly full color.

Table 12. ANNUALS FOR WISCONSIN GARDENS

Plant	Height (inches)	Best Uses	Remarks
Ageratum	6 to 20	Edging	Tall varieties grown for cut flowers. Good rock-garden plant. Pot and bring in house for winter bloom.
Amaranthus	36 to 72	Beds, Borders	Brilliant red to deep-red leaves. Shrublike.

Anchusa	up to 18	Beds, Borders	Deep blue flowers in June and July. Needs full sun.
Arctotis (African daisy)	up to 36	Beds	Large daisylike blooms all summer and fall. Prefers sandy soil and full sun.
Babysbreath	12 to 18	Borders	Source of cut flowers and plants for drying. Grows well on alkaline soils.
Balsam	20 to 28	Bedding	Good window-garden plant. Will not tolerate wet or cold weather.
Brachycome	9 to 12	Edging, rock gardens	Profusion of small flowers all summer and fall. Prefers full sun.
Browallia	10 to 24	Borders	Blooms blue to lavender. Likes moist soil and partial shade.
Calendula	14 to 18	Bedding	Source of cut flowers. Good window-garden plant. Needs full sun, cool, moist soil.
California poppy	10 to 12	Beds, borders	Free-flowering and easy to grow. Likes sandy soil and full sun.
Callispsis	18 to 24	Bedding, edging	Blooms quickly, lasts all summer. Needs full sun.
Candytuft	9 to 12	Edging, bedding	Good rock garden plant and filler. Select dwarf varieties for bedding.
Carnation	15 to 18	Beds, borders	Popular cut flower. Is biennial, but will bloom first year if planted early.
China-aster	12 to 24	Bedding	Good source of cut flowers.
Clarkia	up to 24	Beds, borders	Easy to grow, does best in cooler areas. Prefers dry semishade.
Cockscomb	16 to 40	Bedding	Source of cut flowers and plants for drying. Will tolerate partial shade.
Coleus	20 to 24	Bedding	Perennial, really; grown for its decorative foliage.
Cornflower	16 to 36	Bedding	Source of cut flowers. New double blossoms are impressive.

Cosmos	30 to 48	Screens, bedding	Source of cut flowers. Good background plants. Needs full sun.
Dahlia (seed-grown)	18 to 40	Bedding, edging	Source of cut flowers. Blooms early. Needs good soil, full sun.
English daisy	up to 6	Borders, rock gardens	Likes moist, well-drained soil, partial shade. Not really an annual, but nursery plants will bloom the first year.
Everlasting flower	12 to 36	Beds, borders	Will grow almost anywhere, but prefers dry soil and full sun.
Forget-me-not	8 to 12	Beds, borders	Source of cut flowers. Does not withstand intense heat.
Four-o'clock	20 to 24	Beds, borders	Neat, regular, closely-branching; multicolored blossoms. Plant in sun or partial shade.
Gaillardia	12 to 18	Borders	Source of cut flowers and plants for drying. Needs full sun.
Geranium	up to 24	Beds, borders	Easy to grow from seed. Likes full sun.
Globe-amaranth	18 to 24	Borders	Good for cut flowers and for drying. Likes hot, dry location.
Godetia	10 to 36	Beds, borders	Likes moist, cool soil and partial shade.
Heliotrope	12 to 24	Bedding	Will succeed in any good soil in full sun.
Hollyhock	24 to 96	Screens, beds	Dwarf varieties now available. Likes warm weather and full sun. Plant annual varieties early.
Impatiens	10 to 12	Bedding	Perennial grown as annual. Good plant for window gardens. Will take deep shade.
Kochia	30 to 60	Beds,	Also called burning bush. Green foliage turns brilliant red in autumn.

Larkspur	18 to 48	Screens	Source of cut flowers and plants for drying. Make successive sowings for cut flowers.
Lobelia	4 to 18	Borders, edging, rock gardens	Blooms well in partial shade.
Lupine	18 to 24	Borders	Source of cut flowers. Prefers dry, sandy soil.
Marigold	6 to 30	Bedding	Most popular of all annuals. Good for cut flowers, window gardens. Likes full sun. Excessive nitrogen delays blooming.
Mignonette	6 to 18	Beds, borders	Good fragrance. Likes moist soil and partial shade.
Morning-glory	(climber)	Screens	Vine grows 8 to 12 feet tall. Vigorous once started.
Nasturtium	12 to 72	Beds, borders, screens	Blooms one month after sowing. Likes full sun. Poor soil will produce more blossoms, less foliage.
Nicotiana	15 to 48	Beds, borders	Ornamental tobacco. Easy to grow, blooms profusely summer and fall. Likes moist soil and partial shade.
Nigella	18 to 24	Beds, borders	Short blooming season, but a fine range of colors.
Pansy	6 to 10	Beds, borders	Source of cut flowers. Pot plants after bloom, protect for over winter. Replace with petunia for summer bloom.
Petunia	8 to 24	Bedding	Good plant for window gardens. Long blooming period.
Phlox	6 to 15	Bedding	Withstands heat. More compact than petunias.
Pink	6 to 16	Edging, borders	Source of cut flowers. Long-blooming, bright colors.

Poppy	12 to 16	Borders	Source of cut flowers, Make successive sowings for longer bloom.
Portulaca	6 to 9	Bedding, edging, rock gardens	Bright colors. Withstands heat.
Rudbeckia	20 to 24	Borders, bedding	Source of cut flowers. Loves heat.
Salpiglossis	24 to 30	Bedding	Source of cut flowers. Does not withstand heat. Blooms midsummer to frost.
Salvia	7 to 24	Beds, borders, edging	Blooms profusely and brilliantly from midsummer until frost. Best to buy started plants to set out when weather and soil have warmed up.
Scabiosa	18 to 36	Borders	Source of cut flowers. Remove dead flowers for greater bloom.
Scarlet sage	14 to 36	Borders, bedding	Short varieties bloom early and are best for Wisconsin.
Snapdragon	10 to 36	Bedding	Source of cut flowers. Dwarf varieties good for window gardens. Sun or partial shade.
Spider plant	30 to 36	Borders, hedges	Long blooming period.
Stock	24 to 30	Bedding	Source of cut flowers. Good plant for window gardens.
Strawflower	30 to 40	Bedding	One of best plants for drying. Grows well in a variety of locations, but prefers hot sun.
Sunflower	48 to 84	Screens, borders	See cultural directions in chapter on vegetables.
Sweet alyssum	6 to 10	Edging, borders	Grow in well-drained soil. Damps off easily. Neat and free flowering. Long blooming period.
Sweetpea	(climber)	Screens	Vine, grows 4 to 8 feet long. Source of cut flowers.

Tithonia	36 to 72	Screens, hedges	A large and vigorous plant with three-inch orange-colored blossoms. Good for cut flowers.
Torenia	8 to 12	Borders, rock gardens	Compact and bushy plants will do well in full sun or partial shade. Blooms during summer and fall.
Verbena	9 to 12	Bedding	Source of cut flowers. Cover spots left by spring-flowering bulbs.
Vinca	15 to 18	Bedding	Perennial grown as annual. Good plant for window gardens.
Zinnia	18 to 36	Bedding	Popular source of cut flowers. Endures heat. Foliage frequently mildews. Wide choice of colors.

(Note: In the listings above, you will see some plants—such as dahlia and geranium—that we do not usually think of as annuals. They are included because certain varieties of these species can be grown from seed and will produce as annuals. They will also be treated in later parts of this chapter, however, under the classifications in which we usually expect to find them.)

BIENNIALS

Biennials are plants which require two seasons to complete their life cycle. Generally, flowering biennials are planted during the summer of the first year, and they bloom during the second year.

The use of biennials in home gardens is not so popular as it once was, probably because the extra care they require is not thought to be worth the results they bring — and also because it is so simple and inexpensive to buy second-year biennials from the nursery, ready to bloom. Also, there seems to be a general lack of desire to prepare a bed and sow flower seeds in June and July, when we are already surrounded by blooming annuals and perennials. Last, plant breeders have developed annual varieties of some of the popular biennials, so that the extra effort in starting and overwintering plants is seldom necessary.

The most popular biennials are canterbury bells, sweet william, foxglove, hollyhocks, rose campion (these, the more hardy), pansies, forget-me-not, English daisies, and English wallflowers (these, less hardy). Others include Siberian wallflower, cup-and-saucer, steeple-bellflower, honesty, and hornpoppy.

The cultivation of biennials in Wisconsin is a chancy thing, at any rate, because of our severe winter climate. In southern areas of the United States, the young plants can overwinter without much difficulty. Here, however, special winter protection is an absolute necessity. Seeds are sown in June or July, depending on the variety, and the young plants are transplanted into a cold frame in September, where they are covered with straw and left to overwinter in a dormant state. In spring they are transplanted into their permanent garden locations.

The only advantage of growing biennials in this way is that they will provide some nice color early in the season, when the annuals are just getting started. Even this advantage, however, is largely obviated by the efficient services of the local garden center or nursery, which can supply the same plants in ready-to-bloom state, at the same time of the year.

PERENNIALS FOR BUSY GARDENERS

Perennials should form the backbone of the flower garden. They produce a maximum of bloom with a minimum of care, and they reappear year after year, soon becoming old and trusted friends.

Strictly speaking, perennials are plants which live for more than two years. Under this definition, trees and shrubs qualify as perennials — and, indeed, they are. But when the gardener speaks of perennials, he is speaking of herbacious flowering plants whose tops die down each fall, but whose roots remain alive to produce new top growth and bloom during the following year. Some of the most popular perennials in Wisconsin are chrysanthemums, asters, delphiniums, peonies, phlox, and daylilies. But there are scores of perennials that will find a happy home in Wisconsin's rugged climate — especially if they are given a little winter protection. Your selection of varieties should be dictated only by the growing conditions in your garden and your aesthetic sense.

Planning for perennials. Since you hope to keep your hardy perennials in one location for a number of years, you should exercise considerable care in planning the beds. Perennials can be divided and transplanted, of course, but there is no sense in doing this unless and until the plant really needs it. Take into consideration, then, each variety's expected mature height, sun and shade requirements, time of blooming, and hardiness. In this section we will recommend only the more hardy perennials that can take Wisconsin's winters, although gardeners in the colder areas of the state should be conscientious in providing extra winter protection — while those in the southern portion of Wisconsin can find many additional options in garden catalogs.

Soil. Nearly all perennials like a light, rich, and well-drained soil, one that is capable of holding adequate moisture without being heavy. It will reward your efforts to prepare the perennial beds carefully in advance. Till the soil eighteen to twenty-four inches deep and incorporate plenty of compost, manure, peat moss (or leaf mold), and bone meal (four to seven pounds per 100 square feet).

Sun and shade. Most perennials prefer full sun. Many will grow in light shade, while only a few will bloom in the deep shade of large trees and buildings.

The perennials that will do best in deep shade are bugleweed, bleeding heart (*Dicentra eximia*), and several varieties of phlox (including *Phlox arendsi* and *Phlox divaricata*).

There are many perennials that will do well in partial or light shade, and these are cited in the listings of individual perennials, beginning on page 249.

Hardiness. Most common garden perennials are hardy in Wisconsin, although some are naturally hardier than others. The best way to discover which are definitely hardy in your area is to check with your local nursery or observe those plants in other local gardens. Don't be afraid to ask friends and neighbors about their own favorite perennials. The conversation might even lead to the neighbor's sharing some root divisions with you.

Planning for continuing bloom. Many perennials have comparatively short blooming periods, even though the blooms during these times may be spectacular. A typical example familiar to nearly all of us is the peony, which is found growing everywhere in Wisconsin because of its remarkable hardiness and vigor. Its blooming period is short — only a week or two — while that of marigolds, the popular annual, lasts from spring right up until the first hard frosts of autumn. But we grow peonies because of the breathtaking glory of that short bloom, just as we welcome marigolds for their long and cheerful service.

The perennial garden, then, should be planned so that there is some bloom during as much of the growing season as possible. The following guide will help. Remember, though, that this is a guide and not a guarantee. These perennials might bloom a week or two earlier or later, depending on which section of the state is their host. Generally, however, you can assure a continuing parade of bloom (although not continuous bloom) by choosing at least one perennial from each of the following groups:

April-blooming perennials: Anchusa, arabis, bleeding heart, dwarf anchusa *(Brunnera macrophylia)*, forget-me-not, primrose, and Virginia bluebell *(Mertensia virginica)*.

May-blooming perennials: Anchusa, anthemis, arabis, armeria, artemisia, aubrietia, bleeding heart, bugleweed, daylily, dwarf anchusa *(Brunnera macrophylia)*, forget-me-not, gas plant, iberis, painted daisy, primrose, trollius, and Virginia bluebell *(Mertensia virginica)*.

June-blooming perennials: Achillea, agrostemma, alyssum, anthemis, armeria, artemisia, astilbe, baby's breath, balloon flower, blue flax, bugleweed, columbine, coral bells, coreopsis, cupid's dart *(Catananche caerulea)*, daylily, cornflower, delphinium, forget-me-not, gaillardia, gas plant, geum, heliotrope, iberis, lychnis, myrtle, nepeta, oenothera, oriental poppy, painted daisy, penstemon, peony, pink, shasta daisy, sidalcea, snow-in-summer *(Cerastium tomentosum)*, sweet william, trollius, verbena, and viola.

July-blooming perennials: Achillea, agrostemma, alyssum, anthemis, artemisia, astilbe, baby's breath, balloon flower, beebalm, blue flax, cimifuga, columbine, coral bells, coreopsis, cornflower, cupid's dart *(Catananche caerulea)*, daylily, delphinium, gaillardia, geum, harebell, heliotrope, hosta, lupine, lychnis, lythrum, myrtle, nepeta, cenothera, oriental poppy, painted daisy, penstemon, peony, perennial pea *(Lathyrus latifolius)*, phlox, physostegia, pink, scutellario, shasta daisy, sidalcea, sweet william, trollius, verbena, veronica, and viola.

August-blooming perennials: Alyssum, anthemis, artemisia, baby's breath, balloon flower, beebalm, boltonia, cimifuga, coreopsis, cupid's dart *(Catananche caerulea)*, daylily, cornflower, gaillardia, geum, golden glow, harebell, helenium, hosta, lythrum, monkshood, myrtle, nepeta, oenothera, penstemon, perennial pea *(Lathyrus latifolius)*, phlox, physostegia, pink, scutellario, sedum, verbena, veronica, and viola.

September-blooming perennials: Anthemis, artemisia, aster, baby's breath, boltonia, chrysanthemum, coreopsis, cornflower, gaillardia, golden glow, harebell, helenium, hosta, lythrum, monkshood, myrtle, nepeta, penstemon, perennial pea *(Lathyrus latifolius)*, physostegia, pink, verbena, and veronica.

October-blooming perennials: Aster, chrysanthemum, coreopsis, gaillardia, nepeta, penstemon, and pink.

November-blooming perennials: Gardeners in the southern part of the state can hope for some November bloom, particularly if they take precautions against the first hard frosts. When frost is forecast, cover your favorite perennials with large plastic trash bags. Anchor the bags at the bottom so that the heat rising from the soil cannot escape readily. After the sun is well up in the sky the next day, the bags can be removed easily and the plants can again receive the warm rays of the sun. You can prolong bloom for several weeks in this way — but the day will come when you will at last have to put the perennials to bed for the winter.

Starting perennials. There are various ways in which you can build up a collection of perennial flowering plants. The least expensive is to prevail upon your friends and neighbors to share clump divisions, or to give you cuttings. Perennials usually should be divided about every three years, anyway, in order to keep the plants vigorous and thriving. The best time for dividing is in the early spring, although it can be done in fall, too, if you can do it at least four weeks before the first hard frosts. (Fall-blooming perennials, however, should not be divided in the fall.)

When a perennial has been in one spot too long, the center of its root clump will become crowded and weak. You will want to discard the center of the clump, while dividing the vigorous outside shoots into new plants. To divide roots, dig up the entire clump, getting as much of the root as you can, wash most of the soil away, and examine the clump to see where the most vigorous growth is taking place. Make the divisions by inserting two garden forks into the clump, back to back, and gradually prying the clump apart. Try to get good-sized divisions, so that they will grow quickly. Then replant these divisions in newly prepared soil.

You can start perennials also by taking and rooting cuttings, although this is sometimes a little tricky. Select vigorous new shoots in spring, and cut them as far down as possible — below the soil line, if they extend beneath the soil. Insert these in moist sand, indoors or in a hotbed, until they have established good roots. Expose the young plants gradually to outside temperatures to harden them off, until they are ready to be transplanted into the perennial beds by midsummer. (The care of young plants is covered in detail in the chapter on vegetables. The principles are the same.)

You can also grow many perennials by sowing seed in the open garden, and these often grow quickly into strong and vigorous plants, since you will not have to nurse them along. Seed should be sown after all danger of frost is past, in finely prepared beds, and the young plants should be thinned and spaced according to directions for the individual variety. You can get an earlier start by sowing seed indoors or in a hotbed or cold frame, although the added burden does not seem to be justified for plants which you hope to establish as permanent plantings.

Perhaps the safest and easiest way to start perennials (although the most expensive) is to buy started plants at a local nursery or garden center. These will have a good chance of growing, even for the beginner, and you will know that the plants you buy are suited for growing in your locality. Also, the plants will probably be in bloom when you buy them, and so you will see the exact colors of the blossoms. Buy plants that are bushy, compact, dark green, and vigorous looking.

Assuring moisture. After your perennials have been established, they should be mulched, in order to conserve moisture and keep down weeds. The best mulch material will be one that is light, porous, and attractive. Buckwheat hulls and cocoa bean shells are two good ones that fill all three requirements. During a particularly long dry spell, you might find that the soil has become dry, despite the mulch. Water the perennials at this time, and be sure to water thoroughly and deeply. A soaker hose is perfect for a perennial bed.

Fertilizing. If you have composted the soil well during the preceding fall, you will not have to feed the plants during the season. However, they will respond to a few applications of compost or manure tea, particularly when they begin to bloom. Older plantings should be fertilized more often — once, when they have begun to make active growth in the spring, again in three weeks, and still again just as they begin to bloom. These feedings, too, can be made in the form of compost or manure tea. In addition, older plants will respond to a light side dressing of compost in the early spring.

Staking. Modern perennials have been bred to bloom heavily, and so the taller of them will need staking for support. Any stakes will do, although the most inconspicuous will be the green cane types sold by garden centers. Tie the stems to the stake with some soft material or with green plastic strips made especially for the purpose. Loop the strip loosely around the plant stem. Make a knot between the stem and the stake, and another around the stake to secure it tightly. Do not endanger the stem by tying a knot tightly around it, or by using wire.

Removing wilted flowers. As with other flowering plants, you should remove wilted flowers regularly, in order to encourage the plant to produce more blossoms.

Winter protection. All but the hardiest of perennials will appreciate a heavy winter mulch to protect their roots from hard freezing and — more important — to prevent root damage during the alternate freezing and thawing of the ground during late winter and early spring. A good mulch keeps the soil temperature at a more constant level, preventing the heaving of the ground that can tear roots apart.

Wait until the ground freezes hard before applying the winter mulch. (The summer mulch need not be removed at all.) When the ground is hard, apply a ten-to-fifteen-inch layer of straw or hay, or even pine boughs, over the plants. When the weather has moderated in April, remove the straw, but do not remove the light summer mulch. Loosen up the summer mulch and, after the plant has made some good growth, replenish the summer mulch to make up for any that might have composted itself into the top layer of soil. The winter straw mulch which you removed can be used to mulch vegetables a little later in the season.

THREE DOZEN PERENNIALS FOR WISCONSIN

The following thirty-six selected perennials (with cultural recommendations based mainly on USDA materials) will constitute a well-rounded group for Wisconsin gardens. All are hardy and most are easy to grow — which is perhaps why this group includes many of the more popular perennials in this section of the country.

This list is, to be sure, far from comprehensive. You can get many more ideas by scanning the seed and nursery catalogs and by checking with your local nursery. But do make sure that any other perennials you choose are hardy in your area.

Achillea. *Achillea millefolium* (yarrow, milfoil) grows about two feel high. It looks best in borders that bloom from June to September. Achillea is grown also for cut flowers. Plant seed in early spring or late fall. Choose a sunny spot in your garden. Space plants thirty-six inches apart. Seed germinates in seven to fourteen days. Because seed is very small, water with a mist. Achillea is easy to grow.

Alyssum. *Alyssum saxatile* (golddust) grows nine to twelve inches high. It is used in rock gardens and for edging and cut flowers. It blooms in early spring. Alyssum is excellent in dry or sandy soil. Plant seed in early spring in a sunny spot. Space plants twenty-four inches apart. Seed germinates in twenty-one to twenty-eight days.

Anchusa. *Anchusa italica* and *Anchusa myosotidiflora* (alkanet, dropmore) grow four to five feet high. They are used for borders and backgrounds, as well as a source of cut flowers. Refrigerate seed for seventy-two hours before sowing. Plant seed anytime from spring to September in a semishaded part of the garden. Shade summer plantings. Space plants twenty-four inches apart. Seed germinates in twenty-one to twenty-eight days.

Anthemis. *Anthemis tinctoria* (golden daisy, golden marguerite, Saint John's daisy) grows about two feet high. It looks best in borders that bloom from midsummer to frost. Anthemis is grown also for cut flowers, which are slightly aromatic. Plants can be started indoors eight weeks before planting outdoors. Or, you can plant seeds outdoors after the soil has warmed in the spring. Anthemis grows well in dry or sandy soil. Plant in a sunny spot. Space plants twenty-four inches apart. Seeds germinate in twenty-one to twenty- eight days.

Arabis. *Arabis alpina* (rockcress) grows eight to twelve inches high. It is used for edging and in rock gardens. Plant seed in well-drained soil anytime from spring to September. It grows best in light shade. Shade summer plantings. Space plants about twelve inches apart. Seed germinates in about five days.

Armeria. *Armeria alpina* (sea pink, thrift) grows eighteen to twenty-four inches high. It is used in rock gardens, edging, and borders. The dwarf tufted plants are also used as cut flowers. Plant seed in dry, sandy soil anytime between spring and September. Space plants twelve inches apart in a sunny part of the garden. Shade the seed bed until plants are sturdy. Seed germinates in about ten days.

Artemisia. *Artemisia stelleriana* (wormwood, dusty miller) grows about two feet high. It is used in beds, borders, and rock gardens. Plant seed in full sun from late spring to late summer. It grows even in poor and dry soils. Space plants nine to twelve inches apart.

Asters. Fall-blooming asters grow from one to five feet high. They are used in rock gardens, borders, and for cut flowers, as one of our most popular late-blooming perennials. Plant seed in early spring in a sunny spot. Space plants about three feet apart. Seed germinates in fourteen to twenty-one days.

Astilbe. *Astilbe japonica* (florists' spirea) grows one to three feet high. It is used in borders. Plant seed in early spring in rich, loamy soil. Space plants twenty-four inches apart. Seed germinates in fourteen to twenty-one days. Likes partly shady spot.

Aubrieta. *Aubrieta deltoidea graeca* (rainbow rockcress) grows about six inches high. It is grown in borders and rock gardens and along dry walls. Aubrieta is a dwarf, spreading plant. Sow seed anytime from spring to September in light shade. Space plants about twelve inches apart. Seed will germinate in about twenty days. Shade plants in summer. To propagate, divide mature plants in late summer.

Baby's breath. *Gypsophila paniculata* grows two to four feet high. It is used for borders and as a source of cut flowers and flowers for drying. It does best in a deeply prepared soil that is

Asters provide late-season bloom in a variety of forms. Included above are decorative, button, and dwarf varieties.

high in lime content. Plant seeds anytime from early spring to September in a sunny spot. Space plants about four feet apart. Seed germinates in about ten days.

Bleeding heart. *Dicentra spectabilis* grows two to four feet high. A smaller variety, *Dicentra cucullaria* (Dutchman's breeches) grows one foot tall. They are used for borders, in front of shrubbery, and as pot plants. Plant seed in late autumn. Space plants twelve to eighteen inches apart. Seed will germinate in the following spring.

Cerastium. *Cerastium tomentosum* (snow-in-summer) grows about six inches high. It is used in rock gardens and for ground cover. Plants form a creeping mat. Cerastium does well in dry and sunny spots. Plant seed in early spring. Space plants about eighteen inches apart. Seed germinates in fourteen to twenty-eight days. Cerastium is a hard, tough plant, and a rampant grower. Do not allow it to crowd out other plants.

Chrysanthemums. Mums are popular all over Wisconsin, because of their profusion of fall bloom and their great variety. The major types include the singles, pompons (the kind associated with football corsages), anemones, spoons, and spiders, depending on the form of their blossoms. Plant mums in a rich and well-drained soil, in a sunny location. You can buy field-grown clumps in spring (which generally must be divided before planting) or you can start cuttings. Gift plants which you receive can be planted, too. Let the gift plants finish blooming indoors, then cut them back to two to three inches above the pot rim. Plant them outside in spring, after danger of frost has passed. Chrysanthemums winterkill quite easily, and so a heavy mulch is necessary. Do not choose the late-blooming varieties, which might have trouble reaching the blooming stage in Wisconsin's short growing season.

Columbine. Columbine hybrids (Aquilegia) grow thirty to thirty-six inches high. They are used for borders and for cut flowers. Columbine needs fairly rich, well-drained soil. Plant seed anytime from spring to September in sun or partial shade. Space plants twelve to eighteen inches apart. Seed germinates in about thirty days, but germination is irregular. It is often grown as a biennial to avoid leaf miner and crown rotting.

Coral Bells. *Heuchera sanguinea* grows up to two feet high. It is used for rock gardens, borders, and cut flowers. It grows best in a limed soil. Plant seed in early spring or late fall in partial shade. Space plants about eighteen inches apart. Seed germinates in about ten days. Propagate by division.

Coreopsis. *Coreopsis grandiflora* grows two to three feet high. It is used in borders. Plant seed in a light loam in early spring or late fall. Choose a sunny spot in the garden. Space plants about thirty inches apart. Seed takes about five days to germinate. Coreopsis is drought resistant. It is best grown as a biennial.

Daylily. Hemerocallis grows one to four feet high. To have daylily flowers throughout the growing season, plant various species of this perennial. Daylily is used in borders and among shrubbery. Plant seed in late fall or early spring in full sunlight or partial shade. Space plants twenty-four to thirty inches apart. Seed germinates in fifteen days.

Delphinium. *Delphinium elatum* grows four to five feet high. It is used for borders, background, and cut flowers. Plant seed anytime from spring to September in a well-drained and sunny spot. Plants tend to rot in wet, heavy soils. Space plants twenty-four inches apart. Seed germinates in about twenty days. Shade summer plantings. Foliage tends to mildew. Early staking is recommended.

Dianthus. *Dianthus deltoides* and *Dianthus plumarius* (pinks) grow about a foot high. They are used for borders, rock gardens, edging, and cut flowers. Plant seed anytime from spring to September in a sunny spot. Space plants twelve inches apart. Seed germinates in five days. Dianthus is best when grown as a biennial. It is winterkilled in wet locations and is very susceptible to rotting at the soil line.

Gaillardia. *Gaillardia grandiflora* grows twelve to thirty inches high. It is used in borders and for cut flowers. Gaillardia is easily grown from seed, which you can plant in early spring or late summer. Choose a sunny spot in your garden. Space plants twenty-four inches apart. Seed germinates in about twelve days.

Geum. *Geum chiloense* grows six to twenty-four inches high. It is used in borders and rock gardens and for cut flowers. Geum will grow in many different locations. You can plant seed in spring or summer in a sunny spot. Space plants about eighteen inches apart. Seed germinates in twenty-five days. Geum is winter hardy if you give it plenty of protection.

Lupine. *Lupine polyphyllus* grows to about three feet high. It is used in borders and for cut flowers. Plant seed in early spring or late fall in a sunny spot that has perfect drainage. Soak seeds before planting, and inoculate them with the same bacterial agent used for peas. Plant seed where lupine is to flower, since it does not transplant well. Space plants about thirty-six inches apart. Seed germinates in about twenty days.

Lythrum. Lythrum (blackblood) grows four to six feet high. Use it scattered in gardens and yards or among trees and shrubs. Plant seed in late fall or early spring in a moist, lightly-shaded area. Space plants eighteen to twenty-four inches apart. Seed germinates in fifteen days.

Oriental Poppy. *Papaver orientale* grows about three feet high. It is used in borders and for cut flowers. Plant seed in early spring in a permanent location, because it does not transplant well. Choose a sunny spot. Space plants two feet apart. Seed germinates in about ten days.

Penstemon. *Penstemon murrayanus grandiflorus* (beardlip, pagoda flower, beard-tongue) grows eighteen to twenty-four inches high. It is used in borders and for cut flowers. It grows best in well-drained soil and does well in rather dry soil. Plant seed in early spring or late fall in a sunny spot that is sheltered in winter. Space plants eighteen inches apart. Seed germinates in about ten days.

Peony. Peony grows two to four feet tall. It is used in borders and for cut flowers. It is difficult to grow from seed. Plant tubers in late fall at least three feet apart and two to three inches deep.

Phlox, summer. *Phlox paniculata* grows to about three feet high. It is used in borders and for cut flowers. Plant seed in late fall or early winter in a sunny spot. Keep seed in refrigerator one month before seeding. Space plants about two feet apart. Keep soil moist. Germination takes about twenty-five days and is very irregular. Plants grown from seed are very variable in color and form.

Phlox, moss. *Phlox subulata* grows four to five inches high and is used in borders. It is normally grown from stolons (shoots). Plant in a sunny spot. Space plants about eight inches apart. Moss phlox is drought resistant.

Platycodon. *Platycodon grandiflorum* (balloon flower) grows about two feet high. It is used for borders and cut flowers. Plant seed anytime between spring and September in a sunny spot. Space plants about twelve inches apart. Seed germinates in ten days. In the fall, dig roots and store in moist sand in a cool (but frost-free) cold frame. Replant in early spring.

Primrose. *Primula polyantha* grows six to nine inches high; *Primula veris* grows six inches high. Primrose is used in rock gardens. Early in the year, sow seed on soil surface in pots; water with mist; cover with glass; place outside to freeze; bring inside to germinate. Seed also can be planted outside in spring if it is first frozen in ice cubes. Usually, seed is planted in late autumn or early winter. Choose a spot in partial shade. Space plants about a foot apart. Seed germinates in about twenty-five days, but is very irregular.

Shasta daisy. *Chrysanthemum maximum* grows twenty-four to thirty inches high. It is used for borders and for cut flowers. Plant seed anytime from early spring to September in a sunny spot. Space plants about thirty inches apart. Seed germinates in about ten days. Shasta daisy is best grown as a biennial. Winter protection, in any case, is essential in Wisconsin.

Sweet william. *Sweet william* grows twelve to eighteen inches high. A dwarf form also is available. It is used for borders, edging, and cut flowers. It is very hardy, but grows best in well-drained soil. Plant seed anytime from spring to September in a sunny spot. Space plants about a foot apart. Seed germinates in five days.

Trollius. *Trollius ledebouri* (globe flower) grows about twenty inches high. It is used in borders. Trollius requires extra moisture.

Plant seed in late fall, in order to allow it to overwinter before germination in the spring. If you want to plant seed in early spring, soak it in hot water for thirty minutes before sowing. Space plants about a foot apart.

Veronica. *Veronica spicata* (speedwell) grows about eighteen inches high. It is used in borders and rock gardens and for cut flowers. It is easily grown. Plant seed anytime from spring to September in a sunny spot. Space plants eighteen inches apart. Seed germinates in about fifteen days.

Viola Cornuta. Tufted pansy grows about six inches high. It is used for bedding, edging, and window boxes. It is easily grown from seed and is very hardy. Plant seed anytime from spring to September in partial shade. Space plants about twelve inches apart. Seed germinates in ten days.

ROSES

The rose stands in a class by itself. It is undoubtedly the most cherished garden flower in America. And its popularity stems not from its ease in growing (it is not easy to grow), nor from its resistance to insects and diseases (it is notoriously susceptible to both), nor for its economy (it is one of the most expensive garden flowering plants to buy and maintain). No, its popularity can be attributed to one reason and one reason only — the sheer magnificance of its bloom. The rose is a delight to the sight and to the scent, and that is the reason why thousands of Wisconsin gardeners take up the challenge of rose growing each year.

The literature on rose growing is so extensive that the books written on this single flower would fill several library shelves. We cannot hope to do justice to rose culture here, for the subject would require an entire book of this size to give it fair treatment of any kind. The best we can hope to do is to present a bare skeleton of information, and then to recommend those rose varieties that are best for Wisconsin's climate. And that is what we will do.

Classes of roses. For all practical purpose, there are five classes of roses: bedding roses, climbing roses, creeping roses, shrub roses, and tree roses.

The bedding roses include the teas and hybrid teas, hybrid perpetuals, and floribundas. Of these, the hybrid teas are by far the most elegant and the most prized by *aficionados*.

There are two general kinds of climbers — ramblers, which produce flowers in clusters, and large-flowered climbers, which produce single blossoms.

Creepers are really climbers which are suited to training along banks and walls. They are hardy and suited to the Wisconsin climate, although their flowers are not spectacular.

Shrub roses are, as their name states, shrublike in structure. They are hardy, and their blossom colors are limited to red, white, and pink. The most famous member of the family, at least to avid organic gardeners, is the *Rosa rugosa*, which provides large and vitamin C-rich rose hips after the blossoms have faded. Many organic gardeners grow *Rosa rugosa* not for its flowering beauty (it isn't that attractive) but for its fruit or hips, which are discussed in greater detail on page 222.

Tree roses are a product of the breeder's art, featuring tall and slender trunks, bushy tops, and many single blossoms of good form and large size.

Growing conditions. Roses need plenty of sun, good air circulation, deeply-prepared and well-drained soil (pH 5.0-6.0), and a lot of attention. The soil should be tilled to a depth of twenty-four inches, and large amounts of aged manure and/or compost should be incorporated into the planting hole or trench. A season-long mulch is advised.

Moisture should be assured throughout the growing season, and the plants should be fertilized monthly, beginning in early spring and ending on August 1. A compost tea, providing that it is a rich mixture, is good for roses.

Pruning. Roses are pruned very much like fruit trees. The old and dead wood should be pruned away in spring. In addition, all branches of bedding, shrub, and tree roses should be cut back to encourage bushier growth and greater blossoming. The wilder kinds of roses need be pruned little, except to remove their deadwood each year.

Hybrid teas in Wisconsin should receive special winter protection. This burlap shield will do the job nicely, especially if straw is then packed around the rose bush.

Winter protection. In Wisconsin, winter protection of roses is absolutely essential. Prize hybrid teas should be cut back to thirty inches in the late fall, and soil should be mounded up to a height of ten to twelve inches. Then, a burlap cover supported by stakes should be placed around each bush. For ultimate protection, you may fill this burlap with hay or straw, so that the bush is entirely encased.

Climbers and ramblers, depending on the hardiness of the variety, might also need protection. If so, remove them from their supports, tie the long canes in a bundle on the ground, and cover them with soil for the winter.

Tree roses are most difficult to protect. The best method is to build a burlap shelter large enough for the plant, and to mound soil and add a heavy mulch to protect the trunk. The trunk can also be wrapped with the material that is used for young trees.

Insects, diseases, and other enemies. Intense breeding has deprived many modern roses of their natural resistance to insects and diseases. The battle will be a continuing one, worthwhile only to those whose love affair with roses is absolutely hopeless. We will begin with field mice and other small rodents, who will gladly set up house in the straw-filled burlap shelters which you erect around the plants for winter protection. The mice will be quite snug in the shelters, and will feast on the rose bark all winter long. The best defense is a delay action — do not add the mulch until the ground has frozen hard and the mice have made other living arrangements.

Fungus diseases that attack roses include black spot, mildew, rust, leaf spot (anthracnose), chlorosis (mosaic), and canker. These can be controlled somewhat by clean cultivation (removing diseased plant parts, removing fallen leaves promptly, removing mulches in spring, etc.) and by buying varieties that are somewhat resistant to attack — but you will probably have to resort to rose dust for really effective control.

The insect enemies of roses are legion: Aphids and rose leaf hoppers will suck the juices from the leaves. Rose saw-fly and rose chafer will, together, attack and eat leaves, buds, and flowers. Rose curculio and climbing cutworm will destroy the buds. Add leaf cutters, leaf rollers, stem girdlers, and rose midge, and you will have some idea of how you will spend your summer in the rose garden. You can keep reasonable control of the situation by handpicking the insects and by clean cultivation — and by applying some of the techniques recommended in Chapter 8 — but you might well have to resort to rose dusts or sprays if you are after perfect plants with perfect blossoms.

(Another consideration is that the insects and diseases that roses attract will often spread to your vegetables, fruit trees, and other flowering ornamentals.)

With all the problems entailed in rose growing, you may wonder why anybody would attempt it in the first place. And the answer is, again, that there is simply no flower in America that can match the classic and timeless grace and beauty of this magnificant flower. Thousands of Wisconsin gardeners will continue the noble struggle for rose perfection — and, each time they succeed in producing a perfect blossom, fresh with morning dew, their victory will be that much sweeter. They will have beaten the odds, overcome adversity, and been rewarded with ultimate beauty.

Roses for Wisconsin. The world-famous Boerner Botanical Gardens in Hales Corners (Milwaukee) features more than three thousand growing rose bushes in their gardens at Whitnall Park. There are 350 varieties included in their impressive collection. Of these, the Boerner staff has named 84 as being "dependably outstanding" for growing in Wisconsin. And, of these 84, only 26 were cited for "above average hardiness." These 26, then, are the very best for all Wisconsin gardens. Here is a listing of them, as reported in the *Milwaukee Journal* (February 17, 1974):

El Capitan. A medium-red grandiflora of medium height.

San Antonio. A tall orange red grandiflora that performed here as a medium red.

Tamango. A dark red floribunda of medium height.

Lucky Lady. A light pink grandiflora of medium height and a 1967 All-America winner.

Manuel Pinto de'Azevedo. A tall pink blend hybrid tea with a fruitlike fragrance.

Marie Antoinette. A medium-pink, tall hybrid tea with a fruitlike fragrance.

Nearly Wild. A medium-pink, low-growing floribunda.

Poulsen's Bedder. A light pink, medium-height floribunda.

Show Girl. A medium-pink, medium-height hybrid tea.

Tip Toes. A pink blend, tall, hybrid tea with a fruitlike fragrance.

Vogue. A pink blend, medium-height floribunda with fruitlike fragrance — a 1952 All-America winner.

Golden Slippers. A yellow blend, low-growing floribunda.

Medallion. A tall-growing, apricot-blend hybrid tea — an All-America winner in 1973.

Golden Jubilee. A medium-yellow, medium-height floribunda.

Golden Wings. A medium-yellow, medium-height shrub rose.

Irish Gold. A low-growing, medium-yellow hybrid tea.

Lemon Spice. A medium-height, medium-yellow hybrid tea with true rose fragrance.

Soeur Therese. A tall, yellow-blend hybrid tea that grows like a grandiflora here.

Deesse. A tall-growing, multicolor pink blend hybrid tea.

Simon Bolivar. A medium-height, orange red hybrid tea.

Iceberg. A medium-height white floribunda with a fruitlike fragrance.

Ice White. A medium-height, white floribunda.

Lily Pons. A medium-height, white hybrid tea with petals that are sometimes light yellow.

Mount Shasta. A medium-height, white grandiflora that grows like a hybrid tea.

White Prince. A medium-height, white hybrid tea.

Heirloom. A medium-height, mauve-colored hybrid tea that grows like a grandiflora and has a fruitlike fragrance.

The other roses included in Boerner's "top 84" included:

Red: Americana, Christian Dior, Chrysler Imperial, Crimson Glory, Grand Slam, Kentucky Derby, Lichterloh, Mister Lincoln, Old Smoothie (a thornless variety), Proud Land, and Scarlet Knight.

Pink: Betty Prior, Camelot, Century Two, Dainty Bess, Electron, First Prize, Garden State, Helen Traubel, Miss All-American Beauty, Permanent Wave, Pink Favorite (very glossy foliage), Pink Parfait, Portrait, Queen Elizabeth, Royal Highness, Rubaiyat, Sonoma, Swarthmore, Sweet Afton, Tiffany.

Orange: Contempo, Old-Timer.

Yellow: Eclipse, Golden Girl, Handsome, King's Ransom, Peace, Yellow Cushion.

Multicolor: Confidence, Flaming Peace, Granada, Little Darling, Redgold, Snowfire, Sunrise-Sunset.

Orange Red: Command Performance, Fragrant Cloud, Fire King, Firelight, Gypsy, Montezuma, Tropicana, Villa de Madrid.

White: Garden Party, John F. Kennedy, Pascali.

Lavender: Lady X.

TENDER BULBS, CORMS, AND TUBERS

There are bulbous plants, such as tulips, daylilies, and daffodils, that can be left in the ground all year-round with perfect safety. These are hardy plants. There are others, however, that are not hardy in Wisconsin, and that must receive special attention. They must be removed from the soil in the fall and brought indoors, there to be stored over the winter. In spring, they can be put back outside.

These tender bulbs, corms, and tubers do require special attention and extra care. But many Wisconsin gardeners are more than happy to give them that care because of the beauty of their bloom. The most popular plants in this category are gloxinia, gladiolus, canna, begonia, anemone, and — far above the others — the glorious and versatile dahlia.

Following is a descriptive list of ten tender bulbs, corms, and tubers, with cultural tips based on the advice of USDA horticulturists. Although these are in alphabetical order, we will leave the dahlia until last, because we will give it special attention.

Anemone. There are many varieties of this cheerful tuberous plant, from dwarfs right up to the tall Japanese forms. Most anemones flower in May or June in Wisconsin, although the tall Japanese varieties may bloom later in the summer and right up until frost. The stems of the plant are erect and the flowers are showy, fully suitable for cutting. Anemones are used in rock gardens, beds, and borders.

A rich, well-drained, and sandy loam is best for anemones. They should be planted as early in spring as possible, since they do best in cool weather. Some varieties are at home in partial shade, although most prefer full sun. Propagation is by seed or root division.

After the blooming period has finished and before the first hard frost, the anemone tubers should be dug up and stored in the manner described for dahlias on pages 264-67.

Begonias are especially well adapted for planting in pots and tubs. They will brighten up any porch or patio.

Begonia. Begonias are popular houseplants, but many varieties will thrive outside and will bloom in the summer. They grow from one to two feet tall. The flowers are red, pink, orange, salmon, yellow, or white, and they grow up to thirteen inches in diameter. Begonias are good pot plants, some varieties especially adapted for hanging pots on porches and patios. Other varieties are good for lightly shaded flower beds.

The USDA offers this good growing advice for begonias: Plant the tubers in February or March in flats indoors. Use a mixture of equal parts of peat moss and coarse sand. Press the tubers into the mixture; make sure the "growing eyes" are upward. Space them two to three inches apart.

Keep the flats in a dark room at sixty-five degrees. Water the tubers often enough to keep the sand and peat moss mixture damp. When pink shoots appear, add one-half inch of the mixture over the tubers and move them to a lighted room that is kept at a minimum of sixty-five degrees.

In six weeks after you put the plants in a lighted room, transfer them to five- to six-inch pots or outdoors in the garden. Use a mixture of equal parts of garden soil, sand, and leaf mold. Grow the plants in a cool, lightly shaded area.

If you put pot plants under fluorescent lamps for sixteen hours a day, they will continue to bloom throughout the winter. Keep the room temperature at a minimum of sixty-five degrees.

Fertilize begonias at least every other week after you have replanted them in pots or in the garden. The USDA recommends a 20-20-20 soluble mixture, one teaspoon per gallon of water, but organic gardeners will want to substitute a liquid fish fertilizer or, outdoors, a well-made manure tea.

Water often enough to keep the soil moist. Water early in the day so that the flowers and leaves will dry quickly; they rot easily.

When the leaves turn yellow in the late summer or early fall, dig the tubers in the garden. Store the potted tubers in the pots and the dug tubers with the dirt around them in a cool and dry place away from frost. Start the growing cycle again in February or March.

Caladium. Caladium is grown for its showy and colorful leaves. The flower buds should be removed as soon as they appear, so that the leaves can develop fully.

Many varieties of caladium are available. Dwarf varieties grow up to nine inches tall. Ordinary tall varieties grow up to eighteen inches, and elephant's ear grows up to six feet. Use caladium in front of shrubs, as foundation plantings, and as pot plants.

Plant the tubers close together in a flat from January to mid-May. Use a mixture of peat moss and coarse sand. Cover the planted tubers with a one-inch layer of peat moss.

Water the tubers often enough to keep the soil mixture damp. Roots grow from the tops of the tubers; they must be kept moist and covered with peat moss. Keep the room temeprature no lower than seventy degrees. Tubers often rot in cool soil.

As soon as roots develop, replant the tubers of elephant's ear outdoors or in tubs or boxes; replant the tubers of other varieties outdoors or in six-inch pots. Use a mixture of equal parts of garden soil and peat moss. Grow the plants in a lightly shaded area, never in direct sunlight. The leaves burn easily.

Try to balance the light and shade to get the most color in the leaves. When plants are grown in deep shade, the leaves will have more green coloring and less pink and red.

Water and fertilize caladium at least every other week. Do not allow the soil to become dry. Fertilize as recommended for begonias.

When the leaves turn yellow in the fall, dig the tubers from the garden and store them with the soil around them. Store potted tubers in the pots. Keep the storage area dry and at no less than sixty degrees. Start the growing cycle again the next year.

Canna. Cannas are spectacular plants that will serve anywhere in the garden where bright color is needed. Many types are grown, from the dwarfs (eighteen to thirty inches) to the tall varieties (five to seven feet). Canna blooms for many weeks in the summer. Flowers are red, pink, orange, yellow, and cream. Use canna in flower beds.

Plant rhizomes (underground stems) from March to May in flats filled with peat moss. Cover the rhizomes with one inch of peat moss and water them often enough to keep the peat moss damp.

When shoots appear, replant the rhizomes in four-inch pots. Use a mixture of equal parts of garden soil, peat moss, and sand. Leave the pot plants indoors until all danger of frost has passed. Then plant them outside in full sunshine.

Dig the planting site thoroughly and mix well-rotted cow manure into the soil. Plant the rhizomes just below the soil surface. Space them twelve to eighteen inches apart.

Water and fertilize the plants at two-week intervals throughout the growing season. Side-dress lightly with aged manure or compost, or use a tea solution. Stake the tall varieties; they fall over easily.

After the first light frost, cut off the stems of the plants. Then dig the rhizome clumps and let them dry. Store them with the soil around them away from frost. If your storage conditions are dry, embed the rhizomes in flats of dried peat moss for the winter. The next spring, clean the rhizomes and start the growing cycle again.

Gladiolus. Gladiolus grows two to four feet high. It blooms in summer and fall and produces flowers of all colors. The kinds of gladiolus that are commonly grown are grandiflora, primulinus, primulinus hybrids, and colvilleii. Use gladiolus for cut flowers or in beds.

Plant gladiolus bulbs in rows thrity-six inches wide or in flower beds. Prepare the beds the year before you plant, incorporating plenty of manure and/or compost.

Start to plant as soon as the soil is dry enough to work in the spring. Plant the bulbs four to seven inches deep and six to eight inches apart. Continue planting every seven to ten days, until early July, in order to assure a continuous supply of flowers.

When shoots are six to ten inches tall, fertilize the plants with compost tea. Water the soil around the plants every ten days in dry weather.

Dig the bulbs every year, about six weeks after the plants

have bloomed. Wash the soil off the bulbs and spread them in a shaded area to dry for several weeks. When they are dry, separate them by size and keep only those that are more than one inch in diameter. Store them in a well-ventilated area at thirty-five to forty-five degrees.

Gloxinia. Gloxinia are good plants for pots or window boxes. They are often grown as a winter houseplant, but they will bloom outdoors in the summer, too. They produce both single and double flowers, depending on the variety, and they come in many colors.

Plant the bulbs in five- to six-inch pots in early spring. Use a mixture of equal parts of peat moss, sand, and garden loam. Keep the bulbs indoors at sixty-five degrees until after the last killing frost. Grow the plants in a lightly shaded area away from direct sunlight.

Water the plants often enough to keep the soil mixture damp throughout the growing season. Fertilize every other week with compost or manure tea.

When the leaves turn yellow in the fall, gradually withhold water and allow the bulbs to dry. Store the potted bulbs in a cool and dry area at fifty degrees. Repot the bulbs in the spring and start the growing cycle again.

Ismene. The Peruvian daffodil grows about two feet high and produces large, funnel-shaped, white flowers that have green stripes running down the funnel. Use ismene in front of shrubs, as foundation plantings around the home, and as pot plants. They will bloom during the summer.

Plant the tubers close together in a flat anytime from January to mid-May. Use a mixture of peat moss and coarse sand. Cover the planted tubers with a one-inch layer of peat moss.

Water the tubers often enough to keep the soil mixture damp. Roots grow from the tops of the tubers; they must be kept moist and covered with peat moss. Keep the room temperature no lower then seventy degrees. Tubers often rot in cool soil.

As soon as roots develop, replant the tubers in six-inch pots or outdoors. Use a mixture of equal parts of garden soil and peat moss. Grow the plants in a lightly shaded area, never in direct sunlight.

Water and fertilize ismene at two-week intervals. Do not allow the soil to become dry. Fertilize with compost or manure tea, or side-dress lightly with well-aged manure.

When the leaves turn yellow in the fall, dig the tubers and store them with dirt around them. Store the potted tubers in the pots. Keep the storage area dry and at no less than sixty degrees. Start the growing cycle again the next year.

Montbretia. Montbretia grows to about three feet in height. It blooms in August and September and produces flowers about four inches in diameter. Blossoms are orange, gold, red, or yellow. Use montbretia in borders and as cut flowers.

Plant montbretia bulbs in rows thirty-six inches wide. Prepare the rows the year before you plant, applying plenty of compost and/or manure, dug ten inches into the soil.

Start to plant as soon as the soil is dry enough to work in the spring. Plant the bulbs four to seven inches deep and six to eight inches apart. Continue to plant every seven to ten days until mid-June, to assure a continuous supply of flowers.

When the shoots are six to ten inches tall, fertilize the plants again with compost or manure tea, or with a light side-dressing of compost or manure. Water the soil around the plants every ten days in dry weather.

In side-dressing, or in weeding, be certain not to injure the corms that lie just below the surface of the soil. It is really best to fertilize with tea, and to remove weeds by hand.

Dig the bulbs about six to eight weeks after the plants have bloomed. Wash the soil off the bulbs and spread them in a shaded area to dry for several weeks.

When the bulbs are dry, separate them by size and keep only those that are more than one inch in diameter. Handle the bulbs carefully to avoid damaging them. Store them in a well-ventilated area at thirty-five to forty-five degrees.

Tigridia. The Mexican shell flower grows to about two feet in height and blooms in midsummer. The tripetaled flowers are a mixture of white, red, yellow, and rose colors.

Plant tigridia bulbs in rows thirty-six inches wide or in clumps of twelve bulbs, eight to twelve inches apart. Prepare the soil well during the year before planting, incorporating plenty of compost and/or manure.

Start to plant as soon as the soil is dry enough to be worked in the spring. Plant the bulbs three inches deep and four to eight inches apart. Continue to plant every seven to ten days until mid-June, in order to assure continuous bloom.

Mulch the bulbs with two inches of pine bark, ground leaves, peat moss, or hay to keep the soil from drying. Remove the mulch in the fall.

When shoots are six to ten inches tall, fertilize the plants well with compost or manure tea, or with a side-dressing of compost or manure. Water the soil around the plants every ten days in dry weather.

Dig the bulbs about six to eight weeks after the plants have bloomed. Wash the soil off the bulbs and spread them in a shaded area to dry for several weeks.

When the bulbs are dry, separate them by size and keep only those that are more than one inch in diameter. Handle bulbs carefully to avoid damaging them. Store them in a well-ventilated area at thirty-five to forty-five degrees.

A cactus dahlia grown by Joe Thompson of Madison, Wisconsin.

DAHLIAS

No other garden flower comes in a greater variety of shapes, sizes, and colors than the dahlia, a favorite of thousands of Wisconsin gardeners. By one count, there are more than two thousand individual varieties available commercially — and more than *fifteen thousand* dahlia varieties in all! There is a dahlia for everyone.

The size of dahlia blossoms ranges from the miniature but perfectly-formed pompons, as little as one-half inch in diameter, to the huge informal decorative varieties that can grow to more than fifteen inches across! The plants themselves range from eighteen inches to seven feet tall. There are hundreds of varieties in between these extremes, so that a dahlia can be found to fit into any garden space. Color range is equally wide, covering hundreds of shades of red, yellow, orange, white, pink, buff, lavender, bronze, and nearly infinite variations of all of these, plus the many variegated varieties that show contrasting colors within each blossom. Everyone's favorite color can be found in a dahlia.

Dahlias can be divided into six general types: formal decorative, informal decorative, cactus-type, semicactus, dwarf pompons, and dwarf single, double, and semidouble varieties. Generally, the informal decoratives produce the very largest blooms, if it is size you are looking for, while the formal decoratives form blossoms not quite so large but incredibly perfect in form. The cactus varieties range greatly in size and feature petals that are numerous, long, and often curled into tubelike structures. The dwarf varieties come in many choices, far more so now than only a few years ago, since the dahlia breeders have stopped going for enormous size (a limit — at least within good taste — was reached in that area some years ago) and have begun to improve their offerings of dwarf varieties for every garden taste and purpose.

Dwarf dahlias bloom from early July on into heavy frost, while the large varieties start blooming later — usually in August — and continue until hard frosts have blackened their foliage. In the colder reaches of Wisconsin, where early frosts threaten to nip dahlias just when they have begun to bloom heavily, the season can be stretched by covering the plants with large plastic trash bags. Anchor the bags firmly on the ground, to retain ground heat, and remove them when the air warms up the following day. Quite often, the early cold snap will be followed by a week or two of Indian summer, when the plastic will not be necessary at all.

Dahlia culture. Dahlias are grown from tubers. They are planted in the spring, when danger of frost is past, and the tubers are taken up in fall, after frost has killed the tops of the plants but before the ground has frozen hard. The tubers are then packed in sand, garden loam, or peat, and are held indoors until the following spring.

The best dahlia grower I know, barring none, is Joseph Thompson of Madison. Joe has been growing dahlias since 1938 and, after his family, dahlias are his greatest love. I was so impressed with his expertise in this area, in fact, that I shared it with the readers of *Organic Gardening and Farming* magazine in the November 1972 issue. From that article, I will excerpt some salient points of Joe Thompson's technique — with fair warning that Joe's methods differ somewhat from the standard advice given in most garden books and horticulture bulletins. (Your county agent has an excellent booklet on dahlia culture, prepared by University of Wisconsin horticulturists, which gives standard advice.)

Joe Thompson usually has the first dahlia blooms of the season in Madison, weeks ahead of others. The secret is in starting out early.

Joe Thompson loves dahlias so much that he is impatient to get them going in the spring — and so he breaks tradition by taking his boxes of stored tubers from under his basement work-bench in mid-February (he stores them in ordinary garden soil) and placing the boxes under the basement windows. He waters the boxes about once a week, and in a few weeks the tubers begin to sprout. They make steady progress for the next two months. By April 15, when the danger of hard frost is still with us in southern Wisconsin, Joe begins to move the plants outside. (Standard advice tells us not to move them out until the middle of May, but Joe is working for earlier bloom. If he finds frost on the plants early in the morning, he washes it off with a gentle spray from the garden hose. He has never lost a plant to spring frost.)

From the middle of April through the middle of May, Joe moves his dahlias gradually outside. The planting process is very special and always the same: "Air is as important as any nu-trient," says Joe. "You've got to work the soil well, keep it loose, and let plenty of air into it."

After choosing a spot that will get plenty of sun, he digs a hole twelve inches deep for each plant, and as big around as the plant foliage will get — which often is several feet. He puts seven to eight inches of well-rotted and screened manure into the bottom of the hole and fills the rest with topsoil. Then he gently works the tuber shallowly into the topsoil, exposing the green shoots, which are large and strong after their early start in the basement. (Rec-ommended planting depth is four to six inches.)

Next, Joe takes the subsoil he had dug from the bottom of the hole, and with it builds a circular wall around the edge of the hole, about three inches high and sloping gradually towards the center of the plant. This forms a basin which will catch rainwater and direct it towards the center of the plant. It also helps to hold down weeds. The subsoil walls resist breaking down, too, since the sub-soil is a heavy clay.

Water is vitally important to dahlia success. Only a temporary lack of moisture can set plants back as much as three weeks, or even stunt them permanently. A long soaking during dry spells will do wonders for dahlias.

Joe doesn't do very much after planting time, except to watch the soil moisture carefully, stake and tie the plants when they become several feet tall, and work the soil at least every third week, adding a little sheep manure.

Buds begin to appear around the first week of July. Joe then knows it will be only three weeks until the first blossoms burst forth. (Most people's large-variety dahlias in the Madison area don't bloom until much later.) If he wants to groom a blossom for showing, he observes the usual garden-book rules about cutting off suckers and disbudding. If not, then he doesn't take these pains, for he likes a profusion of bloom as well as individual champions.

In any case, though, he likes to encourage one strong stalk for each plant. If one blossom shows particular promise for exhibiting, he may cut a gunny sack and build a little sun shelter over it to protect the blossom from being bleached out by the sun.

The fall storage process is simple. Joe half-fills a wooden box with garden soil, places the dahlia tubers on top of the soil, and covers them with sand — an inch over their tops. Then he slides the box under his workbench where it is cool and dark. He waters the box lightly after about three weeks, then once a month thereafter — until the first of February rolls around, when he pulls out the box and sets it under the basement window. The cycle begins anew.

Dividing. Dahlias are most easily propagated by dividing the tubers. In the very early spring, when the shoots are just beginning to show, separate the clumps with a sharp knife, being sure to get at least one good bud with each clump. You can also take cuttings from the first shoots in spring, after the third set of leaves has developed. Plant the cuttings in coarse sand or vermiculite until they have developed roots — about three to four weeks — then pot them in good garden loam and keep them indoors in a shaded spot until it is time to set them outdoors.

HARDY BULBS, CORMS, AND TUBERS

There are more than a score of flowers in this category that are suitable for Wisconsin's gardens. Most are the eagerly-awaited spring-flowering bulbs — including crocus, tulips, and daffodils — that signal the ending of winter and the renewal of outdoor gardening activity. No wonder, then, that they hold a special place in our hearts.

Here, we will treat nine hardy bulbs, corms, and tubers, eight of which can brighten your home grounds during spring, when it is still too cold to plant your tender annuals. Of the following, only the lilies bloom later in the season, but they are included here because of their unusual hardiness. All can be left in the ground year-round.

Planting and general culture. Hardy bulbs, corms, and tubers can last for as little as two years or as long as ten or more, depending on the variety. Generally, they should be dug up and divided every third year or so, then replanted. When your hardy bulbs begin to produce stunted flowers, it is a sign that they need dividing; they have produced little bulbs which are crowding each other.

Spring-flowering bulbs are always planted in the fall, from September up through November. It will do no good for you to plant them in early spring, since they need a winter of cold temperatures to activate their blooming in the spring.

All the following plants like a fairly light, fertile, slightly acid, and well-drained soil. Full sunlight is not essential, but certainly is preferable. (Lily-of-the-valley will bloom in shade.) Those bulbs planted close to the house on the south side will bloom earliest in spring.

Prepare the beds well in the fall, preparing the soil deeply (twelve inches) and adding generous amounts of well-aged compost or manure, and a little bone meal. Remember, though, that these bulbs can easily be damaged by coming into contact with fresh manure. Be certain that it is fully composted before using it.

A winter mulch is not absolutely necessary for these hardy bulbs, but in the colder regions of the state it is a good safety precaution. Apply the mulch when the ground has frozen hard. If you put it down before the ground has frozen, mice may take up residence in the mulch and feed on your bulbs. The purpose of the mulch is not to keep the soil warm, but rather to keep it cold. An unusual warm spell during the winter can force your bulbs into premature growth; and, alternate freezing and thawing during winter's late days can heave the soil and crush the bulbs. In the spring, when the weather begins to moderate (March, in southern Wisconsin) the mulch can be removed.

The blossoms and stems of spring-bloomers can be cut at any time for indoor display. However, the foliage must never be cut, for it is the foliage that carries nutrients down to the bulb, where they are stored to make possible the following year's bloom. The foliage must be allowed to turn yellow and die back gradually. You can prevent this dying foliage from becoming an eyesore by planting annuals in among the bulbs after — or during — spring flowering. Petunias are particularly good for this purpose, since they spread so rapidly.

A summer mulch is also a good idea, for it will both protect the bulbs from summer heat and hold down weeds for the interplanted annuals. But do not cover the foliage of the spring-bloomers with the mulch.

Crocus. This is the first garden blossom to greet us in the spring. Ours usually begin to bloom in the middle of March, here in Madison, often peeking up from under a diminishing blanket of snow. The crocus is a tiny plant, as garden flowers go, and its bloom is short-lived — but certainly no other flower brings greater joy to winter-weary Wisconsin gardeners.

Plant crocus in the fall, anytime up until the ground freezes. Remember that they are small and, for best results, should be planted in mass groupings. You can plant crocus almost anywhere — even scattered here and there in the lawn, for the foliage will have matured and died back before the lawn needs its first cutting. The crocus will appreciate a winter mulch, although it should not be applied until after the ground has frozen hard. Remember also to remove it in the very early spring. Crocus needs very little, if any, dividing. Many gardeners simply add a few dozen more bulbs to the ground each year, to improve the spring showing year by year.

Crocuses (or *croci*, if you took Latin in high school) are available in many shades of blue, violet, yellow, orange, and white.

Daffodil. The daffodil (*Narcissus*), also called jonquil, is traditionally planted in October in Wisconsin, because its roots must become established before the ground freezes hard. They are planted deeply, about six inches under the soil surface, and about six to eight inches apart.

Daffodils are fast growers and they appreciate a nutrient-rich soil. Be sure to incorporate plenty of well-aged manure or compost when planting. But do be aware that they are very susceptible to injury when coming into contact with manure that has not fully decomposed.

As with crocuses, it is best to plant daffodils in very informal groupings or clumps, so that they appear to have wandered naturally into your garden. Many gardeners simply scatter the bulbs in the chosen area, and then plant them where they have fallen. In any case, do not plant them in rows, for this arrangement does not become the free spirit of the daffodil. Divide the bulbs after a few years, when they appear to be losing vigor and size.

There are many varieties to choose from, including both single-flowering and double-flowering types, in shades of yellow and white.

Grape hyacinth. These little plants, which grow only six to twelve inches tall, flower early in the spring. Most varieties are dark blue to dark violet, but there are blue-and-white, white, and pink varieties, too. They are good complements to the other spring-flowering bulbs because of their novel appearance.

Plant grape hyacinths in October, in fertile soil and in a sunny spot. These small bulbs are set two inches deep and two to three inches apart. They can be mixed in with the crocus bulbs and planted at the same time.

Hyacinth. The hyacinth, with its many delicate and fragrant blossoms, has become our traditional Easter plant. It will bloom before the daffodils, and will come along quite early if planted on the south side of the house, close to the wall, in full sun. Varieties are available that offer various shades of blue, purple, yellow, and pink blossoms, both single-flowered and double-flowered.

Hyacinths are often planted in formal arrangements, but I still prefer to scatter them informally. They are good for planting in front of shrubs, along fences and walls, or at either side of the front steps to the house. They grow to about eight inches in height.

Hyacinths send down roots more deeply than do the other spring-bloomers, and so you must prepare the soil to a depth of two feet if you want the best results. Incorporate plenty of well-aged compost or manure, along with a handful of bone meal. Plant

the bulbs five to six inches deep and six to eight inches apart.
Plant an inch or two more deeply in very light soils, an inch or two
less deeply in heavy soils. Late September and early October are
good times to plant hyacinths.

Like other spring-blooming bulbs, hyacinths will appreciate a
winter mulch, applied after the ground has frozen hard. Remove it
in the early spring, to allow the plants free access to the air. After
blooming has stopped, plant annuals in among the hyacinths. By
the time the foliage begins to die back, the annuals will have
covered them.

The bulbs of hyacinths last for a shorter time than those of
any other spring-blooming bulbous plant. For best results, they
should be taken up every two or three years, divided, stored in a
cool and dry place for the summer, and replanted in fall. Usually,
you will want to replace a third to a half of them at this time,
since hyacinth bulbs tend to be short-lived. When you dig up the
bulbs, you will find many little bulblets attached to them. These
can be separated and planted in an unused part of the garden,
there to be nursed into full size — or, they can be discarded.

Iris. The iris has not taken very readily to improvement by the
plant breeders, and so the varieties we grow today are very much
like those grown in Europe hundreds of years ago. Fortunately,
the iris is such a beautiful flower that it hardly needs improvement. It has a rich history, and is in fact named after the Goddess
of the Rainbow. Medieval France adopted the iris (*fleur-de-lis*) as
its emblem, and it has since adorned the gardens of crowned heads
and peasants throughout the Western world. It is undoubtedly a
regal beauty, worthy of your close attention.

Irises are offered in both rhizome-rooted varieties (which include the tall beardeds, Japanese, and Siberians) and bulbs (the
Dutch, English, and Spanish). A large variety of colors and sizes
tempt the iris lover. Some dwarf varieties compete with the crocuses for early blooming, while some of the giant Japanese varieties flower well into July. Blue and lavender are the traditional
colors of iris, although there are many varieties in yellow, orange
copper, pink, red, and white.

Planting time for the tall beardeds is in late June or July.
Japanese and Siberians should be planted in September or early
October. All bulb irises should be planted in September.

Select a sunny spot for your irises, prepare the soil deeply
(fifteen inches), and incorporate plenty of well-aged compost or
manure. The rhizome-rooted irises are planted shallowly — barely
an inch of soil covering the top of the root clump — and about
twelve inches apart. The bulb varieties are planted from three to
six inches deep, depending on the particular variety.

A good winter mulch is important for the shallowly planted
rhizomes. And, in fact, a mulch is a good safety precaution for all
irises.

Around the end of March, sprinkle equal parts of bone meal and lime over the iris beds. The spring rains will wash the mixture down to sweeten the soil and feed the roots.

Although irises are subject to more disease and insect attack than other spring-flowering plants, you can control these with a little individual attention. The iris borer, often a problem, can be controlled by a three-step program: (1) the cleaning up of all dead foliage in the fall; (2) the prompt removal of any torn or diseased leaves and stems during the season; and (3) the application of a paste of flour and water if the borers become numerous. They will eat the paste, bloat, and die.

Lily-of-the-valley. Here is a little flower so eager to please that it can often become a nusiance (but never to those of us who love it). It will grow virtually anywhere, even in total shade. It never really needs dividing, although it will benefit from it, and it will spread cheerfully and rapidly where other plants will not grow. Lily-of-the-valley prefers at least some shade during the heat of the day, and it will take well even to moderately wet soils which would drive out other flowers. You can plant lily-of-the-valley in either fall or spring; it doesn't much care.

This said, I will also say that lily-of-the-valley appreciates the same attention as you heap upon other spring bloomers, and that it will respond to your extra attention with larger blossoms. (Incidentally, if you are looking for a large-flowered lily-of-the-valley, try *fortunei*.)

Madonna lily. *Lilium candidum* grows three to four feet high and has beautiful white, classic blossoms. It is a true lily.

All the cultural suggestions given for other spring-flowering bulbs apply to the Madonna lily, as well. Prepare the soil deeply and add plenty of aged compost or manure. Plant the bulbs from one to two inches deep (or according to package directions), one foot apart. Mulch when the ground has frozen hard. The plants will bloom in June, and will dazzle you with their waxy brilliance.

Snowdrop. *Galanthus* is another early-spring bloomer, growing from five to nine inches high and producing lovely white blossoms with a green interior. They like a partly shady location, and will respond to fertilization. Giant snowdrop (*Galanthus elwesi*) grows to eighteen inches and prefers a sunny location.

Everything that has been said about other spring-blooming plants can be said about snowdrop. They look best when planted in mass, informal groupings. Plant them in early-to-mid-September, two or three inches deep and two to four inches apart. They will need little care after they have been established, and will spread quite easily.

Tulip. No spring flower is quite so regal as the tulip, which plant breeders have improved greatly in the past few decades. There are several hundred varieties on the market today, ranging

Springtime visitors to the State
Capitol in Madison are rewarded with breathtaking
views of brightly colored tulips in well-tailored beds.

from the dwarfs to the giant hybrids which grow to three feet in
height and sport brilliant and enormous blossoms.

There are single-flowering and double-flowering tulips, Darwin
tulips, cottage tulips, lily tulips, and peony-flowering tulips. There
are parrot tulips and botanical tulips, and just about any kind of
tulip you could want, in a wide range of colors — golden yellow,
brilliant crimson, pristine white, blushing rose, flaming orange,
baby blue, and infinite varieties of these and other colors. There
are many varigated varieties, as well.

Like other spring-flowering bulbs, tulips are best planted in
mass groupings. Their formal structure, however, lends itself to
planting in formal arrangements.

Tulips like a well-drained and light garden loam, and plenty of
sunlight. Plant them in the fall, from two to four weeks before the
ground is expected to freeze in your area. In Wisconsin, this generally means during November. The ground should be deeply prepared, and plenty of well-aged compost or manure should be added
to the soil. A winter mulch should be applied after the ground
freezes, and removed in early spring.

Bulbs should be planted according to specific directions given
for each individual variety. Pay close attention to these directions,
for too-deep planting will result in smaller blossoms, while too-
shallow planting will subject the bulb to damage from heaving of
the soil in late winter and early spring.

Tulips will have to be dug up, separated, and replanted every
three or four years. They may also be stored over the summer for
fall replanting, and if you do this, choose an airy, shady, and cool
storage place. Some gardeners lift the bulbs each year, after the
foliage has died down completely, in order to protect the prized
bulbs from summer rot and rodent damage — but most gardeners
will find it easier to take their chances with tulips, replacing any
that are lost. Tulips do not have a very long life span, in any case,
and this temporal nature gives us a perfect opportunity to try new
varieties every year or so.

Location is important for wild flowers. Bloodroot needs shelter from the heat of summer, which overhanging tree branches can provide. It blooms in the early spring, when the leafless branches allow the sun to filter through.

WILD FLOWERS FOR WISCONSIN

The beauty of wild flowers is a special one. Gardeners who encourage and cultivate Wisconsin's native flora are not likely to be impressed by the sight of a flaming red dahlia the size of a dinner plate — but they will go into quiet ecstasy upon spotting the blushing pink blossoms of a wild-growing bleeding heart (*Dicentra eximia*).

Wild flowers are precious to many of us because they have the independence of other wild creatures, and we respect that independence. We feel more fortunate to catch a glimpse of a bald eagle high above a Mississippi bluff, than to see a lion in a zoo. And we feel a similar thrill when a family of trillium consents to live with us — even though we may love our hybrid tea roses for entirely different reasons.

The growing of wild flowers is often difficult, requiring patience, devotion, study, and careful planning. Many wild flowers have very particular needs, and we can grow them only by studying those needs and meeting them in our own gardens. Sometimes, we can adjust the conditions in our gardens to provide a suitable environment for wild flowers. Sometimes, conditions in parts of our gardens will be just right for certain wild flowers, with no further adjustment. And other times, nothing we can do will create the right environment. When it comes to wild flowers, our attitude is important. We cannot simply "buy 'em and grow 'em," but we must invite them, make them feel at home, and then hope for the best. If they like it in our gardens, they will flourish forever, with no further help from us.

If you have a burning desire to invite wild flowers to your garden, there are three essential books you should have: Norman Fassett's *Spring Flora of Wisconsin* (University of Wisconsin Press, 4th ed., 1975) which will aid you in identifying wild flowers in the woods and fields, give you their time of blooming, and their distribution within the state; Marie Sperka's *Growing Wildflowers* (Harper & Row, 1973); and *Wild Flowers of Wisconsin*, which is distributed free by the Department of Natural Resources.

While Fassett's book is primarily for hikers with a nodding acquaintance with botany, Sperka's is for the home gardener. It is a beautiful book, well worth its price, and it tells you how to create the conditions for growing more than two hundred wild flowers, including all our favorites — black-eyed Susan, bleeding heart, bloodroot, salvia, wild columbine, cattail, downy skullcap, Dutchman's-breeches, rock geranium, jack-in-the-pulpit, lady's slipper, pasque flower, trillium, Solomon's seal, star-of-Bethlehem, violet, and many more.

The author of *Growing Wildflowers* runs the Woodland Acres Nursery (Route 2, Crivitz, Wisconsin 54114) in the Nicolet Forest region. She has been studying wild flowers for forty years and has operated her wild flower nursery for twenty-five, thus providing a broad background from which to advise us all. Fortunately, too, the advice she gives is based on the climatic conditions of Wisconsin's northeast region, where winters can bring temperatures of thirty degrees below zero. Too many garden books are written for us by people in places like Virginia and lower New York, and they reflect a climatic and geographical bias. Here is a book we can trust.

Conditions for wild flowers. It is vitally important, in encouraging wild flowers, that you recreate, to the best of your ability, the conditions in which each species thrives naturally. Highly bred garden flowers, such as marigolds and dahlias, can grow in a fairly broad range of garden conditions. Not so, wild flowers — or, at least, not most of them. They will thrive under very narrow conditions, and they will not survive at all unless these conditions are met.

Soil and sun are the two most important considerations for wild flowers. You must remember that most woodland wild flowers grow in the shade — or partial shade — of trees, and that their soil is rich, dark, humusy, and very likely acid. The flora native to Wisconsin's northern regions will likely demand an acid soil, whereas in the south, where sugar maples and basswoods flourish, the soil will be more towards the alkaline side and its native wild flowers will demand a higher level on the pH scale. Sunlight is an equally important consideration. Some wild flowers, such as those native to Wisconsin's natural prairie and meadow areas, need full sun and hot days, whereas others demand cool, moist, and largely shaded conditions. Know the native habitats of the wild flowers you are considering, and be sure that you can do a good job in simulating those conditions in your own garden.

In the limited space available to us, we cannot list the conditions necessary to the cultivation of Wisconsin's several hundred wild flowers. Again, I suggest Marie Sperka's fine book for those seeking to introduce wild flowers into the home grounds, and Norman Fassett's *Spring Flora of Wisconsin* as an infallible identification guide. The Sperka book lists plants for nineteen different garden environments, so that — whatever the conditions in your garden — you will be able to find those wild flowers best suited to them.

Getting wild flowers. It is a great temptation to roam the woods, fields, marshes, and streams of Wisconsin to gather wild flowers for later transplanting at home. Unless you have a great deal of experience in this area, I would advise against it. First, your chances for success are not very great, considering the exacting growing conditions which most wild flowers demand. Many will not survive the trip home. Second, with man's continuing encroachment upon nature's wild preserves, there are some wild flower species that are endangered — and, in fact, it is against the law even to pick some species, and certainly illegal to dig up plants in any state park. Third, there are wild flower nurseries — such as Mrs. Sperka's — that will supply you with seeds and plants of those species which have the greatest chances of flourishing in your garden.

If you do choose to collect wild flowers in wood, field, bog, or marsh, be aware that there are some plants protected by law. The following plants may never be picked, much less dug up and transplanted, from any public land or from any private property without the written permission of the owner: trilliums, wood lily, purple-fringed orchid, pitcher plant, bittersweet, trailing arbutus, turk's cap lily, lady's slipper (orchid), and American lotus. In addition, even though they are not protected by law, gentians and Indian paintbrush do need protection and should not be picked or dug from their natural habitat.

One way in which you can pick or dig wild flowers with impugnity is in saving them from destruction by bulldozers. If you are certain that an area is about to be levelled for building construction, ask for permission to remove wild flowers before the bulldozers come. Generally, you will have no problem in obtaining such permission, and you will be providing a real service, even if only a small percentage of the plants survive transplanting.

Go, little book, and wish to all
Flowers in the garden, meat in the hall
A bin of wine, a spice of wit,
A house with lawns enclosing it,
A living river by the door,
A nightingale in the sycamore!
　　　　　　　　—Robert Louis Stevenson
　　　　　　　　Underwoods (1887)

Chapter Seven

Lawns, Trees, and Ornamental Plantings

A well-landscaped home, enclosed by a thick, green lawn, healthy shrubs, and flourishing shade trees, is both a balm for the soul and a shrewd economic investment. The trick is to maintain your lawn and ornamental plantings with a minimum of care, so that you will have more time to devote to your flowers and vegetables — and the pursuit of this goal will dictate the direction of this chapter.

If you live in an older home, your landscaping is probably pretty well set, and your lawn is established. True, there are changes you would like to make in the landscaping plan — shrubs you would like to replace, bare areas you would like to fill in — and the lawn may be far from the country-club ideal you have always cherished — but you are still many years ahead of those who must start from scratch in a newly built home.

If your home *is* newly built, your problems are entirely different. You have a major landscaping job on your hands, which probably calls for the advice of a professional. Whether or not you do the job with professional counsel, you will want to get hold of several good books on landscaping, either at your local library or your bookstore. You will also depend heavily on the advice of your local nurseryman, who can tell you exactly which plants are suitable for your soil and climate.

LIVING LAWNS

Many homeowners approach the lawn as if it were some sort of animated carpet, one that has to be trimmed weekly, watered, fed with chemicals, and sprinkled with herbicide granules in order to keep it at the proper thickness and shade of green. Plant food manufacturers have nurtured this notion by flooding the market with "miracle-working" fertilizer/herbicide products that, according to the ads, will virtually solve all your lawn problems.

In truth, a lawn is a collection of thousands of tiny plants, some fifty to the square foot. On a fifty-by-fifty foot lawn, one hundred twenty-five thousand such plants will be growing. Important, however, is that each of these is an *individual plant* and, like any other plant in your garden, each reacts to the particular conditions of soil, sun, and climate of its immediate location. Pay attention to the needs of these plants as you would those of any other garden perennial, and your chances for lawn success will be improved considerably.

Grasses for Wisconsin lawns. Of the many kinds of lawn grasses in America, three are most suited for growing in Wisconsin's climate: *Kentucky bluegrass, red fescue,* and *bentgrass.* The chances are that your lawn is made up mostly of bluegrass, although there are doubtless other kinds mixed in with it.

Kentucky bluegrass, of which there are a number of varieties, is popular in the north because it is a vigorous and attractive grass, well suited to cool and humid conditions. During dry spells, bluegrass will turn brown and wiry, but with the return of rain or artificial watering, it will come back bright and green. Bluegrasses are slow to become established, and therefore any lawn seeding mixture will also contain a certain percentage of "nurse" grasses, whose purpose it is to grow quickly, crowd out weeds, look attractive, and give the permanent bluegrass a chance to become established. (These nurse grasses, which include redtop and ryegrass, are not permanent, or are not vigorous and attractive after the first year — but they do serve a valuable purpose in getting a new lawn established.) Kentucky bluegrass will react best to a slightly alkaline soil — pH around 7.5. Since most of our Wisconsin soils will tend to be on the acid side, it is vitally important that you test your lawn soil regularly and, if indicated, add limestone during the spring or early fall until the condition is corrected. Bluegrass does not do well in heavy shade or on dry soil. It should never be cut lower than two inches (ideally, 2½ to 3 inches), especially during hot and dry weather. It needs fertilization in midspring and early fall, and very thorough soakings (six inches deep) during dry weather.

The fescues — especially the red fescues — are far better than bluegrass in shady areas and on poorer soils. Most lawn seed mixtures will contain a percentage of red fescue. However, if your

The appearance and value of an older home can be improved greatly by thoughtful landscaping.

lawn area is under large shade trees, you should ask your dealer for a mixture containing a far higher percentage of this grass. A good lawnseed for a shady area might contain only 20 percent bluegrass, 60 percent fescue (often, of several kinds), and 20 per- cent of nurse grasses. Or, the percentage of red fescue might run as high as 75 percent. A sunny-area mixture, however, might contain 50 to 75 percent bluegrass. When buying lawnseed, go to a garden center or nursery — not to a supermarket or discount house — and take advantage of the expert advice of your nurs- eryman. Explain your needs to him, and get a mixture made especially for those needs.

Bentgrass will produce the most beautiful lawn of all. Unfor- tunately, it demands such close attention that it is rarely used for home lawns. Although Kentucky bluegrass and red fescue can be mixed freely, bentgrass is not compatible with either. If you want the perfection of a bentgrass lawn, you must plant straight bentgrass, and you must be prepared to spend a major part of your total gardening time in looking after it. Bentgrass costs much more than other common lawn grasses. It will not stand heavy foot traffic. It can be injured easily by adverse climatic conditions, and it is prone to diseases more than other grasses are. During the summer months, bentgrass must be watered daily, or at least every other day, for its shallow roots must not be allowed to dry out. If you go on vacation, be prepared to hire a babysitter for your bentgrass lawn. More likely, however, you will avoid bentgrass completely.

Establishing a new lawn. Late summer to early fall is the best time to seed a new lawn in Wisconsin. James C. Schroeder, Dane County horticultural Extension agent, recommends the period from August 15 to September 15 as the ideal, although in northern Wisconsin this time may be pushed back a week or two. The idea is to give the new grass plants a chance to become established before winter sets in. If you cannot seed at this time, satisfactory results may be achieved by spring seeding — although, in this case, you will have to give the new lawn more attention during the hot days of summer. In any case, avoid the hot summer months as a time for seeding a new lawn.

Jim Schroeder also gives the following good advice on seeding preparations for the new lawn:

The contour and slope of a lawn will be determined primarily by fixed installations such as the house foundation, driveway, walks, and streets. The lawn grade should slope away from the house at least six inches in 100 feet. Rocks and building debris should be removed before the soil is turned over. Cultivate to a depth of three to four inches. Periodic soaking and drying will enable the soil to settle naturally. At this time, level the lawn by scraping soil from high spots and filling in holes and depressions.

Prior to seeding, the soil should receive a shallow cultivation. The seed bed should be firm, but not packed. The ideal seed bed should consist of moderately coarse particles from a pea to golf ball in size. These particles prevent washing, reduce crusting, and provide crevices in which the seeds can lodge.

While mulching is not essential for lawn establishment, a thin, uniform, weed-free covering can be beneficial in establishing grass, particularly on sloped areas. Benefits derived from mulching include conservation of moisture and reducton of seed loss due to washing, wind, and birds. Clean straw, salt hay, shredded bark, burlap bags, wood shavings, and peat are some mulching materials that can be used with success. Apply the material evenly and lightly so soil can be easily seen.

Germination depends upon a continuous presence of light, moisture, and warmth. Without water, seeds cannot germinate even when other conditions are ideal. Apply water as a gentle spray. Keep soil moist, but not flooded. Try to set sprinklers so that there is a minimum of walking over the wet surface. Once the seedling has sprouted, a continuous supply of moisture is essential. This will involve frequent, light waterings, especially during the hot period of each day. An example of a watering schedule would be ten o'clock, two o'clock, and four o'clock. On days when there are drying winds or high temperatures, additional waterings are advisable. As seedlings develop, watering frequencies should be reduced until the total water, including rainfall and irrigation, equals approximately one to 1½ inches per week.

Start mowing as soon as growth of any kind is tall enough to cut. Try to do so when the soil surface is fairly dry, otherwise muddy mower wheels may pull out some seedlings. Set your mower to cut at 1½ to 2 inches. Mow frequently to reduce weed competition. For best results, catch or sweep up the clippings.

Maintenance of established lawns. The three most important considerations in caring for an established lawn are feeding, mowing, and watering.

A lawn can be fertilized regularly by either chemical or organic methods. There is little doubt that chemical preparations will get the nutrients to the roots and help the grass plants to vigorous growth — but there are several disadvantages to consider in chemical fertilization. First, these preparations are expensive, as most homeowners know. They can run from five to ten dollars or more for a bag large enough to take care of an average urban lot. Second, these preparations are quick releasing and short-lived. You must keep on spoon-feeding your lawn to maintain it, your wallet growing thinner while your lawn grows thicker. Third, chemical fertilizers do absolutely nothing to improve the quality of your soil — and it is the soil which eventually will determine the condition of your lawn. Constant use of chemicals brings diminishing returns because it does not improve the texture of the soil. Last, the use of nitrogen chemical fertilizers on lawns is a major cause of weed pollution of urban-area waterways. In Madison, for instance, every heavy rainfall washes tons of nitrogen fertilizer from lawns into sewers, and eventually into the Madison-area lakes, fouling them with rampant weed and algae growth. The nitrogen which the homeowner buys to fertilize his lawn often supports the aquatic weeds that foul up his fishing boat motor.

Organic fertilizers, on the other hand, are slow acting and long lasting, and they are apt to be less expensive. They will not produce instant results, but they will build up the soil's natural fertility, providing a storehouse of nutrients that grass plants can call upon as their need dictates. They work constantly to improve the texture of the soil, making it spongy and humus-rich, eventually forming a soil environment that can support a rich, green, and healthy lawn.

What organic fertilizer? You will work towards the best interests of your lawn by slowly weaning it from chemical fertilizers while changing over to organic methods. You can do this gradually, over two or three years, eventually depending entirely on organic fertilizers and soil conditioners.

What organic fertilizers? Sewage sludge is generally considered to be the best organic lawn fertilizer. Check with your local sewage disposal plant to see whether dried sludge is available free. If not, then you can depend on Milorganite, a sludge product made commercially right in Milwaukee. Use according to directions on the bag.

Other good organic lawn fertilizers are cottonseed meal (for its high nitrogen content), tobacco stems (potash), bone meal (phosphorus and nitrogen), castor pomace (balanced formula), cattle manure, and sheep manure. Not all of these products are easy to find (whereas Milorganite is available at nearly all garden centers). Sometimes you will have to do a little detective work to find them locally; however, the list of organic fertilizer sources on pages 45-48 will be a good place to begin.

How to apply organic fertilizers. If you are establishing a new lawn, it is important to incorporate a good supply of organic material into the topsoil before sowing the lawnseed. Be sure, however, that all manures are fully composted and that all materials are finely screened. If your lawn is an older one, you may simply topdress with organic matter in spring or fall, or you may go over the lawn with a spiked roller and then spread the organic materials so that they will work themselves into the spike holes. A thorough soaking after application of materials will help to wash the nutrients down into the soil. Remember, also, that every time you add organic materials you will be slowly building up a layer of humus. Eventually, the entire soil foundation of your lawn will be transformed into an ideal one.

Mowing. The most common mistake homeowners make in mowing is in setting the mower blades too close to the ground. Although grass grows from the crown of the plant and not from the top of the leaf or blade, the plant still must manufacture its own food from its blades. If you reduce the length of the blades by more than one-third at any one time, their ability to manufacture food will be impaired, disease will be invited, and the plant will suffer. Kentucky bluegrass should not be cut lower than 2½ inches during the summer, or 2 inches in the fall.

It doesn't matter much whether you use a reel or rotary type mower, although a reel type will give you a neater cut and a better looking lawn. A rotary mower, on the other hand, can be used for other garden purposes, such as cutting down tall weeds, shredding leaves and plant wastes for mulching or composting, and "sheet-mulching" your autumn leaves on your lawn. If at all possible, you should own both a hand-operated reel mower and a gasoline-driven rotary.

Watering. A lawn based on a deep, rich, and humusy soil will withstand dry conditions with relative ease, because the grass roots in such a soil will penetrate deeply to bring up moisture. If the soil is lacking in good texture, tending to become hard and baked at the first sign of drought, the roots will likely be shallow and will demand frequent artificial watering. Again, the secret lies in establishing a good soil under that lawn. All efforts should be made to upgrade the soil quality by the carrying out of a year-round organic feeding program.

If you must water, be sure to soak the soil thoroughly, four to six inches deep. You will get far better use from each gallon of water by these infrequent-but-thorough soakings than by sprinkling the lawn frequently. The water from sprinklings will be taken up by the air in short order, by evaporation, and the roots of the grass plant will be forced to grow laterally and shallowly, where they will bake out as soon as dry conditions reappear.

Weed control. Weeds in the lawn drive some homeowners crazy. They see each dandelion as a criminal trespasser, each plantain as a sinister intruder seeking to mock their weed control programs. Other gardeners, doubtless more happy, see dandelions as a nice spring salad plant, and plantain as good and cheap rabbit food. Weeds, obviously, are in the mind of the beholder, and part of the answer to the "weed problem" rests in the homeowner's attitude.

Nevertheless, weeds do crowd out the lawn grasses you are attempting to cultivate, and you should make reasonable attempts to keep them within reasonable numbers. (If your goal is to eliminate lawn weeds entirely, on the other hand, prepare yourself for a life of frustration and misery.)

When it comes to lawn weeds, the best defense is a good offense. Build your soil organically, seed the lawn well, feed your lawn grass, and it will drive out most weeds by its own aggressiveness. If your lawn is not too large, dig weeds by hand. The job will not take more than a good afternoon of work, and it is a great job for the kids, too. Keep your mower blades set high, also, for weeds are encouraged by close cropping of the lawn. Regular mowing is equally important, because it will trim most weeds before their seed has had a chance to set.

Use herbicides if you absolutely cannot stand the sight of weeds. But first, try this: Simply mow the lawn carefully, then stand back and ask yourself, "Are the weeds *really* that horrible looking?" If the answer is yes, then stand back a little farther. Eventually, you will get far enough away to be unable to distinguish the weeds from the grass. And that, after all, is how most people see your lawn.

Patching bare spots. This job is not difficult. Define the exact area you wish to renew, then dig up the soil in that area to a depth of six inches. Add screened compost and bone meal to the soil, rake it smooth, top it with a thin layer of potting soil or fine garden loam, and sow the seed. Water the area regularly with a fine spray, so that the soil is kept moist but not saturated, and then treat it just as you would a new lawn. The lawnseed you choose should, of course, be dictated by the location of the lawn area.

The beauty of ground covers is in their versatility. Here, a low-growing and shade-loving cover is used as a graceful border for a wooded path.

TWENTY GROUND COVERS FOR WISCONSIN

Lawn grass is actually a kind of ground cover — obviously, the most popular of ground covers. But there are others, many of which can find a welcome place in your landscaping program. The beauty of these other ground covers is that they are easy to maintain (no mowing every Saturday), they add interest to many outdoor areas with their variety of heights, colors, and form, and they will grow in places where lawn grasses will fail or are impractical — on difficult slopes, in irregular places difficult to mow, in total shade, under taller shrubs, etc.

Here are twenty ground covers, growing from two inches to three feet tall, one or more of which will certainly solve a problem on your home grounds. All of these ground covers have been recommended as suitable for growing in Wisconsin by Professor Edward R. Hasselkus, University of Wisconsin landscape architect. Professor Hasselkus also wrote the following comments in *Ground Covers for Wisconsin* (Special Circular 130, University of Wisconsin Cooperative Extension Programs):

FOR SUNNY AREAS

Bearberry *(Arctostaphylos uva-ursi)*. Evergreen, growing six to twelve inches high. Pinkish flowers, red fruits. For dry sites and acid soil.

Crownvetch *(Coronilla varia)*. Herbaceous plant, growing twelve to twenty-four inches high. Pinkish pealike flowers; wide-spreading. For dry bank plantings.

Cranberry cotoneaster *(Cotoneaster apiculata)*. Deciduous plant, growing twelve to eighteen inches high. Large red fruits and wine-red autumn foliage. The hardiest of the low-growing contoneasters.

Creeping juniper cultivars *J. Horizontalis* "Bar Harbor," "Douglasi," "Plumosa," and "Wiltoni." Evergreen plants, growing from eight to twelve inches high. Most cultivars turn purple in winter. They tolerate dry and poor soil.

Japgarden juniper *(J. procumbens)*. Evergreen, growing eight to twelve inches high. Tufted needles on trailing stems, bluish-green year-round.

Canby pachistima *(Pachistima canbyi)*. Evergreen, growing eight to twelve inches high. Tiny hollylike leaves turn bronze in fall. Plant spreads by underground shoots.

Moss phlox *(Phlox subulata)*. Herbaceous plant, growing to about six inches in height. Forms needlelike carpet with white, pink, or red flowers.

Reynoutria fleeceflower *(Polygonum reynoutria)*. Herbaceous plant, growing four to six inches high. Pink flowers in late summer, red fall color. A very aggressive plant.

Wineleaf cinquefoil *(Potentilla tridentata)*. Evergreen, growing two to twelve inches high. White flowers in spring, purple autumn foliage. For dry areas.

Stonecrops *(Sedum* species). A herbaceous evergreen, growing from two to six inches high. Summer bloom, fleshy leaves that may turn red or purple in winter.

FOR SHADED AREAS

Silveredge bishop's groutweed *(Aegopodium podograria,* "Variegatum"). Herbaceous plant, growing from six to fourteen inches high. Leaves with white margin and white flowers. Aggressive on any soil.

Carpet bugle *(Ajuga reptans)*. A herbaceous evergreen, growing from four to twelve inches high. Blue flowers, evergreen foliage when protected from winter sun, purple and variegated leaf form are available.

Wild ginger *(Asarum canadense)*. A herbaceous plant, growing to eight inches in height. Large heart-shaped leaves. Needs ample moisture.

Lily-of-the-valley *(Convallaria majalis)*. A herbaceous plant, growing to eight inches in height. Fragrant white flowers. Foliage may be unattractive in late summer.

Purpleleaf wintercreeper *(Euonymus fortunei* "Colorata"). Evergreen, growing six to twelve inches tall. Shiny, dark green leaves which turn purple in winter.

Bulgarian ivy *(Hedera helix* "Bulgaria"). Evergreen, growing six to eight inches tall. Hardiest of the English ivies; best in rich, moist, organic soil.

Plantainlily (Hosta species). Herbaceous plant, growing eighteen to thirty-six inches tall. White or purple flowers. Forms distinct mounds.

Canby Pachistima. (See description under Sunny Areas.)

Pachysandra *(Pachysandra terminalis)*. A herbaceous evergreen, growing up to eight inches in height. Sparse white flowers. Prefers a moist, organic soil.

Periwinkle *(Vinca minor)*. A herbaceous evergreen, growing up to six inches in height. Blue flowers; white and purple flowered varieties available.

Violets *(Viola* species). Herbaceous plants, growing to six inches in height. Violet, white, pink, or yellow flowers. Some remain evergreen.

SHRUBS FOR BEAUTY AND PRACTICALITY

An intelligently planned collection of shrubs can serve many purposes on the home grounds. Shrubs can break up the harsh vertical and horizontal lines of a house, softening and enhancing its appearance. They can filter the sunlight that enters certain rooms, thus reducing summer heat and improving the view from both inside and outside those rooms. They can provide backyard privacy for family barbecues, or simply for sitting and relaxing. They can provide nesting, refuge, and food for birds. And they can — well, just make a house look warmer and more inviting.

Shrubs are woody plants that grow from several stems instead of one. It is this characteristic, plus their generally smaller size at maturity, that distinguishes shrubs from trees. Shrubs rarely grow taller than ten feet in Wisconsin, and they can grow as low as two feet. When choosing shrubs, be certain that you know how tall each is expected to grow, so that you can choose each to fit your particular needs. Tall-growing shrubs should not be forced down to an unnatural size by pruning, lest they lose their natural grace and beauty of form.

Shrubs, like trees, are either evergreen or deciduous, and for the most interesting effect every home should feature some of each. Some deciduous varieties flower beautifully in the spring, and others produce brilliant autumn foliage, while the evergreens add color to the home grounds all winter long.

Choosing shrubs. In addition to the above considerations, there are four factors to consider when choosing shrubs:

1. **Foliage.** What is its shade of green? What is its texture? How large are its leaves? Will it produce autumn color? Choose shrubs that have foliage to your liking.

2. **Flowering.** Will this shrub flower in the spring? At what time? Will the blossom color complement your house color?

3. **Fruiting.** Is food for birds important to you? If so, choose at least several shrubs which are good for this purpose.

4. **Soil, sun, and climate requirements.** Will this shrub be absolutely hardy in your area of Wisconsin? Is it particularly sensitive to drainage conditions — and does the particular location you have in mind offer suitable drainage? Does this shrub need full sun? Remember that shrubs are comparatively expensive plantings, and you hope that they will become permanent residents. Know their needs and be certain that you can provide them.

Planting shrubs. Shrubs can be planted either in spring or fall in Wisconsin. In the harsher regions of the state, the less hardy shrubs are better planted in spring, so that they will have an entire summer to become established before facing the rigors of their first winter. On the other hand, fall-planted shrubs are less likely to face insect and disease problems for the first seven or eight months of their establishment. Your nurseryman can tell you whether it is better to plant any particular variety in spring or fall.

Shrubs should be planted with the same care as you would give in planting a tree. The hole should be dug very generously, so that the roots can be spread out with no cramping at all. A moderate amount of well-aged compost may be mixed with garden loam and a few good handfuls of bone meal and wood ashes. (Skip the wood ashes if the shrub requires a very acid soil.) Line the hole with several inches of this mixture, and then spread the roots out naturally in the bottom of the hole. Fill in the hole with the planting mixture, packing it carefully around the roots in order to leave no air spaces. Water the hole thoroughly several times during the planting operation, so that no air spaces remain. When the hole is filled, make a small basinlike depression around the plant, with the walls of the basin extending beyond the reaches of the roots, in order to catch rainwater and direct it down to the roots.

Pruning. The pruning of shrubs is not a difficult task, nor need it be done very often. Deadwood should be pruned regularly, of course, and those branches that get out of hand can be trimmed back, preferably when the plant is dormant, either in early spring or late fall. Spring-blooming shrubs (lilac, dogwood, mock orange, honeysuckle, etc.) should not be pruned in fall, but just after the blooming period in spring, or many of the latent flower buds will be cut off. Summer- and fall-blooming shrubs can be pruned before spring growth begins.

Fertilization. Shrubs do not need much fertilization, since their roots drive vigorously into the ground to bring up minerals from deep within the subsoil. They will, however, respond favorably to fertilization, especially in the first few years when their root systems are becoming established. An annual topdressing of compost, spread out to the drip line, will be sufficient for all shrubs, while a year-round mulch will slowly increase the organic matter content of the soil. Once established, shrubs need very little care at all.

Forty-eight shrubs for Wisconsin. Hardiness, as we have said, is a vitally important factor in choosing any shrub. You want your shrub plantings to be permanent garden residents, and the only way you can assure this is to select varieties that will make it through every Wisconsin winter with ease.

The following list of forty-eight shrubs was drawn up by University of Wisconsin landscaping expert George Ziegler. Of these forty-eight, there are four which are of doubtful hardiness in the colder sections of Wisconsin, and these are so indicated. The others, however, will withstand our typical winters with scarcely a whimper.

TALL SHRUBS — EIGHT TO TEN FEET
(Plant Five to Six Feet Apart)

Siberian peashrub *(Caragana arborescens).* Very hardy, good on sandy soil.

Gray dogwood *(Cornus racemosa).* White flowers, white berries. Native to Wisconsin.

Redosier dogwood *(Cornus stolonifera).* Hardy red twigs, white flowers. Native to Wisconsin.

Winged euonymous *(Euonymous alatus).* Excellent accent shrub.

Peegee hydrangea *(Hydrangea p.g.).* Large white to pink flowers.

Tartarian honeysuckle *(Lonicera tatarica).* Fast growing.

Sweet mock orange *(Philadelphus coronarius).* Single, fragrant flowers.

Common ninebark *(Physocarpus opulifolius).* White flowers, red seeds. Native to Wisconsin.

Double flowering plum *(Prunus triloba plena).* Pink flower.

Chinese lilac *(Syringa chinensis).* Lavender flowers.

Common lilac *(Syringa vulgaris).* Lavender or white flowers.

Hybrid lilac *(Syringa in varieties).* Many colors.

Arrowwood *(Viburnum dentatum).* Good fall colors. Plant in sun or shade. Native to Wisconsin.

American cranberry bush *(Viburnum trilobum).* White flowers, red fruit.

Wayfaring tree *(Viburnum lantana)*. White flowers, red fruit.

Nannyberry *(Viburnum lentago)*. White flowers, colored berries. Native to Wisconsin.

MEDIUM SHRUBS — FIVE TO EIGHT FEET
(Plant Three to Four Feet Apart)

Peking cotoneaster *(Cotoneaster acutifolia)*. Good for hot, dry spots.

Many flowered cotoneaster *(Cotoneaster multiflora)*. Pink bloom and red berries.

Dwarf winged euonymus *(Euonymus alatus compacta)*. Excellent accent shrub.

Forsythia *(Forsythia* in varieties). Early yellow flowers. Check for hardiness in your area.

Morrow honeysuckle *(Lonicera morrowi)*. Fast growing, white blossoms.

Zabel honeysuckle *(Lonicera zabeli)*. Red flowers.

Double mock orange *(Philadelphus* in varieties). Many kinds are available. Check for hardiness in your area.

Golden currant *(Ribes aureum)*. Yellow flowers, very hardy.

Father Hugo rose *(Rosa hugonis)*. Yellow flowers, hardy.

Rugosa rose *(Rosa rugosa)*. Different colors, hardy.

Bridal wreath *(Spirea vanhouttei)*. White flowers.

Double bridal wreath *(Prunifolium)*. Double white flowers. Check for hardiness in your area.

Weigela *(Weigela* in varieties). Pink and red flowers. Check for hardiness in your area.

LOW SHRUBS — TWO TO FIVE FEET
(Plant Three Feet Apart)

Potentilla *(Potentilla* in varieties). Yellow flowers.

Snowhill hydrangea *(Hydrangea arborescens)*. White flowers. Likes shade.

Dwarf ninebark *(Physocarpus op. nana)*. White flowers. Native to Wisconsin.

Fragrant sumac *(Rhus aromatica)*. Good fall color. Native to Wisconsin.

Avalanche mock orange *(Philadelphus lemoinei)*. White flowers, fragrant.

Alpine currant *(Ribes alpinum)*. Very hardy. Good in shade.

Froebel Spirea *(Spirea froebeli)*. Red flowers, hardy.

Common snowberry *(Symphoricarpos albus)*. White berries in winter.

Coralberry *(Symphoricarpos orbiculatus)*. Red berries. Native to Wisconsin.

Clavey dwarf honeysuckle *(Lonicera claveyi)*. Good in almost all situations.

EVERGREENS — MEDIUM HEIGHT

Pfitzer juniper and varieties *(Juniperus phitzeriana)*. Spreading habit. Needs sun.

Olfield common juniper *(Juniperus communis depressa)*. Use in sun. Native to Wisconsin.

Savin juniper *(Juniperus sabina)*. Semiupright in growth.

Mugho pine *(Pinus mughus)*. Semiball shaped. Needs sun.

Spreading yew *(Taxus cuspidata)*. Thrives in shade.

Dwarf yew *(Taxus cuspidata nana)*. Thrives in shade.

Globe arborvitae *(Thuja occidentalis globosa)*. Good at house entrances.

EVERGREENS — LOW

Andorra juniper *(Juniperus h. plumosa)*. Purple in fall. Needs sun.

Other varieties of creeping types of juniper.

(Note: These are the most popular species, but there are many other suitable shrubs for Wisconsin gardens.)

SHADE TREES
— A GIFT TO FUTURE GENERATIONS

Shade trees play an important part in our lives. They provide protection from the hot sun in the summer and they shelter us from the wind in the winter, making our homes more comfortable throughout the year (while saving heating and cooling costs). They, along with other plants, produce all the oxygen that we need for survival. They are an important part of our water cycle, bringing water from deep within the earth and releasing it into the atmosphere, where it later returns as welcome rain. Trees trap and filter dust, and they reduce noise pollution from the street. Most of all, trees fill that deep need within all of us to be among living and growing things, and therefore they are beautiful. We need trees for our happiness.

There are important considerations in choosing shade trees for your home grounds. Here are ten to think about:

1. **Hardiness.** A tree is planted not only for your lifetime, but for future generations. It is your gift to those who will come after you, just as our giant oaks of today are gifts to us from those who lived many generations ago. The shade trees you plant, therefore, should be absolutely hardy in your climate zone. Table 13, which lists thirty-one street trees for Wisconsin, will be a dependable hardiness guide in your selection process — but it will always be worth your while to check with your nurseryman or Extension

agent to see which trees are most dependable in your particular area.

2. **Mature size.** Survey the location for your proposed tree, and then choose one which — after it has reached maturity — will fit nicely into that area. Allow at least half the diameter of the tree as the space between that tree and any other tree. If you are planting a tree by the street curb, check the city regulations which govern such plantings, and consider overhanging utility lines that might be injured or broken by the tree's growth in a few years. In any case, do not plant trees closer than twenty-five feet from the corner of an intersection, for reasons of auto safety.

3. **Shade patterns.** Know the route of the sun in both the summer and winter skies, and calculate the shade patterns that the tree will cast at maturity. Will it shade the only good garden location on your lot? If so, perhaps you should choose a lower-growing variety or change the proposed location. You will also want to choose a location wherein the tree will offer cooling shade to the house during summer. It has been estimated that one mature shade tree has the cooling power of ten room-size air conditioners running twenty hours a day. It would be nice of you to offer this cooling power to your neighbor's house, but perhaps you would rather plan the location so that your own house receives the benefit.

4. **Tolerance to pollutants.** If you live in the country or in a sparsely settled suburb, you will not worry very much about this factor. City dwellers, however, must pay attention to it. Norway maples, for instance, are very adaptable to all city conditions, but sugar maples are intolerant to salt; if the city habitually salts your street during winter, a sugar maple is not the wisest choice. Other city trees that are especially tough are the Washington hawthorne, ginko, honeylocust, sycamore, and littleleaf linden.

5. **Soil conditions.** Although trees send their roots deeply into the subsoil to bring up moisture and nutrients, you should pay attention to basic soil conditions if you wish your tree to make it to maturity. Consider soil fertility, moisture, and pH. You can get good clues to the suitability of any variety by checking to see whether others of its kind are growing nearby. Your nurseryman or county Extension agent also will be willing to advise you in this area.

6. **Resistance to insect and disease damage.** One can never tell when a plague might spread among any tree species. Years ago, our American chestnuts were virtually wiped out by blight. Now, many midwestern cities are being stripped of their elm populations because of Dutch elm disease. Oak wilt has become a serious problem in Wisconsin, striking especially red and black oaks. One never knows what might come next, but we can lessen the chances of heavy tree loss in the future by planting a broad variety of different trees, and by avoiding those which do not show good

resistance to diseases currently active. Certain trees attract harmful insects, also, and these insects can harm not only the tree but
your other garden plants as well. Chief among these is the box
elder, which brings the box elder bug (which in turn will eat many
fruits and flowers in your garden, as well as invading your house),
and the black locust, which is subject to borers.

7. **Tolerance to light, heat, and wind conditions.** Certain trees
will be harmed by sweeping winter winds in an unprotected location. Others cannot withstand intense heat, and therefore can be
harmed if planted against a highly reflective white house. Check
with your nurseryman or Extension agent for advice.

8. **Potential refuse.** All deciduous trees shed their leaves in fall,
of course, but others deposit inedible fruits, nuts, pods, flowers, or
twigs, as well. The chief offenders in this area are the catalpa,
poplar, willow, and many nut trees and ornamental fruit trees.
Many people are not bothered by these natural tree products, but
others prefer arboreal tidiness.

9. **Natural strength.** Some trees, including the box elder, poplar, and willow, lack the natural wood strength to see them easily
through to maturity. It will be best to avoid these, unless one of
them happens to be your very favorite.

10. **Root behavior.** The roots of some trees cause inordinate
trouble on city lots. The roots of the poplar and willow, for instance, are known to block sewers more than those of other varieties, while silver maple roots tend to heave pavements. Avoid
these along sidewalks.

Using these ten broad considerations and the accompanying
table as your general guide, study your likes, your needs, and the
restrictions of your location, narrowing your choices down to a few
likely candidates. Then go to your nursery and try to discover
more about these finalists. Talk to the nurseryman, look at his
saplings, and try to find out where mature varieties might be
growing nearby. Eventually you will find the right tree for the
right place — one that you can plant with every good hope for the
future.

Planting trees. Shade trees are planted in either spring or fall
in Wisconsin. Tree planting advice is given freely on pages 194-97,
in the chapter on fruit and nut trees. The same advice applies
to the planting of shade trees, for the needs of both are the same
at this stage of the game. I will repeat only one piece of advice,
because I think it is so important: "It is better to plant a one-
dollar tree in a five-dollar hole, than to plant a five-dollar tree in a
one-dollar hole." Do it right.

Pruning shade trees. Any tree should come from the nursery
properly pruned for planting. If the top growth seems particularly
large and the root system very small, you might have to cut back
the top after planting. Do not cut back the main leader, but trim
the side branches by as much as one-third. For the first several

years, prune away only deadwood, crossing branches, and suckers which appear on the main leader. Although shade trees do not require the care in pruning that fruit trees do, you might check on pages 198-200 for a rundown of pruning principles.

Fertilizing. Your shade tree will appreciate an annual application of compost or well-rotted manure, at least for the first several years when it is becoming established. You can most easily apply this as a topdressing, simply spreading it around the tree out to the drip line of the branches, and then shallowly raking it into the soil. If you cannot rake in compost because of a lawn, then it will be better to give the tree several applications of compost or manure tea. This will be washed down into the soil, reaching and stimulating the roots. After the tree is several years old, it will need no more fertilization, since its top growth and root system will then be large enough for the tree to manufacture ample food for itself.

Table 13. STREET TREES FOR WISCONSIN

Botanical and Common Name	Height	Spread	Growth Rate	Remarks
Acer platanoides Norway maple	50'	50'	Medium	Greenish yellow flowers before leaves. Avoid using in areas where turf is to be maintained; withstands adverse city conditions.
var. "Columnare" or "Erectum" Columnar Norway maples	40'	10-15'		Columnar forms of the species.
var. "Emerald Queen" Norway maple	50-60'	30'	Fast	Oval form of the species with crisp, dark green, glossy foliage.
var. "Globosum" Globe Norway maple	20'	20'	Slow	Low-crowned globe form of the species.
Acer rubrum Red maple	50-60'	30-40'	Fast	Prefers moist acid soil; bright red flowers before leaves; brilliant autumn foliage; smooth gray bark. New varieties are available with superior autumn color.
var. "Armstrong" or "Columnare" Columnar red maples	40'	10-20'		Columnar forms of the species.
var. "Bowhall" red maple	50-60'	30'		Oval form of the species with orange autumn foliage.
Acer saccharum Sugar maple	60'	50'	Slow	Avoid using in congested city areas or on sandy soils; excellent fall foliage. Intolerant of salt.
var. "Newton Sentry" or "Temple's Upright" Columnar sugar maples	45'	15-20'		Columnar forms of the species.

Name				Description
Aesculus hippocastanum "Baumannii" Baumann horse chestnut	30-60'	30'	Medium	Bears double white sterile flowers. Casts dense shade.
Celtis occidentalis Common hackberry	30-50'	40'	Medium	Interesting pebbled bark; hard black fruits; "Witches broom" may be a problem; similar in habit to the elm. Tolerant of both dry and wet soils.
Crataegus phaenopyrum Washington hawthorn	20-30'	15-20'	Medium	Bears thorns; white flowers, tiny orange fruits and red to orange autumn foliage. Tolerant of adverse city conditions.
Fraxinus americana White ash	50-80'	50'	Medium	Broad-headed tree with diamond-shaped fissures in bark and yellow to purple autumn foliage.
var. "Autumn Purple" white ash	50'	50'		Seedless form of the species with orange purple autumn foliage.
Fraxinums pennsylvanica subintegerrima "Marshall Seedless" green ash	50-60'	30-40'	Fast	Dark green, glossy foliage turning yellow in autumn; uniformly pyramidal in habit. Tolerant of salt and both dry and wet soils.
Ginkgo biloba Ginko	60'	30-40'	Slow	Picturesque growth hebit; fan-shaped leaves turn yellow in autumn; tolerant of city conditions. Adapted only to southern and eastern Wisconsin.
var. "Fastiglata" Sentry ginko	60'	10-15'		Narrow columnar form of the species. Adapted only to southern and eastern Wisconsin.
Gleditsia triacanthos inermis varieties: "Imperial" honeylocust and "Skyline" honeylocust	60'	40'	Fast	Podless and thornless varieties; fine textured foliage that casts a light shade. Tolerant of salt, adverse city conditions, and both dry and wet soils.

Gymnocladus dioica Kentucky coffeetree	60'	40'	Medium	A picturesque tree with unusual deep furrowed twigless branches.
Malus varieties: Flowering crabapples: Chinese pearleaf (*rinki*), columnar siberian, strathmore, Van Eseltine	20-30'	to 15'	Medium	Use only where fruits up to ¾" in diameter can be tolerated. Flowers are white, purplish red, or pink; fruits are yellow, red, or purple, depending on variety.
Ostrya virginiana Hophornbeam or ironwood	25'	20'	Slow	Similar in appearance to American elm, but much more refined; interesting fruits. Tolerant of dry soil and shade.
Phellodendron amurense Amur corktree	45'	30'	Fast	A sturdy tree with ashlike leaves, yellow autumn color, and a thick corky bark. Tolerant of dry soils.
Platanus occidentalis Sycamore or American planetree	60'	50'	Fast	Mottled gray green exfoliating bark; pendulous ball-like fruits; tolerant of city conditions; use only on moist soils. Adapted only to southern and eastern Wisconsin.
Quercus palustris Pin oak	40-50'	30-40'	Medium	Symmetrical in form; fine autumn color; avoid using on alkaline soils. Tolerant of wet soils.
Quercus rubra Red oak	60'	40-50'	Medium	Dark red autumn foliage. Intolerant of heavy or poorly drained soils.
Tilia cordata Littleleaf linden var. "Chancellor" or "Greenspire" Pyramidal littleleaf lindens	40'	30'	Medium	Oval to pyramidal in form; tolerates adverse city conditions. Uniformly pyramidal in form.
Tilia euchlora "Redmond" linden	50'	40-50'	Medium	Pyramidal form; coarse and lustrous foliage.

SOURCE: University of Wisconsin-Extension

Chapter Eight

Insects and Diseases — Control without Poison

It is not my purpose in this chapter to make an impassioned attack against chemical pesticides. Thirteen years after the publication of *Silent Spring*, such warnings hardly seem necessary — except perhaps to a surprising majority in the governmental and university ranks of agriculture and horticulture, and an unsurprising majority in the pesticide industry — those, in other words, who most often advise us on matters of insect and disease control.

Home gardeners, on the other hand, are well ahead of their advisers. They have turned to nonchemical controls in legion, and have found that it is not really necessary to wage chemical warfare in order to attain gardening success.

A University of Wisconsin-Extension pamphlet I recently picked up recommends the use of 2,4,5,-T for at least nine common lawn weeds. Then, stamped above the recommendations, is the caution, "DON'T USE 2,4,5,-T — THE FOOD & DRUG ADMINISTRATION HAS DISAPPROVED ITS USE ON LAWNS."

Now, the potential hazards of 2,4,5-T have been known for years. Just why it has been condoned for all this time, in government and university publications, is something I certainly cannot understand — especially when such use has been strictly for ornamental purposes. The USDA and our universities have apparently been willing to let us risk our health in order that we may control crabgrass.

The mistake that too many of us have been making for too long is in letting our advisers do our thinking for us. We have been too eager to believe that, "if a product would hurt us, the government wouldn't allow it on the market." We have also placed undue credence in that well-worn manufacturer's phase, "Safe When Used as Directed." More and more — with DDT, with 2,4,5-T, and with other hydrocarbon and organic phosphate poisons — we have discovered that the government is often the last to recognize a public health hazard, and that the manufacturer's safety precautions, as well as his assurances, are based not upon current knowledge of product safety or hazard, but upon the most extreme allowances of the law. The pesticide-maker's record of public concern has been as appalling as the government's snaillike response to findings of danger, when it comes to pesticides. It has been the individual actions of a few individuals — pioneers such as J. I. Rodale and Rachael Carson, consumer advocates such as Ralph Nader, and foward-looking public officials such as Senator Gaylord Nelson — and gardeners and farmers — thousands, at first, then millions — who have recognized the dangers of pesticides and sought alternatives to them in both agricultural and horticultural areas. We are ahead of our leaders — or, at least, most of them.

Tempting as it is, it is not my purpose here to warn against the dangers of chemical pesticides. Those warnings are being issued almost daily by others, and it is up to us to listen and to evaluate. We are here to get some practical, down-to-earth tips on controlling insects, plant diseases, and other pests in our gardens.

I have no statistics to support it, but I believe firmly that organic gardeners are bothered less by insects and diseases than are those who carry out regular pesticide application programs. Nor am I alone in this belief. Thousands of organic gardeners report the same experience — that, after changing over to organic methods, insects and diseases become less and less a problem, until they simply cease to be a major problem at all. To look over the pamphlet rack in the county agent's office, you would swear that insect control is absolutely the most essential, time-consuming, and expensive of all garden operations. According to the advice in these pamphlets, the home gardener should have a dozen separate pesticides for the vegetable garden, and still more for the fruit trees and ornamentals. I would be uncomfortable with an arsenal such as this in my home, in the first place, and in the second place I couldn't find enough insects on which to use them all. In the past year, I had a little trouble with cabbageworms on both cabbage and broccoli plants. I dusted twice with rotenone (a natural, plant-derived agent, short lasting and of very low toxicity to warm-blooded animals) and I picked a few by hand after that, but the plants were not otherwise bothered. I saw a few asparagus beetles on the asparagus ferns, but I did nothing about them and they never amounted to anything. (I tilled the asparagus patch just before the ground froze, to upset winter hibernating places.) Beyond that, none of my plants were bothered at all — tomatoes, eggplants, cauliflower, beans, peas, lettuce, herbs, onions, garlic, carrots, potatoes, and squash. Nothing appeared on the flowers or the ornamental shrubs and trees. (An old, inherited apple tree is another story — and a project for rejuvenation next year.)

There will be times, of course, when insects and diseases will be a problem, and we should be ready to put controls into effect at that time. But we can do much in the way of *prevention*, to begin with — and, when forced to use specific controls, there are many safe ones to consider. They are less expensive than chemicals, although they often require a little imagination and experimentation to put into effect.

INSECTS, GOOD AND BAD

Scientists have, thus far, identified more than one million different insect species on this earth, and they are identifying more than ten thousand new ones each year. But don't let these figures overwhelm you. In North America north of Mexico, there are not many more than one hundred thousand identified species, and many of these don't come as far north as Wisconsin. Of those that do, there are probably fewer than one hundred which are likely to be garden pests. And so — lesson number one — *there are far more harmless insects than harmful insects.* Wholesale chemical warfare makes little sense, even if it were not for the potential dangers to man, so long as safe alternatives are available to us.

Lesson number two is that many insects perform valuable services for mankind. Chief among these is the pollination of the flowers of literally thousands of plant species, many of which we depend upon for food. Honeybees are most noted for this service, perhaps because they have gained out affections through the production of honey, but actually there are many other flying insects which perform pollination services — either by accident or design — therefore permitting the survival of valuable plant species.

Insects are also soil builders. Those which live in the soil help to break down raw organic matter into plant-supporting humus. Insects which burrow into the earth create spaces for life-giving air, and they bring nutrients to the upper soil layers where hungry plant roots can feed. Still other insects prey on some of the insects which give our gardens the most trouble. These insect allies — including lady beetles, dragonflies, praying mantids, aphis lions, wasps, and spiders — must be given the chance to establish their places in the natural order of the garden. They cannot do so under continual chemical bombardment.

Ecologists have barely scratched the surface of the insect

world. We have very little concept or understanding of insects' relationship to each other or to other life forms. We do know, however, that there are "good" bugs and "bad" bugs — i.e., those that aid or hinder our gardening efforts — and that a wholesale assault on the insect world of our backyard can upset delicate systems, often creating more harm than good. It is up to each of us to act as pioneers in safe insect control, to learn what we can, where we can, and to share the knowledge of any personal observations with others. Our universities and government research centers are not moving fast enough in this area. We home gardeners, however, are helping each other by sharing our ideas. Often, our ideas are far from scientific, and sometimes a successful control method for one will fail for another. But, through trial and error, we are making progress.

The nation's chief clearinghouse for the exchange of information in this area is *Organic Gardening and Farming*. The magazine's nearly one million readers are encouraged to send in the results of personal observations and trials in safe insect control, and these ideas are often shared with other readers. The editors of the magazine also keep in close touch with professional researchers in the area, and with manufacturers who are attempting to develop safe insect control products. In addition, the Rodale organization maintains two experimental farms where insect control is a major focus of research. The results of many years of these efforts have been summarized admirably in a book, *The Organic Way to Plant Protection* (Rodale Press, 1966). Much of the solid information in this chapter is drawn from that book, which is one I certainly would recommend for the library of every Wisconsin gardener.

The other outstanding book in this area is *Gardening without Poisons*, by Beatrice Trum Hunter (Houghton Mifflin). It contains many ideas for home insect control that will benefit Wisconsin gardeners.

RESISTANT VARIETIES
FOR DISEASE PREVENTION

Disease in plants is very similar to disease in man. Diseases affect the health of the plant in one way or another, and they are carried by minute organisms — fungi, viruses, bacteria, slime-molds, and other low forms, including nematodes. There are hundreds of different plant diseases that might affect Wisconsin home gardens. Some of the more familiar are scab, rust diseases, mildew, anthracnose, fusarium and bacterial wilts, mosaic, and — in seedlings — damping-off.

By far, the most effective way of fighting plant diseases is to choose disease-resistant varieties to begin with. I have, insofar as possible, indicated those resistant varieties in the various chapters of this book dealing with individual plants and plant species. But you can get further clues by studying seed and nursery catalogs, government and university bulletins, and by consulting with your nurseryman or county agent whenever in doubt. Good strides have been made in recent years in developing disease-resistant varieties, and the home gardener should take full advantage of these efforts.

PREVENTING DISEASE IN THE GARDEN

The key to disease control is in providing a garden environment where the trouble-causing organisms cannot live. Choosing resistant varieties is one way of effecting this control, since these varieties act as poor hosts for the fungi, bacteria, and other organisms that carry the diseases. But there are other methods to be used, the combination of which can keep disease damage to a minimum in your garden.

Removal of diseased tissue. Diseased tissue is a breeding ground for disease organisms. Remove all diseased plants or plant parts promptly. Either burn them or bury them deeply in the hot part of the compost pile, where the organisms will be destroyed. This action alone will reduce the number of organisms, and the incidence of disease, tremendously in your garden.

Clean cultivation. Various weeds act as hosts for disease organisms. In some cases, a disease could not exist if it were not for its host weed, and yet gardeners unknowingly tolerate such weeds. Tomato and cucumber mosaic, for instance, is encouraged by the overwintering of the virus in the roots of milkweed, ground cherry, pokeweed, and catnip. Keep your garden cleared of weeds, to reduce the number of possible disease hosts.

Crop rotation. This is difficult for small-space gardeners, but essential for those with larger plots. Rotate crops annually. If any crop is bothered by a disease one year, move that crop as far away as possible next year and fill the diseased area with a crop which is totally resistant to the particular disease. Having no plants to live on, the disease organisms will die out.

Air and moisture control. Many diseases thrive when the weather is wet and the air is still. You cannot control the weather, but you can follow spacing directions carefully so that every plant will have optimum air movement around it, and you can work for good soil drainage so that your soil will not become waterlogged for long periods. In the case of some diseases — tomato blossom-end rot, for instance — the trouble is caused by an overly dry soil. The addition of copious amounts of compost will correct this problem within a few years, since it will build a soil texture capable of holding moisture adequately.

Companion planting. This is an area just beginning to be understood, and more is said about it on pages 94-97. There are, however, a few suggestions worth heeding in companion planting for disease prevention. The first is that members of the same family — cabbage and broccoli, for instance, or any other two crops that are subject to the same diseases — should not be planted next to each other. If this rule is followed, a disease that strikes one crop will not easily spread to another.

You may also plant rows of tall crops in between shorter, disease-prone crops, in the hope of reducing the spread of airborne diseases. This method might well be more effective than it appears to be, on the surface. Some gardeners have gone so far as to erect sheets of cheesecloth on all sides of plantings that are particularly susceptible to an airborne disease, in order to reduce the number of organisms entering the area. A great deal more research is needed in this area, and it seems to be the duty of the gardener/scientist, or at least the gardener with an active interest in scientific exploration, to conduct most of this research for us.

Companion planting for insect control is important, also, since insects are among the major carriers of disease organisms. More is said about companion planting for insect control later in this chapter.

SAFE INSECT CONTROL

There are two approaches to safe insect control. One is to create conditions in your garden which will keep the number of insects within reasonable bounds. These are general controls, aimed at no particular insect, and they should be worked into your regular gardening schedule just as mulching, fertilizing, or any other necessary activity. The other is to put into effect controls for particular insects when they present serious problems. If you are conscientious in carrying out a program of general control, however, the times you will have to use specific controls should be fairly few.

GENERAL INSECT CONTROL METHODS

Soil fertility. The late J. I. Rodale expressed, for many years, the belief that insects and diseases prefer to attack sick plants, being repelled by healthy plants. He observed this phenomenon in his own experience at his farm in Emmaus, Pennsylvania, and he received confirmation from other gardeners and farmers. The theory seemed to fit well into the evolutionary concept (survival of the fittest, etc.), and yet there was little scientific evidence to back up his belief, and so scientists dismissed the concept or openly scoffed at it. As with so many of Rodale's concepts, however,

Purple martins are among the most voracious of insect eaters. In addition to providing garden services, they will keep the yard free of mosquitoes.

science is now catching up to observations that seemed obvious to J. I. Rodale twenty or thirty years ago.

The beginnings of this scientific confirmation are well exemplified by Dr. Selman A. Waksman, discoverer of streptomycin (who is *not*, I must add, one of the scoffers): "Plant deficiency diseases are usually less severe in soils well supplied with organic matter not only because of the increased vigor of the plants but because of antagonistic effects of the various soil microorganisms which become more active in the presence of an abundance of organic matter."

Other plant scientists have reported, also, that sick plants seem to draw more than an average number of attacking insects and diseases, while healthy plants are bothered less. Again, we do not know all the reasons, but we must heed the observations.

If you build your soil to a peak of health, by the incorporation of organic matter and natural mineral substances, you will raise healthy plants that will show greater resistance to the attacks of both insects and diseases.

I cannot prove this statement by the presentation of scientific evidence, but I believe it firmly. I can point to evidence showing that the fungi which live in decaying organic matter are the worst enemies of nematodes, and I can dig up other bits of evidence that support my belief. But that would not serve my purposes. I do not want to argue with scientists, or take the position of some scientists in an argument with others — I just want to grow healthy plants, and I know that organic methods will help me to do this. Each gardener must make his own decisions.

Clean cultivation. The prompt removal of weeds, plant debris, and other garden clutter — including boards, old seed packages, pieces of clay pots, etc. — will remove many of the harboring and breeding places of insects and will aid in reducing their populations. Fall plowing or tilling is also important, since the turning of the soil just before the ground freezes will overturn many insect eggs, exposing them to the cold air and destroying them. Another tilling in the spring, as soon as the ground can be worked, will accomplish more of the same purpose.

Encouragement of birds. It is difficult to overestimate the importance of birds in the natural order of the garden. They should be encouraged by the building of houses, birdbaths, feeders, shelters, and nesting places. When choosing hedges and shrubs, choose some that will offer attractive berries for the birds.

In building birdhouses, you might concentrate on attracting the house wren. It is a common summer resident throughout Wisconsin, in the first place, and it is one of the birds which will consent to live in a birdhouse. Most important, the house wren is a voracious consumer of insects. Other Wisconsin birds which prefer insects over seeds and berries are barn swallows, swifts, gnat-catchers (southern Wisconsin only), purple martins, flycatchers, brown creepers (uncommon in Wisconsin, but welcome), and some warblers. It is unfortunate that the ubiquitous English sparrow does not like insects.

Our friend, the toad. Toads, admittedly more rare than birds, are also hungry pursuers of insects, particularly cutworms, grubs, and slugs. You should encourage neighborhood children to bring a few toads into your garden. If you pen them up for a few days, they might adapt themselves to the area and decide to stay. To encourage their staying, you should provide brush cover for them, some water, and perhaps a toad house (described on page 202). Toads toil while we sleep, gathering up insects that carry out night raids on our garden plants.

Insect allies. Do all you can to encourage the presence of the predator insects — those which feast on other insects, many of which are harmful. The two most important of these allies are *praying mantids* and *lady beetles*, both of which can be purchased commercially (see page 328). The others can be encouraged simply by the avoidance of poisonous sprays.

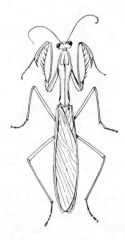

Praying mantids, fearsome-looking creatures, attack and eat a variety of destructive insects, including the large ones that no other insect will dare to attack. Mantid egg cases can be purchased during the dormant season — late fall to midspring — and should be tied to trees or other plants where you want them to hatch. They will withstand subzero temperatures without harm, and each case will produce from 50 to 400 young mantids. So great is the appetite of the female mantid that she habitually devours her own mate after fertilization has taken place, and she often will eat her own young. We overlook these excesses, however, since the rest of her diet is so beneficial to the growth of our garden plants.

Lady beetles are perennial favorites of small children, who delight in the examination of tiny things. The lady beetle is easy to spot in the garden because of its bright red wing covers with black polka dots. It should not, however, be confused with the harmful Mexican bean beetle, which is slightly larger than the lady beetle, copper colored, and has sixteen black spots on its wing covers. Lady beetles, which have fewer spots, feed on soft-bodied insects, particulary aphids, spider mites, scales, and mealybugs.

Other helpful insects, probably unavailable through commercial sources, include *aphis lions* (which eat aphids, mealybugs,

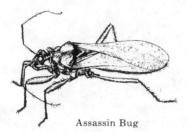

Assassin Bug

Minute Pirate Bug

scales, thrips, and mites), *damsel bugs* (eat ahpids, fleahoppers, and small larvae of other insects), *assassin bugs* (feed on the immature forms of many insects), *ground beetles* (eat caterpillars and other insects), *minute pirate bugs* (mites and other small insects, and the larvae of larger insects), *spiders and mites* (many harmful insects), *syrphid flies* (the larvae eat insects, including aphids), and *wasps*. (Tiny parasitic wasps lay eggs in the bodies of insects, the developing larvae killing the insects; large wasps feed on young caterpillars.) Learn to recognize these insects and do not kill them when you see them. If you do not have an insect identification guide, you may obtain one for forty cents by asking your county agent for USDA Home and Garden Bulletin Number 46 — *Insects and Diseases of Vegetables in the Home Garden*. This fifty-page booklet will also tell you how to kill insects and disease organisms by the application of chemicals, if you are inclined in this direction.

Companion planting. Any kind of companion planting will reduce your insect problems significantly. Why any kind? Because the very fact of mixing different plants together in the garden seems to make it more difficult for insects to locate their favorite plants. Experiments at Cornell University comparing insect populations between interplanting and monoplanting, concluded in 1970, demonstrated this principle without much doubt. "The amount of total plant-eating insects turned out to be significantly higher in the monoculture," said Dr. Richard B. Root, a Cornell entomologist. By monoculture, of course, he means the large-area planting of a single crop.

Entomologists still do not understand very well the sensory apparatus of insects. The key might or might not be in the odor that each plant releases. But we do know that strong-smelling plants such as onions, garlic, marigolds, and many herbs and spices seem to repel many harmful insects.

When planting your garden, therefore, do not plant large areas of a single crop, but work for diversity. By all means, ring your garden with marigolds, which are easy to grow and which have perhaps the most effective insect repellent qualities of any plant — and intersperse your vegetable garden with other plants that have shown repellent qualities.

Table 14 lists some common garden pests and some of the plants that have been reported to repel them. I cannot vouch for the effectiveness of each companionship, but there certainly can be no harm in trying these in your own garden and noting the results. (See also the table on companion planting on pages 96-97.)

Table 14. INSECTS AND THEIR PLANT REPELLENTS

Ants	Tansy
Aphids, bean beetles	Nasturtiums
Cabbageworm	Tomatoes, sage, catnip
Cucumber beetle	Radishes, marigolds, nasturtiums
Cutworms	Onions
Spider mites	Coriander, anise
Verticillium wilt in potatoes	French marigolds
Many harmful bacteria	Garlic
Many harmful insects	*Artemisia* family, asters, chrysanthemums, marigolds, other members of the aster family

SPECIFIC INSECT CONTROLS

Safe insecticides. There are some insecticides that are of such low toxicity, and of such short-lasting effect, that they are considered safe to use even by avid organic gardeners. Chief among these are dormant oil sprays, Ryania, rotenone, pyrethrum, and microbial preparations.

Dormant oil sprays are used mainly on fruit trees, although sometimes on other trees, shrubs, and evergreens, too. The oil, applied in early spring before leaf growth begins, spreads a film over the eggs of hibernating insects, suffocating them. The leaves, blossoms, and fruit which later emerge are in no way affected by the oil. Much more is said about dormant oil sprays on page 203.

Ryania, a plant-derived insecticide made from the South American *Ryania speciosa*, is effective against corn borers, cranberry fruitworms, codling moths, Oriental fruit moths, and some other insects. Ryania does not always kill the insects on contact, but it often makes them too sick to eat and they eventually starve to death.

Rotenone is another plant-derived insecticide, this one made from one or more of several tropical plants, including derris, cube barbasco, and timbo. It is effective against asparagus beetles, twelve-spotted beetles, flea beetles, thrips, cabbageworms, cucumber beetles, tomato fruitworms (corn earworms), pea weevils, and Europeans corn borers. Its toxicity to warm-blooded animals is very low.

Pyrethrum, made from the flower heads of *Chrysanthemum coccineum*, a popular summer-blooming perennial, is effective against a number of soft-bodied insects. You can grow your own pyrethrum insecticide by drying the flower heads and grinding them as finely as possible. Pyrethrum is often mixed with rotenone — but, like rotenone, it is sometimes mixed with toxic chemical insecticides. Always read the label of any product carrying the names pyrethrum or rotenone, to see whether it is the pure product. If you cannot find the pure product, go to a pet store or veterinarian and ask for it.

Microbial insecticides contain millions of microorganisms that are lethal to one or more harmful insects. Biotrol, Bio-Guard, and Thuricide are the brand names of some of the more popular of these preparations, which are effective against gypsy moths, oak-moth larvae, cankerworms, tent caterpillars, cabbage loopers, imported cabbageworms, tomato hornworms, and grape leaf folders (not all of which are problems in Wisconsin). The active ingredient in these products is the *Bacillus thuringiensis*, which paralyzes the digestive tract of the insect, causing it to stop eating and starve to death over a period of several days.

Last, there are many homemade insecticides or repellents that can be made from plants growing right in the garden. Many of these are listed in the two books mentioned previously — *The Organic Way to Plant Protection* and *Gardening without Poisons* — but you can experiment with your own recipes, starting with the plants recommended previously as repellents and going on to the strong-smelling parts of other plants, including garlic, onions, chili peppers, etc. One good way to begin is to use a plant that is absolutely unaffected by the insect you wish to repel. Grind up parts of that plant, mix with water, and wash the affected plants with it. If the harmful insect is not airborne, then sprinkle the mixture liberally around the plants on the ground. Note the results carefully. Constant experimentation by thousands of gardeners in this area will build a mountain of data, which can then gradually be refined into genuine garden guides. You can be a leader in insect control, instead of a follower!

Traps. Traps have been used for centuries in controlling insects both on farms and in gardens. It has just been since the introduction of chemical pesticides that we have lost much of our knowledge in this area, but now most of that knowledge is being recaptured, and much is being added by modern technological methods.

Simple traps include the laying down of a board or an inverted cabbage leaf, under which snails and slugs will hide during the day to escape the heat of the sun. Simply remove the board or leaf and shovel up the insects into a jar of kerosene.

A shallow pan of kerosene set under a shaded light, outdoors, will kill many night-flying moths and other insects. They will dive into the pan and be killed in short order.

Bands of sticky material are available commercially. Wrapped around the trunks of trees, they trap insects which crawl up the trunks to lay eggs in the bark.

There are also commercially available a variety of traps which attract insects with light and then dispose of them in one of several simple ways, including electrocution.

SPECIFIC CONTROL METHODS FOR TWENTY COMMON GARDEN INSECTS

The following twenty insects are among the most common pests in Wisconsin gardens. The general control principles presented earlier will go far in eliminating any serious trouble from these garden attackers. However, if any of them should become uncommonly numerous and destructive, you might wish to use one or more of the following specific control methods.

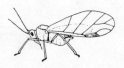

APHIDS (plant lice)

Description. There are many species of aphids, but all are tiny, green to black, and soft bodied. They cluster on the undersides of leaves or on stems or roots.

Damage. Aphid damage results in curled and distorted leaves and stunted plants. Aphids attack turnips, melons, cucumbers, peas, beans, tomatoes, potatoes, celery, peppers, spinach, and cabbage. Aphids transmit certain virus diseases of vegetables.

Control. Aphids are repelled by soil that is high in organic matter. They are repelled also by chives, garlic, nasturtiums, and tobacco. Many tobacco-containing preparations are used in repelling or killing aphids. Lady beetles, available commercially, are the aphid's natural enemy. Aphids are attracted to the color yellow; a shallow, yellow pan, filled with water and a thin film of detergent, will destroy thousands of them when the pan is set on the ground near the plants. Aphids can easily be washed off plants with a forceful stream from the garden hose. On woody perennials, a dormant oil spray will control them.

ASPARAGUS BEETLES
Description. The adult is a metallic blue to black, with orange to yellow markings, ¼ inch long. The larvae are olive green to dark gray, 1/3 inch long. The eggs, which are laid on spears by female beetles, look like shiny black specks.

Damage. Both adults and larvae eat the foliage of the asparagus. The shoots are disfigured.

Control. Fall plowing or tilling will upset the beetles' winter environment, seriously reducing their population. Country gardeners can turn a few chickens loose in the asparagus patch for effective control. Tomatoes planted next to asparagus are said to repel the beetles. Garden cleanliness is also vitally important in control of the asparagus beetle. Rotenone dust will provide effective control if the infestation is serious.

CABBAGEWORMS (imported cabbageworms)
Description. This worm is velvety green, up to 1¼ inches long. It is often difficult to spot because its body blends in so well with the foliage. It is the larva of the white cabbage butterfly.

Damage. The cabbageworm feeds on the undersides of leaves, producing ragged holes in cabbage, broccoli, and related plants.

Control. The butterfly is repelled by tomatoes, sage, tansy, rosemary, sage, nasturtiums, catnip, mint, hemp, and hyssop. Any or several of these plants grown around the cabbages will help to reduce the incidence of egg laying. Yellow jacket hornets kill cabbageworms, and so does *trichogramma*, a commercially-available parasite. Several homemade preparations repel the cabbageworm and its parent butterfly: sour milk spooned into the center of the plant; a mixture of two parts flour and one part salt sprinkled on the heads while dew is present; plain salt sprinkled on the heads; and rye flour sprinkled on the heads, also when dew is present. The worms are large enough to be picked off by hand and dropped into a jar of kerosene. Rotenone, pyrethrum, and *Bacillus thuringiensis* are effective and safe insecticides.

CORN BORERS (European corn borers)

Description. This caterpillar is pale pink or brown, with a dark brown head, growing to one inch in length. It is the larva of a night-flying moth.

Damage. The corn borer feeds in the stalks and ears of corn, entering at the base, side, or tip. It is also a serious attacker of peppers, lettuce, potatoes, and other garden vegetables, as well as ornamentals and even some fruiting trees and plants.

Control. Traps with daylight blue lamps have been found to be effective in reducing the night moth population. More important, however, is the removal of plant debris — especially cornstalks — in fall. The borer overwinters in the corn stubble and emerges in early May as a moth. Fall removal of debris will destroy many of the caterpillars. *Bacillus thuringiensis* is effective against the caterpillars, as well as Ryania, rotenone, and pyrethrum.

CORN EARWORMS
(See FRUITWORMS.)

CUCUMBER BEETLES (striped cucumber beetles)

Description. The adult is yellow to black, with three black stripes down the back. It is approximately 1/5 inch long. The larva is white, slender, brownish at the ends, and up to 1/3 inch long.

Damage. The adults feed on leaves, stems, and fruit, and they also spread bacterial wilt. The larvae bore into roots and stems below the soil line. The cucumber beetle usually attacks young plants, causing them to wilt and sometimes die. Plants most commonly attacked are cucumbers, muskmelons, squash, and watermelons.

Control. Try a mixture of three parts colloidal phosphate and one part wood ashes. Sprinkle the young plants generously with the mixture. (It is a good fertilizer, as well as a cucumber beetle repellent.) A Mississippi gardener reported success by interplanting radishes among his melons. Nasturtiums, marigolds, and castor beans are also reported repellents. Rotenone is an effective safe insecticide.

CUTWORMS

Description. There are many species. The worms are dull gray, brown, or black, and may be striped or spotted. They are stout, soft bodied, and smooth, up to 1¼ inches long. They curl up tightly when disturbed.

Damage. Cutworms are among the worst threats to very young plants. They cut off the stems above, at, or just below the soil surface. Some cutworms feed on leaves, buds, or fruits, while others feed on the underground portions of plants. Those plants most often attacked are peppers, tomatoes, members of the cabbage family, peas, and beans.

Control. Fall tilling will do much to disturb the overwintering places of the cutworm. When setting out plants in spring, cardboard collars placed around the young stems, pushed one inch into the ground, will bar the cutworm's entrance. A ring of wet ashes around each plant is also said to be effective. Toads are especially fond of cutworms. A pie pan, filled with stale beer and sunk into the ground to the brim, will trap and kill cutworms during the night.

FLEA BEETLES

Description. There are many species, black, brown, or striped. These are beetles with great jumping ability, about 1/16 inch long.

Damage. Flea beetles attack potatoes, tomatoes, eggplants, peppers, beets, spinach, turnips, radishes, and members of the cabbage family. Young plants, especially transplants, are severely damaged, looking as they had been shot full of holes.

Control. Rotenone dust is effective, although its use should be discontinued before the plants begin to blossom. More important is clean cultivation. Remove all weeds and plant debris in which the tiny beetles hide. The flea beetle is also repelled by shade, and so susceptible crops should be interplanted among shade-giving ones.

FRUITWORMS (tomato fruitworms)

Description. The tomato fruitworm is green, brown, or pink, with light stripes along the sides and on the back. It grows up to 1¾ inches long. When the same insect appears on corn, it is called the *corn earworm.*

Damage. The fruitworm eats holes in both the fruits and buds of tomatoes. On corn it feeds on the central shoot early in the season, later burrowing through the silk and feeding on kernels near the tip of the ear. On beans the fruitworm eats holes in pods, attacking usually in the fall. It will also attack okra.

Control. Fruitworms are easily picked by hand from tomatoes, beans, and okra. On sweet corn, a few drops of mineral oil dropped into the top of the ear will eradicate the worm. (Do it when the ears are small, and repeat every two weeks.) Rotenone is an effective safe insecticide.

GRASSHOPPERS

Description. There are many species of grasshoppers, one of the most easily recognized of Wisconsin insects. They are brown, gray, black, or yellow, up to two inches long, with strong hind legs. Most grasshoppers are strong flyers.

Damage. Grasshoppers are voracious eaters of vegetation, and they are not particular about their diet. When abundant, they may destroy complete plantings of such crops as lettuce and potatoes.

Control. Frequent cultivation is important, since grasshoppers lay their eggs in the top three inches of soil. Fall tillage will expose many eggs and kill them. Deep cultivation in spring will kill further numbers. Birds are especially fond of the meaty grasshopper, and this insect is very easy prey for the birds, too. A good homemade trap for grasshoppers consists of a high backboard (about four feet) attached to a ground-level trough, any length you wish. The trough is filled with water and covered with a good film of kerosene. Put the trap at one end of the garden. Then gather together the neighborhood children, and perhaps your dog, and begin a shoulder to shoulder march through the garden, preferably banging on pots and pans. The grasshoppers will be stampeded towards the trap, crashing into the backboard, falling into the trough, and dying in the kerosene. (If this doesn't work, it will at least delight the kids and arouse the curiosity of your neighbors.)

GRUBS (white grubs)

Description. There are several species of white grubs. They are white or light yellow, with hard brown heads. They are curved in structure, ½ to 1½ inches long. White grubs, which are the larvae of May beetles, live in the soil and require three years to mature.

Damage. The larvae feed on roots and underground parts of potato and many other plants. Adults feed on tree foliage.

Control. Grubs will likely be a serious problem on lands that have grown heavy crops of weeds or grasses during the previous season. Try to avoid planting vegetables in newly plowed grass-lands. If grubs are a real problem, till the soil repeatedly in both spring and fall, uprooting as many grubs as you can for the birds to eat. Let the land lie fallow for a year, if it has been in grass for a long time. This will reduce the grubs' food supply and thus reduce the population. Grubs are also a favorite food of toads, when the toads can find them.

HORNWORMS (tomato hornworms)

Description. There are two species of hornworms. Both are green, with diagonal lines on the sides and a prominent horn on the rear end. They grow up to four inches in length.

Damage. Hornworms eat the foliage and fruit of the eggplant, pepper, and tomato. They are large worms with hearty appetites, and they work quickly.

Control. Since hornworms are so large, they may easily be picked off plants and destroyed. *Bacillus thuringiensis* is an effective and safe insecticide.

LEAF MINERS

Description. The larva is yellow, about ⅛ inch long, and lives in leaves. The adult is a tiny fly, black and yellow in color. Several generations of this insect develop in a summer.

Damage. The larvae make long, slender, winding, white tunnels in the leaves of tomato, pepper, and spinach plants.

Control. It is not difficult to spot the infected leaves, for they have a distinct blotchy appearance. Remove these leaves as soon as you spot them, and bury them deeply in the compost heap where the miners will be destroyed. Clean cultivation is also important in control of the leaf miner, since weeds harbor them.

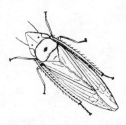

LEAFHOPPERS

Description. There are several species of leafhoppers. The adults are green, wedge shaped, and up to ⅛ inch long. They fly quickly when disturbed. Nymphs resemble the adults, but are smaller. They crawl sidewise like crabs.

Damage. Adults and nymphs attack beans, whose leaves curl, or roll downward, crinkle, and tend to become yellow or bronze. Some plants are dwarfed and may die. The six-spotted leafhopper spreads the virus of aster yellows to lettuce, carrots, and asters. Leafhoppers also attack potatoes and cause hopperburn. Tips and sides of potato leaves curl upward, turn yellow to brown, and become brittle.

Control. Plants, or parts of plants, should be removed immediately upon discovery of infestation. Pyrethrum is an effective and safe insecticide.

LOOPERS (cabbage loopers)

Description. This caterpillar, an inchworm or measuring worm, is pale green with light stripes going down its back, growing to 1½ inches in length. It doubles up, or loops, when it crawls.

Damage. Loopers feed on the undersides of leaves, producing ragged holes. Large loopers burrow into the heads of cabbage. They also attack collards, Brussels sprouts, broccoli, and kale.

Control. *Trichogramma*, a commercially available Lepidoptera egg parasite, is very effective in controlling the looper, as is *Bacillus thuringiensis*.

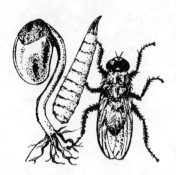

MAGGOTS

Description. A maggot is the larva of a fly, and there are many species to cause trouble in the garden, including root maggot, onion maggot, seed-corn maggot, and pepper maggot. All are white or yellowish white, legless, and ¼ to ⅓ inch long.

Damage. The seed-corn maggot bores into sprouting seed and prevents the development of plants. Root maggots attack the very young plants and transplants of cabbage, peas, and radishes, tunneling into roots and stems and causing rot. The onion maggot burrows into the young bulbs, causing them to rot.

Control. Eggs are laid on the soil surface near the stems of the plants. If the eggs can be found and destroyed, damage will be avoided. Tar paper collars will reduce the incidence of egg laying around plants. Wood ashes sprinkled around the young plants is also said to discourage egg laying. If onion maggots are a recurring problem, scatter the onion sets throughout the garden instead of planting them in rows. Damage will be reduced greatly. Rotation of crops is also important, as it is for the protection of any crop against underground insect attackers. Pepper maggots are the larvae of the barred-wing fly. Some gardeners have reported success by sprinkling a little talc right on the growing fruits of the pepper plant. This should be done during the egg-laying season, in July and August. Fall cultivation will also help to disturb winter hibernating places.

SLUGS AND SNAILS

Description. There are many species of slugs and snails, which are grayish insects, legless, with wormlike bodies. Snails differ from slugs in that they have a protective shell.

Damage. Slugs and snails attack a wide variety of garden vegetables and flowering ornamentals, doing their dirty work at night.

Control. Slugs and snails are easily trapped under boards. They must find a cool and moist place to rest during the day, and old boards placed on the ground offer this refuge. Simply lift the boards daily and dispose of the insects. They are repelled by sharp sand (which irritates their soft bodies), and also by slaked lime and wood ashes. Sprinkle one or more of these around any area you wish to protect. Toads are also nocturnal enemies of snails and slugs, and will dispose of hundreds of them in your garden.

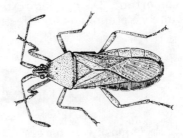

SQUASH BUGS

Description. The adult is brownish, flat-backed, about ⅝ inch long, and is otherwise known as the stink bug (a name you will appreciate, if you will crush one of these bugs). The nymph varies from bright green with a red head and legs, to a dark greenish gray with black head and legs, and grows up to ⅜ inch long. The egg clusters, found on leaves, are shiny brick red.

Damage. Both adults and nymphs feed in colonies, sucking sap from the leaves and stems of many plants, particularly squash and pumpkins. Often, the plants wilt and die.

Control. Radishes, nasturtiums, and strong-smelling marigolds will repel the squash bug. Handpicking is also effective. Boards placed on the ground can also trap the squash bug, since he finds refuge in cool, dark, and moist places.

THRIPS (onion thrips)

Description. The adult is yellow or brownish, winged and active, about 1/25 inch long. The larva is white and wingless, looking like a smaller version of the adult, but is almost too small to be seen with the naked eye.

Damage. Both the adult and larvae suck out juices from onion plants, as well as from beans, cabbages, and many other garden plants. White blotches appear on the leaves, and the tips of the leaves wither and turn brown.

Control. Some onion varieties, including Spanish onions, show resistance to damage by thrips. Both larvae and adults overwinter on onions and other plants, including weeds. Eliminate their over-wintering places by clean cultivation and by the prompt removal of weeds during the growing season. If thrips are a major menace to any particular crop during one year, try to eliminate that crop the next year, and plant a nonsusceptible crop in its place. This, plus clean cultivation, can starve out the population. Fall tillage is also very important. Do not let rotted onions remain in the soil over the winter. Rotenone is an effective and safe insecticide.

VINE BORERS (squash vine borers)

Description. This larva is wormlike, white, up to one inch long.

Damage. The larvae bore into vines, eating holes in stems near the base of the runner. The runner wilts and either dies or is unproductive.

Control. The USDA recommends: "Locate points of injury. Split one side of stem with razor blade or sharp knife and puncture worm. Put a mound of moist dirt around each cut stem to prevent drying and to induce root growth beyond point of injury." The eggs are laid in July, and the sprinkling of black pepper around the plants before this time may reduce egg laying. (At the current price of black pepper, however, you might prefer to take your chances with the insects.) Butternut varieties of squash have shown some resistance.

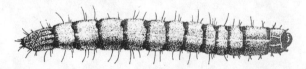

WIREWORMS

Description. There are many species of this slender, rather hard-shelled worm. It is colored yellow to white, with a dark head and tail, growing ½ to 1½ inches long.

Damage. Wireworms puncture and tunnel into stems, roots, and tubers of many garden plants, including beans, carrots, beets, celery, lettuce, onions, potatoes, and turnips.

Control. Wireworms will be particularly troublesome in soil that had been planted to sod the previous year. Four to six plowings or tillings of the soil in fall, at one-week intervals, will reduce populations and disturb winter hibernating. Poor soil drainage will also encourage wireworms, and so additional organic matter should be incorporated into the soil, in order to open it up and improve drainage. One trap involves the placing of a piece of potato slightly underground, a stick running through it and poking up out of the ground. In a few days, the potato is removed by gently pulling the stick. As many as twenty wireworms have been found adhering to the potato.

Tools and Sources

CLUBS, SOCIETIES,

AND ORGANIZATIONS

ORGANIC PRODUCTS FOR THE SOIL

SAFE INSECT CONTROL MATERIALS

COUNTY EXTENSION AGENTS

MAIL ORDER NURSERIES

AND SEED HOUSES

SUGGESTED READING

CLUBS, SOCIETIES, AND ORGANIZATIONS

NATIONAL ORGANIZATIONS

North American Fruit Explorers
1848 Jennings Drive
Madisonville, Ky. 42431
  Henry Converse, Pres.
  (for hobbiest fruit growers and
    breeders)

Men's Garden Clubs of America
5560 Merle Hay Rd.
Des Moines, Iowa 50323
  Lyman E. Duncan, Exec. Sec.
  Wisconsin Affiliates:

MGC of Beloit
Thomas Giralomo, Pres.
2249 Shopiere
Beloit, Wis. 53511

Fond du Lac MGC
Jerry Severson, Pres.
1507 Eleanore Lane
Fond du Lac, Wis. 54935

Gardeners of Green Bay
John Boerschinger, Pres.
RFD 6
Green Bay, Wis. 54301

Milwaukee County MGC
Charles Schneck, Pres.
2179 N. 74th St.
Milwaukee, Wis. 53212

Sheboygan MGC
Terry Nelson, Pres.
2018 Lakeshore Dr.
Sheboygan, Wis. 53081

Superior MGC
Andrew Osterheim, Pres.
5502 Hughett Ave.
Superior, Wis. 54880

Woman's National Farm and
  Garden Association
% Mrs. Richard D. Latham, Pres.
170 Bittersweet Dr.
Findlay, Ohio 45840
  (geared towards country life)

African Violet Society of America
Box 1326
Knoxville, Tenn. 37901
  (twenty Wisconsin affiliates; write
  for the one nearest you)

American Amaryllis Society
Dr. Thomas W. Whitaker, Sec.
Box 150
La Jolla, Calif. 92037
  (affiliated with American Plant Life
    Society)

American Begonia Society
% Mrs. Margaret B. Ziesenhenne,
  Pres.
1130 N. Milpas St.
Santa Barbara, Calif. 93103

American Daffodil Society
10 Othoridge Rd.
Lutherville, Md. 21093
  Mrs. E. E. Lawler, Sec.

American Dahlia Society
345 Merritt Ave.
Bergenfield, N. J. 07621
  Mrs. Irene B. Owen, Exec. Sec.

American Gloxinia and Gesneriad
  Society
58 Hill St.
Tewksbury, Mass. 01876
  Miss Janis I. Langston, Sec.

American Horticultural Society
Mount Vernon, Va. 22121
  O. Keister Evans, Exec. Dir.

American Iris Society
Missouri Botanical Garden
2315 Tower Grove Blvd.
St. Louis, Mo. 63110

American Peony Society
250 Interlachen Rd.
Hopkins, Minn. 55343

American Rock Garden Society
90 Pierpont Rd.
Waterbury, Conn. 06705
  M. S. Mulloy, Sec.
  (for growers of wild or native species
    of plants)

Wisconsin-Illinois Chapter
Mr. Iza Goroff
622 W. Wellington St.
Chicago, Ill. 60657

American Rose Society
Jefferson-Paige Rd.
Box 30,000
Shreveport, La. 71130
    Harold S. Goldstein, Exec. Dir.
    North Central District Office
    Charles L. Coens, Dir.
    609 Anthony Lane
    Madison, Wis. 53711

Aril Society, Int.
10427 Samoa Ave.
Tujunga, Calif. 91042
    Herbert H. McKusick, Pres.
    (for iris growers)

Delphinium Society
% Mr. J. H. Seager
'Birklands', Douglas Grove
Lower Bourne, Farnham,
Surrey, GU10 3HP.
England

Dwarf Iris Society
% Mrs. Elsie Zuercher
121 E. Union St.
Portland, Ind. 47371

American Gourd Society
Box 274
Mount Gilead, Ohio 43338

Herb Society of America
300 Massachusetts Ave.
Horticultural Hall
Boston, Mass. 02115

International Geranium Society
11960 Pascal Ave.
Colton, Calif. 92324
    Mr. Arthur Thiede, Membership
    Sec.

Median Iris Society
26231 Shaker Blvd.
Beachwood, Ohio 4122
    Anthony Willott, Pres.
    (for growers of medium-sized irises)

North American Gladiolus Council
30 Highland
Peru, Ind. 46970
    Bob Dorsam, Sec.

North American Lily Society, Inc.
Mrs. Betty Clifford, Exec. Sec.
Rt. 1, Box 395
Colby, Wis. 54421
    Wisconsin-Illinois Lily Society
    Mr. Leonard D. Byerly, Pres.
    1525 Lincoln Place
    Calumet City; Ill. 60409

Wisconsin Garden Club Federation, Inc.

(This is the largest gardening organization in the state, with too many local chapters to list on these pages. Membership information may be obtained by writing to Mrs. Bud Brendle, Membership Chairman, Wisconsin Garden Club Federation, Inc., 445 N. Shore Dr., Onalaska, Wis. 54650. The federation publishes a small bimonthly magazine filled with news of club activities and some gardening hints; it is available at one dollar per year and may be ordered from Mrs. Eugene Kanabay, Circulation Manager, *Wisconsin Gardens*, 1564 Woodcrest Dr. Neenah, Wis. 54956.)

WISCONSIN ORGANIC GARDENING CLUBS

Cumberland Organic Gardening
    Club
% Paul Wilson
Cumberland, Wis. 54829

Organic Gardening Club
% S. Hensley
Student Life Programs, UWGB
Green Bay, Wis. 54302

The Waukesha County Organic
  Gardening Club
% John A. Greenwood
S. 94 W. 13876 Ryan Dr.
Hales Corners, Wis. 53130

Milwaukee Organic Gardening
  Club
% Mrs. Michael Cavatis
2850 S. 128th St.
New Berlin, Wis. 53151

Milwaukee Organic Gardening
  Club
% Bernard Dziedzic
7644 Geralayne Circle
Wauwatosa, Wis. 53213

ORGANIC PRODUCTS FOR THE SOIL

It would be most difficult, and very unfair, to attempt a listing of
all Wisconsin dealers who carry organic soil-improvement products.
The next best thing is a list of manufacturers who supply organic
products to local dealers. The reader can ascertain the local dis-
tributor nearest to him by writing to any of these manufacturers
— or he can ask his local dealer to order some of these products
and keep them in stock. No endorsement is implied by the inclusion of any product or manufacturer, here, and the author will
appreciate information concerning good organic products that are
not included in these listings. Thank you.

ROCK MINERAL PRODUCTS

Thompson Sales Co.
Calphos
Box 246
Montgomery, Ala. 36101
205:263-6696

Lonfosco Colloidal Phosphate
Loncala Phosphate Co.
High Springs, Fla. 32643

The Hybro-Tite Corp.
Box 527
Lithonia, Ga. 30058
404:482-1334

Sunnylawn Farm
Soft Rock Phosphate
Box 101
Steward, Ill. 60553

Hy-Brid Sales Co.
1124 S. Sixth St.
Council Bluffs, Ia. 51501
712:323-5022

Florida Phosphate Rock
Grand Rapids Growers, Inc.
401 S. Ionia Ave.
Grand Rapids, Mich. 49502

Zeolite Chemical Co., Inc.
Greensand Zeolites
Clayton, N. J. 08312

The North Carolina Granite Corp.
Gran-I-Meal
Mount Airy, N. C. 27030
919:786-5141 or 786-5155

Glauconite Green Sand
3505 Mozart Ave.
Cheviot
Cincinnati, Ohio 45211
513:481-0982

Ruhm Phosphate & Chemical Co.
Ruhm's Phosphate Rock
Box 361
Columbia, Tenn. 38401

Robin Jones Phosphate Co.
Arrow Brand Rock Phosphate
Box 50236
Nashville, Tenn. 37205
615:292-5604

Key Minerals Corp.
Box 2364
Salt Lake City, Utah 84110

SEA PRODUCTS

Wachters' Organic Sea Products
Corp.
1550 Rollins Rd.
Burlingame, Calif. 94010

Atlantic & Pacific Research, Inc.
Box 14366
North Palm Beach, Fla. 33408
305:842-1911

Maxicrop USA, Inc.
Box 964
Arlington Heights, Ill. 60006

Sea-Born, Inc.
2000 Rockford Rd.
Charles City, Ia. 50616
512:257-2530

Samoset Sea-Crop
Liquid Sea Weed
Box 98
Boothbay, Me. 04537
207:633-4144

Mer-Made
Liquid Fish Fertilizer
The Hy-Trous Corp.
Boston, Mass. 02109

Liquid Fertrell, Fertrell Super,
Fertrell Super N
The Natural Development Co.
Bainbridge, Pa. 17502

Tangier Sea Organism Co.
Tangier Island, Va. 23440

Alaska Fish Fertilizer, Inc.
865 Lind Ave., S.W.
Renton, Wash. 98055
206:228-5910

MULCH, COMPOST, AND SLUDGE PRODUCTS

Mosser Lee Co.
Millston, Wis. 54643

Milorganite
Box 2079
Milwaukee, Wis. 53201
414:271-2403

Earth-Rite-Pfeiffer Process
Composted Soil Conditioner
Zook & Ranck, Inc.
R.F.D. 1
Gap, Pa. 17527

The Charles H. Lilly Co.
109 S.E. Alder St.
Portland, Ore. 97214
503:232-5135

Organic Compost Corp.
Box 217
Germantown, Wis. 53022

Western Peat
Box 3006
Houston, Tex. 77001
713:522-0711

Ever-Green Soil Aids Co.
Rt. 13, Box 210 TA
San Antonio, Tex. 78218
512:651-6115

EARTHWORMS

Clear Creek Farms
5300 Clark Rd.
Paradise, Calif. 95969

Bronwood Worm Gardens
Bronwood, Ga. 31726

Worm Enterprises
1624 W. Edinger
Santa Ana, Calif. 92704

Beatrice Farms
Dawson, Ga. 31742

Homegrown
Star Rt., Box 11
San Bernardino, Calif. 92407

West World Organic Worm Farms
Box 23
Upland, Calif. 91786

The Worm Firm
3139 Duffy St.
San Bernardino, Calif. 92405

Brazos Worm Farms
Box 4185
Waco, Tex. 76705

Sundance Ranch
17803 Glen Helen Rd.
San Bernardino, Calif. 92407

Bud Kinney
Rt. 1, Box 438
Chico, Calif. 95926

SAFE INSECT CONTROL MATERIALS

ELECTROCUTORS
Insect Electrocutor Co.
Western Hills Station
Box 53
Cincinnati, Ohio 45238

Detjen Corp.
Electrocuting Fly Screen Div.
Pleasant Valley, N. Y. 12569

B & G Depot
141 E. State St.
Westport, Conn. 06880

LIGHT TRAPS

Alexander Sales
125 Marbledale Rd.
Tuckahoe, N. Y. 10707

Insect Control Co.
6 Meadow Lane
Freeport, Long Island, N. Y. 11520

Insect-O-Lite Co.
1925 Queen City Ave.
Cincinnati, Ohio 45214

Hall Industries
407 S. Dearborn
Chicago, Ill. 60605

Agrilight Systems, Inc.
404 Barringer Bldg.
Columbia, S. C. 29201

LADY BEETLES

Bio-Control Co.
10180 Ladybird Dr.
Auburn, Calif. 95603

California Bug Co.
Rt. 2
Auburn, Calif. 95603

L. E. Schnoor
Box 148
Yuba City, Calif. 95991

Insect Pest Advisory Service
762 S. First St.
Kerman, Calif. 93630

PRAYING MANTIDS

Eastern Biological Control Co.
104 Hackensack St.
Wood-Ridge, N. J. 07075

Gothard, Inc.
Box 367
Canutillo, Tex. 79835

California Bug Co.
Rt. 2
Auburn, Calif. 95603

BIOLOGICAL CONTROLS

Gothard, Inc.
Trik-O (Trichogramma)
Box 367
Canutillo, Tex. 79835

Nutrilite Products, Inc.
Agricultural Division
Bio-Guard Dust (*Bacillus thuringiensis*)
5606 Beach Blvd.
Buena Park, Calif. 90620

Agrilight Systems, Inc.
Biotrol (*Bacillus thuringiensis*)
404 Barringer Bldg.
Columbia, S. C. 29201

Thuricide (*Bacillus thuringiensis*)
Science Products Co., Inc.
(At most garden centers.)

PLANT-DERIVED INSECTICIDES

Ryania
Hopkins Agricultural Chemical Co.
Box 584
Madison, Wis. 53701

Threefold Farm
B. D. Tree Spray
Spring Valley, N. Y. 10977

Rotenone and Pyrethrum
(At most garden centers.)

Scalecide (dormant oil spray)
B. G. Pratt Co.
206 Twenty-First ave.
Paterson, N. J. 07503

Tanglefoot (tree bands)
The Tanglefoot Co.
314 Straight Ave., S.W.
Grand Rapids, Mich. 49504

Fred Howe
(plastic netting)
Box 267
Somerville, N. J. 08876

Protect-O-Net
O. W. Stewart
Elm St., R.F.D. 2
Kingston, Mass. 02364

WISCONSIN HORTICULTURE AND AGRICULTURE EXTENSION OFFICES

University of Wisconsin-Extension office faculty members are standing by to help home gardeners in every county. They have the keys to research information and the resources of the University of Wisconsin system, the USDA, and other federal agencies. Get to know your county agent, and take advantage of the services and materials he provides. But do be aware that the demands on his time are enormous in the spring. At that time, some Extension offices get as many as a thousand telephone calls a day from farmers and gardeners. Some offices have installed a series of tape recordings on various gardening topics, which the caller can request to be played for him. If your county office has installed such a system, use it before asking specific questions, because the chances are that the tape will have the answer to the question you had in mind. In any case, treat your Extension agent with care — for he is a hardworking public official and a valuable ally in time of need. (Note: The listing of these offices does not imply any endorsement by the University of Wisconsin-Extension.)

Adams County
Agricultural Extension Agent
County Courthouse
Friendship, Wis. 53934
608: 339-3341

Ashland County
Agricultural Extension Agent
County Courthouse
Ashland, Wis. 54806
715: 682-2804

Barron County
Agricultural Extension Agent
County Courthouse
Barron, Wis. 54812
   715: 537-3124

Bayfield County
Horticulture Extension Agent
County Courthouse
Washburn, Wis. 54891
   715: 373-2221

Brown County
Horticulture Extension Agent
Northern Building
Box 518
Green Bay, Wis. 54305
   414: 437-3211

Buffalo County
Agricultural Extension Agent
County Courthouse Annex
Alma, Wis. 54610
   608: 685-4560

Burnett County
Agricultural Extension Agent
County Office Building
Webster, Wis. 54893
   715: 866-3101

Calumet County
Agricultural Extension Agent
County Courthouse
Chilton, Wis. 53014
   414: 849-2361

Chippewa County
Agricultural Extension Agent
Box 310
Chippewa Falls, Wis. 54729
   715: 723-9195

Clark County
Agricultural Extension Agent
County Courthouse
Neillsville, Wis. 54456
   715: 743-3118

Columbia County
Agricultural Extension Agent
County Administration Building
Portage, Wis. 53901
   608: 742-2191

Crawford County
Agricultural Extension Agent
Post Office Building
Prairie du Chien, Wis. 53821
   608: 326-8615

Dane County
Horticulture Extension Agent
City-County Building
Madison, Wis. 53709
   608: 266-4271

Dodge County
Agricultural Extension Agent
County Office Building
Juneau, Wis. 53039
   414: 386-2626

Door County
Horticulture Extension Agent
County Courthouse
Sturgeon Bay, Wis. 54235
   414: 743-5511

Douglas County
Agricultural Extension Agent
County Courthouse
Superior, Wis. 54880
   715: 394-0363

Dunn County
Agricultural Extension Agent
County Courthouse
Menomonie, Wis. 54751
   715: 232-1636

Eau Claire County
Agricultural Extension Agent
County Courthouse
Eau Claire, Wis. 54701
   715: 835-5134

Florence County
Agricultural Extension Agent
Forest County Courthouse
Crandon, Wis. 54520
   715: 478-2212

Fond du Lac County
Agricultural Extension Agent
Federal Building
Fond du Lac, Wis. 54935
   414: 921-5600

Forest County
Agricultural Extension Agent
County Courthouse
Crandon, Wis. 54520
715: 478-2212

Grant County
Agricultural Extension Agent
Youth & Agriculture Center
Fairgrounds
Box 31
Lancaster, Wis. 53813
608: 723-2125

Green County
Agricultural Extension Agent
Agricultural Building
Box 120
Monroe, Wis. 53566
608: 325-5181

Green Lake County
Agricultural Extension Agent
County Courthouse
Green Lake, Wis. 54941
414: 294-6573

Iowa County
Agricultural Extension Agent
Agricultural Center
Dodgeville, Wis. 53533
608: 935-3354

Iron County
Agricultural Extension Agent
County Courthouse
Hurley, Wis. 54534
715: 561-2695

Jackson County
Agricultural Extension Agent
County Courthouse
Black River Falls, Wis. 54615
715: 284-5391

Jefferson County
Agricultural Extension Agent
County Courthouse
Jefferson, Wis. 53549
414: 674-2500

Juneau County
Agricultural Extension Agent
County Courthouse
Mauston, Wis. 53948
608: 843-1341

Kenosha County
Horticulture Extension Agent
714 Fifty-Second St.
Kenosha, Wis. 53140
414: 658-2044

Kewaunee County
Agricultural Extension Agent
County Courthouse
Kewaunee, Wis. 54216
414:388-2542

La Crosse County
Agricultural Extension Agent
County Courthouse
La Crosse, Wis. 54601
608: 784-9494

Lafayette County
Agricultural Extension Agent
County Courthouse
Darlington, Wis. 53530
608: 776-4494

Langlade County
Agricultural Extension Agent
Fairgrounds
Box 460
Antigo, Wis. 54409
715: 623-4156

Lincoln County
Agricultural Extension Agent
County Courthouse
Merrill, Wis. 54452
715: 536-7151

Manitowoc County
Agricultural Extension Agent
County Offices Building
1701 Michigan St.
Manitowoc, Wis. 54220
414: 682-8877

Marathon County
Agricultural Extension Agent
County Courthouse
Wausau, Wis. 54401
715: 842-2141

Marinette County
Agricultural Extension Agent
County Courthouse
Marinette, Wis. 54143
715: 735-3371

Marquette County
Agricultural Extension Agent
County Courthouse
Montello, Wis. 53949
    414: 297-2717

Menominee County
Agricultural Extension Agent
County Courthouse
Keshena, Wis. 54135
    715: 799-3311, Ext. 44

Milwaukee County
Horticulture Extension Agent
9722 Watertown Plank Road
Wauwatosa, Wis. 53226
    414: 257-5351
    (also)
Todd Wehr Nature Center
5879 S. 92nd St.
Hales Corners, Wis. 53130
    414: 425-8550

Monroe County
Agricultural Extension Agent
County Courthouse
Sparta, Wis. 54656
    608: 269-6718

Oconto County
Agriculture Extension Agent
County Courthouse
Oconto, Wis. 54153
    414: 834-5322

Oneida County
Agricultural Extension Agent
County Courthouse
Rhinelander, Wis. 54501
    715: 362-6314

Outagamie County
Agricultural Extension Agent
County Courthouse
Room 102
Appleton, Wis. 54911
    414: 739-7741

Ozaukee County
Agricultural Extension Agent
County Courthouse
Room 21
Port Washington, Wis. 53074
    414: 284-9411 (or) 377-6400

Pepin County
Agricultural Extension Agent
County Courthouse
307 W. Madison St.
Box 39
Durand, Wis. 54736
    715: 672-8664

Pierce County
Agricultural Extension Agent
County Courthouse
Ellsworth, Wis. 54011
    715: 273-4376

Polk County
Agricultural Extension Agent
Agricultural Center
Balsam Lake, Wis. 54810
    715: 485-3136

Portage County
Agricultural Extension Agent
County-City Building
Stevens Point, Wis. 54481
    715: 346-3573

Price County
Agricultural Extension Agent
Normal Building
Phillips, Wis. 54555
    715: 339-2555

Racine County
Agricultural Extension Agent
Rt. 1
Sturtevant, Wis. 53177
    414: 886-2744

Richland County
Agricultural Extension Agent
123 E. Mill St.
Box 440
Richland Center, Wis. 53581
    608: 647-6148

Rock County
Agricultural Extension Agent
County Courthouse
Janesville, Wis. 53545
    608: 752-7471

Rusk County
Agricultural Extension Agent
County Courthouse
Ladysmith, Wis. 54848
    715: 532-5539

St. Croix County
Agricultural Extension Agent
Agricultural Center
Baldwin, Wis. 54002
715: 684-3301

Sauk County
Agricultural Extension Agent
Box 46
Baraboo, Wis. 53913
608: 356-5581

Sawyer County
Agricultural Extension Agent
County Courthouse
Box 351
Hayward, Wis. 54843
715: 634-4876

Shawano County
Agricultural Extension Agent
County Courthouse
Shawano, Wis. 54166
715: 526-6136

Sheboygan County
Agricultural Extension Agent
111 First St.
Sheboygan Falls, Wis. 53085
414: 457-5521

Taylor County
Agricultural Extension Agent
Agricultural Center
Medford, Wis. 54451
715: 748-3327

Trempealeau County
Agricultural Extension Agent
County Courthouse
Whitehall, Wis. 54773
715: 538-4341

Vernon County
Agricultural Extension Agent
County Courthouse Annex
Viroqua, Wis. 54665
608: 637-2165

Vilas County
Agricultural Extension Agent
County Courthouse
Eagle River, Wis. 54521
715: 479-4797

Walworth County
Agricultural Extension Agent
County Courthouse
Elkhorn, Wis. 53121
414: 723-4900

Washburn County
Agricultural Extension Agent
County Highway Building
Spooner, Wis. 54801
715: 635-3192

Washington County
Agricultural Extension Agent
Courthouse Annex 2
515 E. Washington St.
Box 537
West Bend, Wis. 53095
414: 334-3491

Waukesha County
Plant Life Extension Agent
County Courthouse
Waukesha, Wis. 53186
414: 547-2711

Waupaca County
Agricultural Extension Agent
County Courthouse
Waupaca, Wis. 54981
715: 258-7681

Waushara County
Agricultural Extension Agent
County Courthouse
Wautoma, Wis. 54982
414: 787-2226

Winnebago County
Agricultural Extension Agent
County Courthouse
Oshkosh, Wis. 54901
414: 235-2500, Ext. 74

Wood County
Agricultural Extension Agent
County Courthouse
Wisconsin Rapids, Wis. 54494
715: 423-3000

MAIL ORDER NURSERIES AND SEED HOUSES

Catalogs are not only fun, but they are valuable in planning the garden. The catalogs of most nurseries and seed houses are available free for the asking. A few, which are particularly large and sumptuous, do cost up to two dollars, although the fee is applicable to any order. Spring catalogs are usually available in December, while fall catalogs come out in midsummer. If you make a purchase from any nursery or seed house, you will doubtless receive a catalog automatically the following year.

WISCONSIN FIRMS

J. W. Jung Seed Co.
Randolph, Wis. 53956
    Large variety of fruit, vegetable, flower, ornamental, and landscaping plants and seeds.

McFarland House
5923 Exchange St.
McFarland, Wis. 53558
    Specialists in herbs and begonias.

Olds' Seeds
Box 1069
2901 Packers Ave.
Madison, Wis. 53701
    Wide variety of flower and vegetable seeds; supplies.

Woodland Acres Nursery
Rt. 2
Crivitz, Wis. 54114
    Specialists in wild flowers.

OUT-OF-STATE FIRMS

Andrews Nursery Co.
Box 8
Faribault, Minn. 55021
    Apple specialists.

Antonelli Brothers
2545 Capitola Rd.
Santa Cruz, Calif. 95060
    Begonia specialists; other flowering perennials.

Armstrong Nurseries, Inc.
Box 473
Ontario, Calif. 91761
    Rose specialists; fruit and ornamental trees.

Bountiful Ridge Nurseries, Inc.
Princess Anne, Md. 21853
    Fruit tree specialists.

Joseph Breck & Sons
440 Summer St.
Boston, Mass. 02210
    Specialists in Holland bulbs; flower seeds; supplies.

W. Atlee Burpee Co.
Box 6929
Philadelphis, Pa. 19132
    Large variety of fruit, vegetable, and ornamental seeds and plants; supplies.

The Conner Co., Inc.
Box 534
Augusta, Ark. 72006
    Strawberry specialists.

Emlong Nurseries, Inc.
Stevensville, Mich. 49127
    Fruit trees and ornamentals.

Farmer Seed & Nursery Co.
Faribault, Minn. 55021
    Fruit, nut, and ornamental plants and seeds.

Earl Ferris Nursery
Hampton, Iowa 50441
    Fruit, nut, and ornamental trees; perennials and landscape plants.

Henry Field Seed & Nursery Co.
407 Sycamore St.
Shenandoah, Iowa 51601
    Fruit, nut, and ornamental trees; flower and vegetable seeds.

Gurney Seed & Nursery Co.
Yankton, S. D. 57078
 Wide variety of seeds and plants.

House of Wesley, Inc.
Rt. 1
Bloomington, Ill. 61701
 General nursery stock.

Inter-State Nurseries, Inc.
Hamburg, Iowa 51644
 Rose specialists; fruits, nuts,
and ornamental plants.

Jackson & Perkins Co.
Medford, Ore. 97501
 Noted rose specialists.

P. de Jager & Sons, Inc.
188 Asbury St.
South Hamilton, Mass. 01982
 Specialists in Holland bulbs.

Johnny Apple Seeds
Acton, Mass. 01720
 Exotic and unusual seeds.

Joseph Harris Co., Inc.
Moreton Farm
Rochester, N. Y. 14624
 Vegetable and flower seeds;
supplies.

Forrest Keeling Nursery, Inc.
Elsberry, Mo. 63343
 Large variety of trees and
shrubs.

Kelly Brothers Nurseries, Inc.
Dansville, N. Y. 14437
 Specialists in fruit trees; com-
plete nursery stock.

The Krider Nurseries, Inc.
Middlebury, Ohio 46540
 General nursery stock.

Lakeland Nurseries Sales
Hanover, Pa. 17331
 Fruits, nuts, and ornamental
flowering plants.

Henry Leuthardt Nurseries, Inc.
Montauk Highway
East Moriches, N. Y. 11940
 Specialists in dwarf and espalier
fruit trees.

Lounsberry Gardens
Box 135
Oakford, Ill. 62673
 Wild flowers, ferns, perennials.

Earl May Seed & Nursery Co.
Shenandoah, Iowa 51601
 Specialists in hybrid seed corn;
general nursery stock and seeds.

Mellinger's Inc.
2310 W. South Range Rd.
North Lima, Ohio 44452
 General garden nursery plants,
trees; supplies.

J. E. Miller Nurseries, Inc.
Canandaigua, N. Y. 14424
 Fruit, dwarf fruit, and nut
trees; small fruits.

Musser Forests, Inc.
Indiana, Pa. 15701
 Tree specialists; also perennials
and landscape plants.

Nichols Garden Nursery
1190 North Pacific Highway
Albany, Ore. 97321
 Exotic and unusual seeds; herb
plants.

Geo. W. Park Seed Co., Inc.
Box 31
Greenwood, S. C. 29646
 Specialists in flower seeds, vege-
table seeds, bulbs, and plants.

Putney Nursery, Inc.
Putney, Vt. 05346
 Specialists in wild flowers and
ferns.

Rayner Brothers, Inc.
Salisbury, Md. 21801
 Strawberry specialists; fruit and
nut trees.

Seedway, Inc.
Hall, N. Y. 14463
 Fruit and vegetable seeds.

R. H. Shumway Seedsman
628 Cedar St.
Rockford, Ill. 61101
 General nursery stock, house
plants, seeds, bulbs, and plants.

Spring Hill Nurseries Co., Inc.
Tipp City, Ohio 45371
  General nursery stock.

Stark Bros. Nurseries
Louisiana, Mo. 63353
  Fruit tree specialists; also orna-
  mental plants and trees.

Stern's Nurseries, Inc.
Geneva, N. Y. 14456
  Rose specialists; general nursery
  stock.

Stokes Seeds Inc.
Box 548
Buffalo, N. Y. 14240
  Wide variety of flower and vege-
  table seeds; supplies.

Otis S. Twilley Seed Co.
Salisbury, Md. 21801
  Large variety of flower and
  vegetable seeds.

Van Ness Water Gardens
2460 N. Euclid Ave.
(Crescent West)
Upland, Calif. 91786
  Specialists in plants for pools
  and ponds.

The Wayside Gardens Co.
Mentor, Ohio 44060
  Huge selection of ornamental
  plants.

Gilbert H. Wild & Sons, Inc.
Sarcoxie, Mo. 64862
  Specialists in peonies, iris, hem-
  erocallis (daylilies), and liriope.

Wilson Bros. Floral Co., Inc.
Roachdale, Ind. 46172
  Geranium specialists; other house
  and patio plants.

Zilke Brothers Nursery
Baroda, Mich. 49101
  Fruit trees, ornamentals, peren-
  nials.

SUGGESTED READING

Of the hundreds of gardening books on the market today, it would be difficult or impossible to choose "the best" of the lot — and the following list is no attempt to do so. Instead, these are books known personally to the author which have been of help in answering problems. The selections are, like this book, slanted toward the organic approach to gardening. It is hoped that some of them might be helpful to the reader, and might lead to a trip to the nearest public library or bookstore where new worlds of gardening are waiting. (Note: Government and university publications are not included here because, first, they are so numerous, and, second, because they are so often revised or out of stock. For current selections of these publications, pay a visit to the office of your county Extension agent.)

GENERAL GARDENING

Encyclopedia of Organic Gardening
J. I. Rodale & Staff
Rodale Press, 1959, $10.95
   Undoubtedly the most useful of all garden books; a treasure-house of information on all subjects.

Organic Gardening and Farming (magazine)
Monthly publication
Rodale Press, Emmaus, Pa. 18049, $6.85 per year
   More than 20,000 Wisconsin gardeners already subscribe to this magazine; the number should be still higher.

The Organic Way to Plant Protection
Organic Gardening & Farming staff
Rodale Press, 1966, $7.95
   The best book on insect and disease control without poisons.

Taylor's Encyclopedia of Gardening
Edited by Norman Taylor
American Garden Guild-Doubleday, rev. ed. 1961, $12.95
   Although its formal style is not very entertaining, this classic still provides a mountain of useful gardening information; keyed to Latin nomenclature.

10,000 Garden Questions
Edited by F. F. Rockwell
American Garden Guild-Doubleday, 1959, $8.95
   An enormous book, 1400 pages, and one of the most valuable you will ever own; every gardener should have one handy.

Gardening with Nature
Leonard Wickenden
Fawcett Publications, rev. ed. 1972, 95c (paper)
   A minor classic; useful and entertaining.

Gardening without Poisons
Beatrice T. Hunter
Houghton Mifflin, $6.95 (Medallion paperback $1.25)
   Many useful tips on insect and disease control.

How to Have a Green Thumb Without an Aching Back
Ruth Stout
Cornerstone, 1955, $1.45 (paper)
   Ruth's original classic. No gardener should be without it.

Gardening without Work
Ruth Stout
Devin-Adair Co., 1961, $4.95
   Ruth's "other" book — just as entertaining and valuable as her first.

The Organic Gardener
Catharine Osgood Foster
Vintage Books (Alfred A. Knopf),
1972, $7.95 (paper $2.95)
   One of the better of the genre to
   come out in the last five years;
   many useful tips; charming
   illustrations.

Working with Nature
John Brainerd
Oxford University Press, 1973,
$15.00
   How to treat a piece of land after
   you have bought it.

SOIL TREATMENT

The Complete Book of Composting
J. I. Rodale & staff
Rodale Press, 1960, $10.95
   Everything you have always
   wanted to know about compost-
   ing, and maybe a little more.

Organic Fertilizers
Organic Gardening & Farming staff
Rodale Press, 1973, $2.95 (paper)
   Which organic fertilizers to use
   and how to use them.

The Organic Way to Mulching
Organic Gardening & Farming staff
Rodale Press, 1972, $5.95
   The complete mulching book.

VEGETABLES AND HERBS

Step-by-Step to Organic Vegetable
   Growing
Sam Odgen
Rodale Press, 1971, $7.95
   An old Vermont gardener's
   approach — practical, no non-
   sense, and valuable especially
   to Wisconsin gardeners because
   of the similarity in climates.

The Rodale Herb Book
Edited by William H. Hylton
Rodale Press, 1974, $12.95
   Valuable tips on selecting, rais-
   ing, and using herbs of many
   kinds.

FRUITS AND BERRIES

Grow Your Own Dwarf Fruit
   Trees
Ken and Pat Kraft
Walker & Co., 1974, $8.95
   For the small-space gardener
   who wants a variety of fruit
   trees.

Successful Berry Growing
Gene Lodgdon
Rodale Press, 1974, $7.95
   A valuable little book for berry
   lovers.

FLOWER GARDENING

Flower Growing in the North
George E. Luxton
University of Minnesota Press,
   1956, $4.95
   An old favorite in this country
   which is, unfortunately, running
   out of print; thousands of useful
   tips for flower gardeners in Wisconsin as well as Minnesota.

Gardening with Wild Flowers
Frances Tenenbaum
Charles Scribners' Sons, 1973, $7.95
   A good book for the wild flower
   enthusiast.

Growing Wildflowers
Marie Sperka
Harper & Row, 1973, $8.95
   The best book on wild flowers for
   Wisconsin gardeners because it
   is written by a Wisconsin gar-
   dener with decades of experience;
   beautifully produced.

Spring Flora of Wisconsin
Norman C. Fassett
University of Wisconsin Press,
   4th ed. 1975, $3.95 (paper)
   A classic identification manual
   for the field.

TREES, SHRUBS, LAWNS, AND GROUND COVERS

Deciduous Garden Trees and
  Shrubs
Anthony Huxley
Macmillan, 1973, $4.95

Evergreen Garden Trees and
  Shrubs
Anthony Huxley
Macmillan, 1973, $4.95
  Both books are informative and
  useful in planning for landscap-
  ing.

Lawn Beauty the Organic Way
Organic Gardening and Farming
  staff
Rodale Press, 1970, $7.95
  The only book that really tells
  you how to grow a good lawn
  without resorting to chemical
  fertilizers and pesticides.

The Pruning Book
Gustave L. Wittrock
Rodale Press, 1971, $6.95
  No gardener with more than one
  tree on his place should be with-
  out this practical volume.

REFERENCE WORKS

The Dictionary of Useful Plants
Nelson Coon
Rodale Press, 1974, $10.95
  Aside from its value as a refer-
  ence, it is great browsing mate-
  rial.

The Green Thumbook
Edited by Marion Schroeder
Valley Crafts (Box 99, Cary, Ill.
  60013), 1974, $2.95 (paper)
  Listings of sources for garden
  supplies and information.

The Vegetation of Wisconsin
John T. Curtis
University of Wisconsin Press,
  1959, $12.50
  The definitive guide to native
  plants in Wisconsin; tells you
  whether any plant grows
  naturally in your particular
  area.

MISCELLANEOUS

Gardening in the Shade
H. K. Morse
Charles Scribners' Sons, $8.95
  (paper $2.45)
  A "must" volume for those gardeners who love their trees too
  much to part with any of them.

Stocking Up
Edited by Carol Hupping Stoner
Rodale Press, 1973, $8.95
  How to preserve all the fruits
  and vegetables you have worked
  so hard to produce.

Index